Gender and the First World War

CH00923366

This page intentionally left blank

Gender and the First World War

Edited by

Christa Hämmerle

Oswald Überegger

and

Birgitta Bader Zaar

First published 2014 by
PALGRAVE MACMILLAN

Palgrave Macmillan in the UK is an imprint of Macmillan Publishers Limited, registered in England, company number 785998, of Houndmills, Basingstoke, Hampshire RG21 6XS.

Palgrave Macmillan in the US is a division of St Martin's Press LLC, 175 Fifth Avenue, New York, NY 10010.

Palgrave Macmillan is the global academic imprint of the above companies and has companies and representatives throughout the world.

Palgrave® and Macmillan® are registered trademarks in the United States, the United Kingdom, Europe and other countries.

ISBN 978-1-349-45379-5   ISBN 978-1-137-30220-5 (eBook)
DOI 10.1057/9781137302205

This book is printed on paper suitable for recycling and made from fully managed and sustained forest sources. Logging, pulping and manufacturing processes are expected to conform to the environmental regulations of the country of origin.

A catalogue record for this book is available from the British Library.

A catalog record for this book is available from the Library of Congress.

Typeset by MPS Limited, Chennai, India.

Contents

List of Illustrations and Maps

Illustrations

Maps

Acknowledgements

We would like to acknowledge the contributions of a range of institutions and persons who, by financing and/or supporting the preceding conference and the preparation of this volume, helped us to realize the project. Alongside all the lecturers and participants in the conference, from whom we learned so much, we thank the University of Vienna (Faculty of Historical and Cultural Studies, Department of History, and the Research Platform on 'Repositioning of Women's and Gender History in the New European Context'); the Department of History at the University of Hildesheim (the project 'Militärische Normübertretungen und Kriegsführung: Kriegsgräuel der Mittelmächte im Ersten Weltkrieg', funded by the Deutsche Forschungsgemeinschaft); the Austrian Federal Ministry for Science and Research; the city of Vienna; the journal *L 'Homme: Europäische Zeitschrift für Feministische Geschichtswissenschaft*; and the Association for Historical Peace Research. We would also like to express our gratitude both to the staff at Palgrave Macmillan, especially Clare Mence and Penny Simmons as an excellent copy-editor, and the reviewers of the typescript. Finally, we thank Michaela Hafner (Vienna), whose organizing abilities are just wonderful, and Christine Brocks, who very proficiently edited the English in all the chapters written by non-native speakers and prepared the index.

Notes on Contributors

Tina Bahovec is Assistant Professor at the Department of Eastern and Southeastern European History of the Alpen-Adria University of Klagenfurt, Austria, and focuses on ethnicity/nation and gender in modern southeastern Europe in her research. Publications include 'Engendering Borders: The Austro-Yugoslav Border Conflict Following the First World War', in A. Schwartz (ed.) *Gender and Modernity in Central Europe: The Austro-Hungarian Monarchy and Its Legacy* (2010), and the edited volume *frauen.männer* (2007).

Bruna Bianchi is Associate Professor at the Department of Comparative Linguistic and Cultural Studies of the University Ca' Foscari Venice, Italy. Her research interests include war and militarism, reflections on war and peace, and war violence. Among Bianchi's latest books is *Crimini di guerra e contro l'umanità: Le violenze ai civili sul fronte orientale (1914–1919)* (2012) and she is the author of 'Psychiatrists, Soldiers and Officers in Italy during the Great War', in M. Micale and P. Lerner (eds) *Traumatic Pasts: History, Psychiatry, and Trauma in the Modern Age, 1870–1931* (2001).

Jason Crouthamel is Associate Professor of History at Grand Valley State University in Allendale, Michigan, and centres on memory, trauma, and masculinity in Germany during the age of total war in his research. He is the author of *The Great War and German Memory: Society, Politics and Psychological Trauma* (2009), '"Comradeship" and "Friendship": Masculinity and Militarization in Germany's Homosexual Emancipation Movement after the First World War', *Gender & History*, 23:1 (2011), pp. 111–129, and 'Male Sexuality and Psychological Trauma: Soldiers and Sexual "Disorder" in World War I and Weimar Germany', *Journal of the History of Sexuality*, 17:1 (2008), pp. 60–84.

Matteo Ermacora is an independent scholar. His research interests include the history of labour, migration, refugees, and the World Wars. Publications on the First World War include *Cantieri di Guerra: Il lavoro dei civili nelle retrovie del fronte italiano (1915–1918)* (2005) and 'Assistance and Surveillance: War Refugees in Italy, 1914–1918', *Contemporary European History*, 16:4 (2007), pp. 445–59.

Alison S. Fell is Professor of French Cultural History in the School of Modern Languages, University of Leeds, UK, where she works both on French women's life-writing and on women's experiences during and after the First World War. She is the author of *Back to the Front: Women as Veterans in France and Britain, 1916–1933* (forthcoming 2016) and has co-edited *Studies in First World War Nursing: New Perspectives* (2013) with C. Hallett and *The Women's Movement in Wartime: International Perspectives 1914–1919* (2007) with I. Sharp.

Susan R. Grayzel is Professor of History at the Department of History and Director of the Sarah Isom Center for Women and Gender Studies of the University of Mississippi. Her research focus is on gender in modern Europe. Publications include *Women's Identities At War: Gender, Motherhood, and Politics in Britain and France during the First World War* (1999), *Women and the First World War* (2002), and *At Home and Under Fire: Domesticating the Air Raid in Britain from the Great War to the Blitz* (2012).

Christa Hämmerle is Associate Professor of Modern and Women's and Gender History at the University of Vienna, Austria, co-founder and co-editor of *L'Homme: Europäische Zeitschrift für Feministische Geschichtswissenschaft*, and chair of the *Sammlung Frauennachlässe* (Collection of Women's Written Papers). Among her fields of research are war and the military, auto/biographical writings and the history of love. Her latest publications include *Heimat/Front: Geschlechtergeschichte(n) des Ersten Weltkrieges in Österreich-Ungarn* (2013) and 'Between Instrumentalisation and Self-Governing: (Female) Ego-Documents in the European Age of Total War', in F.-J. Ruggiu (ed.) *The Uses of First Person Writings: Africa, America, Asia, Europe* (2013).

Virginija Jurėnienė is Professor at the Department of Philosophy and Culture Studies of Vilnius University, Lithuania, and has worked on feminism, representations of women, and the history of women's movements in Lithuania. Publications include *Lietuvos moterų judėjima XIX amžiaus pabaigoje – XX amžiaus pirmojoje pusėje* (2006) and 'The Development of Women's Rights in Lithuania: Striving for Political Equality', in B. Rodríguez-Ruiz and R. Rubio-Marín (eds) *The Struggle for Female Suffrage in Europe: Voting to Become Citizens* (2012).

Julia Barbara Köhne is Visiting Professor at the Humboldt Universität zu Berlin. Her research focus is on cultural studies, media culture and film theory in the twentieth and twenty-first centuries, the history of the body, and the history of military psychiatry. Köhne is author of *Kriegshysteriker: Strategische Bilder und mediale Techniken militärpsychiatrischen Wissens, 1914–1920* (2009) and has co-edited, among others, *Trauma und Film: Inszenierungen eines Nicht-Repräsentierbaren* (2012) and *The Horrors of Trauma in Cinema: Violence, Void, Visualization* (2014) with M. Elm and K. Kabalek.

Manon Pignot is Assistant Professor at the University of Picardie, France, and a member of the Historial de la Grande Guerre's Research Centre. She has studied the wartime experiences of children in two books: *La Guerre des crayons: Quand les petits Parisiens dessinaient la Grande Guerre* (2004) and *Allons enfants de la patrie: Génération Grande Guerre* (2012). As a Junior

Member of the Institut Universitaire de France (IUF), she works mainly on youth and war and has recently edited *L'enfant-soldat XIXe–XXIe siècle: Une approche critique* (2012).

Ingrid E. Sharp is Senior Lecturer in German at the University of Leeds, UK, and researches gender relations in German history. Sharp has co-edited *Aftermaths of War: Women's Movements and Female Activists, 1918–1923* (2011) with M. Stibbe and *The Women's Movement in Wartime: International Perspectives 1914–1919* (2007) with A. S. Fell, she is the author of 'Feminist Peace Activism 1915–2010: Are We Nearly There Yet?', *Peace and Change*, 38:2 (2013), pp. 155–80.

Claudia Siebrecht is Lecturer in Modern European History at the University of Sussex, UK, and has a research focus on the cultural history of war and violence in twentieth-century Germany and Europe. Her book, *The Aesthetics of Loss: German Women's Art of the First World War, 1914–1919*, is published by Oxford University Press (2013). Other publications include the chapter 'Martial Spirit and Mobilisation Myths – Bourgeois Women in Germany and their "Ideas of 1914"', in A. Fell and I. Sharp (eds) *The Women's Movement in Wartime: International Perspectives, 1914–1919* (2007).

Oswald Überegger is Director of the Research Centre for Regional History at the University of Bozen/Bolzano, South Tyrol, Italy. He has worked on regional and military history as well as the history of the First World War. Publications include *Erinnerungskriege: Der Erste Weltkrieg, Österreich und die Tiroler Kriegserinnerung in der Zwischenkriegszeit* (2011) and *Der andere Krieg: Die Tiroler Militärgerichtsbarkeit im Ersten Weltkrieg* (2002). Currently, he is leading a research project on war atrocities carried out by the German and Austro-Hungarian armies in the First World War.

Dorothee Wierling is Professor of Contemporary History and Deputy Director of the Research Centre for Contemporary History at the University of Hamburg, Germany. She has worked on social, gender, generational, and oral history. Publications include *Geboren im Jahr Eins: Der Geburtsjahrgang 1949 in der DDR, Versuch einer Kollektivbiographie* (2002). Forthcoming is *Eine Familie im Krieg: Leben, Sterben und Schreiben 1914–1918* (2013).

Birgitta Bader Zaar is Assistant Professor in the Department of History at the University of Vienna, Austria. Her research centres on comparative legal history, specifically women's suffrage, citizenship, and foreigners. Forthcoming is *Zur Einführung des Frauenwahlrechts: Großbritannien, Deutschland, Österreich, Belgien und die USA im Vergleich* (Böhlau). Published articles include 'Women's Suffrage and War: World War I and Political Reform in a Comparative Perspective', in I. Sulkunen, S.-L. Nevala-Nurmi and P. Markkola (eds) *Suffrage, Gender and Citizenship: International Perspectives on Parliamentary Reforms* (2009).

This page intentionally left blank

1
Introduction: Women's and Gender History of the First World War – Topics, Concepts, Perspectives

Christa Hämmerle, Oswald Überegger and Birgitta Bader Zaar

The starting point of this volume was the observation that the upcoming centenary of 2014 has already evoked a wide range of memorial activities, book projects, conferences, and so on, so that a historiographical revisiting, re-discussing, and rewriting of the First World War can be expected in the near future. With this in mind, we are convinced that it is essential to incorporate gender issues from the very outset. Neither the societies of the belligerent nations between 1914 and 1918 nor the consequences of the First World War can be sufficiently documented and understood without considering the analytical category of gender. Historians of women and gender have impressively revealed this fact over the last decades,[1] albeit quite disparately for different European countries and national historiographies. Nevertheless, mainstream history of the First World War all too often still ignores a gender perspective, which seems to be especially true for the context of Eastern and south-eastern Europe. Motivated by international imbalances of current gender approaches to the history of the First World War and the consequential difficulty of taking up a transnational perspective, we organized a conference on 'The First World War in a Gender Context – Topics and Perspectives', held in Vienna from 29 September to 1 October 2011. This volume presents some of the revised and extended papers of that conference.

In most European countries, the total war of 1914–18 led to extensive support by women not only at the so-called 'home front' – which was mainly conceived as a woman's sphere – but also in the battle zones. In addition and always corresponding to war-related constructions of womanhood, soldierly masculinity was idealized in a far more powerful way than ever before. This had implications for the hegemonic gender order and the structure of society in all belligerent nations. What is more, it also hampered pacifist efforts and activities, which were carried out by only a minority in those years. The transformation of the nation into a collective body of warriors in combat and the associated war mongering and ideological blindness were in fact international phenomena, as was the experience of bellicose violence which varied between different types including gender-differentiated forms.

1

Nevertheless, the question remains to what extent and under which representations those phenomena shaped the warring European societies, which themselves were fractured and riven by numerous divisions, high levels of inequalities, and conflicts. Furthermore, it can be asked what role the concepts of masculinities and femininities, as well as related subjectivities, played for mass mobilization, perseverance, protest, and resistance. And following on from this, in what way did the idea of citizenship, which was strongly embedded in the war discourses of the time, change? Which current research topics and theorizations can be outlined in these contexts? Is it possible to detect general phenomena and experiences transgressing the framework of national history? And finally, which are the main research desiderata; that is to say, which are the key topics and aspects worthwhile examining, in particular against the background of mainstream First World War history?

Far from answering all these questions, the chapters in this volume lead us towards a broader comparative perspective which will hopefully be fleshed out in the future. Their topics are of paramount significance for a women's and gender history of the First World War: gender concepts of the relationship between front-line and 'home front', violence, pacifism, contemporary peace movements, and the issue of citizenship. These aspects are examined not only in regard to well-researched fields such as the Western Front and the war societies of Britain, France, and Germany, but also for Lithuania, Italy, Austria, and Slovenia – the latter two being part of the Habsburg Monarchy during the war – which are less familiar in the international context and far more marginalized.

'Home front' and front lines – femininities and masculinities

At an earlier stage of interest, historians primarily focused on those places where the presence of women became more apparent during the First World War; that is, at the so-called 'home front' (a term invented at the outbreak of war in 1914). The higher public visibility of women was a result of the fact that they joined the labour market to an unprecedented extent and took on previously more or less exclusively male professions and jobs. In addition, many of them, led by feminists and pre-war women's associations, also entered the public sphere supporting their warring home nations. The state not only fostered these activities including a broad range of public relief and pro-war work, but also developed new paternalistic political concepts towards women and families in order to substitute for the fighting male breadwinner. For that purpose, some European states such as Germany, the Habsburg Monarchy, and Britain, introduced allowances for soldiers' wives and families and, at the same time, used them as disciplinary measures in order to control women.[2] In tension with these benefits, a new form of social policy aimed at supporting female employment, be it in the munitions industry, where working conditions and self-conceptions of women seem to have been quite different throughout Europe,[3] albeit in offices and shops, public service, and so on. In this process, the war-related extension of female work had always been considered merely temporary. This was accompanied by a dense discursive 'mobilization of femininity', developed and propagated both by the women involved and by male-dominated politics and (visual) media. Therefore, despite the obvious contradictions to reality, discourses on motherhood and allegedly natural female roles and tasks such as devotion, self-abandonment, love, and care for others prevailed or were even reaffirmed during wartime, as research has revealed in detailed studies.[4]

On the other hand, historians' attention has also been attracted by women who, more obviously, seem to have transgressed traditional gender roles and spaces in the opposite direction – towards the front lines. At least for the Western Front and the warring countries engaged here, namely France, Britain, Germany, and the United States, much has been written about mobilization, organization, and experiences of wartime nurses and the few female doctors, who very often were deployed directly in or just behind front areas. We also have a number of accounts of women who became well known in their own countries as car-drivers, spies, or resisters against occupation due to specific heroic events.[5] In addition, there are some detailed studies on those women who, in a very concrete sense, were militarized by wearing uniforms and being integrated into military contexts. For instance, the Women's Army Auxiliary Corps (later Queen Mary's Army Auxiliary Corps), which was founded by the British government in 1917, or its less known equivalents, the German 'Etappenhelferinnen' and the Austrian 'weibliche Hilfskräfte der Armee im Felde', established in the same year, supported combatant soldiers and released men for the trenches.[6] Some women were even active soldiers, either officially acknowledged as in the case of Polish and Ukrainian women's units in the Habsburg Army and the Russian Women's 'Battalion of Death'[7] or in some individual cases when women cross-dressed and/or their presence at their husband's or lover's side was as well accepted as their fighting at the front lines.

To be sure, these are only a few examples of the complex relevance and dimensions of substantial female involvement in the war. However, they indicate that researchers inevitably had to address the contested issue of women's 'emancipation' as a consequence of the war, not least because military history has successfully supported this view for a long time. Historians had to acknowledge that women's war efforts did not cause a profound change of the hegemonic gender order or long-term improvements of the status of women, even though they might have been of great importance for the contemporaries themselves. Also, dichotomous and hierarchically constructed concepts of femininity and masculinity prevailed in the public sphere of the 'home front' and the theatres of war, where women faced being denounced and sexualized. These insights led historians to believe that the war did not, in fact, have any long-term implications on political gender transformations. On the contrary, its impact in this respect was, as Françoise Thébaud has

argued, deeply conservative.[8] By comparing both World Wars and their aftermath, other scholars developed the theory of the 'double helix'. It combines
more explicitly research findings on women's commitment and advanced
status in wartime societies with the category of masculinity, stating that soldierly masculinities were valued far more than women's partially expanded
roles. Thus, women always remained subordinated within the gender
system. In the words of Margaret R. and Patrice L.-R. Higonnet, who proposed
the concept of the 'double helix' with its intertwined strands in the late
1980s: 'The female strand on the helix is opposed to the male strand, and
position on the female strand is subordinate to position on the male strand.
The image of the double helix allows us to see that, although the roles of
men and women vary greatly from culture to culture, their relationship
is in some sense constant.'[9]

Since then, research has often referred to this influential model. Many
scholars have confirmed the permanent tendency of social and ideological
reproductions of the 'double helix' in times of total war. The model seems
to be particularly valid in regard to the contemporary construction of the
front/'home front' dichotomy that was strongly advocated by state authorities
and (male as well as female) agents of war propaganda by using – or rather
misusing – a polarized set of gender concepts for the purpose of maintaining
order. Here, gender was a weapon of modern warfare, putting immense moral
pressure on men and women. However, this is only one side of the coin: These
polarized gender concepts had their limitations, ambiguities, and disruptions,
and ultimately led to the dissolution of the dichotomizing power system – not
least because of the chaos of war. Following such insights, the model of the
'double helix' has also been criticized, above all for being too mechanistic and
focusing exclusively on the discursive structure of the hegemonic gender order,
thus underestimating experiences or agencies on the one hand, and ambivalences or ambiguities, as well as war-related 'gender troubles', on the other.

As this volume shows, these discussions are still ongoing and taking on
more and more dimensions. They have particularly developed in recent years
due to approaches based on personal narratives, such as war correspondence
or diaries,[10] and the by now dense work on the history of masculinities,
which has emphasized an immense variety and fluidity in the category of
masculinity.[11] In this respect, R. W. Connell's ground-breaking work on masculinity needs to be mentioned. Connell has coined the term 'hegemonic
masculinity', which is defined as the most influential, most accepted, or
most idealized variation of masculinity permanently re/constructed by the
ruling alliance of economy, military, and politics. In contrast, other forms
of masculinity are subordinated and marginalized (as well as all forms of
femininity). Until today, Connell's theoretical concept has been discussed,
criticized, and further developed in a stimulating way – also regarding topics
such as military and war.[12] As a consequence, and closely related to feminist
theories of gender in general such as in Joan W. Scott's influential approach,

our view of gender as a category of power which establishes differences and hierarchies (also between men) has been sharpened.[13] Similarly, and again rather implicitly than explicitly, current research on the 'home front' and the battle zones as well as on the dissolution of these spheres, also applies to the concept of gender performativity. This theoretical approach, introduced by J. Butler, focuses on the permanent – and therefore always shifting – re/construction of various forms of masculinity and femininity in given contexts, transgressing sexes and causing permanent 'gender trouble'.[14]

Thus, by examining different aspects of the complex relationship between front line and 'home front', current research clearly demonstrates that these spheres were closely linked and intertwined in many ways. The chapters in this volume confirm such a view most strikingly. Matteo Ermacora, for instance, in Chapter 2 offers a micro-study of Italian women from the rural Friuli region near the Austrian–Italian front. These women were mobilized for work in factories, on farms, for relief activities, and as so-called *portatrici* who brought fresh supplies to the soldiers in the Alpine trenches. While we have evidence that many were proud of their support, local authorities and the Church also feared their potential 'masculinization' due to their war experience, and tried to control them in moral terms. Susan R. Grayzel, in Chapter 8 deconstructs the myth of a dichotomy between battle zone and 'home front' by using a different angle. She explains the dramatic dissolution of both spheres by pointing out the effects of modern war technology such as air raids and gas attacks against soldiers and civilians 'at home' alike. Grayzel analyses British and French gendered rhetoric on this issue by focusing on the widespread use of the shocking image of the 'Baby in the Gas Mask' and related representations of the maternal body.

The involvement of children as part of the mobilized 'home front' is emphasized in Manon Pignot's chapter on girls and boys in wartime France. In Chapter 10, she describes how they were guided by teachers and parents to support both the soldiers in battle and their families at home. Propaganda discourse addressed these children in a clearly gendered fashion. However, their experiences were not exclusively shaped by gender, but also by categories such as family constellation, social background, and location as Pignot can show, particularly in regard to the children's strained situation in the occupied territories. Claudia Siebrecht's Chapter 9, on the figure of the female mourner in Germany, focuses on women who perceived the brutality of war in a different way. In her approach to this elusive topic, which again transgresses the front line/'home front' divide, Siebrecht not only draws on letters exchanged between soldiers and their families, but also on female art and literature. She shows that the propagated ideal of the proud mourner as part of a moral economy indeed prevailed in contemporary discourses and was often adopted. Yet hegemonic gender models for bereavement were, in fact, also undermined in various and more complex ways than the male–female dichotomy of the 'double helix' suggests.

Three further chapters of the volume give illuminating insights into gender shifts at the battle front. They furthermore underline the important fact that the front line cannot be equated with masculinity or with men in general. As Julia Köhne maintains in Chapter 5, the image of the soldier as a masculine hero and the concept of soldiering as a hegemonic ideal were fragile. She examines the visualizations of shell-shocked and mentally wounded men, the so called 'war hysterics', in scientific films produced by medical officers. Alison S. Fell, on the contrary, in Chapter 7 offers a case study of female war heroines who were active at or near the Western Front, namely Emilienne Moreau, Elsie Knocker, and Mairi Chisholm. Comparing the highly patriotic function of their wartime glorification in France and Britain with their post-war autobiographies, Fell reveals a more complex story. She points out that in general, the heroines' status as war veterans was disputed and dependent on class affiliation and political contexts. This is also true of homosexuals, whose war and post-war history is ambiguous and has been widely ignored. Jason Crouthamel's study breaks new ground by connecting the foci on both homo- and heterosexual German soldiers. In Chapter 4, he examines 'gender trouble'; that is to say, the shifting concepts of masculinities *and* feminini-ties at the battlefront, showing how hegemonic masculinity was frequently threatened and undermined in the trenches by potentially homoerotic behaviour, relations, and experiences, which were considered to be 'feminine' or 'deviant'. Nevertheless, in the interwar period and pre-fascist political atmosphere in Germany, organized homosexual veterans distanced them-selves from any conception of homosexuals as 'effeminate'. On the contrary, they used the militarized rhetoric of the hypermasculine warrior, hoping to gain political momentum.

Having reflected on these issues, furthermore, different levels of time and temporality might be considered to an even greater extent than previous research has done when comparing war- and post-war evidence. How can we explain the dynamics of the interwar period, when changes such as 'gender troubles' and, in particular, dissolving gender dichotomies, which were brought about during the war, simply disappeared from cultural memory afterwards? What is the conclusion of our findings on disparate functionalities and practices of gender in total war regarding its mainly one-dimensional use for propagandistic, political, and war-affirming purposes? More in depth research of the complex relationship between front line and 'home front' should, in our view, examine the political contexts and pressure groups which had the (discursive) power to publicly interpret war and war experiences. This includes studying, in detail, wartime interpretations in comparison with developments in the post-war period, when 'wars' of commemoration were led and won by (nationalist) right-wing groups in many European countries.[15] Furthermore, the discussion should be widened to include more Eastern and Southern European case studies. Another interesting topic, the relation between gender and emotions, has been developed in the context of the promising history of emotions.[16] It seems to us – and this volume hints at this in various ways – that such research could considerably improve our understanding of the complex relationship between the battlefields and 'home fronts' of the First World War.

Gendered dimensions and experiences of war violence

This statement seems equally true for the pivotal topic of violence. In contrast to its importance, the history of violence in the First World War has, for a long time, been neither in the focus of public nor historiographic interest; in particular when it comes, more specifically, to the history of violence against international and common law. Violations of war rules in modern military conflicts are commonly seen as part of the crises and wars of the twentieth century, which followed the First World War. This is particularly true for a gendered perspective on violence. Studies over the last two decades pursuing this angle have mainly referred to the Second World War and the Yugoslav Wars. They primarily investigated war rape as a well-established topic of research on gender and violence.[17] With reference to the current state of gender research on violence of the First World War, which, in general, is insufficient, a substantial regional imbalance is particularly deplorable. Whereas the territories of the Western Front again are examined in greater depth, there have been no profound studies on the complex relations of violence between armies, soldiers, and civilians in other theatres of war. In contrast, for the countries involved in the war of the West, research has focused on gendered war violence.[18]

As mentioned above, several of these studies address the issue of war rape, which, in comparison with the Second World War, has been neither sufficiently nor systematically examined for the time between 1914 and 1918. So far the majority of academic research has concentrated on rape conducted by German soldiers in the occupied territories of Belgium and France. Regardless of the vast extent of rape during the German invasion for which exact figures cannot be ascertained, recent research has increasingly examined the question of how this phenomenon was sometimes deliberately overdrawn and of how rape victims were instrumentalized. In this context, rape served as a general metaphor for the German occupation of the Belgian and the French nation.

Overall, research findings on war rape demonstrate that sexual crimes on a large scale did not only occur during the chaotic phases of invasion at the beginning of the war, as some historians assume.[19] Rather, they were a common and significant phenomenon throughout the entire course of the war and closely linked to the operative dynamic of warfare, in particular to mobile warfare. The fact that in many cases women were raped deliberately in front of their relatives and other uninvolved bystanders indicates that monocausal explanations of war rapes such as the argument of the sex drive fall short, which is confirmed by recent studies. Instead, complex, in some cases even subliminal, clusters of code and meaning can be outlined as underlying reasons for rape with aspects such as humiliation and degradation conducted by a mainly male and hostile 'we-community'.[20] In-depth research on rape during the First World War from a modern cultural sciences and gender studies perspective still remains a desideratum, particularly with respect to the underexplored situation on the Balkan and the Eastern Fronts.[21]

However, beyond the well-established topic of war rape, there remains the more general question about the complex nature of the relation between gender and violence in times of war. Three aspects are to be considered in this respect: firstly, the act of inflicting and the suffering of violence as a consequence of warfare and occupation. In this context, the character of violence conducted by soldiers – that is to say, the type of violent acts – and the identification of victims and perpetrators as well as the narratives of different contexts of violence play a significant role. It has to be examined in what situations and under what circumstances violent acts against civilians, however involved in the war, took place, in particular against women. Apart from sexual assaults, women in the territories of warfare and occupation – especially in the East and the South – fell victim to several forms of violence, for instance when they got injured or killed in the context of the scorched-earth policy, when they became victims of mass executions of civilians as a consequence of the fight against guerrilla warfare, when they got caught up in hostage-takings which were carried out by all armies on a massive scale, in evacuations and deportations throughout the territories of the front, or when they were recruited as forced labourers.

The second aspect reflects on the wide field of violence experience as a specific type of war experience. The issue of individual perception and interpretation of excessive military violence by soldiers in the context of modern mass warfare has been largely ignored. This is also true for approaches to the suffering of violence and its consequences focused on the victims – or the role of soldiers as victims – as Christa Hämmerle's contribution in this volume demonstrates. In Chapter 6 she focuses on narrations of violence in war accounts of nurses serving in the Habsburg Empire, who were often deployed directly behind or even in the midst of the battlefields, like nurses of other belligerent countries, and thus witnessed much of the cruelty and barbarity of industrialized warfare. Their autobiographical texts can be read, in a paradoxical way, as an attempt to inscribe their war experiences into (always gendered) hegemonic war interpretations and legitimizations on the one hand, and as individual lamentations and critique of the traumatizing mass killing on the other. In this context several further questions arise: How important was personal suffering and participation in physical and mental violence for the overall war experience of men and women? In what ways was violence interpreted in the context of certain situations and what gender-related differences can be observed? How did war societies deal with mass killings and what patterns of remembrance in terms of both perpetrators and victims evolved? How should national and regional differences and characteristics be addressed?

Military societies on the one hand, and civilian societies on the other experienced war violence (such as war imprisonment, sexual, or other forms of war violence including active killing) sometimes in a very different, sometimes in a rather similar way. The process of imagining, experiencing, and carrying out (even excessive) war violence affected prevalent concepts of masculinity and femininity. Thus, the third aspect of future research projects – ideally with an interdisciplinary focus and within the scope of a broad concept of violence – would have to deal with the question of how the routinization of violence altered, damaged, redefined, and radicalized gender constructions in the long term. In this context, violence and discourses on violence have to be examined beyond the typical forms of inflicting or suffering of physical violence during military conflicts in war-affected areas. Gendered discourses on violence, violence projections by media, and propaganda interpretations of violence gained momentum during the war and changed discourses on violence and war of the 'home front'. Thus, it may be worthwhile to examine these discourses on violence and to point out their characteristics, which in part depend on social strata. For this purpose, the continuous discursive communication between front and 'home front' and between various roles of combatants and non-combatants should be taken into account. Notably, Dorothee Wierling's contribution in this volume demonstrates the benefits such an approach can provide. In her analysis of the complex communication network of an intellectual Berlin family and their war experiences in Chapter 3, Wierling renders differing styles and levels of communication and analyses various interpretations of war. She reflects on divergent perceptions of violence and masculinity by different family members and traces how their narrative strategies redefine the genre of war communication – especially in a heroic-martial sense, and, in the case of military violence, are oriented towards the respective recipients of their communication.

Women's war effort and feminist goals: pacifism – internationalism – citizenship

Military violence and war in general challenged the pre-war women's movements' hopes for a moral reorganization of the world based on women's values of equilibrium and motherhood. The outbreak of the war also contested the internationalism of the women's movement and exerted a great strain on the latent tension between national interests and the peace agenda within international women's organizations, such as the International Council of Women and the International Woman Suffrage Alliance. Only a few scholars have reflected on this topic so far.[22] The minority of feminists who opted for pacifism and objected to the war has merely appeared in side-notes on splits in the women's movements during the war. In Chapter 11, Bruna Bianchi reviews some of the pacifist journals edited by these internationally minded women and argues that a new pacifism emerged during the war, whose representatives insisted that nurturing motherhood was the most important impediment to war. Backing such an argument implied an either/or decision concerning membership in women's associations in some countries. It could also affect the question of whether to attend the women's peace conference held in The Hague in April 1915, where the forerunner committee of the Women's International League for Peace and Freedom was founded. As Ingrid Sharp's contribution in Chapter 12 shows for the case of Germany, commitment to peace also had repercussions on those parts of the women's movements which supported the war effort. Their relationship to the nation state was potentially jeopardized by their pacifist sisters, and the ensuing controversies and oppositions had a far-reaching impact on the interwar period. In this way, pacifist efforts also affected women's claims to citizenship based on their patriotic commitment.

The question of the war's impact on women's emancipation has already been briefly mentioned above in the context of women's war efforts on the 'home front'. Access to equal citizenship is a point that has been widely discussed among historians, at least regarding suffrage. The idea that women's commitment to war relief and their mobilization for the war economy resulted in the right to vote is both sustained and contested in this context. It is, on the one hand, widely accepted that those parts of the women's movement championing their nation's war effort were in fact convinced that their relief work would prove 'women's patriotism and their fitness for citizenship'.[23] However, the assertion that parliaments actually ceded suffrage to women because of this commitment has been challenged. Criticism was not only based on the Anglocentrism of this argument; a modified version of this concept was also discussed particularly in British historiography itself.[24] Thus, a differentiated view, which ties in an understanding of citizenship as subjectivity,[25] has evolved acknowledging the fact that the war changed cultural concepts and discourses on political rights and gender, as Susan Grayzel and Nicoletta Gullace in particular have argued. On the one hand, wartime rhetoric de-radicalized women's enfranchisement by defining political rights through women's 'contributions to the "public" and "national" good'. On the other hand, the war could also establish a masculine basis for the parliamentary vote when patriotism and military service were explicitly considered as qualification for the vote, as in the British Representation of the People Act of 1918.[26]

To be sure, historians' early emphasis that the war can be viewed as a catalyst for women's legal rights insofar as it put women's suffrage on the political agenda is still true for a number of countries.[27] Yet the war did not necessarily result in full political, not to say citizenship, rights as is, for instance, well known to be the case for France and Italy, and even for Britain. Political interests still prevailed and ultimately decided whether women were enfranchised or not, whether they achieved equal constitutional rights or not.[28] Two contributions in this volume explore this issue by including gendered concepts of citizenship in the formation of new nation states in the aftermath of the war. Virginija Jurėnienė emphasizes the liberal model of citizenship as a legal status endowed with certain rights in Chapter 13 on Lithuania. The Baltic state was occupied by German troops during the war and experienced a division of women's war activities due to the emigration of a part of the Lithuanian women's movement to Russia. These constraints consequently shaped efforts to attain equal citizenship in post-war independent Lithuania. Tina Bahovec looks at the Slovene case. In Chapter 14 she takes up the republican model of citizenship that emphasizes national participation and is closely connected to the state's interest in creating a national community and identity. Her chapter addresses the discourse on the gendered meanings of citizenship in times of peace and war during the plebiscite campaigns of 1920. She examines how Slovene women of Carinthia were influenced in their decision on whether parts of Southern Carinthia were to be integrated into the newly founded Austrian republic or rather into the Kingdom of Serbs, Croats and Slovenes.

As we have argued for the other topics of a gendered perspective of the First World War, here again, further studies on citizenship and war for as yet marginalized regions are to be desired. However, it is not only the question of political rights that requires attention. A few researchers have already critically discussed the impact of the war on the developing welfare state in a gendered perspective; for instance, as already mentioned above in regard to allowances for soldiers' wives and families.[29] Still, more in-depth research examining the relationship between civil and social rights and the war remains necessary.

In any case, the 1914 centenary is an opportunity to motivate such studies, to close gaps, and to systematically analyse and research a more detailed and comparative women's and gender history of the First World War. It thus offers the chance of rewriting the history of the First World War in general and of re-evaluating the high potential of the gender category for this topic in particular.

Notes

1. Due to limited space, this introduction cannot offer an extensive bibliography of the research on women's and gender history and the First World War. Instead, it cites only some selected studies: G. Braybon and P. Summerfield (1987) *Out of the Cage: Women's Experiences in Two World Wars* (New York: Routledge & Kegan Paul); M. R. Higonnet, J. Jenson, S. Michel and M. C. Weitz (eds) (1987) *Behind the Lines: Gender and the Two World Wars* (New Haven: Yale University Press); F. Thébaud (1986) *La femme au temps de la guerre de 14* (Paris: Éditions Stock); F. Thébaud (1992) 'La Grande Guerre: Le triomphe de la division sexuelle', in F. Thébaud (ed.) *Histoire*

des Femmes en Occident 5: Le XXe siècle (Paris: Plon), pp. 31–89; M. C. Adams (1990) *The Great Adventure: Male Desire and the Coming of World War I* (Bloomington, IN: Indiana University Press); J. Bourke (1996) *Dismembering the Male: Men's Bodies, Britain and the Great War* (Chicago, IL: University of Chicago Press); U. Daniel (1997) *The War from Within: German Working Class Women in the First World War* (Oxford: Berg); S. R. Grayzel (1999) *Women's Identities at War: Gender, Motherhood, and Politics in Britain and France during the First World War* (Chapel Hill, NC: University of North Carolina Press); M. H. Darrow (2000) *French Women and the First World War: War Stories of the Home Front* (Oxford: Berg); B. Davis (2000) *Home Fires Burning: Food, Politics, and Everyday Life in World War I Berlin* (Chapel Hill, NC: University of North Carolina Press); S. R. Grayzel (2002) *Women and the First World War* (London: Pearson Education); K. Hagemann and S. Schüler-Springorum (eds) (2002) *Home/Front: The Military, War and Gender in Twentieth-Century Germany* (New York: Berg); É. Morin-Rotureau (2004) (ed.) *1914–1918: Combats de femmes. Les femmes, pilier de l'effort de guerre* (Paris: Éditions Autrement); N. M. Wingfield and M. Bucur (eds) (2006) *Gender and War in Twentieth-Century Eastern Europe* (Bloomington, IN: Indiana University Press); A. Fell and I. Sharp (eds) (2007) *The Women's Movement in Wartime: International Perspectives, 1914–19* (Basingstoke: Palgrave Macmillan); A. S. Belzer (2010) *Women and the Great War: Femininity under Fire in Italy* (Basingstoke: Palgrave Macmillan); M. Szczepaniak (2011) *Militärische Männlicheiten in Deutschland und Österreich im Umfeld des Großen Krieges: Konstruktionen und Dekonstruktionen* (Würzburg: Könighausen & Neumann).

2. For Germany, see the comparative study on allowances in the First and Second World Wars by B. Kundrus (1995) *Kriegerfrauen: Familienpolitik und Geschlechterverhältnisse im Ersten und Zweiten Weltkrieg* (Hamburg: Christians).

3. In former Austria and the German Empire, the situation of female workers in the war industry became dramatically bad during the conflict. See Daniel, *War from Within*; and for Austria, S. Augeneder (1987) *Arbeiterinnen im Ersten Weltkrieg: Lebens- und Arbeitsbedingungen proletarischer Frauen in Österreich* (Wien: Europaverlag).

4. On the discursive meaning of motherhood, see especially Grayzel, *Women's Identities*.

5. See studies mentioned in note 1 as well as, for example, C. Antier, M. Walle and O. Lahaie (2008) *Les espionnes dans la Grande Guerre* (Rennes: Éditions Quest-France); S. Das (2005) *Touch and Intimacy in First World War Literature* (Cambridge: Cambridge University Press), pp. 175–203; C. Hallett (2010) *Containing Trauma: Nursing Work in the First World War* (Manchester: Manchester University Press).

6. France, for example, did not establish a uniformed women's military auxiliary corps, although many women demanded it; instead, they worked for the military as civilians – again from 1917 on, when the number of soldiers decreased dramatically; see Darrow, *French Women*, pp. 229–67. For Germany, see B. Schöneberger (2002) *Mobilising 'Etappenhelferinnen' for Service with the Military: Gender Regimes in First World War Germany* (u-Thesis, University of Oxford); for the Habsburg Monarchy, M. Healy (2004) *Vienna and the Fall of the Habsburg Empire: Total War and Everyday Life in World War I* (Cambridge: Cambridge University Press), pp. 204–9.

7. S. R. Grayzel (2010) 'Women and Men', in J. Horne (ed.) *A Companion to World War I* (Malden, MA: Blackwell), p. 272.

8. Thébaud, 'La Grande Guerre', p. 74.

9. M. R. Higonnet and P. L.-R. Higonnet (1987) 'The Double Helix', in Higonnet, Jenson, Michel and Weitz, *Behind the Lines*, p. 34.

10. See, for example, C. Hämmerle (1999) '"You let a weeping woman call you home?" Private correspondences during the First World War in Austria and Germany', in

R. Earle (ed.) *Epistolary Selves: Letters and Letter-Writers, 1600–1945* (Aldershot: Ashgate), pp. 152–82; J. Meyer (2009) *Men of War: Masculinity and the First World War in Britain* (Basingstoke: Palgrave Macmillan); M. Roper (2009) *The Secret Battle: Emotional Survival in the Great War* (Manchester: Manchester University Press); B. Ziemann (2003) 'Geschlechterbeziehungen in deutschen Feldpostbriefen des Ersten Weltkrieges', in C. Hämmerle and E. Saurer (eds) *Briefkulturen und ihr Geschlecht: Zur Geschichte der privaten Korrespondenz vom 16. Jahrhundert bis heute* (Vienna: Böhlau), pp. 261–82.

11. For example, S. Dudink, K. Hagemann and J. Tosh (eds) (2004) *Masculinities in Politics and War: Gendering Modern History* (Manchester: Manchester University Press); U. Frevert (2004) *A Nation in Barracks: Modern Germany, Military Conscription and Civil Society* (Oxford: Berg); Meyer, *Men of War*; Roper, *The Secret Battle*.

12. R. W. Connell (2005 [1995]) *Masculinities* (2nd edn, Berkeley: University of California Press); see also J. Tosh (2004) 'Hegemonic Masculinity and the History of Gender', in Dudink, Hagemann and Tosh, *Masculinities in Politics and War*, pp. 41–58; M. Dinges (2005) (ed.) *Männer – Macht – Körper: Hegemoniale Männlichkeiten vom Mittelalter bis heute* (Frankfurt am Main: Campus).

13. J. W. Scott (1986) 'Gender: A Useful Category of Historical Analysis', *American Historical Review*, 91:5, pp. 1053–75.

14. J. Butler (1999 [1990]) *Gender Trouble: Feminism and the Subversion of Identity* (2nd edn, New York: Routledge).

15. See, for example, the micro-studies by O. Überegger (2011) *Erinnerungskriege: Der Erste Weltkrieg, Österreich und die Tiroler Kriegserinnerung in der Zwischenkriegszeit* (Innsbruck: Universitätsverlag Wagner) and B. Ziemann (2012) *Contested Commemorations: Republican War Veterans and Weimar Political Culture* (Cambridge: Cambridge University Press), as well as J. Winter (1998) *Sites of Memory, Sites of Mourning: The Great War in European Cultural History* (Cambridge: Cambridge University Press).

16. See, for example, U. Frevert (2011) *Emotions in History – Lost and Found* (Budapest: Central European University Press).

17. See the footnotes of the chapter 'Sexuelle Gewalt im Ersten Weltkrieg', in B. Beck (2004) *Wehrmacht und sexuelle Gewalt: Sexualverbrechen vor deutschen Militärgerichten 1939-1945* (Paderborn: Schöningh), pp. 42–3. On the history of sexual violence against women in general, see S. Brownmiller (1975) *Against Our Will: Men, Women, and Rape* (New York: Simon & Schuster). On the Second World War, I. Eschebach and R. Mühlhäuser (eds) (2008) *Krieg und Geschlecht: Sexuelle Gewalt im Krieg und Sex-Zwangsarbeit in NS-Konzentrationslagern* (Berlin: Metropol); R. Mühlhäuser (2010) *Eroberungen: Sexuelle Gewalttaten und intime Beziehungen deutscher Soldaten in der Sowjetunion, 1941–1945* (Hamburg: Hamburger Edition). Gender studies have addressed the issue of war rape especially in the aftermath of the Yugoslav Wars, for example, A. Stiglmayer (1994) (ed.) *Mass Rape: The War Against Women in Bosnia-Herzegovina* (Lincoln, NE: University of Nebraska Press).

18. R. Harris (1993) 'The "Child of the Barbarian": Rape, Race and Nationalism in France during the First World War', *Past and Present*, 141, pp. 170–206; S. Audoin-Rouzeau (1995) *L'enfant de l'ennemi, 1914–1918: Viol, avortement, infanticide pendant la Grande Guerre* (Paris: Aubier); N. Gullace (1997) 'Sexual Violence and Family Honor. British Propaganda and International Law during the First World War', *American Historical Review*, 102, pp. 714–47; J. Horne (2000) 'Corps, lieux et nation: La France et l'invasion de 1914', *Annales*, 1, pp. 73–109. See also: J. Horne and A. Kramer (2001) *German Atrocities, 1914: A History of Denial* (New Haven, CT: Yale

University Press); Grayzel, *Women's Identities at War*; N. Gullace (2002) *'The Blood of Our Sons': Men, Women, and the Renegotiation of British Citizenship During the Great War* (Basingstoke: Palgrave Macmillan); R. S. Fogarty (2008) 'Race and Sex, Fear and Loathing in France during the Great War', in D. Herzog (ed.) *Brutality and Desire: War and Sexuality in Europe's Twentieth Century* (Basingstoke: Palgrave Macmillan), pp. 59–90. Italian historians in particular have addressed the issue of rape during the First World War: A. Gibelli (2001) 'Guerra e violenze sessuali: il caso veneto e friulano', in *La memoria della Grande Guerra nelle Dolomiti* (Udine: Gaspari), pp. 195–206; L. Calò (2005) 'Le donne friulane e la violenza di Guerra durante l'occupazione austro-tedesca 1917–1918. Alcuni esempi per la Carnia' in E. Folisi (ed.) *Carnia invasa 1917–1918: Storia, documenti e fotografie dell'occupazione austro-tedesca del Friuli* (Udine: Gaspari), pp. 111–31; D. Ceschin (2006) '"L'estremo oltraggio": La violenza alle donne in Friuli e in Veneto durante l'occupazione franco-germanica (1917–1918)', in B. Bianchi (ed.) *La violenza contro la popolazione civile nella Grande guerra: Deportati, profughi, internati* (Milano: Unicopli), pp. 165–84. For a more general perspective, see also M. Geyer (1998) 'Gewalt und Gewalterfahrung im 20. Jahrhundert – Der Erste Weltkrieg', in R. Spilker and B. Ulrich (eds) *Der Tod als Maschinist: Der industrialisierte Krieg 1914–1918* (Bramsche: Rasch), pp. 241–57.
19. Beck, *Wehrmacht und sexuelle Gewalt*, p. 44.
20. To mention just a few: R. Seifert (1995) 'Der weibliche Körper als Symbol und Zeichen: Geschlechtsspezifische Gewalt und die kulturelle Konstruktion des Krieges', in A. Gestrich (ed.) *Gewalt im Krieg: Ausübung, Erfahrung und Verweigerung von Gewalt in Kriegen des 20. Jahrhunderts* (Münster: Lit), pp. 13–33; C. Hämmerle (2000) 'Von den Geschlechtern der Kriege und des Militärs: Forschungseinblicke und Bemerkungen zu einer neuen Debatte', in T. Kühne and B. Ziemann (eds) *Was ist Militärgeschichte?* (Paderborn: Schöningh), pp. 260–1.
21. On Serbia, see B. Bianchi (2010) 'Gli stupri di massa in Serbia durante la Prima guerra mondiale', in M. Flores (ed.) *Stupri di Guerra: La violenza di massa contro le donne nel Novecento* (Milano: Angeli), pp. 43–60, and the volume by B. Bianchi (2012) *Crimini di guerra e contro l'umanità: Le violenze ai civili sul fronte orientale (1914–1919)* (Milano: Unicopli).
22. For example, L. J. Rupp (1997) *Worlds of Women: The Making of an International Women's Movement* (Princeton, NJ: Princeton University Press); A. Wilmers (2008) *Pazifismus in der internationalen Frauenbewegung (1914–1920): Handlungsspielräume, politische Konzeptionen und gesellschaftliche Auseinandersetzungen* (Essen: Klartext). Women as peace activists in general are dealt with in A. Wiltsher (1985) *Most Dangerous Women: Feminist Peace Campaigners of the Great War* (London: Pandora); D. S. Patterson (2008) *The Search for Negotiated Peace: Women's Activism and Citizen Diplomacy in World War I* (New York: Routledge).
23. Effie McCollum Jones (1917) 'Report on Winona meetings', 8–9 May, in *Minnesota Woman Suffrage Association Records*, Minnesota Historical Society, St Paul. See also M. G. Fawcett (1920) *The Women's Victory and After: Personal Reminiscences, 1911–18* (London: Sidgwick & Jackson), p. 88, and for similar quotes B. Bader-Zaar (2009) 'Women's Suffrage and War: World War I and Political Reform in a Comparative Perspective', in I. Sulkunen, S.-L. Nevala-Nurmi and P. Markkola (eds) *Suffrage, Gender and Citizenship: International Perspectives on Parliamentary Reforms* (Newcastle upon Tyne: Cambridge Scholars), p. 198, n.19.
24. For example M. Pugh (1978) *Electoral Reform in War and Peace 1906–18* (London: Routledge & Kegan Paul); S. S. Holton (1986) *Feminism and Democracy: Women's Suffrage and Reform Politics in Britain 1900–1918* (Cambridge: Cambridge

University Press); for Europe in general, see B. Rodriguez-Ruiz and R. Rubio-Marin (2012) 'Transition to Modernity, the Achievement of Female Suffrage, and Women's Citizenship', in B. Rodriguez-Ruiz and R. Rubio-Marin (eds) *The Struggle for Female Suffrage in Europe: Voting to Become Citizens* (Leiden: Brill), pp. 26–7.

25. That is, 'a multidimensional discursive framework' that 'consists of the languages, rhetorics, and formal categories of claims-making that are accessed and deployed not only by those who are endowed with formal citizenship rights, but also by those excluded from them', K. Canning (2006) 'The Concepts of Class and Citizenship in German History', in *Gender History in Practice: Historical Perspectives on Bodies, Class, and Citizenship* (Ithaca, NY: Cornell University Press), p. 208.

26. Grayzel, *Women's Identities at War*, pp. 206 and 224; Gullace, 'The Blood of Our Sons', p. 169.

27. For example, Higonnet and Higonnet, 'The Double Helix'.

28. Bader-Zaar, 'Women's Suffrage and War', pp. 193–218.

29. For example, S. Pedersen (1993) *Family, Dependence, and the Origins of the Welfare State: Britain and France, 1914–1945* (Cambridge: Cambridge University Press), ch. 2; Kundrus, *Kriegerfrauen*, pt. 1; Healy, *Vienna and the Fall of the Habsburg Empire*, ch. 4.

2
Women Behind the Lines: The Friuli Region as a Case Study of Total Mobilization, 1915–1917

Matteo Ermacora

During the First World War, the northeastern border region of Italy known as Friuli became a rear area of the Italian front.[1] In this period people experienced 'total war' not only due to an extensive use of civilian workers in the context of the logistic efforts of the Italian Army, but also through the militarization of society, through air strikes, internments, and new forms of military control. After the defeat of Caporetto in October 1917,[2] part of the population managed to flee towards other Italian regions, while the others had to bear the harsh Austro-German occupation until the end of the war.[3]

Within this framework, women were deeply involved in the war. In this chapter I examine wartime mobilization of women from the lower class, their changing role, and the relationship between women and wartime society. In addition, I consider the question of how the state and religious authorities tried to maintain traditional gender roles behind the front. Finally, I will compare wartime representations of women and women's subjective perspectives. For this purpose, I refer to various sources such as military and civil administration records, letters and diaries, parish books, newspapers, and interviews conducted between 1999 and 2000.

When analysing women's changing role, we must consider some aspects of the area during both the pre-war years and wartime. Friuli was a rural, barely industrialized region, and characterized by a high level of male seasonal migration with 80,000–100,000 men working in the Habsburg Empire and Germany. Mass migration introduced elements of secularization and socialism to this traditionally Catholic society, which, to a certain degree, challenged patriarchalism and, in consequence, strengthened the position of women within families, especially in the foothills and alpine part of the region called Carnia.[4] As a workforce, women and girls were mainly employed in the countryside, in textile factories, and as servants and housemaids, whilst some of them emigrated abroad and worked in brick kilns. August 1914 had a traumatic effect on the region, as migrants had to return home and the local economy got out of balance. Hunger and unemployment as a consequence of these events led to huge social unrest in 1914/15, in which women were in the first line protesting against high prices and shortages of goods. Issues such as social and welfare benefits, peace, and neutrality as discussed by the socialist movement also contributed to the uproar, which lasted until March 1915.[5]

From May 1915, the region became a 'war zone', divided into 'operation zones' 10–20 kilometres behind the lines and 'rear areas'. In both these areas military authorities had special powers over civilians.[6] The rural society in Friuli was considerably transformed by the deployment of 1.5 million Italian soldiers and by 200,000–250,000 workers who came from other regions to build trenches, barns, roads, and railways.[7] Thus, everyday life, space, time, economy, and relationships were fundamentally changed by militarization. Due to male enlistment, women and children had to cope with the loss of their family income, shortages of essential goods, increasing prices, and inflation. Unprepared for a long-lasting war, the Italian Army exploited the rear area for workforce and raw materials. Within this general framework, the mobilization of society and workforce was implemented, firstly, by the army itself and army organizations such as the 'Segretariato per gli Affari Civili', which took orders directly from the Supreme Command of General Cadorna; secondly, by local authorities (prefetti, mayors); and thirdly, by agrarian institutions and private committees.

The military efficiency of the whole country was closely linked to the economic effort and the capacity to mobilize the civilian population. As Friuli was near the front line the entire society was mobilized in the war effort. While middle- and upper-class women participated in the patriotic effort by joining local committees for work relief and aid to poor people, refugees, soldiers and their families,[8] lower-class women remained indifferent or even hostile to the war they received with both rage and resignation. Their support of the war agenda was improvised and military authorities, especially in the zone near the front line, initially distrusted the local population and accused them of disloyalty. However, the rear area soon became a resource for workers to fill the gaps of the military logistics effort. Women kept on working in the local textile factories and were involved in farming, where they replaced called-up farmers. In Carnia, on the other hand, the logistic needs of the Italian Army and the scarce agricultural resources attracted women to work for army units behind the front lines. The mobilization of the workforce was conducted to different degrees by military and local authorities. In 1915–16, landowners and mayors sought to encourage peasant women to take up jobs in farm work in order to improve agricultural production. Another type of mobilization was promoted by the state itself and realized by local committees which involved adult women with small children, whose husbands were soldiers, in sewing uniforms and knitting woollen scarves, sweaters, and socks. Between 1915 and 1917, in Udine alone, about 1500 women were employed in this task. It was a form of aid through work, but wages were not sufficient to allow the survival of the families. However, this kind of work was used for propaganda purposes to confirm women's traditional domestic role.[9] Women had to fend for themselves and showed great adaptability. During the war, women worked alternatively in the agricultural and industrial sectors, in textile factories, for the army's logistics services and in small businesses. This implied that women, especially young girls, had to move to the interior of the region, and to change their jobs to search for better wages and suitable working conditions.

Women's mobilization in the countryside

Concern regarding the 'collapse' of agricultural production was common to all rural areas of Italy, as the debates in the Chamber of Deputies illustrate. The situation in Friuli was marked by increasing difficulties, such as a shortage of labour due to enlistment in the army and to the involvement of younger and older male labourers in the logistics effort, as well as infrequent use of farm machinery. From March 1916, the main agrarian association (Associazione Agraria Friulana) urgently advised mayors, priests, and teachers to mobilize the countryside in order to keep up supplies.[10] It was somewhat of a mass draft: 'The land must not be left abandoned. [...] Behind every army an army of workers is absolutely indispensable [...]. It is therefore necessary that the work of the absent men is replaced by old men, women, and children.'[11]

There are no figures available for this increase in involvement. Nevertheless, during 1916–17 women, young girls, and children replaced men on almost every farm. They performed men's work, such as ploughing, threshing, mowing, fertilizing, driving cars, looking after the cattle, and they had to use machinery for the first time.[12] Observers pointed out that the work in the fields and stables was taken care of 'entirely by women'.[13] Local authorities and landowners emphasized that female work required not only 'compensation' but also 'public recognition'; landowners and priests played an important role in mobilizing women. Following the French example, mayors and the Agrarian Association started to award silver medals to peasant women as patriotic symbols of cooperation. In June 1916, the Minister of Agriculture also decided to deliver diplomas, medals, and prize money to peasant women.[14] In 1917, agricultural production was stimulated through incentives.

These initiatives were accompanied by intensive propaganda: Agrarian bulletins applauded women's new roles and tasks in the countryside and celebrated peasant women within a traditional framework as role models of patriotism and self-sacrifice, sobriety and renouncement.[15] These articles demonstrated that women could do men's jobs. They were called 'female heroes of the fields' and portrayed as soldiers' mothers or wives who were waiting for their sons and husbands. In the meantime, they looked after house and land, they were attending to housekeeping and farming and in so doing they emulated the soldiers at the front. Rhetorically, the fields became 'battlegrounds', and women were depicted as 'wilful', 'strong', 'energetic', and 'heroic' as they were 'quietly' responding to the 'fatherland's call'.[16]

The first topic that was highlighted by propaganda in 1916 was the notion of 'cooperation'; that is to say, the involvement of women in the national war effort as a 'patriotic duty'. By using dialogic texts and didactic poems which were often written in the local Friulian language to suggest a sort of closeness, propaganda presented women's new roles as recognized and endorsed by God and the nation itself.[17] Loneliness, separation, and even death of their relatives at the front line became noble reasons for their activities. The second notion was 'stability': stability of production, of gender roles, of families. Even male peasants recognized women's resistance to fatigue, their dedication to the family and to their loved ones at the front as 'patience' and 'obedience'.[18]

Although female labour was not a novelty given women's wartime industrial employment, this development also raised concerns in Friulian society. For that reason, propaganda paid particular attention to gender hierarchy and presented this female work as temporary and exceptional in order to avoid women's masculinization. Photographs depicting women who did 'men's jobs' and used tools and machinery from the 'male world' were not usually published. The few pictures showing women using wagons and machinery presented these tasks as the necessary process of mechanization and the modernization of agricultural production. Abstract and rhetorical ideas were personified and real people shown as examples, such as the 'courageous' Santina Mantovani from Codroipo, mother of eight children, whose husband had been called up and who worked on her own on her large estate.[19]

Due to increasing difficulties, the tone of propaganda changed in 1917. The image of peasant women gradually became militarized. It was used to disseminate the ability to endure suffering, discipline, sobriety, and to rationalize food consumption,[20] in stark contrast to the image of young urban female workers who were accused of unnecessary spending.[21] Another propaganda keyword in 1917 was 'strength'. The nation needed 'strong' wives and mothers who would dry their eyes and could cope with mourning and weakness. The increasing atmosphere of resistance and war-weariness among soldiers is well portrayed by a poem, entitled 'Madre Friulana' (Friulian Mother), published by a leading newspaper: A patriotic mother takes her deserter son back to the battlefront. In so doing, she symbolizes every woman's duty.[22]

Local churches contributed to this discourse. In fact, the Archbishop of Udine Anastasio Rossi, who was a patriot, loyally supported the Italian war effort in the official bulletin *Rivista diocesana udinese* (Journal of the diocese of Udine) between 1915 and 1919. He also played an important role in the representation of women. He mobilized peasant women in public letters, prompted them to subscribe to the national war loan (in January 1916) and accepted that people had to work on Sundays (in April 1916). In February 1917, Rossi asked parish priests to urge congregants to reduce their consumption: The keyword 'rationing' was associated with the moral issue of 'renunciation'.[23] A few months later, he requested them to improve agricultural production. Although parish priests in their diaries underlined the massive work of women and children, labour conditions were not challenged in general, yet nurseries for small children were introduced in almost every village from 1915 onwards to facilitate women's work.[24] Nevertheless, in 1917 the Catholic authorities started denouncing unnecessary spending and alcoholism among women in the countryside. Furthermore, they condemned defeatism and women who refused to work in order to hasten the end of the war.[25] In so doing, priests joined the paternalism of civil authorities and landowners who praised only women who sacrificed themselves for their families and the nation.[26] As had already happened with the demonstrations of 1914, newspapers in 1917 portrayed women protesting against shortages of food and of state benefits as 'imboscati' (slackers) and as being hysterical and irrational. By using a sarcastic tone, articles ridiculed and discredited the unrest. Rural women who stole wood, wheat, and maize were dehumanized and depicted as 'rats'.[27]

All in all, local authorities 'discovered' the female workforce in the countryside during wartime. Their astonishment about women's capabilities was the expression of a deeply bourgeois and patriarchal culture which had confined women to emotional space, devalued female productivity, and feared women's presence in society outside of the private sphere.[28] For this reason, their work was officially recognized for the first time in special celebrations in village town halls. However, a paternalistic tone prevailed in public discourse, in which women were treated as children who needed to be educated. This public recognition did not improve their everyday lives.

Government and landowners counted on women to accept any hardship in order to make working the land as cheap as possible. Wages (0.80–1.50 lire per day, from dawn to dusk) as well as prizes distributed for seasonal work (5–10 lire per woman) remained extremely poor.[29] Moreover, there was no national accident insurance for peasants until late 1917.

Beyond propaganda: Linda's and Maria's wartime correspondence

A close reading of letters that women sent to their relatives at the front allows us to analyse women's changing roles during wartime and to point out their social and cultural meaning. In the following, I refer to letters written by Linda Ellero from Variano, born in 1881 and mother of seven children, to her husband Giuseppe Merlino, a soldier at the front, and those by Maria Nardin from San Vito al Torre, born in 1876, to her father Michele Nardin, who was interned by the Italian Army in Ascoli Piceno. Using the example of these letters, we can learn about the living conditions of peasant women. Both of their families owned and rented small estates of land. Linda Ellero lived in the Italian rear area, Maria Nardin in the territory that was occupied by the Italian Army in 1915 and very close to the battlefront.[30]

These two women clearly accepted the challenges posed by the war. Their letters show how women had to cope with new tasks. Women became the main labour force along with the young and the old. They had to leave the domestic space (housekeeping, gardening, raising chicken, harvesting fruit) to go outside to the fields to look after the cattle, drive cars, plough, plant, fertilize, harvest, thresh all types of crops, and take care of the vineyards. Both women did 'men's work' and used 'men's tools' (shovels, hoes, sickles, wagons, ploughs), which could also be interpreted in a symbolic way.[31] They also had to take on new responsibilities on their own, such as managing labour, selling cattle and foodstuff, buying seeds, distributing food rations to eight family members, accounting as well as handling and saving money. In their letters they described their work and what the situation was like in the countryside, complaining about the lack of workforce and the increasing involvement of the elderly and children in agricultural production. Men, on the other hand, were in a state of passivity and helplessness. In spring 1916, for example, Linda Ellero tried to reassure her husband at the front: 'Keep calm Giuseppe, don't worry, neither about us because we're safe, nor about the agricultural work, because if the weather is good, we'll do what we are able to do.'[32]

Their role implied a new visibility as they attended new spaces such as the marketplace and the town hall.[33] This involved the establishment of new relationships: Maria Nardin, for instance, had to attend local authorities to sign petitions for her absent father and to obtain benefits: 'Now, dear father, I am always in the town hall, for one thing or another.'[34] Linda Ellero, on the other hand, often asked the local authorities for leave for her husband and an authorization to visit him at the front, or she had to negotiate requisitions of cattle with military officials. Their relationship with state and local authorities was characterized by diffidence and submissiveness, but also by anger and the determination to fight for their rights.

Both women were in a state of constant nervousness and tension due to the war. They faced the new situation courageously, yet with feelings of uncertainty. Occasionally, when they were not sure about how to handle a certain situation, they discussed the problem with husband or father, asked for their permission to decide or took decisions together with them. Relatives tried to give suggestions and advice, yet these women, who were well aware of the local situation, acted on their own and proudly claimed their independent choices: 'So, if I had followed uncle's decisions, I would have done bad business, then, dear father, I did it all on my own, I didn't ask anyone, I want to do it by myself.'[35] This new kind of female attitude and behaviour pattern can't be stressed enough, all the more given the fact that everyday life in the rear area was hard, a 'bad life', 'full of sorrow and worries', as these two women wrote.[36] Women sometimes confessed weakness and increasing fatigue, sometimes they felt powerless and inadequate, especially because of the double workload of family and outside work. In October 1916, Linda Ellero wrote: 'To tell you the truth, dear husband, I haven't got enough breath to thank God for giving me and the children health, as we had to work the whole season.'[37] Maria Nardin, too, grieved and declared her weakness. She wrote in June 1917: 'Dear father, if you knew what my head is like... a drunk's is better than mine.'[38] Sometimes both women were so lonely, tired, and confused that they wanted to give up making decisions. However, they were also happy to tell about their decisions, and proudly claimed their increasing business skills.[39] Female behaviour patterns were characterized by a progressive awareness and growing empowerment, yet always accompanied by uncertainty and the continuous search for male approval. This is shown by the fact that both women in their letters of 1917 devoted increasing space to their personal feelings, yet mentioned farm matters less frequently because women's work tasks ceased to be extraordinary. As we have seen, the years 1915 and 1916 were marked by significant changes in women's lives.

The letters also underline the transformation of the rural landscape brought about by the war. In October 1915, Maria Nardin wrote that soldiers had dug trenches in the fields and cut trees, while cars and trucks were passing by. She was not allowed on the fields, soldiers examined passports at military checkpoints and officers banned the cutting of the corn.[40] Maria witnessed damage, destruction of crops, and also thefts by soldiers. Furthermore, air raids were a source of constant fear.[41] Linda Ellero, in contrast, who lived in an area far away from the front line, experienced the repercussions of the war in terms of labour shortage, enlistment of men from the village, requisitions of cattle, and widespread diseases. In this context they both stressed the deterioration of living conditions, the fragile economy, and the increasing difficulty in finding food. Due to the war both became 'single women': In August 1917, Maria Nardin's interned husband died of tuberculosis in Maribor, and her father, Michele Nardin, did not return from Ascoli until 1919. Linda Ellero lost her husband Giuseppe Merlino who, in September 1917, died at the front of a disease. These circumstances were not uncommon.

Our two examples show how peasant women, who did not necessarily identify with the official war aims or war motives, experienced problems concerning working conditions. Moreover, the war had an intense, existential impact on them. Their main intention was to keep their families together, and their choices were not in accordance with the submissive image of women portrayed by public discourse. They were neither involved in the rhetoric of war, nor *matres dolorosae*. In fact, they tried to take a step across gender roles and acquired a new identity. The tensions they experienced were reworked within the family, as shown by numerous examples in 1917, when other women, who perceived the injustices brought by war, decided to protest publicly and to protect deserters, challenging the strong repressive police apparatus behind the front.[42]

Behind the front lines

Another form of wartime mobilization of women and girls was their employment in war logistics. This occurred especially in Carnia, in the rear of the Alpine part of the front, where people were involved in building military installations from the autumn of 1915 onwards. The villages' close vicinity to the front line as well as the lack of roads and infrastructure were reasons for many to participate. While young people and non-fighting men were recruited for the construction of roads, trenches, barracks, and military stores, women and girls were employed as 'portatrici' (see Figures 2.1–2.3) to transport tools and goods to the soldiers in the trenches up in the mountains.[43]

Mobilization of the female workforce intensified when even young girls aged 11 to 12 and elderly women aged 50 to 60 were recruited. In February 1916, about 1600 women in Carnia worked for the Italian Army (45 per cent of all women at the Italian front line), while in summer 1917, 4000 women were employed (33 per cent).[44] As male migration ceased in 1914/15, work for military units in addition to state welfare benefits and income from gardening was the only way to survive. Women were directly recruited by officers and had to transport food, cognac, pasta, wood, barbed wire, and ammunition in large baskets on their backs towards the lines. While ascending altitudes from 500 to 1000 metres along alpine paths, they were often

Figure 2.1 Inspection of the Alpine post Timau (Zona Carnia – But alto). In the middle are Generals Segato, Airoldi, and Fara with *portatrici* and troops around them
Source: Museo della Guerra di Timau (Udine).

Figure 2.2   Portatrici of Paluzza
Source: Museo della Guerra di Timau (Udine).

exposed to enemy fire. They arrived at the military barracks after walks of two or three hours and then went back to their homes. The pay for each trip was 2.50 lire. The goods they carried weighed between 35 and 50 kilogrammes. The *portatrici* worked in all weather conditions as well as under enemy fire. The case of Maria Plozner Mentil from Paluzza, for instance, is well known; she was shot dead in February 1916 by a sniper while she was transporting food for soldiers. Maria Vigezza from Moggio Udinese, aged 48, died on 18 November 1916 when a bomb was dropped by an Austrian airplane while she was delivering gravel.[45]

General Agostino D'Adamo, chief of the Segretariato Generale per gli Affari Civili, tried to regulate women's employment in military units and protect them from exploitation and excessive risks. On 11 January 1917, he issued a decree that banned the enlistment of women younger than 17 and older than 50 years. These women could not be forced to work in areas 'under enemy shell fire' or do heavy or dangerous work; their wages ranged from 2.50 to 4.00 lire for a ten-hour working day. They were not subjected to the code of military justice, yet lack of discipline and absence without notice were punished with fines and wage deductions. Women were to be recruited in the villages near the front line and were supposed to go back home every day; meals and lodging were provided only if the women worked in isolated places near the front line. However, these regulations were not acknowledged in Carnia. Local army officers refused to dismiss young girls arguing

Figure 2.3   Carnic *portatrici* on a souvenir photograph
Source: Museo Centrale del Risorgimento, Rome, Album O2, 7.32.

that their exclusion would reduce the workforce and push the girls 'into prostitution' because they were not under the control of their fathers.[46]

Poorly paid, this female work was considered mainly as a form of support for army units. As interviews revealed, it was perceived as an extension of traditional jobs held in the mountain estates such as transporting hay or alpine pasture. In the interviews, the women emphasized the danger they faced and the heavy fatigue they experienced. 'Fatigued to death', as Irma Casanova, one of the last survivors, told me in 1999. In fact, during the winter, women had to transport goods in high snow and they had to shovel paths and roads. Their work started early in the morning and at times went on overnight to avoid being discovered and shot. They remembered that they were terrified by artillery fire whilst hauling supplies.[47]

Women therefore had to bear a great burden during wartime: logistic work, farming, mothering, and housekeeping. It is difficult to decide if these women were motivated to work for patriotic reasons; they accepted their mobilization as a duty, but also as a relief from poverty. They often expressed their solidarity and grief for the soldiers who had to live, suffer, and die in the trenches. All in all, their relationship with the military was ambivalent as on the one hand they received food and cigarettes from the soldiers, on the other they were severely controlled by the officers. Especially in the first phase of the war, military units were harsh, because they suspected civilians who lived near the borderline to be spies or enemies. From this perspective, women's work can also be seen as a sort of demonstration of loyalty. Often officers used women's and girls' fear of the enemy to force them to work. In some cases the military brutally requisitioned women, even those pregnant, to tow artillery or shovel snow from alpine roads.[48]

The third year of the war was characterized by a crucial transformation of women's role in the Alpine rear areas. When the army built cableways to transport goods and ammunition to the highest front lines, women were employed to keep roads clear of snow or to transport gravel to maintain roads. Due to the shortage of male workers during spring and summer 1917, women and even girls were employed in heavy labour such as mining, excavating trenches and building roads and railways. This implied medium and short-scale migration to other valleys or towards the military workshops behind the Isonzo front. Work in the rear areas became dirty, heavy, and dangerous; women cut their fingers, got grit in their eyes, fell over and broke their limbs, or had frostbite. Some of them died or were heavily injured by exploding mines or in accidents.[49] It is very difficult to know how many women were injured, killed, or fell ill, not only because these cases were subject to censorship, but also because women were excluded from benefits such as those given to disabled ex-servicemen which were reserved for male military workers only. Few disapproved of the harsh conditions for women. In June 1917, labour inspector Guido Picotti wrote to General D'Adamo that in the yards of Carnia there was 'no military control' of recruitment and officers tried to 'avoid providing tents and beds for the workers'. Picotti criticized 'precarious sanitary conditions, widespread involvement of children, youths, and women without the respect of any law'.[50]

This complaint remained a dead letter. The main problem as perceived by local authorities was women's morality. In fact, in October 1917, the Friulian Catholic deputy Michele Gortani deplored the perils of prostitution among young female workers of Carnia and was worried about the 'honesty' and 'innocence' of married women and children.[51] Similarly, priests of the villages in Carnia described women's deep involvement in military work in their parish books. They did not mention anything about women's 'masculinization' as, due to male migration, women in alpine regions had already been used to hard labour before the war. What bothered priests was that female liberty emphasized 'male' patterns of behaviour such as personal autonomy, lack of control, and absence of family restraints, especially among the young female generation.

Nevertheless, women cooperated with the army and their work allowed the troops to protect the high-lying trenches. In some places at the front in Carnia (Timau, Paluzza Paularo), the transport of supplies and road maintenance was almost entirely conducted by women. Despite their massive involvement, women employed in the army units were neither recognized nor praised as peasant women were. Reports of their work were censored and withheld from public discourse – perhaps to avoid criticism from enemy propaganda, perhaps because it was too heavy, too dangerous, and too 'male'. In fact, women were dangerously invading 'masculine' spaces such as trenches and the war zone, and they approached 'male' jobs par excellence: they were 'making war'. At the same time, this kind of women's work was often accompanied by promiscuity and for this reason was suppressed in public discourse: No article described their heavy work, no photograph was published on this subject. Consequently, propaganda rather chose to glorify a reassuring image of peasant women.

Women without men and men without women

Behind the front, Friulian rural communities had to deal with a large presence of soldiers who, on the one hand, stimulated commerce with civilians, yet on the other transformed mentalities and social mores. In this new 'wartime society', women played an important role and were submitted to severe tensions. Faced with inadequate benefits and increasing prices, women had to leave their homes and earn money. They became street vendors, worked as shop assistants, opened inns, rented out rooms to soldiers and officers, cooked meals, sewed, washed and ironed military clothes, or worked in logistics and workshops. They were paid small sums of money, food, or clothes.[52] Due to the forced absence of men, communities, and families were shaken and the war destroyed traditional rules of community and gender relations. Young girls experimented with new and more open relationships with soldiers and officers, while the stability of marriages was jeopardized by free relationships ('unioni libere') between married women and soldiers. These were characterized by a mutual search for understanding and comfort in view of personal vulnerability and fragility during the war. While men were looking for rest, leisure, and a 'normal life' far from the trenches, women recognized the soldiers' fragile condition and welcomed them as sons, brothers, or husbands. Women escaped from uncertainty and isolation in these relationships, which were also instrumental in improving their quality of life given the worsening living conditions.[53]

Parish priests condemned the 'moral decay' and accused women and girls of immorality, crime, inadequate parental control, bad language, provocative fashion styles, and, above all, sexual relationships with soldiers. Priests were worried because this new behaviour threatened to weaken faith and the moral authority of the Church among peasants.[54] In June and again in December 1916, the Archbishop of Udine, Anastasio Rossi, repeatedly denounced the 'painful consequences' of the soldiers' presence in rural communities because of the number of 'illegitimate babies, broken engagements, and abandoned women'.[55]

Yet there was another side to these new forms of relationships and lifestyle. The amount of rape and clandestine prostitution due to poverty and hardship rose significantly. So many mothers and young servants became occasional prostitutes that venereal diseases were widespread and the army was forced to establish military brothels to prevent diseases among troops.[56] In fact, the province of Udine was the one with the highest rate of illegitimate babies from Italian or, in 1917/18, Austro-German soldiers. Birth ratio increased in the years 1915–18 from 359 to 836 (per 10,000).[57] In Mortegliano, for instance, a typical rural village of the lowlands with 3400 inhabitants, there were about 25 illegitimate births between 1915 and 1918, instead of the two or three cases per year in the pre-war period.[58]

Surveys in newspapers and parish books demonstrate that prostitution was not considered to be as a result of increasing poverty, but as women's desire for 'lust and pleasure', evasion of parental control, and scarce maternal education. However, the 'liberalization' of sexual mores did not constitute women's emancipation. Though there was greater freedom in sexual relationships, there was also a large increase in rape and prostitution. During wartime this behaviour became 'ordinary', due to the fact that people were living in an 'extraordinary' period, in which all social and moral restraints fell and adaptation prevailed. Illegitimate births meant severe problems for girls and women, as they were often marginalized by their families and communities. This resulted in a growing infant mortality rate, due to neglect, abortion, and infanticide.

Concern about social mores and girls' independence was also fed by an increasing juvenile mobility in 1917. As mentioned previously, the shortage of male workers stimulated migration from the mountains and the countryside to military workshops at the Isonzo front, where women produced masks, mats, and coverings for trenches, and mended used uniforms. This weakened parental restrictions and enhanced personal and economic independence. The new situation was perceived as a social threat in as much as women and juvenile workers were seen as criminals or 'irregular' subjects, who jeopardized not only traditional hierarchies between upper and lower classes, but also between the sexes.[59] Female workers and peasant girls were accused of wasting their money on superfluous expenses, such as wine, new clothes, short skirts, stockings. In addition, they were reproached for new behaviours, such as 'male' language, hedonism, provocative clothes, 'immorality', and the lack of religious feeling.

In this context, newspapers condemned promiscuity at the workplace and saw women and young girls as potential prostitutes and as elements of disorder and 'immorality'. Civil and Catholic authorities, on the other hand, wished to maintain, and even to cultivate and glorify, traditional 'feminine' qualities, especially women's maternal 'instincts' towards sons and husbands at the front. Moral and social concerns were used to justify a new repressive wave in rear areas and in the city of Udine during the summer of 1917. Military records show that the arrests of women were often based on anti-female stereotypes such as bad moral behaviour ('cattiva condotta morale'), occasional prostitution, and poverty, and were aimed at assuring social and political control in order to prevent unrest behind the front.[60]

Celebrating a 'sad victory': final remarks

The defeat at Caporetto in October 1917 marked a rupture in the involvement of civilians in the war. About 135,000 people, mostly women and children, fled from Friuli towards other Italian regions, while 500,000 remained under enemy occupation. These events had severe effects on women and on women's public image, which turned women from active participants in the war effort into passive bystanders, from heroines into victims of war. Women who fled the area were depicted as patriotic refugees who escaped 'Teutonic slavery', while women who remained in the occupied territories were represented as having fallen victim to rape by the 'barbarian enemy'. In this understanding, women stood as a symbol for 'the body of the nation'. Both patterns were used to bolster soldiers' resistance at the River Piave battlefront until the end of the war and also to portray the nation as welcoming towards refugees.[61]

After the war, the female image shifted to the 'mourning mother'. In the 1921 celebrations of the 'unknown soldier', in Udine, Gorizia, and Aquileia, women were again considered only as 'soldiers' mothers' or 'soldiers' wives', and depicted as heroic victims who represented the national mourning. The main image was the Catholic *mater dolorosa* or the war widow, which stressed women's domestic and maternal roles and their willingness to sacrifice their husbands and sons for the nation.[62] These ruling class and gender models and the representations of mourning were unacceptable for peasant women. Despite the visibility they had gained as workers, this role was neither recognized nor recalled in public discourse. Female experiences were excluded and women did not find adequate channels to express themselves and their suffering, also due to the fact that even the socialist party in the post-war years supported only returning soldiers.[63] The 'other side of the war' remained hidden in diaries or in letters. These traces of women's experiences were almost completely neglected, overshadowed by the myth of victory and the 'male' nation at war. Fascism later on reinforced this process ideologically by increasing the emphasis on gender differences.[64]

It was not until 1969 that finally state authorities officially awarded the honour of Cavaliere di Vittorio Veneto, to the *portatrici carniche* as a symbol of women's patriotism, maybe because this specific and extreme mobilization could be linked to the soldiers in the trenches. In 1997, Italian president Oscar Luigi Scalfaro rewarded the 'heroine' Maria Plozner Mentil with the gold medal for military valour.[65]

In Friuli, 4 November 1918 was a day of liberation rather than a day of victory. Here, in the 'liberated territories', people celebrated a quasi 'sad victory'. The main issues of 1919 were mourning, reconstruction, but also anger and a desire for social change. The return of refugees and men from the battlefront and the process of reconstruction were traumatic due to devastation, losses, hunger, and disease. About 15,000 soldiers and 5000 civilians had died during the war, thousands came back injured, sick, and wounded. Women had to bear a large part of the burden of caring for men and children.

The war experience can be described as complex and contradictory. Friulian women faced 'total war' and they, too, were directly affected by the violent face of war in this border region, while they were gaining 'liberation' and 'emancipation' to a significant extent. For them, the experience of war meant fatigue, social upheaval, insecurity, fear, diseases, hardships, dislocation, violence, humiliation, and anger. As diaries and letters demonstrate, they were concerned with responsibility for their family and relatives, strain, and loss rather than with patriotic duties. However, despite the militarization of society, hardships, and war violence, women handled their duties very well. In so doing, they surprised civil and military authorities with their ability to undertake heavy work and with their efficiency, both behind the front and in the countryside. Due to women's farming, agricultural production in Friuli was maintained at almost pre-war levels, while the work in the rear area allowed Italian troops to stay in the mountain trenches for three years.

War shook up gender relations, yet only temporarily, especially in rural communities where sexual and gender hierarchies were more stable. Although women's work became more and more important, this process developed within a framework which was still characterized by subordination and devaluation and in which women were still treated as inferior. In public discourse, the war was represented as a 'male war'. Until October 1917, official propaganda emphasized traditional images of women to reassure the stability of gender roles. In addition, some inconvenient facts such as the presence of women at the front line were hidden. Women's work, although effective in boosting the war effort, was considered as temporary almost everywhere. Gender stereotypes were maintained rather than challenged. Military authoritarianism, paternalism, and patriarchalism as well as religious and moral rules preserved and stabilized gender roles. Local and military authorities considered women's work as a 'natural' duty. In so doing, they reinforced the subalternity of women's position in society and contributed to keeping wages to a minimum: In fact, women's wages, routinely portrayed as 'high' in the wartime press, remained significantly lower than male wages. Working in the mountains with military units and sewing uniforms for the soldiers were considered as forms of assistance rather than as 'proper' jobs like men's work. Women's employment and payment were merely to avoid poverty and prostitution. Moreover, the fact that many female jobs were closely linked to the 'war' itself made it necessary to emphasize their being exceptional and temporary, yet also affected the process of emancipation through work negatively and turned into mass exploitation. In some cases, women's labour was viewed as too extreme and, paradoxically, as exceptional rather than as a starting point for emancipation. Overall, the priority given to 'moral' issues, which actually hid any fear of the subversion of gender and class hierarchy, prevailed over labour safeguards. Therefore, women in 1919 considered the end of the war as a relief and a return to 'normality'.

The issue of the troops' homecoming has yet to be fully investigated. We need further research on the early 1920s: Beyond the myth of victory, local sources such as parish reports reveal that violence, hunger, and prostitution characterized the post-war years until 1923.[66] The post-war experience was not free of pain, as high mortality rates, the collapse of marriages, the decline of births, and a growing number of separations show. In the aftermath of the war, new social subjects emerged such as war widows, who had to manage their estates on their own and tried to enter extra-marital relationships ('more uxorio'), as they would have lost their benefits in the event of remarriage.[67]

Although they were reliable and capable, women's 'citizenship' was still considered second class, as the state denied them both the right to vote and special welfare benefits. Public space became narrower in the post-war years, while the private sphere assumed new importance. Nevertheless, during the war women reasserted their position in their families and gained more confidence in their own abilities by demonstrating courage and responsibility. The war only accelerated the ongoing social process of emancipation which had already been initiated by migration. 'Wartime skills' such as self-confidence, autonomy, mobility, the ability to adapt to different tasks were not lost, but could be applied again during the great depression after 1929 and the Nazi occupation between 1943 and 1945. Furthermore, women were more familiar with their role in society and multiplied their relationships with state and local authorities. Those who had experienced mobilization and evacuation developed a sense of citizenship and were well aware of the new rights they had acquired by having contributed to the war effort. These feelings became apparent especially in April and June 1919, when women protested against food shortages and high prices. In this way, the war diminished traditional paternalism between upper and lower classes. Social inequalities, the national war effort, flight, and occupation contributed to making women aware of their rights within society. They became even more inspired and radicalized by the example of revolutionary Russia.

In a generational perspective, the Great War constituted a turning point. This is true in particular for younger women and girls, who attained more autonomy and found their wartime labour experiences in some way 'liberating' because they were able to escape from parental restraints and experienced new patterns of socialization. This critical step was characterized by severe instability and war violence, factors that made this wartime 'transformation' even more remarkable. Even though women's social status did not change permanently in the short term, wartime experience eased the distance between male and female worlds in the long run.

Notes

1. In this chapter I refer to the former 'Provincia di Udine' that belonged to the Veneto region as Friuli.
2. On 25 October 1917, the Austro-German army under General von Below achieved a significant breakthrough by a gas attack against the weak Italian lines in the Isonzo valley near the little village of Caporetto. German and Austrian forces penetrated into Friuli and conquered Udine. They captured 300,000 soldiers, and occupied Friuli and part of the Veneto region within a week. In order to avoid a wide encirclement of the armies placed along the main line of the Carso front, General Cadorna ordered a retreat to the right bank of the River Piave. The Caporetto defeat became somewhat of a 'stain' on the Italian First World War campaign. During the retreat, Cadorna accused his soldiers of cowardice and interpreted the defeat as a soldiers' strike. Although the events of Caporetto were actually due to a military strategic surprise, the defeat became a symbol in public discourse of the 1917 Italian crisis both at the front line and at the home front, and contributed to the repression of and suspicion against 'internal enemies'. Among the broad range of publications, see N. Labanca, G. Procacci and L. Tomassini (1997) *Caporetto: Esercito, stato, società* (Florence: Giunti); N. Labanca (1997) *Caporetto: Storia di una disfatta* (Florence: Giunti).
3. Italian historiography has analysed the situation of women especially in industrial towns (Turin, Milan, Genoa), while research on women from rural districts has been sparse. Since the 1980s, women's industrial work has been selected as a paradigm to analyse women's changing roles, and this approach has affected the understanding of women's wartime experience as a whole. In the late 1990s, historians started to investigate the First World War as a 'total war' and tried to evaluate the impact of war on society behind the front line. See M. Ermacora (2007) 'Le donne italiane nella Grande Guerra: Un bilancio storiografico (1990–2005)', in P. Antolini, G. Barth-Scalmani, M. Ermacora, N. Fontana, D. Leoni, P. Malni and A. Pisetti (eds) *Donne in guerra, 1915–1918: La Grande Guerra attraverso l'analisi e le testimonianze di una terra di confine* (Rovereto: Centro studi Judicaria, Museo storico italiano della guerra), pp. 11–30.
4. See L. Lorenzetti and R. Merzario (2005) *Il fuoco acceso: Famiglie e migrazioni alpine nell'Italia d'età moderna* (Roma: Donzelli).
5. See M. Ermacora (2001) *Un anno difficile: Buja tra pace e guerra (agosto 1914–maggio 1915)* (Udine: El Tomàt); E. Ellero (2007) *Friuli 1914–1917: Neutralità, guerra, sfollamenti coatti, internamenti* (Pasian di Prato: Ifsml), pp. 19–61.
6. N. Labanca (2008) 'Zona di guerra', in M. Isnenghi and D. Ceschin (eds) *La Grande Guerra: Uomini e luoghi del '15–'18*, vol. 2 (Turin: Utet), p. 606.
7. See M. Ermacora (2005) *Cantieri di guerra: Il lavoro dei civili nelle retrovie del fronte italiano (1915–1918)* (Bologna: Il Mulino).
8. See D. Menozzi, G. Procacci and S. Soldani (2010) *Un paese in guerra: La mobilitazione civile in Italia (1914–1918)* (Milan: Unicopli).
9. See 'Commissariato Generale per l'assistenza civile e la propaganda interna' (1917), in *Notizie sull'Assistenza civile in Italia al 30 giugno 1916* (Rome: Bertero), p. 54.
10. 'Agricoltura di Guerra', *L'Amico del Contadino*, 15 January 1916, p. 2.
11. Associazione Agraria Friulana, 'Collaborazione delle donne friulane nel lavoro dei campi', 28 March 1916, *Archivio di stato di Udine, Archivio della deputazione provinciale*, b. 808, I56.
12. A. Roja a don P. Valle, 29 May 1917, *Archivio Roja*, Tolmezzo, b. 149.

13. G. Bubba (1916) 'Il lavoro delle donne nell'alto Friuli', *L'Amico del Contadino*, 7 October, p. 3.
14. 'Premi di produzione per incoraggiare la collaborazione delle donne al lavoro nei campi', *L'Amico del Contadino*, 17 June 1916, p. 3.
15. 'Anute, tu as alvorât par doi!' [Ann, you did the work of two!], *L'Amico del Contadino*, 1 July 1916, p. 4.
16. Quotes from: 'Le donne italiane che sostituiscono i combattenti devono essere additate a pubblica riconoscenza', *L'Amico del Contadino*, published between August and November 1916.
17. See 'Il lavôr das feminis' [Women's work], *L'Amico del Contadino*, 3 September 1916, p. 2; A. Molinari (2008) *Donne e ruoli femminili nell'Italia della Grande Guerra* (Milan: Selene Edizioni).
18. 'Lis feminis. Discors tra Tite e Toni' [Women: Dialogue between Giobatta and Antonio], *L'Amico del Contadino*, 23 September 1916, p. 4.
19. 'Il premio del Ministero dell'Agricoltura alle lavoratrici dei cereali', *Il Corriere del Friuli*, 1 July 1917, p. 2.
20. See, for example, 'Cucina di guerra', *L'Amico del Contadino*, 25 February 1917, p. 3.
21. 'Pes femines. Fat di veretât' [For women. True facts], *L'Amico del Contadino*, 30 December 1916, p. 2.
22. 'Le donne e la guerra', *La Patria del Friuli*, 11 June 1917, p. 3.
23. A. Rossi (1917) 'Lettera pastorale', *Rivista diocesana udinese*, 24 February, pp. 61–77.
24. For example, see: *Libro storico parrocchiale di Fagagna* [Historical parish book], sub 15 June 1916, p. 11.
25. 'Dicerie sciocche e perniciose', *L'Amico del Contadino*, 2 June 1917, p. 1.
26. See, for example, 'Le donne forti', *Il Corriere del Friuli*, 10 July 1917, p. 5.
27. See, for example, 'Tavagnacco. Le donne agitate', *La Patria del Friuli*, 1 February 1917, p. 3; 'Tricesimo. Una donna granivora', *La Patria del Friuli*, 4 February 1917, p. 2.
28. See B. Pisa (2011) 'L'évolution de l'identité féminine en Italie au cours de la Grande Guerre', in F. Bouloc, R. Cazals and A. Loez (eds) *Identités troublées, 1914–1918: Les appartenances sociales et nationales à l'épreuve de la guerre* (Toulouse: Editions Privat), p. 271.
29. These figures are taken from: 'Fagagna, Le donne premiate dal ministero dell'agricoltura', *La Patria del Friuli*, 7 July 1917, p. 5.
30. Linda Ellero and Giuseppe Merlino's correspondance is published by G. Sut (1998) *Torno o non torno: Giuseppe Merlino fante friulano e la grande guerra da lui non voluta* (Pordenone: Edizioni Biblioteca dell'Immagine); Maria Nardin's letters are published in C. Mengozzi (2006) *Raccontare la Grande Guerra: Lettura di un epistolario di San Vito al Torre* (Mariano: Circolo Comunale di Cultura).
31. See L. Scaraffia (1988) 'Essere uomo, essere donna', in P. Melograni (ed.) *La famiglia italiana dall'Ottocento ad oggi* (Bologna: Il Mulino), p. 196.
32. Linda Ellero to Giuseppe Merlino, 28 March 1916, in Sut, *Torno o non torno*, p. 49.
33. Linda Ellero to Giuseppe Merlino, 4 December 1916, in Sut, *Torno o non torno*, pp. 141–2.
34. Maria Nardin to Michele Nardin, 18 January 1916, in Mengozzi, *Raccontare la Grande Guerra*, p. 168.
35. Maria Nardin to Michele Nardin, 24 May 1917, in Mengozzi, *Raccontare la Grande Guerra*, p. 207.
36. Linda Ellero to Giuseppe Merlino, 11 October 1916, in Sut, *Torno o non torno*, p. 111; Maria Nardin to Michele Nardin, 18 January 1916, in Mengozzi, *Raccontare la Grande Guerra*, p. 168.

37. Linda Ellero to Giuseppe Merlino, 11 October 1916, in Sut, *Torno o non torno*, pp. 111–12.
38. Maria Nardin to Michele Nardin, 14 June 1917, in Mengozzi, *Raccontare la Grande Guerra*, p. 207.
39. Sometimes they downplayed their satisfaction in their work due to the absence of their male relatives, whom they missed. In June 1916, Linda Ellero wrote: 'The countryside's good enough. Well, but being unhappy, anything can be appreciated.' Linda Ellero to Giuseppe Merlino, 12 June 1916, in Sut, *Torno o non torno*, p. 63. At the end of 1916, Giuseppe Merlino was concerned about her health and wrote: 'I'm surprised, dear wife, [...] but I wish you didn't have to work so much because, dear wife, if you don't finish today, you'll do it tomorrow. I know that when things are done it's better, but you don't have to die for it.' Giuseppe Merlino to Linda Ellero, 20 October 1916, in Sut, *Torno o non torno*, p. 116.
40. Maria Nardin to Michele Nardin, 24 October 1915, in Mengozzi, *Raccontare la Grande Guerra*, pp. 163–4; about military bans, see also 6 February 1916, p. 169.
41. Maria Nardin to Michele Nardin, 4 April 1916, in Mengozzi, *Raccontare la Grande Guerra*, p. 176.
42. See G. Procacci (1991) 'La protesta delle donne delle campagne in tempo di guerra (1915–1918)', *Annali dell'Istituto Alcide Cervi*, 13, pp. 57–86.
43. This kind of mobilization was common in the Alpine rear areas of the front (Carnia, Cadore, Altipiano di Asiago). Between 1915 and 1917 the Italian army employed about 12,000 female workers in logistic tasks. See M. Ermacora, *Cantieri di guerra*.
44. Minuta gen. D'Adamo, *Archivio Centrale dello Stato*, Roma (hereafter ACS), Segretariato Generale per gli Affari Civili (SGAC), b. 483.
45. Vigezza Maria, 18 November 1916, ACS SGAC, b. 695; *Archivio comunale di Paluzza*, b. 770, fasc. Guerra 1915–1918: Pensioni ai civili. The village of Paluzza was characterized by a shocking death toll amongst civilian workers.
46. ACS SGAC, b. 483, fasc. Mano d'opera femminile: Comando Supremo – SGAC, 11 gennaio 1917, n. 110457; ACS SGAC, b. 483, fasc. 26. For the officers' refusal, ACS SGAC, Zona Carnia, Comando genio militare XII C.d. A., a SGAC, n.5321, 16 February 1917.
47. M. Ermacora (2000) 'Il lavoro dei ragazzi friulani dall'età giolittiana alla Grande Guerra', in B. Bianchi and A. Lotto (eds) *Lavoro ed emigrazione minorile dall'Unità alla Grande Guerra* (Venice: Ateneo Veneto), pp. 132–4.
48. See *Libri storici parrocchiali di Paularo* (sub 1915), and *Monaio* (sub 1915, p. 18).
49. The records of Segretariato Generale per gli Affari Civili provide a lot of cases of injuries and diseases; see, for example, ACS SGAC, b. 685, 688, 689, 692.
50. ACS SGAC, b. 508, Picotti a Comando Genio Zona Carnia, 24 June 1917.
51. *Atti Parlamentari*, 24th leg., 18 October 1917, p. 14621.
52. See L. Fabi (2000) 'Militari e civili nel Friuli della Grande Guerra prima di Caporetto', in G. Corni (ed.) *Il Friuli, Storia e società, 1914–1925* (Pasian di Prato: Ifsml), pp. 125–42.
53. For this 'mass mothering', see C. Fragiacomo (1990) 'Paularo. Un paese in guerra', in L. Fabi (ed.) *La gente e la guerra*, vol. 1 (Udine: Il Campo), pp. 157–88.
54. See Libro storico parrocchiale di Avasinis, 11 March 1917.
55. A. Scottà (1991) *I vescovi veneti e la S. Sede 1915–1918*, vol. 2 (Roma: Edizioni di storia e letteratura), p. 523.
56. See E. Franzina (1999) *Casini di guerra: Il tempo libero dalla trincea e i postriboli militari nel primo conflitto mondiale* (Udine: Gaspari).

57. L. Livi (1921) 'La natalità illegittima durante la guerra', *Rivista internazionale di scienze sociali e disciplina ausiliarie*, 91, pp. 145–55.
58. *Archivio Curia Arcivescovile di Udine* (hereafter: ACAU), Visite pastorali, Mortegliano, 1923.
59. See B. Bianchi (1995) *Crescere in tempo di guerra: Il lavoro e la protesta dei ragazzi in Italia 1915–1918* (Venice: Cafoscarina); M. Ermacora, 'Il lavoro dei ragazzi friulani', pp. 50 and 64.
60. See M. Ermacora (2007) 'Le donne internate in Italia durante la Grande Guerra: Esperienze, scritture, memorie', *DEP. Deportate, esuli, profughe. Rivista telematica sulla memoria femminile*, 7, pp. 1–27, available online at: www.unive.it/dep.
61. See D. Ceschin (2006) *Gli esuli di Caporetto: I profughi in Italia durante la Grande Guerra* (Rome: Laterza); E. Ellero (2001) *Storia di un esodo: I friulani dopo la rotta di Caporetto 1917–1919* (Pasian di Prato: Ifsml).
62. See L. Cadeddu (2006) *La leggenda del soldato sconosciuto all'altare della patria* (Udine: Gaspari), pp. 64, 80, 109–13; A. Baù (2002) 'I figli miei che non son più miei: Note sulla condizione delle vedove di guerra in Padova nel primo dopoguerra (1923–1927)', *Venetica*, 5, pp. 79–104.
63. See M. Casalini (2001) 'I socialisti e le donne. Dalla mobilitazione pacifista alla smobilitazione postbellica', *Italia contemporanea*, 222, pp. 5–41.
64. A. Bravo and A. M. Bruzzone (1995) *In guerra senza armi: Storie di donne 1940–1945* (Rome: Laterza), p. 10. For example, flight and occupation – mainly female experiences – were omitted because they were a symbol of national defeat. These dramatic events became 'local memories' and were removed from the national collective memory until almost the 1990s, when historians started to study war violence in the areas along the Italian border.
65. The decree was signed on 29 April 1997; see Associazione Amici delle Alpi Carniche (1997) *Le portatrici carniche* (Tolmezzo: Moro), p. 16.
66. See ACAU, Visite pastorali, Flaipano 1921, Lusevera 1922, S. Leonardo 1923.
67. In post-war parish reports, widows were often criticized for their 'illegitimate relationships' with men. See, for example, ACAU, Visite pastorali, Resia 1919.

3

Imagining and Communicating Violence: The Correspondence of a Berlin Family, 1914–1918

Dorothee Wierling

The genre of war letters and a family of intellectuals

This chapter examines the correspondence of four people who, during the First World War, wrote approximately 2000 letters to each other: Lily Braun, the well-known feminist, social democratic activist and writer; her husband, the social democrat Heinrich Braun; their son Otto; and a close friend of the family, Julie Vogelstein. All their letters refer, in one way or another, to the 'Great War', in which Otto, a war volunteer, fought as an ensign and later as a young lieutenant. His mother, Lily Braun, supported the cause of Germany and toured the country making public speeches, while his father, Heinrich Braun, saw the war as a step to a future socialist state. Julie Vogelstein, an art historian with expertise on ancient Greece, acted as their dedicated friend and provided the Brauns with an interpretive framework of the war as a modern Greek drama.

Most of the letters they exchanged throughout the war were sent as war letters (*Feldpostbriefe*). It was the young soldier, Otto, who received and sent off the majority of these letters. He was trained in the West Prussian military town of Graudenz from September until December 1914 and served at the Eastern Front until November 1916. After being wounded, he spent the year 1917 in Berlin and volunteered again for the Western Front in February 1918, where he fell on 29 April 1918. War letters from and to the front present an important source for everyday life and death during the war, and are central for the understanding of war experiences and interpretations by soldiers and their families.[1] The vast majority of these letters were written by soldiers and officers, thus they represent the perspective from the front line. Letters from the home front, from parents, wives, and children have been kept and passed on less frequently.[2] In the case of the Brauns and Julie Vogelstein, however, the complete correspondence has survived, which gives us unique access to interpretations of the war and frameworks of meaning as they were exchanged and negotiated between the persons involved.

Moreover, since each of the four correspondents wrote to each other when they were separated, we have a rich body of sources at our disposal with

12 parallel strings of correspondence contributing to a complex network of communication in and on the First World War. To be sure, the war is the predominant topic of the letters, however, what the four correspondents wrote from 1914 to 1918 is only a small part of an even wider correspondence which covers the entire life span of each of the protagonists and which grew even larger during the course of the war – a corpus of about 10,000 letters. Lily and Heinrich Braun alone exchanged around 4000 letters throughout their relationship of 20 years. Today, this correspondence is part of the private papers of Julie Vogelstein, who donated the Braun correspondence to the Leo Baeck institute's archive in New York, as its largest private collection.[3] This enables us to examine how the war affected the letter writers, their relationships with each other and their position in the family. In addition, we can explore how the correspondents communicated their interpretations of the war, in what way it became part of their lives both practically and emotionally, and how it transformed their expectations and claims.

There are several reasons why the letters of the Braun family and Julie Vogelstein have survived in total. For once, all four correspondents were passionate letter writers and felt an even greater urge to express themselves during the war, seeking and offering an understanding of the 'greatness of the time' – as they, like many others in this period, referred to the war. There was not one day without writing or receiving a letter. Letters were written at home, in coffee houses, in trains, in the rear area, and in the trenches. The different circumstances of the act of writing had a vast impact not only on the letters' content, but also on their style. Even during the war, mail was delivered several times a day in Berlin; however, sometimes letters were delayed on their way between the home front and the front line or vice versa. Thus, the correspondence was continuous but irregular and letters often overlapped or were withheld for security reasons.

All four correspondents were fully aware of the historical value of the letters they wrote and read, all the more since all of them were well-known public figures: the politician Heinrich Braun, the writer Lily Braun, the scholar Julie Vogelstein, and the future hero Otto Braun. Thus, these letters were not just 'private', but were written, read, and kept in expectation of a public interest in their authors.

The letters of the Braun family and Vogelstein – dense and intensive as they are – can be placed in a broader historical context. They directly refer to everyday life experiences of the war and its repercussions, both at the front and in Berlin, or other places in Germany where the correspondents happened to travel or stay. In addition, the letters can be linked to other ego-documents by the same authors, in particular to Otto's war diaries which he started to write when he left home as a volunteer. Comparing diary entries with his letters yields striking results, since certain details or interpretations from Otto's diary differ from his letters. Besides, it may well be assumed that the diary served as a kind of draft for the letters to his family. In some cases, Otto reflects in his diary on his communication with his relatives at home. Yet his diaries are by no means more 'authentic' than his letters, since the notebooks, once filled, were sent home with the tacit understanding that his parents and Julie Vogelstein would read them and then carefully store them away. The fact that Otto's parents were already imagined as readers of his diary limits the additional potential of this source.[4] However, it seems as if Otto was not always completely aware of his future readers, since there are some significant differences in his writings about certain events between diaries and letters. Most likely, they derived from a different situational and social setting of writing itself.

As early as during the war, letters and diaries written by soldiers, mostly young volunteers from the educated classes, often university students, became an important text genre.[5] Together with poems and novels they formed a huge body of literary texts, providing their readers with powerful suggestions of how to interpret the war. Lily Braun herself wrote two such texts. It is striking that even these published pieces, which can be used to contextualize her letters, refer to the correspondence with her family. Both texts were printed in 1915: one as a brochure in which she sums up her experiences when travelling through Germany during her lecture tour in late 1914; the second one as a novel, in which a young nobleman – obviously her male alter ego – finds a meaningful life in death on the battlefield.[6]

Our four protagonists wrote letters, diaries, poems, essays, and novels, and in doing so, they used patterns of interpretation to create images and notions about the war which were familiar, acceptable, and in a way typical for their own social and political circles. And yet, their letters are special in comparison with other fictional and non-fictional genres since they represent the only type of texts in which experiences, perceptions, and interpretations could be expressed openly and unsuppressed, unlike in published texts. What people saw and felt in the midst of this violent time did not necessarily fit into public patterns of interpretations and aesthetics of the war.

The members of the Braun family were well known among educated, middle-class circles (*Bildungsbürgertum*) in Wilhelmine Germany. This is true, in particular, for Lily Braun, born in 1865 as the daughter of the Prussian general Hans von Kretschmann. In the mid-1890s, she broke with her family, moved to Berlin, and became involved, first, in the liberal branch of the women's movement, and later in the Social Democratic Party (SPD), where she held some influence in the socialist women's movement, before she retreated from party politics to become a writer of essays and novels.[7] After her first husband had died one and a half years after the wedding, Lily got married to Heinrich Braun, born 1864, a social scientist and social democrat from a Jewish-Austrian family, who was the editor of several socialist journals.[8] Although members of the SPD, both of them were already alienated from the party when the war broke out. The couple lived in Berlin, and in 1897 their only son Otto was born. The highly talented child enjoyed a careful education, initially in a reform boarding school, and later by a private tutor together with the children of the artists Käthe Kollwitz and Sabine Lepsius.[9] In 1913, Heinrich Braun met Julie Vogelstein (born 1883), who in 1914 became his secret lover and at the same time a close friend to Lily. She was also very attached to their son Otto. Vogelstein had a family background of Jewish scholars and businessmen. She married Heinrich some years after Lily Braun's death in 1916 and became the archivist, chronicler, and interpreter of the Braun family for the rest of her life.[10]

To be sure, these four persons were part of an intellectual milieu shaped by their classical education, their orientation towards feminism and towards the ideas of Youth Movement and Life Reform. These circles were characterized by the typical *fin de siècle* mindset consisting of 'cultural pessimism' and criticism of both urban life and the supposed 'nervousness' of the modern condition in general.[11] Yet, the Braun correspondence from before 1914 does not in any way indicate that any of them hoped for a war in order to purify the nation of all these alleged 'unhealthy', 'weakening' phenomena. Nor did any of them express reservations against European neighbours or justify the use of military force as a legitimate or necessary means to enforce Germany's rights or claims. On the contrary, Lily Braun was regarded as a pacifist by some, both before the First World War and after.[12] The Brauns were well travelled, spoke French, and had friends abroad.

In early summer 1914, Lily Braun was in Florence, where she worked on her new novel and spent time with her Italian lover, whom she had met some years before. Heinrich Braun was in Berlin, suffering from depression, yet just about to fall in love with Julie Vogelstein; while Otto, who planned to sit his final secondary school exams (*Abitur*) in autumn, was travelling through southern Germany. He visited his old teachers and met professors from the university of Heidelberg where he intended to read literature and sociology. Julie Vogelstein was commuting between Munich, where she lived with one of her brothers, and Berlin, where she spent time with her new friends. When the Austrian crown prince was murdered in Sarajevo at the end of June, all four returned to Berlin.

Lily Braun and her son Otto in particular identified themselves with the Great War. Lily immediately went on tour through numerous German cities and gave talks on 'The War as Educator' or 'Women and War', using her reputation as a famous writer with an interesting biography and her talent as a public speaker to support the cause. In summer 1916, she died from a stroke. Otto Braun, who volunteered on 1 August 1914, sat his school exams early and received his military training in East Prussia at the Russian–Polish border. In December 1914, he went to the Eastern Front but did not get involved in serious battle before the summer of 1915. His father, Heinrich Braun, tried everything to prevent his son from going to war, and later intervened several times – much to Otto's dismay – to secure a safe position for him. Without military experience himself, Heinrich hoped his son would survive to become a politician. Finally, Julie Vogelstein tried to support each family member financially as well as emotionally.

In the following, I will analyse five text segments from the Braun corre-spondence in which the writers refer to war violence. Rather than focusing on the violence itself, I examine how it is evoked, framed, and presented in the communication about the war and its meaning – and the role each of the four was expected to play in it. None of them was in any way prepared for the physical violence which the war would bring. Having been raised in a Prussian officer's family, Lily Braun understood the military as a code of honour and a lifestyle, yet this had been a military in times of peace. Heinrich Braun had never served in an army or a war; their son Otto was raised in the spirit of humanism; and Julie Vogelstein's intellectual universe was based on antiquity and Weimar classicism. Writing about the war and describing its violence played an important part in constructing, or rather reshaping, their own selves as well as the personal relationships among the four. When dis-cussing these examples, I will also draw on Otto's diary, which, together with his letters, was part of a growing private archive.

Brains

Lily Braun's lecture tour, starting in October 1914, brought her to every major city in Germany over the course of some weeks. Exhausted, she retreated to Lahmann's sanatorium in Dresden[13] to write an essay on Germany and the Germans, in particular German women, and what was called the *Augusterlebnis*, the great experience of August 1914.[14] Her observations and interpretations, but also her critique, formed the basis of her programmatic vision of what women could and should do to support the war effort, and to become an essential part of the nation due to this involvement. In this context, Lily Braun demanded the immediate introduction of a general compulsory national service for all women in order to force them into soldierly discipline in their own realm: motherhood.[15] To be a mother, meant to support the war; for to produce children, meant to produce future citizens and soldiers. Thus, to become a mother was in itself a soldierly act, the only one that women had access to, since children could be regarded as powerful weapons which only women could create.[16] It was in this line that Lily Braun ended her essay on a passionate note and, rather surprisingly, evoked a shocking image:

> For every hand, now clutching their weapons in mortal agony, let's cre-ate new hands, many small children's hands, stretching out towards the sun, which will build the temples of peace in which we will light the eternal flame. And for all the brains, now pierced by bullets, let's create new brains, many small children's brains, which will once take up and complete the vision of liberating humanity from all bonds of slavery.[17]

While Lily Braun was writing these lines, she was well aware of what was happening on the battlefields of the war, as we know from the letters which she wrote daily during her lecture tour. She had seen the wounded on trains and in hotels while travelling through Germany; she had spoken in front of a desperate audience in Marburg right after the news had arrived that a whole unit of students from the local university had been killed in battle. Peter Kollwitz, her son's close friend, had already died in October 1914.[18] Lily Braun did not consider the war an easy campaign, although she certainly expected Germany to be victorious. On the contrary, she deemed war to be an ordeal, yet one she welcomed as the price for its greatness and consequently the greatness of those who suffered. Thus, it seemed important, if not necessary, for her to evoke graphic images of death and physical destruction to make her point: to face and to accept death and violence in order to mobilize for war. In so doing, she broke with the traditional image of the caring mother and reinvented motherhood as a combative disposition.

Bodies

In mid-March 1915, Otto had reached Lodz on the Eastern Front, but his regiment remained in the back area, leaving the young volunteers deeply bored and disappointed. While waiting, Otto read all the essays and books written in the 'spirit of 1914',[19] sent letters and got himself into trouble with an officer. Proud and unfamiliar with military discipline, he became a target of his superiors' harassment. Otto was aware of his precarious situation, presumably aggravated by the fact that his father was Jewish. Although deeply devoted to his parents, he, for the first time, had a serious conflict with them, because he suspected them (rightly) of interfering with his higher ranking superiors on his behalf, but behind his back. His father in particular hoped to make Otto's life easier and to find him a position which would keep him far away from dangerous situations. Otto, however, felt deeply embarrassed and was probably right to assume that such attempts would further weaken his position and cause even more aggression from the officers in his regiment against him.

In the midst of this crisis, a sergeant decided to take the young soldiers out to the nearby trenches, which had just been deserted, first by Russian troops, then by Germans pursuing the Russian army eastwards. Apparently, the sergeant was hoping to provide them with a taste of war as it really was. Back in his base two days later, Otto wrote an enthusiastic letter to his parents:

> Close to the enemy! I was in dugouts only 40, 80 metres away – anyway: right on the edge, where you can hear the sweet sound of the bullets and the barking of the mortars and the buzzing of the shrapnel shells! [...] I have to come back to it again and again, my feelings of sublime happiness, of magnificent ecstasy to finally, finally be close to the enemy, to be allowed to really risk one's life. It is embarrassing how stupid I am, how difficult it is to find words for it, but it was just so very beautiful, beautiful, beautiful, despite all the horrors I have just

seen here [...] never have I wished more to live, felt more intensely and more passionately life's beauty and meaning than here, where for the first time in my young life I encountered death. [...] You can see from the piles of unburied bodies, how close we are to the enemy. Very often they are dug in the walls of the trenches. Sometimes you can still see a hand, or boots. You'll exempt me from describing all this in detail, but it was rather strange, how little these images, horrific as they seem, affected me.[20]

Otto knew how worried his parents were, especially his father who had done everything possible so far to keep Otto away from the front, or at least far away from a dangerous position. By describing the trenches, the sounds of the bullets, the shellfire, and the dead bodies, all in the same letter of 16 pages, Otto evoked the danger he might get involved in. And yet, with his graphic description, he intended to calm his parents and to assure them that he did not feel any fear and that he had a strong will to live. There is one image, however, he only mentions in his diary: the blood-soaked ground where a soldier had recently been killed.[21]

The trenches, deserted twice by two armies, served as a test field, where the young ensigns could make themselves familiar with the reality of war by listening, seeing, touching, and smelling death without immediate danger to themselves. Here, the war was close enough for them to observe their own reactions, such as fear, panic, or courage. Otto was amazed that he did not feel any fear, that he, on the contrary, was overwhelmed by enthusiasm. The detailed description of the scene and its horrors not only served to prove his courage, it was also meant to reassure his parents and convince them of his maturity. No longer was he a boy denying danger. The closer he got towards death, the stronger became his wish to survive. And, finally, the letter was meant to show Otto's creativity and sense of form when it comes to conceiving the war – and violence and death in particular – as a sublime and solemn event, even as a quasi-religious experience. Thus, his letter from 26 March presents an extraordinary proof of his individual education and his fully developed personality. Although he had not yet been under fire, he already felt like a soldier: calm, but passionate, with a cool gaze and heart, already changed from a boy into a man by the war and the first dead soldiers he had seen. The letter was a powerful message to his parents and a strong argument to strengthen his position towards them, because it describes experiences they never had and which he took 'like a man'. In this respect, he had left his childhood and his caring parents behind. The 'trench letter', as it was called by its enthusiastic readers at home, is mainly a statement of his masculine independence, and it was read as such by his parents and their friend. Thus, his mother confessed to Otto that the 'trench letter' had left her 'deeply shaken, thrilled, and delighted. [...] Yet the strongest sensation I felt was pure happiness about you.' Heinrich, too, was 'very pleased' about

Otto's letter and 'how you absorb and take in all these new impressions mentally and emotionally with that magnificent vigour, that death-defying courage and particularly that sparkling love of life'.[22]

Ponies

In August of the same year, Otto's regiment swiftly advanced towards the East and made only few enemy contacts.[23] Eventually Otto experienced his much longed for 'baptism of fire', when the regiment was attacked while crossing a small bridge over a swamp:

> The wild panic, especially among the ponies,[24] was actually an extremely ridiculous sight. There must have been up to 130 carriages, all tangled up in a big mess, squeaking and pushing. They almost overran the big fat sergeant [...], who was in the thick of it swearing and gesticulating wildly. Everybody was trying to escape as fast as possible through and out of the swamp. Somebody's horse sank into the mud up to its belly and its rider burst into tears; [...] Meanwhile, shrapnel shells exploded on the bridge; Bosse [another volunteer] escaped at the last moment, but one bullet hit the head of my good private Knabe and killed him instantly [...]. He was the first comrade to sink to the ground next to me like that; I was surprised how hard it hit me.[25]

Otto describes this potentially slapstick scenario by stressing the key features: surprise, when the ordered advance came to a halt; chaos, when they had to turn around; and finally panic, when they fell into the swamp. The protagonists are comic figures in Otto's description: the ridiculous fear of the ponies, the fat sergeant, the soldier who cried 'just' because his horse fell into the swamp. A turning point marks the scene, when one of them dies. The tone is changing in view of the serious and frightening events. When a comrade 'sinks down next to him', the reader realizes that Otto is in the midst of the action. In changing his narrative position from observer to participant, he himself is taken by surprise about his changing reaction. Thus Otto himself is hit, if only by shock and surprise, and he has ambivalent feelings about his own role. On the one hand, the young ensign wants to feel and show sympathy with 'his good private', whose family name 'Knabe' (boy) underlines Otto's position of superiority; on the other, he wants to be the hardened soldier who cannot be hit by death around him.

In future, Otto would stick to describing the death of somebody close to him (both emotionally and physically) as 'sinking', thus using an established expression. The 'sinking' seemed to be sudden, silent, and soft, as if the sound of the battle came to a halt when the comrade died. 'Sinking' denied the cruelty and the violence of death and turned it into an eternal sleep.[26]

The little Russian

Two weeks later, Otto, with a group of other young ensigns, was on patrol in the woods around Siedlce, the town where they had taken up position on their way to the East. On 25 August 1915, he wrote in his war diary:

> We were chasing three Kosaks, bold guys. A fourth one, who belonged to the group, had been hit. A very young lad, pretty and fine, but clearly a Slavic type. He had been hit four times, one bullet had destroyed his right testicle. A horrible wound, which he endured like a real hero. How strange is the war! We dressed the wound, wished him to survive, or rather die soon, but only because we knew he would never survive this kind of injury. At the same time, we congratulated the happy shooter, all of us hungry for more prey.[27]

The scene is quite a happy one, four comrades enjoying themselves in the woods hunting. It is similar to another diary entry right after the outbreak of the war, when Otto, looking forward to being a volunteer, spent the last week of August in Berlin biking with friends through the Grunewald. 'We tussled a lot, it was just great'.[28] But this time, at the Eastern Front it was more than tussling, and one of them killed the 'lad' they had been 'chasing'. That he was 'a Slavic type' marks a clear distinction between him and his pursuers, although he otherwise appeared to Otto as 'pretty and fine', 'a lad' almost like himself. This enemy earned Otto's respect by his heroic endurance of an injury that deprived the 'little Kosak' of his masculinity before it ended his life. Otto in his war diary reflected openly the 'strangeness' of a war, where respect and sympathy for the enemy as another human being coexisted with his dehumanization as yet another 'prey' for the competitive group of young warriors. Otto made no attempt to dissolve the inconsistency of his reaction.

In his letter to his parents, written shortly after the diary entry, he began: 'We shot down one Kosak.' And he described the young Russian again as a 'very young lad of very fine features, who, according to his wallet, also must have been very well educated. His wound was very ugly, so that I do not want to go into it here, he endured the terrible pain like a real hero, so that we all admired him. He soon died.'[29]

Here the noble features of the enemy and the likewise noble feelings of his killers are emphasized even more than in his diary entry. The scene is cleared of its strangeness and ambiguity, neither the jolly hunting scene, the lust to kill nor the congratulations for the shooter are mentioned and the injury of the 'Russian' is described as nothing more than 'ugly'.[30] Instead, Otto presents himself again as somebody who had seen and endured what is too cruel for his parents to imagine. Hiding the disturbing joy of killing does not mean that Otto wanted to distance himself from the act: in the letter to his parents, there is no single shooter, but a common 'we' that included himself.

A couple of days later, however, after marching further ahead through villages which had been destroyed by the Russian army, he wrote to Julie Vogelstein: 'The little Kosak we killed (I assume you read my letter about him) aroused my sympathy at the time, but I don't believe this could happen again. Looking at the women and children in front of what is left of their former houses, [...] you can really get into the mood for war, so to speak.'[31]

Otto left a record with his parents: the record of himself as a deeply humane, empathetic, noble young warrior, without hatred and cruelty, for whom war was a fair fight without hard, personal feelings. In the following days, he must have recognized how inappropriate this attitude might have seemed, not just in the eyes of his fellow comrades but also in his parents' view. His description of the scene with the young Russian did not mention passion at all – he had not been in the mood for war. A few days later he was: he felt anger in the face of the destruction and misery of the villages, which were deserted by the Russian Army and then taken over by himself. The physical destruction and the suffering of the people allegedly justified his hate and suppressed whatever empathy he had had before. By changing his mood, he had become an even more integral part of a collective 'we' of young killers.[32]

Thus we have here three attempts to write about the same situation. In the diary as the more immediate medium, which has its place in the milieu of male camaraderie and military exercise, Otto described a scene of male amusement and pastime. And yet he showed his respect to the young man his comrade killed, although this was counteracted by defining the body as a trophy. In his letter to his parents, however, Otto focused on the young man from Russia, whom he recognized as somebody very much like himself: a young, well-educated lad with fine features. Otto did not want his parents to think of him as somebody who killed light-heartedly or even found satisfaction in killing. It took some days and some new images to erase this event, however, and to cause what he called the right 'mood for war'. He himself might have felt it inappropriate to show so much empathy with the enemy, and/or he might have suspected his parents of such thoughts and feelings. In any case, he needed to make sure his family knew that he understood that hate was more suitable an emotion than sympathy. In all his following letters and diary entries, he never again mentioned the enemy with so much respect and even admiration.

The friend

During the summer of 1915, Otto met Boye, a young lieutenant from Bremen, who had been educated at Schulpforta, the famous boarding school in Saxony-Anhalt[33] and was trained in classical Greek and interested in philosophy, literature, and history. Otto had found a soulmate in him, somebody with whom he could talk 'about intellectual and philosophical things'. When Boye cited poems by Hölderlin, Otto felt a 'sudden glow of sunshine on these dirty villages in the middle of nowhere'.[34] He and Boye became close friends, shared a room for a while, and read Nietzsche to each other. In summer 1916, they got into heavy fighting. On 7 July, Otto wrote in his diary:

> We had a number of losses. In particular: Boye fell. The good boy; a shrapnel bullet hit his shoulder and went right into his belly. I was with him, closed his eyes, held my friend's hand once more and now it's over. How fast these things go! Last night there were two heavy thunderstorms, they filled our holes with water; sometimes you just want to give up. But never lose your sense of humour![35]

This diary entry again illustrates how Otto felt about the war's strangeness and inconsistency. Initially, Boye's death seems to be merely one of 'a number of losses'. Yet it becomes clear that this event stuck out as something special, the death of his closest friend. By characterizing him as 'a good boy' in the immediately following remark, Otto used a common phrase with which he had already described 'good private Knabe'. The 'goodness' of a friendly soul, a person who never meant any harm to anybody and thus could not be regarded as an enemy by anybody. Otto had the opportunity to stay with his close friend until it was 'over', surprised by the suddenness and the speed of death. With the same speed, Otto moved on and referred to what happened after Boye's death. Thunderstorms and flooded trenches made him wish to give up, yet he ended the description of this event with the remark that all this could, and should, be taken with 'humour'. Boye's death was already covered by the everyday war miseries. The next day he wrote just one sentence: 'Boye's death was very beautiful.'[36]

It reads like the result of a long night without sleep and full of intense reflection. There is no reasoning and no explanation why beauty is the essence of Boye's death. As Otto described the circumstances of Boye's death later to his parents (see below), the 'beauty' of the comrade's death neither arose from the fact that it was meaningful or served a purpose, nor did the description of Boye's injury suggest 'beauty' in a conventional, literal sense. What remains is the love Otto felt for his friend and the fact that he could stay with him when he died.

Lily Braun, who had heard about Otto's friend from an acquaintance, immediately wrote to her son to assure him of her sympathy. Otto then described the circumstances, which had led to Boye's death in detail, both in his diary and in his letters. Boye's death posed an explanatory problem because it seemed unnecessary, and therefore possibly meaningless: there had been a false alarm about a Russian attack, and Boye, eager to get to his unit, had been running across the fields, when he was hit by a random bullet. When Boye had visited Otto and Lily Braun in Berlin in spring 1915, she found him very likeable, 'but certainly not a soldier'.[37] Otto had agreed at the time that Boye was 'the very opposite of a soldier'.[38] But it was this quality, which formed the basis for his love – a love similar to his close friendships before 1914, when it had been the mental and not the military virtues that counted. The character of this friendship might explain why Otto could find beauty in Boye's death.

Understanding violence

In conclusion, I would like to offer a couple of more general reflections. First, there is the question of timing. In the war letters and diary entries analysed here, descriptions of violent scenes belong to the early phases of the war, when these experiences were still new and exciting, an interruption of the basic boredom of the rear area. They presented a sensation and a promise of future challenges. They were the stuff that heroism is made of. In a remarkable way, they offered an experience of the self that was new and disturbing for the young men: the presumed easiness of mind that accompanied the experience of violence, cruelty, and death. Otto was amazed and surprised, as his remarks on the strangeness of the war show. Later he took wounds, death, and the fear of both as a matter of fact. Until the very end he denied feeling fear for himself, but observed it with sympathy in some of his comrades or his 'men'. Deaths around him were mentioned later in the war without describing the injuries, but as a sudden, silent, and dispiriting 'sinking' – a metaphor he had already used at the first encounter with death, as we have seen above.

Secondly, violence is described as a positive, a sublime experience, which transformed the observer into a kind of superhuman being, feeling neither fear nor repulsion. According to this view, it was a necessary, a manly thing to do and to endure. It was the essence of the soldierly man, and the essence of war – thus a proof of having mastered the total break with the norms of a civilized, civilian, effete society, in which one did not know war, or physical danger or aggression. The mood for war was the mood for violence.

Thirdly, there was time for the laconic and the heroic when it came to the description of violence. There are short sentences without adjectives, written down hastily with a pencil on a small notepad – this is in the trenches, amongst comrades, and in the face of the imminent danger of being wounded or killed. In the trenches, there was neither the time nor the need for reflection or literary aestheticism. The situation back in the base was different, however. Time was abundant, there were letters to read and to answer, diaries to fill, and free time that could – and perhaps ought – to be filled with working and writing on the experience of the trenches. It is under these circumstances that violence was glorified as a heroic moment. Diaries and letters also represent different social places: the front and the home front, the military and the civil world, the male group and the family. Sometimes the diary entry served as a draft for a letter. There must have been experiences, however, which could not be communicated at all. In this respect, letters as a source to examine contemporary interpretations and meanings of violence are of limited value.

Fourthly, there is a tendency in the course of the conflict to look at the war as an opportunity for professionalization. This view was shared by many soldiers, especially young officers (to be).[39] Otto began to read military handbooks and treatises, including Clausewitz;[40] he reflected tactics and strategies of the German and other armies; he drew little sketches in his diary to mark positions and movements of battles his regiment had lost or won; he considered seriously what his mother was hoping from the very beginning, that he might become a professional soldier after the war. He swiftly advanced in the hierarchy and had achieved the position of a lieutenant after his nineteenth birthday. To be sure, reflecting on the possibility of becoming a professional soldier, an occupation which required a certain degree of scientific knowledge and practical skills as well as a professional attitude in regard to killing and being killed, also served as a powerful strategy to cope with what in the beginning he again and again described as amazing, or rather confusing: the close presence of death.

All these aspects are closely linked to a concept of masculinity under the conditions of war. The war turned Otto from a boy into a man. As a boy, he was the centre of his parents' attention and love, he grew up with a private tutor, adored by his mother, idealized by his father. But after 1914, the war itself became Otto's educator – thus realizing what his mother was lecturing about. He had to become a man, both physically and mentally, strong, tough, without fear, disciplined, professional. This type of masculinity implied a cool, if not positive attitude towards violence, suffered as well as inflicted.[41]

The war also had an impact on someone like Lily Braun, who in fact pictured herself as a soldier in her novel as well as in her essay on women and war. Masculinity, for her, was not a matter of biology, but of attitude and action. She certainly felt masculine, especially when she idealized motherhood – for the type of mother she evoked was bearing children in the same spirit as soldiers were carrying their weapons. Since she was prevented from fighting herself, Otto volunteered also to fulfil his mother's greatest wish. In this sense, he was her delegate. Significantly, the only man among the four, Heinrich Braun, the father, turned out to be the least masculine of them all. He presented himself – and was referred to by the other correspondents – as anxious and 'nervous'; in this way he never got into the 'mood for war'. He tried to get Otto home due to a harmless infection; he intervened to keep him away from the front; he sank in depression and contacted a fortune-teller to learn about Otto's future and imminent dangers. Lily Braun showed open contempt for his anxiety, only his lover Julie Vogelstein saw in him a Greek god who stood guard over his son – at least that is how he appeared in her dreams. While violence and masculinity were closely linked by the war, the masculinity it demanded and offered was not for all men and not for men only.

Notes

1. K. Latzel (1997) 'Vom Kriegserlebnis zu Kriegserfahrung: Theoretische und methodische Überlegungen zur erfahrungsgeschichtlichen Untersuchung von Feldpostbriefen', *Militärgeschichtliche Mitteilungen*, 56, pp. 1–30; K. Latzel (1999) 'Kriegsbriefe und Kriegserfahrung: Wie können Feldpostbriefe zur erfahrungsgeschichtlichen Quelle werden?', *Werkstatt Geschichte*, 22, pp. 7–23; and B. Ulrich (1997) *Die Augenzeugen: Deutsche Feldpostbriefe in Kriegs- und Nachkriegszeit 1914–1933* (Essen: Klartext).
2. One of these rarer examples is the correspondence of a young couple from Austria: C. Hämmerle (1998) '"…wirf ihnen alles hin und schau, daß du fortkommst." Die Feldpost eines Paares in der Geschlechter(un)ordnung des Ersten Weltkrieges', *Historische Anthropologie*, 6:3, pp. 431–58; see also B. Ziemann (2003) 'Geschlechterbeziehungen in deutschen Feldpostbriefen des Ersten Weltkrieges', in C. Hämmerle and E. Saurer (eds) *Briefkulturen und ihr Geschlecht: Zur Geschichte der privaten Korrespondenz vom 16. Jahrhundert bis heute* (Vienna and Cologne: Böhlau), pp. 261–82.
3. Julie Braun-Vogelstein Collection (JBVC), Leo Baeck Institute Archives, New York. This collection is almost completely digitalized and can be accessed under archive.org/details/juliebraunvogelstein. The *Guide to the Julie Braun-Vogelstein Collection* (http://findingaids.cjh.org/?pID=214055) offers a complete table of contents and a synopsis of series, boxes, and folders. For citation here, I will mainly use the digitalized version. However, Otto Braun's war diaries are not digitalized. Each source is part of series II: 'Otto Braun', the numbers given relate to the old box and folder numbers respectively, the numbering used on archive.org/details/juliebraunvogelstein.
4. Otto wrote seven diaries during the war, each of them consisting of around 120 pages, except the last one, which ended abruptly with his death.
5. P. Witkop (1915) *Kriegsbriefe Deutscher Studenten* (Leipzig: Panther), reprinted after 1918 under the title: *Kriegsbriefe gefallener Studenten*. Witkop was a professor of German literature at the University of Freiburg. As a single author of a published war diary (first print from 1920), Ernst Jünger became famous and widely read after the war: E. Jünger (2010) *In Stahlgewittern* (Stuttgart: Klett-Cotta).
6. L. Braun (1915) *Der Lebenssucher* (Munich: A. Langen); L. Braun (1915) *Die Frauen und der Krieg* (Leipzig: Hirzel). I will refer to this text later in this chapter.
7. The first biography of Lily Braun was published by Julie Vogelstein in 1922: *Lily Braun – ein Lebensbild* (Berlin-Grunewald: Klemm). The most detailed biography is by A. G. Mayer (1985) *The Feminism and Socialism of Lily Braun* (Bloomington, IN: Indiana University Press), which, however, leaves out the period of the First World War.
8. J. Vogelstein (1932) *Ein Menschenleben: Heinrich Braun und sein Schicksal* (Tübingen: Wunderlich).
9. O. Braun (1922) *Aus nachgelassenen Schriften eines Frühvollendeten*, ed. J. Vogelstein (Leipzig: Insel).
10. J. Vogelstein (1966) *Was niemals stirbt: Gestalten und Erinnerungen* (Stuttgart: Deutsche Verlagsanstalt).
11. J. Radkau (1998) *Das Zeitalter der Nervosität: Deutschland zwischen Bismarck und Hitler* (München: Hanser), esp. pp. 357–455.
12. After 1945, she was considered a social democrat by social democrats and a feminist by feminists. Thus, the trade union journal *Welt der Arbeit* printed an excerpt from the autobiography of the French-Jewish socialist Leon Blum, which

he wrote as a prisoner in Buchenwald, the Nazi concentration camp. Here he remembered having met Lily Braun in Paris in 1904, where she told him of an incident with her then almost seven-year-old son. While Otto was watching soldiers marching in the street, he asked her about the war. He prompted her, as she told her French friends, to a passionate anti-war statement and made her promise him in conclusion that she would work hard to prevent him from ever becoming a soldier. Blum kept this memory as the essence of what Lily Braun meant for him as a political friend. *Welt der Arbeit*, 4 May 1951.

13. Lahmann's sanatorium was a famous Life Reform institution situated in the most elegant part of Dresden, Weißer Hirsch.

14. J. Verhey (2000) *The Spirit of 1914: Militarism, Myth and Mobilization in Germany* (Cambridge: Cambridge University Press). See also the detailed study of C. Geinitz (1998) *Kriegsfurcht und Kampfbereitschaft: Das Augusterlebnis in Freiburg. Eine Studie zum Kriegsbeginn 1914* (Essen: Klartext).

15. The idea of social motherhood or motherhood in spirit had long been a political concept of Germany's bourgeois feminist movement. It was, however, not linked to biological motherhood as a personal experience. Indeed, most activists of the feminist movement at the time were not mothers themselves. Rather, it was seen as a disposition of women towards society and state, characterized by a caring, responsible, reconciling attitude, which aimed at creating harmony and understanding in a society full of social and political conflicts. Still, a valid analysis of the politics based on this assumption is I. Stoehr (1983) '"Organisierte Mütterlichkeit": Zur Politik der deutschen Frauenbewegung um 1900', in K. Hausen (ed.) *Frauen suchen ihre Geschichte: Historische Studien zum 19. und 20. Jahrhundert* (Munich: Beck), pp. 221–49; U. Planert (ed.) (2000) *Nation, Politik und Geschlecht. Frauenbewegungen und Nationalismus in der Moderne* (Frankfurt am Main: Campus). The bourgeois women's movement championed the idea of a national service for women; however, the question of whether it should be solely on a voluntary basis was controversial among them. Proposals for mandatory service were more seriously discussed during the war, but Lily Braun's insistence on a national service beyond war times remained a marginal position even among the conservative women's movement. See E. Gnauck-Kühne (1915) *Dienstpflicht und Dienstjahr des weiblichen Geschlechts* (Tübingen: Mohr); for a short overview of the women's movement in the First World War and the debate about national service, see A. Schaser (2006) *Frauenbewegung in Deutschland 1848–1933* (Darmstadt: Wissenschaftliche Buchgesellschaft), pp. 77–96; also B. Guttmann (1989) *Weibliche Heimarmee: Frauen in Deutschland 1914–1918* (Weinheim: Deutscher Studienverlag).

16. It is striking that this argument implies that these children would all be sons.

17. L. Braun (1915) *Die Frauen und der Krieg* (Leipzig: Hirzel), p. 52.

18. Peter Kollwitz, one year Otto's senior, fell on 23 October 1914. The news reached his parents one week later: J. Bohnke-Kollwitz (ed.) (1999) *Käthe Kollwitz: Die Tagebücher 1908–1943* (Berlin: Siedler), entries pp. 172, 174. See also R. Schulte (1995) 'Käthe Kollwitz' Opfer', in C. Jansen, L. Niethammer and B. Weisbrod (eds) (1995) *Von der Aufgabe der Freiheit: Politische Verantwortung und bürgerliche Gesellschaft im 19. und 20. Jahrhundert. Festschrift für Hans Mommsen* (Berlin: Akademie-Verlag), pp. 647–72.

19. Among them M. Scheler (1915) *Der Genius des Krieges und der deutsche Krieg* (Leipzig: Verlag der Weißen Bücher); J. Plenge (1916) *1789 und 1914: Die symbolischen Jahre in der Geschichte des politischen Geistes* (Leipzig: Springer); T. Mann (1916) *Friedrich und die Große Koalition* (Berlin: Fischer).

20. JBVC, ser. II, 5/2, 25/26 March 1915.

21. JBVC, ser. II, 4, Otto Braun War Diaries 2, 24 March 1915, p. 75.
22. JBVC, ser. II, Lily's letter in 6/2, 2 April 1915, Heinrich's letter in 6/1, 2 April 1915.
23. Otto's unit belonged to the 9th army; see Reichsarchiv (ed.) (1932) *Der Weltkrieg 1914–1918: Die militärischen Operationen zu Lande*, vol. 8: *Die Operationen des Jahres 1915* (Berlin: E. S. Mittler), map 6 and pp. 555–7. For military action in the East in general, see also N. Stone (1998) *The Eastern Front 1914–1917* (London: Penguin).
24. Otto used the term 'ponies' for the small horses drawing carriages with the regiment's baggage and ammunition.
25. JBVC, ser. II, 4, Otto Braun War Diaries 2, 11 August 1915.
26. K. Latzel (1988) *Vom Sterben im Krieg: Wandlungen in der Einstellung zum Soldatentod vom Siebenjährigen Krieg bis zum Zweiten Weltkrieg* (Warendorf: Fahlbusch).
27. JBVC, ser. II, 4, O. Braun War Diaries 2, 25 August 1915.
28. JBVC, ser. II, 4, O. Braun War Diaries 1, 26 August 1914.
29. JBVC, ser. II, 5/3, letter O. Braun to L. and H. Braun, 20 August 1915. (This date may be incorrect as the event was only recorded in the diary on 25 August.)
30. J. Bourke (1999) *An Intimate History of Killing: Face to Face Killing in 20th Century Warfare* (London: Basic Books).
31. JBVC, ser. II, 6/3, letter O. Braun to J. Vogelstein, 29 August 1915.
32. The attempt to describe himself as someone who had become a warrior due to the cruelty of the enemy is obviously an attempt to make his emotional development more consistent than it was in real life. Descriptions of burnt houses, for instance, can be found in his diary already, days before the 'encounter' with the group of young Kosaks (see entry in JBVC, ser. II, 4, Otto Braun War Diaries 2, 20 August 1915).
33. An elite school in Naumburg founded in the sixteenth century, with many celebrities among its former students, such as Fichte, von Ranke, and Nietzsche.
34. JBVC, ser. II, 4, Otto Braun War Diaries 2, 16 August 1915, p. 79.
35. JBVC, ser. II, 4, Otto Braun War Diaries 3, 7 July 1916, p. 124.
36. JBVC, ser. II, 4, Otto Braun War Diaries 3, 8 July 1916, p. 125.
37. JBVC, ser. II, 6/2, letter L. to O. Braun, 21 April 1916.
38. JBVC, ser. II, 5/3, letter O. to L. Braun, 25 April 1916.
39. See again, for instance, Jünger, *Kriegstagebuch*.
40. Most likely K. von Clausewitz, *Vom Kriege, 1915* (Leipzig: Insel), an edition of collected essays.
41. G. Mosse is one of the pioneers in studying the meaning of masculinity in the context of war: G. Mosse (1990) *Fallen Soldiers: Reshaping the Memory of the World Wars* (Oxford: Oxford University Press); for a gendered perspective on military history and the history of wars, see C. Hämmerle (2000) 'Von den Geschlechtern der Kriege und des Militärs: Forschungseinblicke und Bemerkungen zu einer neuen Debatte', in T. Kühne and B. Ziemann (eds) *Was ist Militärgeschichte?* (Paderborn: Schöningh), pp. 229–62; also U. Brunotte (2004) *Zwischen Eros und Krieg: Männerbund und Ritual in der Moderne* (Berlin: Wagenbach), and S. Levsen (2006) *Elite, Männlichkeit und Krieg: Tübinger und Cambridger Studenten 1900–1929* (Göttingen: Vandenhoeck & Ruprecht).

4
Love in the Trenches: German Soldiers' Conceptions of Sexual Deviance and Hegemonic Masculinity in the First World War

Jason Crouthamel

Germany's traumatic experience with total war in 1914–18 presents challenges for historians dealing with the history of gender. The responses of common soldiers to the trauma of war, and their conceptions of masculinity and sexuality, were complex. While the all-pervasive image of the steel-nerved, disciplined warrior suggests an easily identifiable, militarized hegemonic ideal, this masculine image was fragile and, as Monika Szczepaniak recently noted, tends to be oversimplified.[1] Sociologist R. W. Connell argues that while hegemonic masculinity was defined in opposition to subordinate forms of masculinity, perceptions and constructions of hegemonic masculinity were elusive, contested and always changing.[2] To what degree did soldiers embrace dominant images of masculinity? As Christa Hämmerle recently observed, it is difficult to uncover the degree to which hegemonic, militarized conceptions of masculinity were accepted by the majority of soldiers who experienced the Great War.[3]

Undoubtedly, war was the 'school for masculinity' in the nineteenth and twentieth centuries,[4] but the war experience educated men in different ways. Germany's military leaders and civil organizations attempted to control and reinforce a dominant image of an emotionally disciplined, heterosexual and self-sacrificing warrior focused entirely on the defence of the nation. Homosexual men were denounced as 'effeminate' threats to this militarized ideal of comradeship.[5] Newspapers produced by front soldiers (*Schützengrabenzeitungen*), letters from men at the front, and post-war periodicals by homosexual veterans suggest that while some of these soldiers embraced the dominant, martial form of masculinity and sexuality, they simultaneously experimented with emotions and behaviours that were potentially 'deviant' and threatening to the hegemonic ideal. This chapter explores how both heterosexual and homosexual soldiers negotiated different forms of masculinity and sexuality, and the ways in which they balanced 'deviant' behaviours and identities with the image of the 'good comrade'. What competing conceptions of masculinity and sexualities emerged in response to the trauma of the trenches? How were these masculinities and sexualities defined and modified in response to prescribed militarized hegemonic masculinity?

I argue that soldiers constructed their own conceptions of a 'good comrade' that did not fit easily into the prevailing paradigm of hegemonic masculinity. Men affirmed homosocial and homosexual behaviours and desires as natural, 'masculine', and even necessary mechanisms for surviving the strains of trench warfare. For heterosexual soldiers, 'comradeship', as historians have recognized, fused 'feminine' characteristics of nurturing with the 'masculine' comradely ideal.[6] Front newspapers also indicate that some men wished to escape martial masculinity as they celebrated and fantasized about gender transgression, including loving other men. These fantasies of gender transgression suggest that heterosexual comrades wished to express 'effeminate' emotions of love and vulnerability that were not acceptable under the prevailing warrior image. In contrast, many homosexual veterans sanctified prevailing images of martial masculinity, and they contested the exclusively heterosexual nature of militarized masculinity. Gay men appropriated militarized, nationalistic ideals of comradeship to counter stereotypes of homosexuals as effeminate 'social outsiders', and they sought acceptance from their heterosexual comrades by making the case that their love of men was the emotional equivalent of, or even superior to, male–female desire. They equated the 'good comrade' and ideal masculinity with love for other men. Some even observed that heterosexual love had become obsolete in the trench environment, and that homosexual love was more suited to modern war. As heterosexual soldiers experimented with and accepted emotional bonds with men, gay men saw this normalization of male–male love as an opportunity to prove that they were not a deviant threat to the nation, but rather were masculine and patriotic soldiers who were proficient with the emotions that were essential to the nation's survival. In aligning themselves with the hegemonic ideal that affirmed 'masculine' as militarized and superior, many gay men reinforced paradigms of male dominance.[7]

Recent historiography on masculinity and sexuality has called for greater focus on marginalized groups and their perspectives on hegemonic gender paradigms.[8] Examining the experiences of homosexual soldiers in the Great War provides an excellent site for uncovering ways in which the dominant gender order was contested, appropriated, and reinforced. The psychological and physical damage caused by the trench experience indeed provoked a crisis of masculinity, as many historians have observed. However, responses to this crisis, as historian Birthe Kundrus argues, cannot be reduced to a 'single common denominator', and the war presented new opportunities to reconfigure gender assumptions.[9] In their humour and entertainment, front soldiers experimented and fantasized about expressing love for other men. Interestingly, while some heterosexual men perceived martial masculinity to be suffocating in ways that are comparable to the narratives of psychologically traumatized men, many homosexual men celebrated the soldierly ideal. As steel-nerved, patriotic warriors for the nation, homosexual veterans could love other men in a framework that they hoped was acceptable to mainstream culture.

Soldiers' conceptions of masculinity also provide a useful site for studying the history of emotions, which has recently drawn increased attention from historians and sociologists. Analysing the emotional universe of British soldiers through their letters home, Michael Roper argues that in their relationships with women at home, men found their primary basis for emotional support as well as survival skills that helped them domesticize the combat front.[10] However, Roper also highlights the unbearable strains of total war that put a wedge between men and women, including the difficulty men had in conveying the traumatic emotional experience of mass violence.[11] This strain pervades German soldiers' letters and front newspapers. Men at the front often resented women complaining about problems on the home front, as Christa Hämmerle has noted in her work on war-time correspondence, and widespread accusations against women as enjoying comfort while men endured stress further destabilized relations between men and women.[12] In the trauma and deprivation of total war, traditional paradigms for love and emotional support became distorted or broke down.

Love between men at the front was a powerful emotional experience. As Thomas Kühne persuasively argues, many soldiers openly embraced feminine feelings of familial love and nurturing in the trenches, and these emotions were widely accepted under the paradigm of 'comradeship'.[13] Robert Nelson's recent impressive overview of front newspapers also supports Kühne's thesis that a 'softer' side to the 'good comrade' became widely accepted as men showed compassion and support for other men, while still conforming to a hegemonic masculinity that demanded sacrifice and self-control.[14] I argue that by destigmatizing the outward display of emotions like love and compassion, soldiers created a space in which men could normalize and humanize 'deviant' homosocial and homosexual inclinations. The liberation of love and compassion under the guise of being 'good comrades' allowed gay men to assert that homosexuality was normal. As historian Emma Vickers uncovered in her work on gay British soldiers in the Second World War, gay men found the opportunity to be considered 'good fellows' if they adhered to a soldierly image in which they did a good job and did not display their homosexuality, or at least did not appear effeminate in a way that threatened their comrades.[15] Gay German soldiers also imagined that they could be accepted if they performed well on the battlefield. Even gay men who internalized the notion that their sexual desires were 'deviant' perceived their emotions of love for other men in the trenches as perfectly natural, as long as they affirmed the warrior image.

Hegemonic masculinity and its discontents at the front

Young men in imperial Germany were indoctrinated to contain and control 'effeminate' emotions, like love and compassion, while sacrificing themselves as warriors for the fatherland.[16] Doctors, teachers, and conservative political leaders reinforced an image of 'manliness' defined in opposition to 'degenerate' groups, including promiscuous men, homosexuals, and other 'deviants' who, critics argued, were too self-absorbed and hedonistic to dedicate themselves to the nation.[17] When the war broke out, soldiers' front newspapers, especially those written at the army corps and divisional level, which were carefully controlled by military censors, contained images of the 'good comrade' as sexually chaste individuals who sacrificed themselves for the nation.[18] In a December 1916 issue of *Der Dienstkamerad* (The Comrade in Service), Chaplain B. Pfister of the 14th Infantry Regiment in Germany's 3rd Army Division encouraged men, after the devastating losses at Verdun and the Somme, to ignore their personal problems and remain cheerful and courageous in the face of stress. 'True manliness', Pfister observed, required men to be 'loyal, obedient and friendly.'[19] Being a 'good comrade' also had a sexual component. Writing for *Der Flieger* (The Flyer), medical corps Captain Dr Fischer chastised soldiers who visited brothels and risked venereal disease infection. He insisted that sexual intercourse was not a necessity for real men, and that the loyal German soldier was too focused on defending the nation to be concerned with sexual needs.[20] The air force issued a booklet to front-line fighter pilots that warned them to practise restraint or, better yet, total abstinence from sex, which allegedly drained them of the strength they needed to fight effectively.[21]

The physical distance between men and women exacerbated the strain between combat and home fronts. From the army's perspective, the most serious social and sexual crisis brought on by the depravations of war was the epidemic of venereal disease (VD). While propaganda disseminated by military and civil authorities celebrated images of soldiers as sexually chaste and loyal to their women at home, the army also carefully regulated a system of brothels behind the front lines to cope with millions of sexually frustrated men.[22] In a March 1915 letter to the State Secretary of the Interior Ministry, Chancellor Bethmann-Hollweg expressed concern about the spread of VD at the front, and he demanded that the state and army intervene aggressively with sex education, condom distribution, and medical evaluations of prostitutes to contain disease.[23] The military's rationing of sex drew the ire of Christian morality groups on the home front, where coalitions of religious, business, and political leaders warned that if men continued to relieve their stress with promiscuous sex, it would lead to national degeneration.[24] A chaplain, and member of a Christian morality association, named Dr Aufhauser argued in the *Allgemeine Rundschau* that 'sexual abstinence is the duty for the entire army and its troops'. Soldiers,

Dr Aufhauser argued, were heroes if they practised self-control and remained 'pure and immaculate' ('rein und makellos'), dedicated only to their families and the nation. Dr Aufhauser called for the shutting down of military-run bordellos, and he encouraged the military to replace them with Christian reading groups and lemonade.[25]

Wives and girlfriends no longer seemed to fill the sexual needs of men at the front, not only because of geographical distance, but because industrialized war and mass violence seemed to erode the emotional bonds between men and women. The front newspaper *Der Flieger*, which by 1917 was being edited by the left-wing writer and soldier Kurt Tucholsky, published articles that frankly described the sexual breakdown experienced by men at the front. Paul Göhre, an ex-Lutheran pastor turned Social Democrat who fought on the Russian front in 1915, argued that the 'moral-preacher standpoint' on sexual promiscuity had nothing to do with the reality of what industrialized violence did to the sexual relationships between men and women. Gone were the days of August 1914, he observed, when heroic masculinity gave men a sense of power that attracted the loyal *Hausfrau*. Instead, sex had become mechanical, and emotional fulfilment was replaced by cynical and even brutal sex as both men and women sought outlets to express their frustrations after three years of stress and violence. Göhre blamed women for no longer providing emotional support for men, and he lamented that men saw sex with women as a primarily physical experience, devoid of spiritual fulfilment.[26]

It is difficult to determine whether Göhre's thesis accurately reflected soldiers' perceptions of intimacy with women. However, in their letters to comrades some soldiers revealed feelings of psychological numbness and expressions of desire for emotional intimacy, including desire for emotional support from men. One soldier, named Wilhelm B. from a Baden-Württemberg regiment, wrote a series of letters in 1917 to his comrade, Johann V., that surreally alternated between expressions of tender feelings for his comrade and graphic descriptions of violence. Wilhelm B. assumed a level of familiarity and intimacy that suggested a close bond between the two men. In one passage, he expressed admiration for Johann V.'s 'beautiful yellow rider's uniform' and 'gladiator's face hidden by stylish hair'. Then he shifted his focus to the horrors of war, which he said was nothing more than 'filth, rats, mice, fleas and lice'. Trench warfare turned men into helpless and dependent beings rather than heroic adventurers: 'In it [the war] the masses are left to be passive heroes [*passive Helden*] bogged down in idleness.' While the aristocrats gave 'lively lectures' about the glories of war, Wilhelm B. wrote, lowly ordinary soldiers had to endure 'sinking into mindlessness and depravity' that had dominated the monotonous trench experience. Wilhelm B. intimated to his friend that there must have been an epidemic of mental illness that drove comrades and civilians to continue this war. Struggling to explain how this disaster could have happened, and how it affected him,

Wilhelm B. adopted an almost stream of consciousness style that mixes humour and the grotesque:

> War psychosis, wrapped into the fog of a meteor, let's just say it: chronic atrophy of the brain, *Dementia militarilis bellicosa*. It's like something being evacuated out, and I'm not talking about the rectum. One no longer lives. One has only fragmented and infrequent feelings. Look, I want to publish a brochure: 'The Inflatable Rubber Cushion [*Das Gummikissen*] in the World War.' Don't laugh [...] I'll send you a really bad photo, in which you can see the stupefied expression on my face as well as the look of my only comrade here, my dog, the only one who still wants to feel emotions.[27]

Images of a stoic, heroic warrior are absent from Wilhelm B.'s narrative on the psychological effects of the war. He describes a man who has become numb and deeply cynical, yet he is also desperate to recover his sense of feelings and love for Johann V. He finished his letter: 'I don't know when the *bellum gloriosum* will come to an end. I hope it's not so soon – imagine the great deal of trouble it's going to be to have to feel again. I remain in love – your devoted Wilhelm B.'[28] Starved for affection and intensely lonely, Wilhelm B. closed his sardonic diatribe against the war and hollow old values with a vulnerable confession of love and self-doubt about whether he would ever be the same after the war.

In their *Feldpost* to women at home, men often appealed to their wives to provide them emotional support. Their letters reveal that they imagined a strict dichotomy between a sense of martial masculinity, which entailed selfless devotion to the fatherland, and the loyal woman, who showed her dedication to the nation by supporting her soldier husband. At the same time, they also grew resentful of women for not sharing the horrifying realities of war. For example, Leutnant der Reserve Otto L. related to his wife, whom he nicknamed 'Berbel', that he took immense pride in fighting for the fatherland and relied on her loyalty as he faced the stress of war: 'I am proud, Berbel, to be able to be part of this fight for my *Heimat* and naturally I cannot require that you have the same feelings for Germany, but it will come in time. Oh Berbel, whenever I think of the horrors [*Schrecken*] of this war and the misery of our French enemies as well, I often think about how good you have it at home.'[29] It was more natural for him to have 'feelings for Germany', Otto L. maintained, with a hint of condescension, while women enjoyed the comfort of the home front. He expected her to give him unconditional support and to think of him when he went to battle. He became increasingly impatient when Berbel complained about how lonely she felt and lamented financial problems at home. He chastised her: 'Even through these major problems we've got to help each other and in the meantime you cannot complain. Stop it! We've got to keep singing our marching songs and

I'm asking you do the same – if we can get through this things will get better.'[30] Otto L. criticized her as a lamenting woman, an image often depicted in *Feldpost*, which soldiers described as infuriating and, after the war, often characterized as a drain on the army's fighting abilities.[31]

Many soldiers struggled to express their feelings in written words to loved ones at home. In some cases, they felt that loved ones did not appreciate or understand the traumatic experiences they endured, especially the emotional pain of losing comrades. This growing psychological and experiential divide can be seen in the correspondence between Leutnant Kurt K., assigned to a Bavarian mortar battalion, and his fiancée, Lotte. After the deaths of several close friends, Kurt K. struggled to maintain his masculine self-control, and he was self-conscious that Lotte would consider him soft or effeminate if he wrote too much about his emotions:

> And now everything that once made me happy is lost in France, and I feel so completely alone. The last of my friends went to East Prussia, because he had to take care of his stepmother. But his brother was killed. Don't think I'm soft [*weichlich*]. But think about it this way: if suddenly all your female friends, with whom you had shared joy and pain, were killed off, wouldn't you also have such thoughts?[32]

Reluctant to shed his masculine armour against such powerful emotions, Kurt K. asked for Lotte's sympathy as his veneer of emotional control broke down. Lotte responded to his news about death and intense loneliness with optimism and encouragement, telling him that surely he would find new friends soon. Though her advice was consistent with preserving the stoic masculine image, Kurt K.'s response indicates that he was not ready to get over his trauma: 'Do you still remember when I wrote in one of my recent letters, that all of my friends had fallen. You wrote back that I would soon find other friends. But this is no comfort, because a friend that one has been with since childhood cannot be so easily replaced.'[33] In a subsequent letter about another friend's burial, he wrote that his friend's fiancée begged him to write about his last hours. He told Lotte that he could not compose the words to express such pain over 'another exterminated life'.[34] Increasingly, Kurt K. felt cut off from Lotte and home. Though he tried to intimate what he was going through, her attempts to be supportive and optimistic seemed increasingly hollow.

In the context of extreme upheaval, physical deprivation, and psychological stress experienced at the front, men sought intimacy with those who best understood their experience – other men. Front newspapers conveyed images of men openly expressing feelings of intimacy and even love for their male comrades, and placed it in the context of humour, which allowed men to safely and vicariously imagine new types of behaviour and gender ideals within the framework of cartoons and feature articles. Feminine behaviour, including nurturing and emotional support, became an integral part of ordinary soldiers' conceptions of comradeship, where martial masculinity and feminine emotions blended to help men survive. However, soldiers' humour suggests another level of gender transgression, including envy for the female gender. Men imagined themselves as women in emotional terms, taking on feminine traits to such an extent that they fantasized they were no longer men. The brutality of war made some men feel repulsed by what they saw as innately masculine characteristics, and they envied the softer, more peaceful characteristics of the feminine. This fantasy of gender crossing can be found in a poem entitled 'We poor men!' in *Der Flieger*. In the poem, Sergeant Nitsche psychologically escapes the trenches by imagining that he is a woman. Lamenting the images of bombed-out landscapes and the tedium of military drill, Nitsche envied women's 'sweet smiles' and beauty, and reflects: 'We poor, poor men are so completely wicked. I wish I were a girl. I wish I weren't a man!' Nitsche fantasized that he turned into a woman: 'If only I were bedecked with curls, with stockings á la jour, I would charm a lieutenant, and I'd dance an extra round.' He imagined himself strolling arm in arm with his lieutenant, displaying an 'enraptured smile', and filled with thoughts like 'being beautiful and performing beauty is my governing law'. Dreaming of cooking wonderful meals and gracefully moving about – 'my breasts would arch themselves as I waltz about in high heels' – Nitsche ended the poem with: 'For a long time I could kiss the entire company, and I would certainly not absorb the fragrances that come out of the frying pan – Oh, if I only were a girl, why am I a man?!'[35] Nitsche's poem reflected a humorous male fantasy of transforming into a charming woman who served soldiers and provided them relief from their stressful environment. He imagined that he could be a better comrade as a woman, providing love and comfort to men who needed it.

Soldiers' newspapers projected images of men who did not fit the 'martial' image of masculinity, but who were nevertheless 'good comrades'. Men who formed intimate relationships, very much like married couples, were depicted with a mixture of humour and acceptance. In *Der kleine Brummer* (The Little Buzzer), which was edited by men in the 2nd Guard Reserve Division, 'Fritz' and 'Emil' visit a health resort on the beach, take off their uniforms and relax in their swim clothes. Fritz tells Emil, 'First I want to rest in the sun', but fails to notice that he's reclining on the porch of a beach hut painted 'for officers only'. When Emil protests that they might get in trouble, since they are enlisted men, Fritz indicates that there is nothing to worry about. They are amused and chuckle when other enlisted men salute as they walk by. Supplementing the humour about social class inversion there is also a measure of gender inversion. Appearing to be a married couple who vacation and bicker, the cartoon hints at homoeroticism as Fritz makes exaggerated effeminate gestures when he suggests they nap together.[36] Though the couple is depicted as an amusing sight, they are also tacitly accepted by their comrades in the cartoon.

Male–male emotional bonds and homosexuality at the front

Many of the emotional bonds between men appear to be temporary responses to war, as heterosexual men felt safe experimenting with homosocial bonds to alleviate the stress of life at the front. At the same time, acceptance of these bonds gave men who identified themselves as innately homosexual a feeling of safety, and confidence, to express their love for men openly in the trenches. The war created an environment in which homosexuals defined their sexuality, masculinity, and their status in society. Like other minorities in Germany, homosexual men saw military service as an opportunity to prove their patriotism and integration into the social fabric. One of the first and largest homosexual rights organizations in the world, the Wissenschaftlich-humanitäres Komitee (WhK, Scientific-Humanitarian Committee), founded in 1897, played a major role in evaluating the experiences of gay men in the army.[37] Dr Magnus Hirschfeld, a co-founder of the WhK and internationally recognized sexologist, argued that homosexuals were a natural, essentially effeminate 'third sex'. Hirschfeld, an advocate for social democracy, called for the dismantling of Paragraph 175, which criminalized homosexuality. Hirschfeld also allied the WhK with the women's movement, including Helene Stöcker's Bund für Mutterschutz und Sexualreform (League for the Protection of Motherhood and Sex Reform), founded in 1905. Stöcker and Hirschfeld co-organized lectures and clinics for sexual reform, forming the groundwork for organizational and ideological alliances between the homosexual and women's movements in Wilhelmian society.[38]

Magnus Hirschfeld was critical of militarization, but he saw the war as an opportunity to mobilize scientists and activists to study the broader sexual effects of this great upheaval. The WhK collected letters from soldiers on their war experiences and sexual behaviour. Based on his data, Hirschfeld argued that the war created circumstances of physical and psychological deprivation that drove men to experiment with their sexuality. In these conditions, otherwise heterosexual men sought sex with other men as a replacement for the lack of women, engaging in what Hirschfeld described as 'pseudo-homosexuality'.[39] At the same time, Hirschfeld emphasized that the front enabled men who were 'constitutionally homosexual' to find other homosexual men in an environment that was more tolerant of same-sex relations than pre-war or mainstream culture.

Comradeship, according to Hirschfeld, had several dimensions of emotional intimacy. He identified three forms of 'intimate comradeship': the consciously erotic, unconsciously erotic, and bonds between men that remained unerotic.[40] Hirschfeld recorded numerous accounts of men who discovered love with other men, and these relationships were often tolerated by their heterosexual comrades as natural examples of tenderness and love experienced between men in combat. While he was convinced that homosexual men could easily adapt to their 'comradely' roles in war, Hirschfeld also pointed to numerous accounts given by men to the WhK that exemplified his theory that constitutional homosexuals were essentially feminine. There were indeed men with homoerotic inclinations who adapted easily to the militaristic culture of war, he argued, but in cases of 'feminine homosexuals' ('feminine Urninge', or the third sex), they were repulsed by the war and preferred the nurturing work of caring for the wounded and other 'feminine' tasks.[41]

In the context of 'comradeship' and increased intimacy between men, homosexual men were able to more openly manifest their pre-existing sexual feelings. One gay soldier told Hirschfeld that he saw the war as an opportunity to show his friends that homosexual men were just as brave and patriotic as their heterosexual comrades, and he worked hard to dispel the 'horrible lies' about allegedly degenerate gay men.[42] The front enabled homosexual men to find other homosexual men in an environment more tolerant of same-sex relations than pre-war culture. Hirschfeld noted that while the physically erotic nature of these relationships usually remained hidden, they were tolerated, even encouraged, as necessary 'bonding' between men. For many men, these relationships seemed to be a natural, logical extension of their military and emotional experience. As one officer wrote:

One day there came an ensign from the cadet corps, Count L., with whom I immediately fell in love [...]. Soon we became inseparable friends and the major and other older officers rejoiced at the splendid relationship which had grown up between superior and subordinate [...]. Karl and I lived together, went into service together, etc. When we didn't go out in the evening, we dismissed the servants and sat for a long time arm in arm, in close embrace, saying many tender and lovely things to each other, spinning golden for the future and building beautiful castles in the air. To you, doctor, I can confess that we also engaged in sexual activity, but only rarely and in a thoroughly fine, aesthetic, but never punishable form. For two whole months we enjoyed our love happiness together [...].[43]

The question of sexual relations, and Paragraph 175, was critical, as men recounted that superiors only tolerated love between men if it was not overtly sexual. In the case of Count L. and Karl, after they were arrested when caught in bed by a superior officer, Count L. was diagnosed as having a 'neuropathic constitution' and discharged. Count L. concluded his letter to Hirschfeld: 'If I were to say I was not sorry that I could no longer wear the King's uniform, I would be telling an untruth [...]. I will not permit myself to be robbed of the idea that the love of urnings is at least as holy and pure, good and noble as any heterosexual inclination.'[44] Though they had to elude Paragraph 175, gay men asserted that homosexuality was a natural inclination.

While some homosexual men felt more confident about expressing their love for other men in the environment of war-time comradeship, many of them still felt self-conscious about their homosexuality. Homosexuals, defined by army doctors as mentally ill criminals who endangered the nation, found themselves prosecuted for 'crimes against morality' (*Sittlichkeitsverbrechen*). This broad term was applied to men prosecuted for rape, pederasty, and bestiality.[45] In the case of Johann R., for example, a 22-year-old enlisted soldier from Würzburg who was arrested in early 1918 for homosexual rape and pederasty (violation of Paragraphs 175 and 176), he confessed that his homosexual inclinations were evidence that he was mentally ill – a 'pederast', in his words. One of his lovers was found dead in a *Gasthaus*, the victim of suicide, Johann R. insisted. He gave a detailed description of their last hours together in his testimony to the court. His narrative provides an interesting glimpse into how some men perceived homosexuality and military service:

Since I was 16 yrs old I've been a pederast. I don't have any feelings at all for feminine charms. I have never had sex with a woman. [...] At the end of 1918 in the train station in Würzburg, while on leave, I got to know D. [the victim in question]. He asked me for a light, and after that we had a conversation and he told me he was a pederast and asked me if I was interested in him. Because I liked him, I said I was interested and went with him into the city up to his apartment [...]. There we masturbated across from each other twice until 3am, and we kissed. Further intimacies did not happen. We lay on top of each other in the bed or hugged each other. Each had the other's sexual parts in their hands and rubbed until the other ejaculated. Touching sexual parts to the anus or any other nearby body region never happened [...]. When I had to leave him on the evening of 8 February and go back to the front, I asked him for my ring back, which I had given to him on his wish, because my mother would have made a fuss about it. That made him really angry, and we departed fighting. I met him later and he explained to me that he had suicidal thoughts and wanted to commit mutual suicide, but I turned him down. He showed me a revolver. I loaned him 5 Marks, because he told me he was completely broke, and then I left him [...]. I've suffered from terrible nervousness [*starke Nervosität*] for a long time. My siblings and parents are normal and healthy, and cases of pederasty or mental illness have never occurred in my family. I don't have sex with anyone at the front.[46]

Johann R.'s detailed description of his homosexual experiences was crucial from a legal defence standpoint. The courts interpreted Paragraph 175 to be specifically a prohibition on anal intercourse, thus R.'s precise statement that he and his partner did not engage in this act, as mutual masturbation was not considered to be a violation of the anti-sodomy law.[47] Johann R. confesses here that he is mentally ill, but he protests that he did not technically violate the law.

The last line of Johann R.'s testimony also reveals that there was an important division in his mind between sexual behaviour at the front and at home. Insisting 'I don't have sex with anyone at the front', a line that stood as its own paragraph at the end of his transcribed testimony, suggests that he believed authorities would be lenient if he did not tarnish the moral sanctity of the front lines with his self-professed sexual deviance and mental illness. Further, his case file refers to his excellent conduct as a soldier, having fought for three years and earning an Iron Cross. While the home front might be a site of immoral sexual behaviour, the combat front remained pure. Johann R.'s testimony highlights the degree to which many men had internalized hegemonic ideals of masculinity that enshrined the front as a site of exclusively heterosexual, albeit celibate, purity. However, the war also gave rise to a movement of homosexual men who saw their military service as evidence that they were normal and essential members of society who deserved respect for the defence of the nation. Many homosexuals argued that they were indeed pillars of hegemonic masculinity, and that love between men was the most pure and ideal form of love at the front. Under the guise of 'comradeship', where expressions of emotion and close bonds were acceptable, homosexual men attempted to legitimize their desires as not only legally permissible, but also essential to the nation's survival.

Homosexual soldiers' perceptions of hegemonic masculinity

During the war, homosexual men were attacked as threats to masculinity and enemies of the nation. Journalists circulated images of gay men as sexually promiscuous, primitive beings who corrupted otherwise moral, heterosexual front soldiers. In his pamphlet *The Sexual Cruelties of Love-Crazy Men*, conservative journalist H. A. Preiss lamented that the war led 'normal men', as well as 'intrinsically degenerate men', to turn to homosexuality, fetishism, and other 'abnormal sexual practices in order to relieve their tense nerves'. Preiss claimed that soldiers had become so focused on their abnormal sexual needs that they were no longer willing to sacrifice for the nation. Their degenerate sexual practices, he claimed, contributed to the weakening of the army.[48] Gay veterans sought to combat accusations of being 'enemies of the nation', and they characterized homosexual men as responsible members of the front community whose war experience entitled them to be accepted members of the national community. Further, gay veterans pointed to the war experience as evidence that they were not 'effeminate' men, but rather battle-hardened, steel-nerved front fighters who, apart from their sexual attraction to other men, conformed to the hegemonic masculine ideal that celebrated men as patriotic soldiers.

Magnus Hirschfeld's movement for homosexual rights represented only one strand of Germany's gay movement, which even before the war was fragmented into different organizations with diverse political ideologies and perceptions of the nature of homosexuality. In contrast to Hirschfeld's WhK, the iconoclastic, nationalistic Adolf Brand, who formed the Gemeinschaft der Eigene (GdE, Community of the Self-Owned) in 1903, celebrated the virtues of militarism and the warrior ideal. Homosexual men, Brand argued, were not an 'effeminate' third sex, as Hirschfeld claimed, but rather elite, spiritually superior, hypermasculine individuals who were the backbone of the nation. Brand perceived the Great War as a site where gay men could relive the glories of ancient Sparta, and Brand's acolytes in the GdE used the war to celebrate an image of gay men as masculine warriors. Brand was hostile toward the Social Democratic Party, which he believed drained the individualism of cultured, spiritually free Germans. Brand's hatred for the new republic was further intensified by Weimar's granting of voting rights to women in late 1918. GdE leaders opposed the political and economic emancipation of women, and considered the women's movement to be a drain on men's freedom and independence. Men, according to GdE activists, had earned their higher status in society by fighting for the nation, in contrast to women who remained relatively secure at home.[49]

Homosexuals on the political right strongly embraced the warrior ideal and denounced Hirschfeld's 'third sex' homosexuals as degenerate, unmanly outsiders. Journalist and philosopher Hans Blüher, for example, was radicalized by the war experience and attacked the 'third sex' theory and women's civil rights as cultural suicide. Blüher idealized gay men as masculine warriors who maintained their superiority through the strengthening of male associations (*Männerbünde*), which excluded 'social outsiders', including effeminate men, Jews, and feminists.[50] Like Blüher, members of Brand's GdE argued that the war was more instrumental than any scientific theory in proving that gay men were the backbone of German cultural life as evidenced by their essential role in the military. In the 1925 booklet *Male Heroes and Comrade-Love in War: A Study and Collection of Materials*, published by Brand, G. P. Pfeiffer argued that 'physiological friendship' was always the foundation for heroism, courage, and sacrifice displayed in war.[51] War did not necessarily cause men to engage in homosexual behaviour, Pfeiffer emphasized, but it did awaken intimate emotional bonds between men, including comradeship, that transcended sexual instincts and made Paragraph 175 irrelevant:

> War educates to camaraderie, i.e., it releases often slumbering characteristics of man, the ability for devoted friendship with the comrades of tent and battle. It does not seduce to 'homosexuality', but it brings a basic

human drive, physiological friendship, to operation. Whether it thereby comes to the prohibited 'sexual acts' is entirely indifferent, at least the law absolutely should not apply![52]

Pfeiffer insisted that the war gave men the opportunity to manifest emotional bonds with other men, which strengthened their fighting ability. 'Comrade-love' was the ideal emotional experience for men: 'We only wanted to prove that comrade-love and male heroism were the most valuable driving forces in all wars, which effected the complete devotion of one's own person to leader and friend, to the fatherland!'[53] Further, Pfeiffer argued that this feeling of love between comrades was not effeminate, but undeniably masculine:

> When one views his almost wild, adventurous-romantic life, one is certainly unwilling to deny his manly characteristics! And yet this full-man loves not woman, but rather his friends! [...] Is anyone nonetheless still willing to assert that the love for a friend is an 'effeminate' (not female! In the sense of Fliess, Weininger and others, who describe precisely the superman as composed of male and female characteristics!), an effeminate, that is, inferior, bad disposition of character?[54]

Here, Pfeiffer reinforces the notion of a strict dichotomy between 'masculine' and 'effeminate', with the latter as inferior, and he rejects notions of blending the two genders. Love between men at war, Pfeiffer observed, was a superior emotional trait that was perfectly consistent with the masculine ideal and national strength.

For soldiers from diverse ideological perspectives, the war experience was the foundation for the struggle for emancipation. Gay men embraced widely celebrated values of comradeship, which they saw as a sacred bond, and their sacrifices entitled their love of other men to be accepted in post-war society.[55] Some veterans writing for *Die Freundschaft* (Friendship), a periodical that published articles by gay men from diverse ideological perspectives, including Hirschfeld's WhK and the new, more politically moderate, Bund für Menschenrechte (BfM, League of Human Rights), went so far as to argue that homosexuals were even better suited for war because they could provide powerful, and needed, emotional support for each other at the front. Gay veteran Richard Hört characterized 'friendship' between men in combat as a deeper bond of trust than love between men and women. Though heterosexual love was more common, he argued, love between men required the highest level of selflessness and loyalty that men in 'associations of friendship' (*Freundschaftbünde*) were privileged to experience.[56]

Gay men claimed that they were comparable to heterosexuals not only in terms of patriotic dedication to the fatherland, but also in terms of their dedication to a hypermasculine warrior ideal. Many gay veterans writing for periodicals like *Die Freundschaft* perceived themselves as 'masculine' rather than as 'effeminate' or part of a 'third sex,' as Hirschfeld described homosexuality's essential nature. In the fight for social emancipation, many gay activists argued, there was no room for 'effeminate' men. In his article 'Manliness', for *Die Freundschaft*, a writer who gave his name as Kurt portrayed the 'unique gender' ('das eigene Geschlecht') as battle-hardened veterans:

> We must fight in a way that befits men, in order to get what it is we want [...] and during these silent, tough battles, there is another fight: the fight for the unique gender. [...] It is an unequal battle, which will be fought against a flood of enemies, hate and suspicion [...] on the other side we stand with our love of friends in our hearts, full of shame and wrath, full of conviction for the purity of our cause.[57]

Kurt also portrayed effeminate men as detrimental to the movement. He mocked effeminate men 'who clean themselves like young girls and go play and dance' as useless in the new fight. Effeminate homosexuals weakened the struggle: 'We need men, real men [*ganze Männer*]. Effeminate men [*weibliche Männer*] are no good for battle and conflict.' 'Weakness and shortcoming', he wrote, played into the hands of 'the enemy'.[58] Similar to how straight men resented women who remained comfortable while men suffered at the front, gay survivors of the front experience resented effeminate homosexuals as self-absorbed and aloof to the sacrifices of 'real men'. Kurt strongly embraced the masculine warrior ideal, and he suggested that the love of male comrades made gay men ideal soldiers, who were at least as dedicated to protecting the fatherland as heterosexual men who fought for their women on the home front. Love for other men, according to Kurt, was the fundamental reason for fighting, and he equated the passion of battle with passion between other men: 'The battle burns intensely. We fight for the young man, because of our love, just as the young man fights for his girl [*Mädel*]. Everything else is vice and unworthy of men.'[59]

Kurt also hinted that homosexual love was the purest form of love, because gay men at the front gave their love to each other unconditionally, without having to buy it or give it up for sale as in the case of comrades going to prostitutes. Male–male love was the ultimate experience: 'Love of man for man is sacrosanct. Whoever possesses the freedom to love a true friend has reached the holy grail. This treasure is guarded by loyal, brave men with strong minds.'[60] Homosexuality, according to Kurt, was ideally suited for modern war. The gay warrior was emotionally intact and he remained faithful to the hegemonic ideal of a 'masculine', steel-nerved, and patriotic defender of the nation. Under this paradigm, the gay soldier's love for his comrades was not a deviant, selfish threat to the nation, but a spiritually fulfilling experience that gave men the emotional foundations they needed to fight courageously. Emancipation for gay men thus became a keystone for the nation's survival. The right-wing Adolf Brand and the GdE had already embraced this hegemonic warrior image, as they celebrated comradeship at the front as an ideal hypermasculine environment, an all-male utopia where 'real men' could explore ideals of *Eros* without the feminine restraints imposed by bourgeois culture. However, even activists from the more progressive gay organizations like the WhK and BfM moved away from Hirschfeld's pre-war characterization of homosexuality as a unique, essentially effeminate gender.

Conclusion

Soldiers' conceptions of the 'good comrade' were flexible enough to accommodate emotions and behaviour that were considered 'deviant'. Disillusioned with prevailing ideals of the steel-nerved, sexually chaste, emotionally disciplined warrior, some men began to mock the masculine image imposed 'from above' and they fantasized about gender transgression in order to escape the pressures of militarized masculinity. Traditional paradigms for love became further strained as men resented women's allegedly comfortable existence on the home front. Seeking more than just familial nurturing and support, some men affirmed love for their comrades out of desire or necessity, characterizing these bonds as natural and perfectly consistent with ideals of being 'good comrades'.

Within this environment of comradeship that included male–male emotional bonds, homosexual men were able to define their love as acceptable, or even ideal, for the military environment. Gay veterans across the political spectrum embraced the hypermasculine warrior image, but modified it to include homosexual men. Gay men idealized their form of love and sexuality as perfectly suited for the emotional strain of modern war. While some gay men tried to convince authorities that they did not taint the front with their 'deviant' sexual behaviour, they asserted that emotional bonds between men were perfectly consistent with the demands of defending the nation. In making their case for integrating homosexuals into the national community via their experience as soldiers, gay veterans aggressively reinforced the hegemonic image of the disciplined, hypermasculine warrior ideal. The gay movement, veterans argued, needed masculine warriors, not the effeminate third sex described by sexologist Magnus Hirschfeld, to push for civil rights.

Similar to the resentment that heterosexual men felt towards the 'lamenting woman' who drained them and did not understand their psychological experience in the war, gay veterans resented the effeminate homosexual, who was perceived not only as an embarrassment to their militant vision of the movement, but also as lesser in status because they were useless in war. While the gay community in the 1920s found its path for arguing that homosexuals were made into 'real men' through the war experience, they were still perceived as enemies of the 'national community', as evidenced by the violence orchestrated by the Nazi regime against gay men after 1933. Embracing the hegemonic image of masculinity did not substantially alter the gay community's status as 'social outsiders'. However, the experience of the war highlighted the degree to which there were competing perspectives on the dominant masculine ideal. The experiences of veterans who tried to normalize love between men suggest that the exclusively heterosexual paradigm of masculinity was not entirely hegemonic.

Acknowledgements

I would like to thank the editors for insightful suggestions that helped me revise this article. Thanks also to Peter Leese and Michael Geyer who provided excellent advice at a conference that helped me reconsider my ideas from different perspectives.

Notes

1. M. Szcepaniak (2011) *Militärische Männlichkeiten in Deutschland und Österreich im Umfeld des Grossen Krieges: Konstruktionen und Dekonstructionen* (Würzburg: Königshausen & Neumann), p. 10.
2. R. W. Connell (1995) *Masculinities* (Berkeley, CA: University of California Press), p. 3.
3. C. Hämmerle (2005) 'Zur Relevanz des Connell'schen Konzepts hegemonialer Männlichkeit für Militär und Männlichkeiten in der Habsburgermonarchie, 1868–1914/1918', in M. Dinges (ed.) *Männer – Macht – Körper: Hegemoniale Männlichkeiten vom Mittelalter bis heute* (Frankfurt am Main: Campus), pp. 116–19.
4. K. Hagemann (1997) 'Of "Manly Valor" and "German Honor" – Nation, War and Masculinity in the Age of the Prussian Uprising against Napoleon', *Central European History*, 30:2, pp. 187–220; U. Frevert (1996) 'Soldaten, Staatsbürger: Überlegungen zur historischen Konstruktion von Männlichkeit', in T. Kühne (ed.) *Männergeschichte – Geschlechtergeschichte: Männlichkeit im Wandel der Moderne* (Frankfurt am Main: Campus), pp. 82–5; U. Frevert (2004) *A Nation in Barracks: Modern Germany, Military Conscription and Civil Society* (Oxford: Berg).
5. G. L. Mosse (1996) *The Image of Man: The Creation of Modern Masculinity* (New York: Oxford University Press), pp. 79–80 and 110–11.
6. See T. Kühne (2006) *Kameradschaft: Die Soldaten des nationalsozialistischer Krieges und das 20. Jahrhundert* (Göttingen: Vandenhoek & Ruprecht).
7. J. Crouthamel (2011) '"Comradeship" and "Friendship": Masculinity and Militarization in Germany's Homosexual Emancipation Movement after the First World War', *Gender & History*, 23:1, pp. 111–29.
8. See, for example, G. Eley (2006) 'How and Where is German History Centered', in N. Gregor, N. Roemer and M. Rosemen (eds) *German History from the Margins* (Bloomington, IN: Indiana University Press), pp. 274–5.
9. B. Kundrus (2002) 'Gender Wars – The First World War and the Construction of Gender Relations in the Weimar Republic', in K. Hagemann and S. Schüler-Springorum (eds) *The Military, War and Gender in Twentieth-Century Germany* (Oxford: Berg), p. 160.

10. M. Roper (2009) *The Secret Battle: Emotional Survival in the Great War* (Manchester: Manchester University Press), p. xi.
11. Roper, *The Secret Battle*, pp. 6–9.
12. C. Hämmerle (1999) '"You let a weeping woman call you home?" Private Correspondences during the First World War in Austria and Germany', in R. Earle (ed.) *Epistolary Selves: Letters and Letter-Writers, 1600–1945* (Aldershot: Ashgate), p. 176.
13. T. Kühne (1996) '"...aus diesem Krieg werden nicht nur harte Männer heimkehren": Kriegskameradschaft und Männlichkeit im 20. Jahrhundert', in Kühne, *Männergeschichte – Geschlechtergeschichte*, pp. 174–91.
14. R. Nelson (2011) *German Soldier Newspapers of the First World War* (Cambridge: Cambridge University Press), especially ch. 3.
15. E. Vickers (2009) '"The Good Fellow": Negotiation, Remembrance and Recollection – Homosexuality in the British Armed Forces, 1939–45', in D. Herzog (ed.) *Brutality and Desire: War and Sexuality in Europe's 20th Century* (New York: Palgrave Macmillan), pp. 109–34.
16. Frevert, *A Nation in Barracks*, p. 183.
17. Mosse, *The Image of Man*, pp. 79–80 and 110–11.
18. A. Lipp (2003) *Meinungslenkung im Krieg: Kriegserfahrungen deutscher Soldaten und ihre Deutung, 1914–1918* (Göttingen: Vandenhoeck & Ruprecht), pp. 27–30 and 273–5.
19. B. Pfister (1916) 'Sei getrost und sei ein Mann!', *Der Dienstkamerad – Feldzeitung der 3. Division*, 2 (December), *Bundesarchiv*, Abt. *Militärarchiv*, Freiburg (henceforth BAMF), PHD 10/37.
20. Stabsarzt Dr Fischer (1917) 'Geschlechtskrankheiten', *Der Flieger*, 30 (1 July), BAMF, PHD 18/6.
21. *Einflüsse des Fliegens auf den menschlichen Körper und ärztliche Ratschläge für Flieger* (Der kommandierende General der Luftstreitkräfte, 1918), *Landesarchiv Baden-Württemberg, Hauptstaatsarchiv Stuttgart* (henceforth HSAS), M635/2 Bü 665.
22. E. Domansky (1996) 'Militarization and Reproduction in World War I Germany', in G. Eley (ed.) *Society, Culture and the State in Germany 1870–1930* (Ann Arbor, MI: University of Michigan Press), pp. 427–30.
23. Reichskanzler Bethmann-Hollweg to Herr Staatssekretär des Innern, 13 March 1915, no. 68, *Bundesarchiv, Berlin-Lichterfelde* (henceforth BAB), Reichsministerium des Innern (RdI) R1501/111868.
24. E. R. Dickinson (2003) 'The Men's Christian Morality Movement in Germany, 1880-1914', *Journal of Modern History*, 75:1, pp. 61–2.
25. Dr Aufhauser (1915) 'Das sexuelle Problem beim Feldheer', *Allgemeine Rundschau*, 13 February, BAB, RdI R1501/111868.
26. P. Göhre (1917) 'Der Krieg und die Geschlechter', *Der Flieger*, 2:2 (30 December), BAMF, PHD 18/6.
27. Letter from Wilhelm B. to Johann V., 2 July 1917, HSAS, Feldpostbriefe von Johann V., P10 Bü 1727.
28. Letter from Wilhelm B. to Johann V., 2 July 1917, HSAS, Feldpostbriefe von Johann V., P10 Bü 1727. He closes: 'Ich bleibe in Liebe – Ihr ergebener Wilhelm B.'
29. Letter from Otto L. to Berbel L., 15 November 1914, HSAS, Nachlass Ltn der Reserve Otto L., M660/147, nos 1–5.
30. Letter from Otto L. to Berbel L., 20 January 1915, HSAS, Nachlass Ltn der Reserve Otto L., M660/147, nos 1–5.

31. Hämmerle, '"You let a weeping woman call you home?"', p. 176.
32. Letter from Kurt K. to Lotte F., 25 May 1915, *Bayerisches Hauptstaatsarchiv, Abt. IV Kriegsarchiv*, Munich (henceforth BHSAKM), Kriegsbriefe 353.
33. Letter from Kurt K. to Lotte F., 23 June 1915, BHSAKM, Kriegsbriefe 353.
34. Letter from Kurt K. to Lotte F., 26 June 1915, BHSAKM, Kriegsbriefe 353.
35. Untffz. Nitsche (1918) 'Wir armen Männer!', *Der Flieger*, 2:35 (23 June), BAMF, PHD 18/6.
36. 'Im Sommer in Ostende', *Der kleine Brummer*, 3:6 (1916), BAMF, PHD 12/57. Fritz says to Emil, 'Emil, hier bett' ick mir erst mal in der Sonne.'
37. J. Steakley (1975) *The Homosexual Emancipation Movement in Germany* (Salem, NH: Ayer Company Publishers), p. 62.
38. A. Grossmann (1997) *Reforming Sex: The German Movement for Birth Control and Abortion Reform* (New York: Oxford University Press), p. 16.
39. M. Hirschfeld (ed.) (1930) *Sittengeschichte des Weltkrieges*, vol. 1 (Leipzig: Verlag für Sexualwissenschaft, Schneider.), p. 274.
40. Hirschfeld, *Sittengeschichte des Weltkrieges*, vol. 1, p. 288.
41. Hirschfeld, *Sittengeschichte des Weltkrieges*, vol. 1, pp. 296–7.
42. M. Hirschfeld (2006) *The Sexual History of the World War* (Honolulu: University Press of the Pacific, reprint of the translated edition of *Sittengeschichte des Weltkrieges* of 1941), p. 131.
43. Hirschfeld, *The Sexual History of the World War*, pp. 135–6.
44. Hirschfeld, *The Sexual History of the World War*, p. 136.
45. The Landesarchiv Baden-Württemberg, Hauptstaatsarchiv Stuttgart and the Bayerisches Hauptsaatsarchiv, Abt. IV Kriegsarchiv in Munich contain a vast collection of military trial records, the majority of which deal with men arrested for fleeing duty without permission. However, about 10 per cent of these trials deal with various forms of sexual crimes.
46. Case of Johann R., BHSAKM, Militär Gericht 7273, Feldbericht, 21 February 1918.
47. R. Beachy (2010) 'The German Invention of Homosexuality', *Journal of Modern History*, 82:4, p. 809.
48. H. A. Preiss (1921) *Geschlechtliche Grausamkeiten liebestoller Menschen* (Frankfurt: Süddeutsche Verlagsanstalt), p. 6.
49. See E. Bab (1903) 'Frauenbewegung und männliche Kultur', *Der Eigene*, and A. Brand (1925) 'Was wir wollen', pamphlet, both found in H. Oosterhuis and H. Kennedy (1992) (eds) *Homosexuality and Male Bonding in Pre-Nazi Germany* (New York: Routledge), pp. 135–44 and 155–66. The title of Brand's short-lived post-war periodical expresses this opposition to women's economic independence: *Freundschaft und Freiheit: Ein Blatt für Männerrechte gegen Spießbürgermoral, Pfaffenherrschaft, und Weiberwirtschaft*. The periodical can be found in Schwules Museum, Archiv, Berlin (henceforth SAB).
50. C. Bruns (2005) 'Der homosexuelle Staatsfreund: Von der Konstruktion des erotischen Männerbunds bei Hans Blüher', in S. zur Nieden (ed.) *Homosexualität und Staatsräson: Männlichkeit, Homophobie und Politik in Deutschland 1900–1945* (Frankfurt: Campus), pp. 103–7.
51. G. P. Pfeiffer (1925) *Männerheldentum und Kameradenliebe im Krieg: Eine Studie und Materialien-Sammlung* (Berlin: Adolf Brand Kunstverlag), trans. Oosterhuis and Kennedy, *Homosexuality and Male Bonding*, p. 221.
52. Pfeiffer, *Männerheldentum und Kameradenliebe im Krieg*, p. 230.
53. Pfeiffer, *Männerheldentum und Kameradenliebe im Krieg*, p. 232.
54. Pfeiffer, *Männerheldentum und Kameradenliebe im Krieg*, p. 225.

55. M. Danielsen (1919) 'Mehr Mut – mehr Idealismus', *Die Freundschaft*, 1:18, pp. 1–2, SAB.
56. R. Hört (1919) 'Liebe und Freundschaft', *Die Freundschaft*, 1:14, pp. 1–2, SAB.
57. Kurt (1920) 'Manneswürde', *Die Freundschaft*, 2:16, p. 1, SAB.
58. Kurt, 'Manneswürde', p. 2.
59. Kurt, 'Manneswürde', p. 2.
60. Kurt, 'Manneswürde', p. 2.

5
Visualizing 'War Hysterics': Strategies of Feminization and Re-Masculinization in Scientific Cinematography, 1916–1918

Julia Barbara Köhne

Male crises – mentally wounded soldiers

From the end of the nineteenth century, medicine started to use scientific cinematography as a new visual technology. This novelty – the medical films by Albert Londe in Paris and Gheorghe Marinescu in Bucharest in 1898/99 were among the first moving images of neuropsychiatric patients[1] – was widely employed in the field of military psychiatry. It played an important role, especially between 1916 and 1918 when officials at military headquarters and hospitals of the belligerent nations saw themselves confronted with an unexpected phenomenon: 'Huge numbers'[2] of mentally wounded soldiers displayed symptoms of what was medically diagnosed as 'war hysteria' – including severe trembling, dizziness, amnesia, and verbal and bodily dysfunctions such as problems with sitting, standing, walking, and speaking, as well as tics, paralysis, and other disabling factors and forms of behavioural disorganization.

Loss of self-control and the inability to operate weapons reduced the fighting efficiency of the combatant armies dramatically and was considered unmanly – and not only by the military authorities. On a massive scale, 'hysterically' acting men were brought to field hospitals, neurological centres close to the front, or, in complicated chronic cases, to psychiatric clinics back in the 'homeland'. Physicians differed about the aetiology for the 'disease': some considered 'war hysteria' as inherent and merely an extension of former neuropsychiatric symptoms; some acknowledged the effect of overwhelming and traumatizing experiences with artillery fire; some defined 'hysteria' as associated with physical, 'functional', or psychological disorders; and others simply accused patients of feigning illness in order to avoid returning to the front.

These psychiatric casualties of 'war hysteria' received a wide range of medical treatment – therapeutic cures and disciplinary interventions such as hypnosis, massages, electrotherapeutic treatments,[3] and drugs, or persuasion and verbal suggestion.[4] The parameters of the applied cure depended on the patient's military rank and career as well as on the physician's nationality, his reputation, his standing in the profession, and his specialization in either psychoanalysis, neurology, or psychiatry.[5] Even after treatment and re-education, patients remained the focus of physicians' attention and their ultimate ambition. Most of them were still unfit for military service and not able to return to the battlefield (regardless, they were sent back to the front in many cases), not to mention to civil life.

Historians have often described the 'strong soldier' as a 'symbol of masculinity',[6] hence these shaking, trembling, falling, crying, blind, stuttering, shrugging, literally impotent 'hysterical men' embodied an army of 'defeated masculinity'.[7] The widespread phenomenon severely threatened the idealized and glorified image of the brave soldier;[8] 'war hysterics' seemed to subvert male myths and ideologies that were associated with warfare such as strength, the display of tough fighting skills, and an unbreakable belief in victory. They also threatened the political significance of the male soldier as embodiment of the nation state, a symbolic level that had developed with universal military conscription.[9] The appearance of 'hysterical' symptoms on a massive scale was not only regarded as individual failure, but as a failure and dysfunction of the entire military collective body and the nation. In military discourse, just as in popular memory and perceptions, 'war hysteria' was considered to be the 'signature injury' of the First World War and this opinion still has its place in current views on the war.[10]

By the beginning of the war, neuropsychiatric knowledge of traumatic injuries was not yet fully developed, and a medical consensus on the origins and nature of these wounds still had to be found. Medical terminology defined 'war hysterics' in different, almost contradictory ways. Psychiatric knowledge about the 'illness' of 'war hysteria' was not yet standardized and there was no clear concept of how to label, name, address, or treat the massive medical, logistical, and symbolic problems caused by 'war hysterics'.[11] In texts and articles published from 1915 onwards, the observed symptoms were named and classified by completely different terms such as 'war hysteria', 'war neurosis', 'neurasthenia', 'mental breakdown', 'melancholia', 'shell shock', 'nervous' or 'mental shock', 'conversion disorder', 'combat fatigue', 'battle trauma', 'psychogenic disorder', 'functional disorder', 'reactive syndrome', or even 'feigning illness'.[12] The hybrid diagnostic and nosological terminology mirrored ambivalence and confusion associated with the medical concept of 'hysterical men', and the difficulties doctors had in deciding which symptoms were 'hysterical'.

Texts written by military physicians, including journal articles and monographs, reveal that symptoms of 'war hysteria' were indeed considered as signs of male softness, anti-heroism, weakness, lack of character, cowardice, and even so-called 'inner desertion'. The uncontrolled behaviour of 'hysterical' soldiers and officers was transformed into a, symbolically speaking, 'feminine' condition that undermined the structure, efficiency, and *image* of the military machinery as a whole. The emergence of the 'war hysteric' implied that masculinity was in crisis and, as George L. Mosse has argued, was interpreted as the 'social disease of the war': 'War was regarded as a true test of manliness.'[13] In his work, Mosse describes 'war hysteria' or 'shell-shock' as

> an excellent example of the fusion of medical diagnosis and social prejudice. [...] The stereotype of those who were thought to menace society's norms, those defined as 'outsiders', on the margins of established society, was in direct opposition to the ideal manhood, the foil to which such 'outsiders' represented in mind and body. Such men were nervous, ill-proportioned, and, above all, constantly in motion.[14]

In addition to this characterization, 'hysterics' also damaged the ordered and structured image of the military collective body, the corps. They symbolized its weakness and failure, considering that the military was supposed to be a composition of male bodies, forming *one* body, as David J. J. Morgan has claimed.[15] The identification of the 'war hysteric' as an allegory of deteriorated manhood was reproduced and confirmed by the new visual technology of scientific cinematography, as will be explored in the next paragraphs.

Scientific cinematography versus male hysteria

While scientific films on 'war hysteria' played an important role during the war, the making and collecting of these films was not yet well organized. In Germany, the cultural division of the *Universum Film AG* (Ufa) was only founded in 1918, with Curt Thomalla and Ernst Krieger as directors. In France, there were 'better' conditions in comparison. From 1915 on, the Section cinématographique de l'armée française (SCA) served as a sub-department of the military information centre of the War Ministry, headed by Jean-Louis Croze. In Britain, British Pathé, which produced numerous medical films, had already come into being in 1896.

The screening context of scientific films and their 'biography' cannot in all cases be clearly identified. The films were shown in military hospitals and training centres, schools, and cinemas, and physicians, officers, patients/soldiers, authorities from military headquarters, or civilians on the 'home front' may have been part of the audience. It can be assumed that each individual spectator held different motivations for watching these films.[16] Therefore, in the reception process, diverse types of cinematic subgenres were created, including further medical education, information, propaganda, or, by targeting other 'war hysterics', encouragement to recover.

More importantly, these films were evaluated as sources of 'evidence'. Although cinematography as such was associated with theatre, illusion, and delusion from its earliest days on, it was also perceived as conveying the impression of 'true-to-life', 'closeness to reality', authenticity, or to depict 'nature' itself. Overall, films were considered as 'living documents'. As Ute Holl has argued, 'illusionary movement, the illusion of vitality hide the gaps of technical intervention. As vitography, as a recording of life itself, cinema overrides the interventions by the machine and reveals itself as evidence.'[17]

The films analysed here served, firstly, to distribute medical knowledge and empirical values about innovative, 'avant-garde' therapies, such as forced physical training or electrotherapy. Secondly, they were used to promote a specific school of thought, research direction, or medical cure. Thirdly, they were also produced by psychiatrists and neurologists to document methods that accelerated and improved the healing process for patients in order to be presented, for instance, at several medical conferences that took place during the First World War.

Thus, scientific cinematography was supposed to help the medical community to take on the fight against the rapidly increasing number of soldiers and also high-ranking officers suffering from 'war hysteria'. Film was seen as an excellent tool to combat the 'hysterization' of the 'soldierly man'. Film was able to represent – or rather imagine, fabricate, and distribute – features and details of the medical diagnosis 'war hysteria' like no other medium could. And, what is more, it could make them miraculously disappear in an instant.

In the following analysis, I will examine how the relation between 'war hysterics' and military psychiatrists was portrayed in selected medical films conceptualized and produced in various military hospitals in France, Great Britain, and Germany during the First World War.[18] This relationship between patient and doctor was highly dependent on questions of power, hierarchy, and gender identity. The sketched scenery taken from the multi-layered history of medicine will be explored from a perspective of cultural and media science as well as gender theory. In particular, I will deal with the question of how mentally wounded 'war hysterics' were perceived as being threatening and counterproductive to military ideology. Cases of 'war hysteria' displayed by medical cinematography, such as the examples show, occurred in all belligerent countries on a massive scale and were captured on celluloid in numerous films.

The belligerent countries showed considerable differences in their conception of the 'patient' in general, and the incessant belief that there was a successful cure for every patient suffering from 'war hysteria' or 'shell shock'. Not all of these differences in terms of culture, ideology, and health politics can be taken into account in detail here. Rather, I focus on the symbolic impact of scientific cinematography as a practice to encode and decode the symptoms of 'war hysteria'. These were presented by the media as signs of 'feigning illness' and therefore 'inner desertion', a serious war 'injury', a tragic mental 'disease', or as a 'lack' of will to recover. At the same time, newspapers and journals showed how to fight them successfully. In particular, I pursue the following questions: Were military physicians affected by the cinematographic depiction and staging of the 'war hysteric'? And if so, how did this 'semiotic construction',[19] this representational, even iconic figure influence their perception and treatment of mentally wounded persons? Was the pictorial/filmic rhetoric of the 'war hysteric' gender coded? Are there elements, which reflect this fact, such as transgression, diversity, and alterity in gender performance as well as a new semiotic system about how to refer to masculinity, which consequently revealed this concept as historically and culturally constructed? By projecting images of feminized 'hysteria' on to male patients medical films caused a gender specific and symbolic production of meaning. Yet it has to be examined by what means they exactly did so and what part visuality and iconography of the films played in this respect. To cut a long question short: What made a man a 'man' and a soldier a 'soldier' and, vice versa, what prevented a man from being a 'man' and a soldier from being a 'soldier' in the cinematography in question?

In the following, I will argue that initially the figure of the male 'war hysteric' was effeminized and made impotent by numerous visual strategies. Subsequently, this figure was re-masculinized and reinstalled to symbolize the military corps, as can be shown by analysing specific scenes. Morgan writes about the military as a theatre in which certain roles of masculinity and steeliness had to be performed and fulfilled.[20] By using teleological narration, scientific films on 'war hysteria' served a two-fold purpose: On the one hand, military psychiatrists and neurologists – in their role as film directors – used different film-rhetorical strategies to feminize the figure of the 'male hysteric' and enable it to look abnormal.[21] Various techniques were invented to alienate, infantilize, de-potentiate, pathologize, in short, *feminize* affected soldiers by stressing their mental violability.[22] Tens of thousands of patients were characterized as 'hysterical', allegedly posing a dangerous threat to the well-structured military corps. In the film language of scientific cinematography, they were shown in various ways: nude, depersonalized, animalistic, infantilized, or faking symptoms, as can be seen in the visual strategies presented below. On the other hand, as already mentioned, it seemed to be more important to restore the image of the fit soldier as a healthy, stable male ready to fight for his country. To achieve this, 'hysterics' were re-masculinized within the frame of the same media technique that had created their pathology in the first place.

Strategies of feminization and pathologization

The male 'war hysteric' has never been stigmatized and pathologized to the same degree as the *female* hysteric had been in the second half of the nineteenth century. Many photographs, pictures, and drawings, for example by the French neurologist Jean-Martin Charcot from the Salpetrière in Paris around 1880, or scientific films by physicians/directors such as the Italian

Camillo Negro in Turin (*La Neuropatologia*, 1908), depict women as wild, mad, acting clownesque, pathetic, and sexually promiscuous.[23] These illustrations seem to match Dorion Weickmann's findings about female stigmatization and the bodies of female 'hysterics' since 1880 in terms of a 'rebellion' of the senses.[24] Rather than transferring the ascribed female wildness to the male 'hysteric',[25] the ex-warriors of the First World War were shown displaying feminine characteristics of madness only to a degree that appeared to be curable. In this ideological framework, 'hysteria' did not mirror the 'true nature' of male patients, as was considered to be the case with females suffering from 'hysteria', but was seen as a temporary aberrance.

Film as a medium against 'malingerers'

In the case of 'war hysterics' since 1915, medical films were supposed to test whether the 'hysterical' symptoms were 'genuine' or 'feigned'.[26] Since its invention, film had always been linked to illusion, imagination, fakery, and theatre and was seen as a technology of deception and 'the unreal'.[27] In the medical context, it promised to unmask malingering, bluffing, faking 'war hysterics' who supposedly – at least according to some psychiatrists – imagined, invented, or exaggerated their symptoms on purpose. Malingering was considered a potential source of demoralization among other soldiers and thus a jeopardy for the war effort. Just like female 'hysteria', 'war hysteria' was described not only as a feigned disease, but also as an 'illness of feigning' – the 'hysteric' was said to 'malinger', imitating other illnesses.[28] Medical film in the medico-military context was seen as an instrument to discover the 'truth', yet not in the sense of producing but of revealing the factual, essential truth. This point is of particular importance here. According to this view, film not only 'spoke' or visualized the truth *per se*, but made it possible to *uncover* it. In 1911, the Italian psychiatrist Osvaldo Polimanti wrote emphatically: 'Beyond all doubt, the swindler, the malingerer will be detected and exposed by the cinematograph.'[29] By recording and rewatching films on 'hysteria' cases again and again, physicians tried to discover if the patients' movements were real or faked in order to detect the malingerers and to separate them from genuinely ill people.

Theatricalization: patients 'acting' symptoms

It might seem somewhat ironic that psychiatrists presented patients in their films as if on a stage, given the prevalent discourse on 'hysterics' as 'acting' their symptoms. Often, the entire set where a film was shot was built like a stage. Both physicians and patients – the latter following a choreography of walking and gazing – played their distinctive parts as in a 'theatre play'. Everything was 'staged' – setting, accessories, costumes, looks, actions, choreography, and so on. Stage sceneries and wooden constructions on the floor were built, curtains and catwalks followed the aesthetics of the theatre. This design resembled scenes from early cinematography, for instance when film director Georges Meliès gave his theatrical performance standing in front of a black curtain or when mesmeric and occult films featured a magically acting doctor. The strategy of presenting 'war hysterics' as performers on a stage entailed – wittingly or unwittingly – that patients appeared as being actors of their symptoms.

In some cases, there was even an unexpected and unscheduled audience at the set. In *Différents types de Boîteries: Les sciatiques organiques* (around 1916–18), some gardeners gathered in the back of the frame in order to witness what was happening on the wooden stage. For the spectators of this film, these uninvited witnesses, this small inner-filmic audience, might form a 'punctum', a term coined by the French philosopher Roland Barthes in 1980 in his essay 'La chambre Claire' on photo reception. As Barthes points out, the punctum irritates, penetrates the viewer of a photograph, it 'wounds' him or her and thereby can open up new dimensions of meaning, sense, and orientation.[30] The staring gardeners symbolize such a punctum. They add a *surplus*, an additional meaning to the scenery, which might not have been intended or even appreciated by its producers. Yet it hit a certain nerve in later audiences. As uninvolved witnesses of this choreographic spectacle, the gardeners offer a reference point or a *passage* to identify with the filmed patient or to think about the ongoing metamorphosis of the production of meaning in films.

Analysing filmic presentations as well as written sources such as articles in anthologies and neuropsychiatric journals between 1915 and the 1920s,[31] it becomes evident that exhaustive rehearsals were scheduled for the patients to demonstrate their symptoms and that they were only filmed afterwards. This implies that 'war hysterics' were told how to walk, what to show, and what to hide when the camera was filming. Obviously, this was not an authentic, 'natural' display of symptoms of 'hysteria'. The highly artificial character of this display, repeated rehearsals, and verbal directions from the start, as well as the later analysis carried out by the physicians, made the patients look like being part of a ballet performance, for instance in view of the synchronized arm lifts and feet being stretched out simultaneously in *Troubles Fonctionnels/ Service du Docteur Paul Sollier in Lyon*. In this context, a set of further questions emerge: To what extent do these synchronized movements resemble ballet choreography and, consequently, must be seen as another pattern of feminization? Or, on the contrary, do they represent a symmetry similar to military patterns such as marching in lockstep, lifting rifles, and standing to attention? If the latter is the case, were these visualizations supposed to highlight the possibility of total recovery, convalescence, and particularly *military* rehabilitation of the patient?

The following contradiction implied by these films is striking: While they were supposed to communicate the symptoms of 'hysteria' with clearly defined outlines and without ambiguity, they also demonstrated that these symptoms could, literally, vanish into thin air. As a result, they offered the possibility to re-humanize the (ex-)patients and, in conclusion, the 'return of the soldier' with all his qualities and capabilities. To sum up: the theatrical setting as a whole had an ambivalent effect. On the one hand, it emphasized the constructed, fictitious character of these medical films *and* the attested illusionary nature of the symptoms of 'war hysteria'. On the other hand, the staging was somehow counterproductive for the intended message that these symptoms were real and threatening, because soldierly 'hysteria' was considered to be contagious, to spread out epidemically among units and platoons and to jeopardize other soldiers' health.

De-personalization and nudeness – costumes: undressing and re-dressing

In addition, depersonalization was another strategy in order to de-potentiate 'war hysterics'. In most cases their names were not revealed, although sometimes the circumstances of their (mental) injuries were displayed in the intertitles. Yet their faces were not made unrecognizable by a black mask like, for example, the female 'hysteric' in *La Neuropatologia*, mentioned above. Just like their hybrid physicians, who represented the health system, medical service, *and* the military sphere alike, signified by their hybrid mode of dressing in boots, caps, and other parts of the military uniform combined with the white doctor's overcoat, 'war hysterics' stood in between the categories of suffering patients and acting malingerers – as in *Troubles nerveux chez les commotionnés*, filmed in the French military hospital in Val-de-Grâce.

In numerous cases, 'war hysterics' were shown naked or dressed-up in a specific way. The spectrum of their 'costumes' ranged from complete nakedness or nakedness combined with military identifications or 'dog' tags – as in *Troubles de la Demarche consecutifs a des commotions par eclatements d'obus*, filmed by Dr James Rayneau in Fleury-les-Aubrais near Orléans – to underwear or partial dress, and to civilian clothes or military uniforms. Thus, the patients' clothing conveyed how their status oscillated between the civilian and the military sphere, between illness and recovery and between the feminine and the masculine domain, even though there was a tendency not to re-dress 'hysteric' patients in uniforms so as not to devalue this military status symbol. In this context, the administration department of the German war ministry sent a letter to the deputy general command I.II.III.A.K. at the end of 1917: 'It is possible to refrain from dressing conscripts [*Wehrpflichtige*] in military clothes. [...] In cases when military prestige might be damaged civil clothing is appropriate.'[32] This specific staging of clothing in films was an aesthetic instrument either to deny or to confer 'hysterics' the status of manhood and to include, or to exclude, patients from the group of soldiers in active service.

In the relation between physician and patient, nudeness often made no medical sense but was used to humiliate the 'war hysteric'. A quote from the controversial German psychiatrist Max Nonne, who used suggestion in hypnosis and faradic electricity as therapeutic methods, confirms this: 'I always made the invalids undress completely because this increased their feeling of dependency, respectively helplessness.'[33] And these feelings of 'dependency' and 'helplessness' were considered useful for suggestive techniques.

Infantilization

A case study from France can serve as another example to illustrate the power structure between patient and physician. In the military hospital in Val-de-Grâce, a 'hysteric' with a 'special dread of red military garments', as the intertitles of *Troubles nerveux chez les commotionnés* reveal, is deliberately frightened by a physician. His fear of the French red 'kepi' is declared as 'pithiatisme', caused by auto-suggestion and 'hysteria'. According to current psychiatric terms, the patient's 'disorder' would probably be classified as an 'anxiety disorder'. The scene shows the 'hysteric' placed in the foreground of the frame, a large beret completely covering his eyes. The beret is pulled away and a kepi, the traditional red cap with a flat circular top and a peak, is placed in front of his eyes. Immediately, the patient starts to clench his hands and puts them over his mouth. Hovering around, he tries to hide from this impressive sign of military authority. The physician's reaction seems to be questionable, inappropriate, and unprofessional as he laughs towards the cinematograph and its operator, distancing himself from this effeminate display of male 'hysteria'. He does not even take his hand out of his coat pocket. (Later, another physician is visible on the right-hand side of the frame, smoking a cigarette and holding a stethoscope as if to prove that he belongs to the medical sphere while the patient is suffering from a panic attack.) Obviously, the physician is ridiculing the patient and minimizing his illness as he portrays him as a 'sissy', while, at the same time, he tries to reinforce his own image as a rational man of science and supreme authority. This filmed incident sheds some light on the conceptualization of pathological masculinity and the physicians' motivations. It shows, furthermore, how wartime medicine mirrored more general cultural assumptions and political goals linked to intact masculinity.

Strategies of re-masculinization and re-militarization: visual healing techniques

Apart from these more or less subtle strategies of infantilization, feminization, and pathologization, psychiatric films also carried opposite 'messages' by using visual and dramaturgical techniques to re-masculinize the ex-soldiers and patients, quite frequently within the very same film. Some of the films reinforced the image of the brave, active, physically fit, and masculine soldier. In so doing, they established a dramaturgy of healing. Their cinematographic code included the (magical) disappearance of the respective patient's symptoms by adopting the before/after technique. Moreover, in the end the patients were dressed again in their uniforms, which, in a metaphorical way, re-idealized and re-militarized the convalescent 'war hysteric' as efficient and combat-ready ('re-dressing'). In several cases, for example in *Reserve-Lazarett Hornberg (und Triberg) im Schwarzwald. Behandlung der Kriegs-Neurotiker* (Germany, around 1917), 're-dressing' was underlined by a sequence of convalescent patients doing physical exercises as a strategy of re-militarization, as instructed by German psychiatrist Ferdinand Kehrer.[34] Taking this into account, films on 'war hysteria' can be identified as highly gendered systems of representation. What is more, they were alleged 'healing machines' which promised recovery without failure – an almost unattainable goal. Thus, films on 'war hysteria' served as medial antidotes against crises of masculinity and the malfunctioning individual.

Before/after techniques

The scientific films usually followed a certain order. In the beginning, the film displayed the manifest symptoms of 'hysteria' by showing either the treatment of the attending physician or the behaviour of the patient. Then, the symptoms vanished by applying a special cutting technique which divided the cinematic narration into a 'before' and an 'after' section. This 'before/after' logic was adopted from scientific photography and became a significant feature of scientific films in general.[35] In a film by Max Nonne, *Funktionell-motorische Reiz- und Lähmungs-Zustände bei Kriegsteilnehmern und deren Heilung durch Suggestion in Hypnose* (Germany, 1918), filmed in the general hospital of Hamburg-Eppendorf, 'hysterical' symptoms were shown in the first part and simply vanished in the next one. By this means, the recovery of the patient was 'proved'. A short intertitle saying 'cured' followed.

Using this montage technique, the transformation from being 'hysteric' to being 'cured' appeared to be inevitable and a matter of routine. The films were intended to prove that 'war hysteria' was curable and used an easy method to demonstrate the 'fact' of healing: they showed the 'war hysteric' standing straight like a plank without trembling for some seconds. These scenes were supposed to convey the impression of a complete recovery. Yet, this short period of motionlessness was, in fact, not that difficult to achieve and reproduce in the film, since symptoms of 'hysteria', even severe tremor, were interrupted by short quiet periods. The majority of films on male 'war hysteria' claimed a rather unlikely immediate recovery, as written (fictional) sources, war poems, photographs, autobiographies, and other post-war material from a multitude of archives indicate.[36] The successful cure allegedly proved by scientific films was effectively faked.

Verticalization – de-animalization

In several films, for example in *Troubles Fonctionnels*, directed by the neuropsychologist Paul Sollier (1861–1933), a number of 'war hysterics' walked in a file through the frame, from the right to the left. Sollier was a student of Charcot and interested in research on emotions, involuntary memory, and re-experience. Between 1914 and 1917, he practised at the Centre Neurologique de la 14e Région Militaire in Lyon. Here, he used 'isolation therapy'[37] and other forms of psychological treatment.[38] In *Troubles Fonctionnels*, the choreography displayed 'war hysterics' walking crookedly and bent down like animals. In so doing, the film suggested the association with evolutionary drawings depicting anthropoid apes developing towards walking upright. This mode of representation clearly characterized 'hysterics' as examples of human regression by 'animalizing' them.

In some examples, as in *Troubles de la démarche consécutifs à de commotions par éclatements d'obus* by docteur Rayneau, a 'psychotherapist' working in Fleury-les-Aubrais, Annexe de Neuropsychiatrie du 5° Corps d'Armée, 'hysterics' are shown bending their limbs. Drawn lines following their moving torso and extremities highlight these gestures. This strategy of visualization implies the assumption that the more twisted and curvier these lines, the worse the condition of the 'hysteric'. And, vice versa, the straighter the lines, the better his state. This ultimately confirmed the formula 'the vertical equals de-animalization'.

Playing the war game again: *The Battle of Seale Hayne* as re-enactment

Apart from numerous takes which show patients doing military exercises to prove their soldierly rehabilitation, a British film pursued the same objective with different means. This piece is the last issue of a longer scientific film compilation entitled *War Neuroses*, which was filmed at the Royal Victoria Hospital in Netley in 1917 and at the Seale Hayne Military Hospital in 1918 by A. F. Hurst and J. L. M. Symns. The fragment is no more than one and a half minutes in duration. According to the written titles, *The Battle of Seal Hayne* was made by convalescent 'war neurosis' patients themselves, who were the 'actors', 'photographers', and 'directors'. Thus, these 'war victims' re-enacted their own experiences – or something very close to that – in the film; that is to say, they reproduced how they were wounded on the battlefield some time before. These mentally and/or physically wounded ex-soldiers were treated and cured in the military hospitals mentioned above, and then asked to shoot this movie. In doing so, they pretended to be able to return to the battlefield, even though this was only a cinematographic one.

To make the scene more authentic, fake hand grenades were used.[39] In the last seconds an actor/(ex-)patient is rolling down a hill and afterwards his comrades carry him away on a stretcher. He is re-enacting his own experience, only this time the injury is physical and not mental, and he is rescued from the battlefield. One could say that the film adds a somehow apotropaic character to the plot, indicating the possibility of reaching back into the past, and pretending to be able to change the soldier's fate through a 'lucky shot' which damages his health without killing him and which is serious enough to take him out of combat (and back home). *The Battle of Seal Hayne* can be seen as typical of those films which showed allegedly cured individual traumata in order to convince military and medical officials that the collective, even nation-wide healing and the reintegration of ex-'war hysterics' was possible.[40]

Conclusion: the invention of the convalescent and cured male soldier

As we have seen, medical films from all belligerent countries tried to establish an immediate and complete recovery of 'war hysterics' as a fact. Needless to say that this success story remained an illusion and turned into one of the many post-war myths. Even in the aftermath of the war, patients' symptoms proved to be 'resistant' and intractable and did not respond to therapeutic and cinematographic attempts to cure 'war hysteria'. Even if the films suggested perfect 'healing', published articles by the same physicians often told another story.[41]

Nevertheless, the narratives and visual rhetorics of 'healing' in medical films, including cutting and montage techniques and a characteristic iconology, intended to show that the (ex-)patient was capable of being reintegrated. In a first step, the films presented the 'hysteric' nude, depersonalized, infantilized, animalized, pathologized, and objectified. In different countries and production contexts, 'war hysterics' were portrayed as victimized, de-potentiated, and effeminated. It should be noted though that this was not a complete, irreversible disempowerment. The retransformation of the patient into a soldier was achieved by using multiple visual strategies of re-masculinization. A 'chorus line' of uniformed soldiers who were ready to fight and, once again, risk their lives for their home countries was the aim of these 'healing symphonies'. For that purpose, they had to be gradually re-dressed, verticalized, de-animalized, de-alienized, normalized, re-militarized, and re-humanized by using specific visual rhetorics.

In this culture and media studies-oriented analysis of specific cases of gender rhetorics in films and their genealogy, wartime 'male hysteria' research was explored as a discursive field in which film language, the physicians' instructions, and the 'hysterical' body language of the patient merge. Analysis has shown the (gender) identity of the ex-soldier and 'war hysteric' as an unstable imaginary effect created by the medical reproduction of concrete semiotic processes. The latter had a strong impact on the epistemological constellation of the abnormal male object of psychiatry and on how the concrete 'hysterical' individual was 'treated' – therapeutically and as a human being. Filmic imagery represented an essential part of the medical fabrication, degradation, and finally elimination of the male 'hysteric'. As the myth of manhood was deeply injured by the mental injury of 'war hysteria', film was supposed to heal it by creating a convincing scenery of convalescence and rehabilitation that strived to reinforce the traditional ideal type: the manly soldier-warrior. In the course of this reaffirmation of male gender identity, the mental androgyny of the male 'hysterical' soldier was deleted. The filmic portrayal of male 'hysteria' presented both transgression *and* recovery of the social functionality of the gender norms of the nineteenth century and of appropriate masculine behaviour. At the same time, it excluded *and* incorporated the shell-shocked patient into medical narratives of the war and its cultural post-war repercussions.

Notes

1. G. Aubert (2002) 'Arthur Van Gehuchten Takes Neurology to the Movies', *Neurology*, 59:10, p. 1614.
2. Depending on the respective nation and the source of information, research literature mentions tens up to hundreds of thousands of cases of so-called 'war hysteria' or nervous and mental shock. Cf. A. Watson (2008) *Enduring the Great War: Combat, Morale and Collapse in the German and British Armies, 1914–1918* (Cambridge: Cambridge University Press), pp. 36, 43, 240. B. Shephard cites British reports of December 1914 claiming that '7–10 per cent of all officers and 3–4 per cent' of all ranks were being sent home suffering from nervous or mental breakdowns: B. Shephard (2000) *A War of Nerves: Soldiers and Psychiatrists, 1914–1994* (London: Jonathan Cape), p. 21; also W. Johnson and R. G. Rows (1923) 'Neurasthenia and War Neuroses', in W. G. Macpherson, W. P. Herringham, T. R. Elliott and A. Balfour (eds) *History of the Great War Based on Official Documents: Diseases of War*, vol. 2 (London), pp. 1–2. One year later, the French physician M. Laignel-Lavastine mentioned a very high number of somatic manifestations of 'hysteria' that had been observed at the neurological centre in Tours: M. Laignel-Lavastine (1914–1915) 'Travaux des centres neurologiques militaires: Centre neurologique de la IXe région (Tours)', *Revue neurologique*, 28, p. 1165. Contemporary reports and medical journal articles used expressions such as 'epidemic' or 'contagious' to describe the high number of mentally injured soldiers. Cf. M. Roudebush (2001) 'A Battle of Nerves: Hysteria and Its Treatments in France During World War I', in P. Lerner and M. S. Micale (eds) *Traumatic Pasts: History, Psychiatry, and Trauma in the Modern Age, 1870–1930* (Cambridge: Cambridge University Press.), pp. 253–5.
3. A. Rasmussen (2010) 'L'électrothérapie en guerre: practiques et débats en France (1914–1920)', in C. Blondel and A. Rasmussen (eds) *Le corps humain et l'électricité* (Paris: Victoires), pp. 73–91.
4. There are numerous sources for different types of treatments. For the British context, see Shephard, *A War of Nerves*, pp. 21–32 and 53–95; for the French context, Roudebush, 'A Battle of Nerves', pp. 253–79; M. Roudebush (2000) 'A Patient Fights Back: Neurology in the Court of Public Opinion in France during the First World War', *Journal of Contemporary History*, 35:1, pp. 29–38; G. M. Thomas (2009) *Treating the Trauma of the Great War: Soldiers, Civilians, and Psychiatry in France, 1914–1940* (Baton Rouge, LA: Louisiana State University Press).
5. F. Reid (2010) *Broken Men: Shell Shock, Treatment and Recovery in Britain, 1914–1930* (London: Continuum).
6. W. Amberger describes and criticizes the ideal of the 'soldierly man' in her 1984 book, *Männer, Krieger, Abenteurer: Der Entwurf des 'soldatischen Mannes' in Kriegsromanen über den Ersten und Zweiten Weltkrieg* (Frankfurt am Main: R. G. Fischer). See also G. L. Mosse (1990) *Fallen Soldiers: Reshaping the Memory of the*

World Wars (New York: Oxford University Press); G. L. Mosse (1996) *The Image of Man: The Creation of Modern Masculinity* (New York: Oxford University Press); G. L. Mosse (2000) 'Shell-shock as a Social Disease', *Journal of Contemporary History*, 35:1, pp. 101–8; R. Seifert (1992) 'Männlichkeitskonstruktionen: Das Militär als diskursive Macht', *Das Argument*, 196, pp. 859–72; R. Seifert (1996) *Militär – Kultur – Identität: Individualisierung, Geschlechterverhältnisse und die soziale Konstruktion des Soldaten* (Bremen: Temmen); U. Frevert (1996) 'Soldaten, Staatsbürger: Überlegungen zur historischen Konstruktion von Männlichkeit', in T. Kühne (ed.) *Männergeschichte – Geschlechtergeschichte: Männlichkeit im Wandel der Moderne* (Frankfurt am Main: Campus), pp. 69–87; U. Frevert (2001) *Die kasernierte Nation: Militärdienst und Zivilgesellschaft in Deutschland* (Munich: Beck); C. Eifler (ed.) (1999) *Militär – Gewalt – Geschlechterverhältnis* (Osnabrück: Frauenbündnis Projekt '350 Jahre Krieg und Frieden – ohne Frauen?'); K. Theweleit (2005 [1977]) *Männerphantasien, I: Frauen, Fluten, Körper, Geschichte* (Munich: Piper). 'Symbol of masculinity' is an expression by Eva Kreisky (2003) 'Fragmente zum Verständnis des Geschlechts des Krieges', lecture at the University of Vienna on 9 December 2003, p. 5, online at http:// evakreisky.at/onlinetexte/geschlecht_des_krieges.pdf (accessed 1 January 2012); see also D. J. Morgan (1994) 'Theater of War: Combat, the Military, and Masculinities', in H. Brod and M. Kaufman (eds) *Theorizing Masculinities* (Thousand Oaks, CA, and London: Sage), p. 165.

7. P. Lerner (2009) *Hysterical Men: War, Psychiatry, and the Politics of Trauma in Germany, 1890–1930* (Ithaca, NY: Cornell University Press), e.g. p. 54.

8. U. Frevert (1997) 'Das Militär als "Schule der Männlichkeit": Erwartungen, Angebote, Erfahrungen im 19. Jahrhundert', in U. Frevert (ed.) *Militär und Gesellschaft im 19. und 20. Jahrhundert* (Stuttgart: Klett-Cotta), p. 159.

9. The link between notions of war and 'masculinity' has been emphasized by several historians, for instance Seifert, 'Männlichkeitskonstruktionen'; K. Hagemann and S. Schüler-Springorum (eds) (2002) *Home/Front: The Military, War and Gender in Twentieth-Century Germany* (Oxford: Berg), pp. i–xi; K. Hagemann (2002) '*Mannlicher Muth und Teutsche Ehre*': Nation, Militär und Geschlecht zur Zeit der antinapoleonischen Kriege Preußens (Paderborn: Schöningh). Universal military conscription was initially introduced during the French Revolution within the context of the newly formed nation state. By implementing compulsory conscription as the prevalent recruiting system in Europe during the second half of the nineteenth century, 'male actors' in warfare were encoded and their biological sex was predominantly read through their gender performance. The ideals of military discipline, norms, and codes of conduct became more and more powerful in the course of this development (see U. Bröckling (1997) *Disziplin: Soziologie und Geschichte militärischer Gehorsamsproduktion* (Munich: Fink), pp. 31, 113, 329). Furthermore, the coordinates of the new reference system were the 'fatherland', the nation, and the state – all masculine institutions producing masculine role models, functions, and encodings. The soldier not only had to match the requirements of these institutions but, at the same time, was supposed to embody them: the individual biological and the political significance of the male soldier were equal on a symbolic level (see Kreisky, 'Fragmente', pp. 4–5).

10. The features of 'war hysteria' were not only part of military psychiatry during the war, but survived in literature and movies: see P. Barker's *Regeneration Trilogy*, written 1991–95; *Mad Love/Orlacs Hände/Wahnsinnige Liebe* (United States 1935), directed by K. Freund; and *Nerven* (Germany 1919) by R. Reinert – to name just a few. E. Jones, N. T. Fear and S. Wessely (2007) 'Shell Shock and Mild Traumatic

Brain Injury: A Historical Review', *The American Journal of Psychiatry*, 164:11, pp. 1641–5.

11. This did not happen until the 1970s as a reaction to soldiers suffering from traumatic mental injuries in the Vietnam War. Today, an elaborate scientific knowledge pool exists about 'post-traumatic stress disorder' (PTSD) and psychotraumatology.

12. 'War hysteria' was only one term among many others. I chose this term which feminized the affected soldier because it signifies the transfer from the female 'hysteria'-context (the Attic Greek word ὑστέρα, 'hystera' means uterus). In the French context, competing terms used were: 'pithiatisme', 'troubles nerveux', 'troubles physiopathique', 'troubles fonctionnels', or 'commotion'. The term used depended on the respective concept of the 'disease'.

13. Mosse, 'Shell-shock', p. 102.

14. Mosse, 'Shell-shock', p. 102.

15. Morgan, 'Theater of War', p. 167. See also E. Jünger (2004 [1920]) *Storm of Steel*, trans. with an introduction by M. Hofmann (London: Penguin), pp. 30–1 and 93, for the claim that soldiers were expected to stand 'as one man', to form a huge collective body. For the original text, see E. Jünger (1990 [1920]) *In Stahlgewittern* (Stuttgart: Klett-Cotta), p. 5.

16. J. C. Wagner states that although many French 'war hysteria' films were intended for a large audience, most of them were not shown in public because their capacity to 'convey trauma and provoke empathy' had been underestimated. J. C. Wagner (2009) 'Twisted Bodies, Broken Minds: Film and Neuropsychiatry in the First World War' (dissertation, Harvard University), p. 121.

17. U. Holl (2006) 'Neuropathologie als filmische Inszenierung', in M. Heßler (ed.) *Konstruierte Sichtbarkeiten: Wissenschafts- und Technikbilder seit der Frühen Neuzeit* (Munich: Wilhelm Fink), p. 230 (trans. J. B. K.).

18. In the French context, military services, the 'Service du Santé des Armées', commissioned and collected nearly one hundred films on neurological and psychiatric conditions. According to J. C. Wagner, 12 of these films survived in viewable condition (Wagner, 'Twisted Bodies, Broken Minds', pp. 120–2). Here, I discuss fragments and scenes from about half of the surviving films.

19. J. Kristeva (1974) *Die Revolution der poetischen Sprache* (Frankfurt am Main: Suhrkamp).

20. Morgan, 'Theater of War'.

21. In written sources, notions like 'deserter' or 'coward' emphasized the hysteric's vulnerability. Cf. K. Singer (1916) 'Allgemeines zur Frage der Simulation', *Würzburger Abhandlungen aus dem Gebiet der praktischen Medizin*, 16:6, p. 141.

22. The term *hystera* (uterus) *per se* implicates a structural feminization. The very transfer of this term onto the male soldier caused 'gender trouble', especially in the context of the army at war and the belligerent nation.

23. For a close reading of this film, see Holl, 'Neuropathologie als filmische Inszenierung', pp. 217–40.

24. See D. Weickmann (1997) *Rebellion der Sinne: Hysterie – Ein Krankheitsbild als Spiegel der Geschlechterordnung (1880–1920)* (Frankfurt am Main: Campus).

25. E. Showalter (1987) *The Female Malady: Women, Madness and English Culture, 1830–1980* (London: Virago); P. Lerner (2003) *Hysterical Men: War, Psychiatry, and the Politics of Trauma in Germany, 1890–1930* (Ithaca, NY: Cornell University Press); M. Micale (2008) *Hysterical Men: The Hidden History of Male Nervous Illness* (Cambridge, MA: Harvard University Press).

26. See S. Ledebur (2012) 'Zur Epistemologie einer Ausschlussdiagnose: Unwissen, Diskurs und Untersuchungstechniken bei Simulation psychischer Erkrankungen', in M. Wernli (ed.) *Wissen und Nichtwissen in der Klinik: Dynamiken in der Psychiatrie um 1900* (Bielefeld: transcript), pp. 17–50. Ledebur traces the discource, genealogy, and history of the medical label 'feigning illness' in relation to clinical patient demonstrations as it unfolds throughout the second half of the nineteenth century, oscillating between its perception as being part of an illness, fakery, play, or evidence for the subjective agency of the patient.

27. See S. Andriopoulos (2000) *Besessene Körper: Hypnose, Körperschaften und die Erfindung des Kinos* (München: W. Fink), for instance pp. 22, 84, 109; S. Andriopoulos (2008) *Possessed: Hypnotic Crimes, Corporate Fiction, and the Invention of Cinema* (Chicago, IL: University of Chicago Press).

28. E. Kretschmer (1918) 'Die Gesetze der willkürlichen Reflexverstärkung in ihrer Bedeutung für das Hysterie- und Simulationsproblem', *Zeitschrift für die gesamte Neurologie und Psychiatrie*, 41, p. 382.

29. O. Polimanti (1911) 'Der Kinematograph in der biologischen und medizinischen Wissenschaft', *Naturwissenschaftliche Wochenschrift*, 26 (n.s. 10):49, p. 770.

30. R. Barthes (1981) *Camera Lucida: Reflections on Photography* (New York: Hill & Wang), pp. 26–7.

31. J. B. Köhne (2009) *Kriegshysteriker: Strategische Bilder und mediale Techniken militärpsychiatrischen Wissens (1914–1920)* (Husum: Matthiesen), p. 213.

32. Cf. *Bayerisches Hauptstaatsarchiv*, San A 142 (Nr. 199103 Kriegsministerium, Verwaltungsabteilung, Munich, 12 December 1917).

33. M. Nonne (1917) 'Über erfolgreiche Suggestivbehandlung der hysteriformen Störungen bei Kriegsneurosen', *Zeitschrift für die gesamte Neurologie und Psychiatrie: Originalien*, 37, p. 201. Cf. J. B. Köhne, *Kriegshysteriker*, pp. 214–16.

34. *Reserve-Lazarett Hornberg (und Triberg) im Schwarzwald. Behandlung der Kriegs-Neurotiker*, Germany c.1917, produced by National-Hygiene-Museum Dresden, directed by Stabsarzt Dr. Ferdinand Kehrer, cf. Köhne, *Kriegshysteriker*, pp. 200–14.

35. For a photograph, see K. Alt (1918) 'Über die Kur- und Bäderfürsorge für nervenkranke Krieger mit besonderer Berücksichtigung der sogenannten Kriegsneurotiker', *Wiener Medizinische Wochenschrift*, 19, p. 847. See also the relevant chapter in Köhne, *Kriegshysteriker*, pp. 145–99.

36. See, for instance, Imperial War Museum in London at http://www.iwm.org.uk/, or In Flanders Fields Museum at http://www.inflandersfields.be/ (accessed 10 January 2013).

37. J. Bogousslavsky and O. Walusinski (2009) 'Marcel Proust and Paul Sollier: The involuntary memory connection', *Schweizer Archiv für Neurologie und Psychiatrie*, 4, p. 130.

38. O. Walusinski and J. Bogousslavsky (2008) 'À la recherche du neuropsychiatre perdu: Paul Sollier (1861-1933)', *Revue Neurologique FMC*, 164:S4 (September), p. 41.

39. As E. Cowie (2001) has pointed out, real hand grenades did not produce that much smoke: 'Identifizierung mit dem Realen – Spektakel der Realität', in: M.-L. Angerer and H. P. Krips (eds) *Der andere Schauplatz: Psychoanalyse – Kultur – Medien* (Vienna: Turia+Kant), p. 174.

40. For further thoughts on the triangle: (1) war veterans and their traumatic experiences; (2) politics of war remembrance and post-war society; and (3) gender issues in Imperial, Weimar, and Nazi Germany, see J. Crouthamel (2009) *The Great War and German Memory: Society, Politics and Psychological Trauma, 1914–1945* (Exeter: University of Exeter Press).

41. In his film *Funktionell-motorische Reiz- und Lähmungs-Zustände bei Kriegsteilnehmern und deren Heilung durch Suggestion in Hypnose* (Germany 1918), Nonne declares 'war hysteria' as perfectly curable, while in a text refering to a time period up to the year 1916, he admits that of 301 patients, only 61.2 per cent fully recovered. Cf. Max Nonne (1917) 'Neurosen nach Kriegsverletzungen (Zweiter Bericht)', in *Verhandlungen der Gesellschaft deutscher Nervenärzte: 8. Jahresversammlung (Kriegstagung) gehalten zu München, am 22. und 23. September 1916* (Leipzig: F. C. W. Vogel), p. 94.

6

'Mentally broken, physically a wreck...': Violence in War Accounts of Nurses in Austro-Hungarian Service

Christa Hämmerle

In the early 1960s Marianne Jarka, who had been a Red-Cross surgery nurse during the First World War in the Austro-Hungarian Army and later emigrated to the United States, started writing her autobiography. A remarkably large part of her memoirs deals with the time between early 1916 and the end of war, when Jarka was stationed at two mobile military hospitals on the Southwestern Front. Here, she witnessed the consequences of industrial warfare for soldiers with all their horrors – an experience she apparently could never overcome: 'Today, I am 72 years old. Until I draw my last breath, the torn bodies will haunt me', she wrote. Towards the end of her autobiographical text, Jarka also discussed the issue of war remembrance during the difficult post-war years. As a single mother of two illegitimate children, one from her relationship with a medical student who used to be her colleague at the Isonzo Front, she had to scrape through life during these years. Impoverished, she was forced to do menial jobs. Her former war commitment, her medical expertise as a nurse, and the war decorations she had received no longer counted. Laconically, Jarka recollects the public absence of praise for her war mission: 'I gave my war decorations to the milk woman for a litre of milk; she gave them to her boys to play with.'[1]

These two passages from an unpublished autobiographical text written by a former Austrian war nurse, as short as they are, insistently hint at what will be elaborated in this chapter. It discusses the history of those women who in the First World War were confronted with the following contradiction: on the one hand, they experienced the cruelty and barbarity of the Great War in close vicinity to the centres of violence and witnessed the suffering and dying of hundreds of thousands of soldiers with severe, incurable injuries. In so doing, war nurses often worked under very difficult and even dangerous circumstances, as we will see later. During the war, propaganda idealized the image of nurses and emphasized their strongly feminized self-sacrificing roles as 'white angels', 'sisters', or 'mothers' of the male warriors[2] and their importance as

89

'comrades' and 'soldiers'.[3] Yet after 1918, nurses' wartime experiences were publicly remembered and appreciated in hardly any belligerent country,[4] apart from only a few exceptions in some Allied States, where some war nurses were acknowledged as 'war heroines'.[5] This is especially true for Austria-Hungary, where officers' war experiences dominated the official and hegemonic war narratives during the entire interwar period.[6] Accordingly, war accounts not only of common soldiers but also of all women who had participated in the war as trained, or untrained, nurses were rarely published and distributed after 1918. Within the German-speaking countries, only a few of them are available today. Marianne Jarka's manuscript found its way into the hands of historians only because her son sent it to an archive specialized in the collection of lower-class autobiographical texts. Other sometimes more, sometimes less voluminous accounts of former Austrian war nurses were self-published (and probably self-financed) after 1918.[7] They include a remarkable book written by Maria Pöll-Naepflin, who together with a group of other young women came from Switzerland to serve in the Austro-Hungarian Army throughout the entire war.[8] Additionally to this corpus, there are some volumes of nurses' war narratives printed by normal publishers. It is striking that these texts appeared during two different periods. The first group was published during the war years themselves and were often accompanied by a flood of propaganda articles on this very popular form of female war commitment; they will not be discussed in what follows. The second group of accounts came out in the warmongering atmosphere of the 1930s, when Austro-fascism and re-militarization had begun to shape retrospection on the First World War.[9]

For obvious reasons, these various autobiographical texts include – some more than others – ideologizing and patriotic or tendentious and apologetic passages, which is especially true for those published in the 1930s.[10] Yet they demonstrate that these very women also experienced psychological problems and trauma as a consequence of their attempts to cope with violence and horror, and that they criticized the war. All in all, their writings represent 'a many-layered and rich corpus of texts'.[11] Even the most glorifying ones – if read across the grain – can be analysed in line with those which were not written or revised for the public, such as the one by Marianne Jarka, who wrote her autobiography merely for her son, and those which could only be self-published after the end of the war. The latter accounted for the majority of all published nurses' memoirs, and it is primarily these texts, which will be discussed in this chapter. The fact that they could not find a publisher indicates all the more the ambivalence between the probably life-long, troubling repercussions of the war experiences of these women and the public or familial indifference towards what they achieved and suffered in the Great War. Against this backdrop, I will focus on the multifaceted experiences of violence which shaped their war perceptions and memories – experiences similar to those of male soldiers, yet at the same time different in terms of gender. Thus, the history of war nurses has to be situated within the context of dissolving gender boundaries linked to the perpetual intersection of front lines/'home front' as one of the main characteristics of the First World War. As these women in many ways transgressed what was (re-)defined as women's sphere in wartime, we must discuss their narratives by emphasizing the tension of prescribed gender norms and antagonistic experiences.[12] This becomes all the more clear given the fact that many of them were stationed directly behind or even in the midst of the battlefields, so that research has rightly labelled their work as 'front-line nursing'.[13]

The nurse in historical research

Likewise, there is no doubt that in all belligerent, and even in neutral countries, which in some cases were far away from the main theatres of war, nurses were engaged on a large scale. Only a minority of them were fully skilled professionals, as institutionalized training of nurses had not started until some decades before the war.[14] The majority volunteered immediately, in summer 1914, when many appeals were published. They, as well as those who signed up later, enjoyed only a short training. Available figures impressively underline their irreplaceable importance. In the German Empire, nurses and assistant nurses of all religious and non-religious organizations, ranging from the Red Cross, the Order of Malta, and the Knights Hospitallers to diaconal institutions, reached at least approximately 92,000 (two-fifths of the whole medical staff).[15] In France, the three branches of the French Red Cross reached their peak with 63,000 fully qualified nurses and, from 1916 onwards, their workforce grew with a new category of around 30,000 lower-class salaried women.[16] For Great Britain, where 'military nursing had powerful antecedents in the myth (and work) of Florence Nightingale'[17] and thus was professionalized quite early and extensively before the war, the number of women who enrolled as nurses was similarly high: The Voluntary Aid Detachments (VAD), founded in 1909, could provide 47,196 nurses in August 1914, a figure that grew to 82,857 by April 1920.[18] In addition, there were more than 23,500 trained, partially trained or untrained nurses of the Queen Alexandra's Imperial Military Nursing Service and Territorial Force Nursing Services.[19] All these were complemented by approximately 25,000 American,[20] 650 New Zealand and 2,500 Australian nurses[21] – haunting figures indicating the global character of First World War nursing. These women not only originated from countries all over the world, but were also present at every theatre of war in and outside of Europe.

Thus, it is hardly surprising that the war nurse, whose commitment was also huge in the Second World War became an 'iconic figure of the twentieth century', as Christine E. Hallett has argued.[22] From the late nineteenth century onwards, nursing had been considered a genuinely female task. During the First World War, it became the ultimate proof of women's patriotism advocated even by contemporary feminists. More or less dense research, which at least in some national historiographies goes back to the early stages of women's history and has developed to a great extent since then, has examined the related gendered discourses of social motherhood and femininity for several belligerent countries. According to their findings mainly upper- and middle-class women volunteered for nursing.[23] They were often enthusiastic at the beginning of their war deployment and convinced that they had left their homes for doing exactly the right thing to support their nation in war. In this respect, nursing was often seen as the equivalent of male soldiering with which women identified to a high degree. Nurses partly developed similar narratives in their war accounts which framed their experiences in official or semi-official discourses on war and war remembrance[24] – again, this is only one side of the coin.

Most of the (already cited) studies also show that the image of war nurses was rather ambivalent and point to some contradictions in this respect, be it regarding the devaluation and sexualization of these women even in mainstream media during the First World War, or be it in the context of their self-perceptions, experiences, and memories. The 'bad nurse' and the attitude of denouncing women who had entered the field of military and war has attracted the interest of gender historians for a long time.[25] Yet researchers have only recently addressed all the horrors and traumatization nursing meant or resulted in – although this is an extremely important topic. Historians have introduced the term the 'second battlefield', for medical staff's place of deployment in war hospitals, a term coined by the American novelist Mary Borden who was a war nurse herself. With this notion, she described her and other nurses' work in the 'Forbidden Zone' of the Western Front. Here, they fought a continuous battle against the 'real' enemies death and pain – often in vain. In this context, Borden later published her literary sketches under the title 'fragments of a great confusion'.[26]

Against this backdrop, Margaret Higonnet has pleaded for a further 'alternate history of World War I traumas'. She has investigated 'traumatic stress' suffered by nurses and orderlies, as they often worked 'under conditions similar to those faced by combatants' and repeatedly had to face 'men's mutilated bodies'. Thus, Higonnet suggests to examine a variety of texts written by these non-combatants, from diaries and letters to written memoirs and fictionalized autobiographies. These 'trauma narratives' with their rhetorical imagery and a fragmented and even surrealistic language of modernism are closely linked to the writings of shell-shocked soldiers.[27] Likewise, the literary scholar Santanu Das has found a close connection between the medical condition of trauma and literary patterns in nurses' war accounts. In his psychoanalytically orientated analysis of a sample of such texts, he looks into their 'fraught relation to traumatic witnessing and the limits of empathy'.[28] In contrast, Christine E. Hallett argues that nurses found meaning in their stressful work by 'containing trauma'. She foregrounds the 'real and profoundly positive effects on the health and well-being of patients' by drawing on women from several allied countries.[29]

The Austrian context and nurses' desire to write

How do war accounts of nurses of the Austro-Hungarian Army fit into these findings? In what ways do they refer to war violence and traumatization and what are the specifics of these narratives? As already mentioned, there is only a small amount of published sources available, whereas most of these accounts were self-published or remained undisclosed. This might be one reason for their being often ignored by First World War historians; another is probably the fact that in Austria, this field of research has been largely dominated by traditional military and political history and is still lagging behind international standards, developments, and debates.[30] Within this context, research literature on the medical system of the Austro-Hungarian army, with its complex structure and its several reorganizations, has mentioned or cited war nurses only rarely and casually.[31] The current state of research is thus insufficient. Besides, women's and gender history has so far focused on several aspects of the professionalization or 'feminization' process of nursing in former Austria, but not on the specific history of war nurses in the First World War.[32] We do not even have any reliable figures on their numbers, although there must have been at least tens of thousands of women.[33] They not only served under the Red Cross and its Patriotic Female Society, but also as nurses of the Order of Malta and the Order of Knighthood, the three pillars of the Austro-Hungarian Supporting Medical Corps Organization,[34] complemented by some other voluntary associations such as the German diaconal institutions. As in other countries, all of them provided experienced as well as quickly trained nurses. At the beginning of the war, the latter were the majority due to the belated start of professionalized female nursing in Austria.[35]

It was, in fact, only after the Balkan Wars of 1912/13 that the Habsburg authorities accelerated the preparations of the medical service for a future war. This led to its reorganization, triggering a law in June 1914 that for the first time regulated female nursing on a larger scale. Needless to say that it also defined nursing as a woman's natural vocation; that is, as the ideal female profession, in particular in times of war.[36] Yet at the beginning of the First World War, Austria faced a dramatic shortage of trained nurses. As a result, a great amount of professional nurses from Switzerland and Germany were recruited, which consequently improved payment regulations for all trained nurses. They were provided with a poor, but at least guaranteed income that was also supposed to attract women from the lower middle classes.[37] By contrast, not all of the untrained, mostly bourgeois and aristocratic women who immediately volunteered in summer 1914 were employed during the early stage of the war, as military authorities and the society were sceptical about them.[38]

This situation changed as quickly as the area of deployment of nurses was expanding, including both clerical and vocational nurses as well as those graduated from a standard biennial training and those with only short-term training. Again, as in the other belligerent countries, it was initially planned to deploy all these women in the rear areas or in hospitals of the hinterland – fully in line with the gender ideology of 'separate spheres'. Yet this objective could not be realized at all. It took only a short time to allow and organize 'army nurses' in mobile sanitary and surgical units in front areas, sometimes situated only in tents.[39] Others worked on military hospital ships or trains, and in specific epidemic facilities again stationed close to the Eastern or Southeastern and Southwestern front lines, in Serbia and Palestine, Syria, Galicia, Russia, and so on. Many of them moved several times from one area of deployment to another. They could not easily terminate their contracts, which usually covered at least three years up to the entire duration of the war.[40] And not all of them survived. Nurses, too, came under shelling and were killed or died due to infection and illness during their war commitment. Therefore, these women have to be included in the statistics of war victims based on estimates. According to official figures, Austria-Hungary at the end of the war registered at least between 1.3 and 1.5 million 'military death cases' and around 4.15 million injuries, which were 'treated and healed' by sanitary institutions during the war.[41] In many cases soldiers were wounded twice or more times, as according to another statistic, 85 out of 100 injured soldiers were made 'fit for action' again[42] – not least with the help of the many nurses and their 'competing ethical and patriotic responsibilities'.[43]

Nevertheless, at the beginning of the war, many women were driven by 'enthusiasm' or the patriotic wish to actively participate in these 'great times'. They were convinced of the importance of their war mission, all the more when they decided to move towards the front lines. Thus, they wanted to document the hardships and efforts, sacrifices and challenges they had to bear – as women who, just like men, were 'mobilized' or 'enlisted', 'moving to the field' or 'staying in the field', according to 'marching orders' and 'lines of approach' they had received. These terms similar to those used by male soldiers can be found frequently in nurses' war accounts. They signify their affiliation to the military and the front line community, where they gave what they could, and even more. In addition, they longed to witness what war – and in particular the Great War – was like. Their motives to write down their war experiences might differ in detail, overall they are the result of what researchers have characterized as the personal need of those who were directly involved in total warfare. Just like soldiers, nurses felt 'the immense urge for self-expression' and tended to 'recount their experiences of war, describe its violence or at least try to say something about it'.[44] For some, however, this urge could also result in a failure to express themselves or in the (conscious or unconscious) silencing of their experiences.

Researchers focusing on other countries have frequently mentioned that many of these women, who volunteered for front-line nursing, started to pen their war experiences from the beginning of their war commitment onwards. This is also true for Austrian nurses who wrote down their war accounts in diaries or notebooks. One of them was R. M. Konrad, who initially worked in hospitals in the hinterland. In late 1915, she decided to move towards the battlefronts, because she 'wanted to directly participate in caring for the wounded afield', to 'search' for them immediately 'after the battle', and to 'apply the first emergency dressing, accompany those in need of help under a protecting roof'. Konrad therefore was delighted when she received her 'marching order' for the 'much embattled town Gorizia' at the Isonzo Front. On her way she even left the train because she wanted to buy a diary for her and her future patients' notes on 'little war episodes'.[45] In her, and many other nurses', view, experiencing 'front-line nursing' and writing down these experiences apparently belonged together. They added entries to their diaries whenever they had time or felt the inner need to do so – a practice that is frequently mentioned in the sources, together with a widespread practice of letter writing.[46] These women went to war not only with their nurses' clothing or uniforms, Red Cross armbands, bags, and books, but also armed with paper and pen. One of them even noted that she regularly took photographs in these years and compiled a 'big war album' with 'hundreds of such pictures', from which she later drew her written memories.[47]

From 'enthusiasm' to the baptism of fire: nurses' disillusionment

It goes without saying that Konrad did not only note 'little war episodes' which could easily be integrated into the tidy frame of popular war narratives. All war accounts examined here are oscillating between two opposite poles: There was, on the one hand, the aim to put their experiences to order and transform them into a coherent story realized by the process of writing and by adopting official or hegemonic (post-)war discourses in regard to content and interpretation. On the other hand, total war and violence, disorder, chaos, and the inability to give meaning to these experiences break through this surface of seeming order time and again.[48] This immediately becomes clear by comparing the ceremonial departures in military order and the representation of neat womanhood and female tidiness at the beginning of the war, similar to the white nurses on propaganda photographs, with the rapid dissolution of this idealization after the nurses had arrived at their area of deployment. The majority of these women were eager to 'serve their beloved fatherland',[49] as Agathe Fessler from Bregenz, who in October 1914 travelled to Sanok/Sjanik on the Eastern Front, put it. In this respect, their statements were similar to those of male soldiers, for whom historians have already investigated the complex process of disillusionment.[50] According to the patterns they have found, an initial willingness or even much-cited 'enthusiasm' to fulfil their war mission clashed with their experiences of industrial warfare. This polarity often constitutes the structure of an autobiographical text or leads to double-bind narratives, which idealize their own or their own nation's war engagement and, at the same time, refer to various situations of disillusionment, chaos, despair, and disorientation.

This also applies to a text written by an Austrian nurse and released by an acknowledged publishing house in 1935; that is, in the era of Austro-Fascism. Unsurprisingly, it contains a lot of propagandistic pro-war references, including the initial lamentation of its author Eveline Hrouda that she regretted being 'only a girl' who could not 'go to the field too'.[51] Thus she volunteered for nursing immediately after the outbreak of the war – first in secret, because she feared the protest of her wealthy parents.[52] After her training, when news about the first wounded soldiers arrived and Hrouda, in her own words, again felt unhappy that she 'was not yet at the front!!!',[53] she tried everything to get there, although her parents told her that front hospitals could be 'attacked by the enemy'.[54] Her wish finally came true in October 1914. Quite in line with the hegemonic gender order of the wartime society she wrote:

> [...] I went there, following an irresistible inner drive, with huge enthusiasm, fully aware of the severity of this step, with the holy resolution to dedicate all my strength to the service of the brave warriors who give their life and blood to protect our hearth and home. That seemed to me to be such a great duty [...] – the more so as I was entirely free and therefore wanted to leave nursing in the hinterland to those who could not go away from home.[55]

Shortly after, Hrouda and her female comrades had their first encounter with death when they witnessed a nurse dying of cholera, a 'heavy stroke of fate' as she described.[56] She then experienced her first dangerous situation, due to the rushed retreat of the Austro-Hungarian Army from Przemyśl/Peremyśl' which also caused the chaotic flight of the local civilians. At the railway station, the nurses were confronted with soldiers' corpses and felt 'horror-stricken'.[57] Incidents like this, however, happened again and again during the following years. Hrouda switched from the Red Cross to the Maltese Order, travelled from Galicia to the Russian part of Poland and Opava/Troppau, and from Bulgaria to the Isonzo Front, where battles were as bloody as the industrialized mass killing at the Western Front.[58]

And let us once again turn to the previously cited R. M. Konrad. In late 1915, she and ten other nurses travelled to the North Italian town Gorizia/Görz/Gorica. Already at the beginning of her text it becomes evident that they could easily come under fire in the field hospitals to which they were deployed. When they arrived in Gorizia, the women heard the 'heavy roaring of the guns' for the first time and quickly had to nurse many seriously injured soldiers. Konrad felt real 'horror'.[59] Afterwards the group was moved to Ljublijana, where their hospital came under heavy fire, as she describes in an entry dated 16 December 1915:

> I almost want to believe that it is a dream, but it is bitter reality! [...] First I could hardly believe it, although I heard a muffled bang, followed by people scurrying about; a nurse, looking completely scared, approached me and said that the surgery had been bombed, two men were dead. The surgery was a heap of rubble. [...] Then, another bang! I got weak in the knees, a chill came over me. [...] I felt as if the angel of death had touched me with its wing.[60]

In her recollections, Konrad referred to this incident as her 'baptism of fire'.[61] The fact that she used military vocabulary is again characteristic of the rhetoric of these women's accounts.

Our next example is the Swiss nurse Maria Pöll-Naepflin.[62] Together with a group of 11 young trained nurses from this neutral country, she started working for the Austro-Hungarian Army in summer 1914. In her self-published book, she wrote that even she and her female companions felt something like patriotism. On their train journey from the border town Feldkirch near Lake Constance across Austria, they observed the officially staged 'enthusiastic salutation in each city', that 'raised our courage and even evoked patriotic feelings for "our" Austria'.[63] The old Austrian emperor, Franz Joseph, personally welcomed the Swiss 'foreign nurses' at his residence in Schönbrunn in Vienna. Shortly thereafter, Pöll-Naepflin experienced her 'baptism of fire' – only a few kilometres behind the Serbian front, where she was stationed when the November offensive of the Austrian Army started. At that point, her 'disillusionment' began. The nurse, who continued to refer to the Austro-Hungarian Army as 'we' and 'our', remembered this incident with the following words: 'Outside the guns howled without ceasing and the noise of the exploding missiles sounded like infernal laughter. But despite all of that we had to go to work, we had our hands full.'[64] Or, even more dramatically:

> Outside at the Sava we saw the entrenchments for the first time, where days ago the battle had raged. In the trenches there were still guns and cartridges, pieces of shrapnel, linen and rags of clothes, and cadavers of animals. We stared into the brown water of the Sava and heard the thundering and echoing of the guns in the distance – horrible! We, the Swiss nurses, had already been completely cured of our enthusiasm for war: devastation, mutilated limbs and blood – oh, it was misery, wherever you looked! [...] Day by day the casualties came from the height of the Kolubra. In the slaughterhouse – as we named the surgery – the bloody work went on without cease.[65]

Horror, destruction, suffering – and the limits of language

With this quote, we come to the topic of war cruelty, which these nurses describe extensively in their texts. Pöll-Naepflin's further writing refers to killed or injured and invalided soldiers, epidemics, conflicts among nurses, gender disorder, extramarital sex and the spread of syphilis, war atrocities, and military despotism. Her account has to be read as a permanent attempt to survive, not to give up, to cope with despair and exhaustion, with the human chaos and tragedy that the war had brought about. Despite all the 'shocking and criminal things'[66] she saw, this trained nurse functioned until the end of the war – not least because of her use of morphine. Pöll-Naepflin describes in detail how she became a morphine addict and regularly used the drug, like many other nurses and doctors of the Great War did.[67] In addition, she had to witness the consequences of an abortion that led to the death of a pregnant young nurse. A number of times Pöll-Naepflin became seriously ill, physically as well as emotionally: 'Mentally broken, physically a wreck, I came back to Vienna in the days of March 1916.'[68]

Jarka, the nurse quoted at the beginning of this chapter, describes similar conditions. She writes about the horrors of war as frankly as Pöll-Naepflin, be it in respect of evacuations and the destruction of entire villages, constant air raids, gas attacks against the enemy, plundering Austrian soldiers after the twelfth battle at the Isonzo,[69] or be it regarding the helplessness of operating surgeons when confronted with masses of injured bodies, the horror of dying in front hospitals, physical and mental exhaustion, illnesses, and diseases. Jarka describes the brutal rhythm of the positional warfare, with its unceasing series of offensives resulting in only slight changes in the front line. Every offensive, whether from the Austro-Hungarian or from the Italian side, meant hundreds of thousands of wounded people, dead bodies, and prisoners of war. Thus, the nurses' experiences were inextricably linked to this rhythm of battle:

> And then the wagons with injured soldiers arrived, harnessed with four poor horses. Four wounded men in each wagon. What a sad burden that was. Friend and supposed enemy side by side tormented with pain [...]. And they were all young, so young. The churchyard, farmyards, the dairy farm with its corridors and open spaces, overcrowded in no time. The doctors in front of me chose the cases which had to go on the operating table immediately. I went around with the syringe of morphine. And then there was stitching up, amputations. Skull and abdominal operations during the whole night, one after another, throughout the day and again at night, until all of them had been cared for or poorly and hastily buried under debris.[70]

Jarka's description reminds us of what has been said before about field hospitals and surgery units as 'second battlefields', where nurses, orderlies, and doctors had to fight – and all too often were defeated. Deciding on whom to help first and whom to count as a hopeless case must have been traumatizing and surely evoked feelings of helplessness and guilt, all the more so in light of the 'absoluteness' of physical pain. This, as Elaine Scarry has argued, is non-communicable and due to its 'unshareability' erects an insurmountable wall between the person who suffers from pain and the others. According to Scarry's important study, physical pain also destroys language and only leaves anguished cries and noises.[71] 'There was pain and ache and screaming which drowned out everything', Fessler wrote.[72] And Hrouda, the enthusiastic nurse from Bohemia, in August 1917 after the beginning of the eleventh Isonzo battle, witnessed: 'Big transports with badly wounded persons had arrived overnight. In the course of 24 hours we had taken in over 200 severely injured soldiers. The entire hospital, all officers' rooms, were filled to capacity; they lay head to foot in the corridors. We could hear groaning and clamour from all sides; an unspeakable misery!'[73]

By focusing on the 'unspeakable misery' of suffering and injuries, the narratives more or less continuously absolutize the soldiers' victimization. They often use medical terminology which, as a professional discourse, connected members of the medical staff. Very rarely, they remember wounded and treated soldiers as individuals by their names and life stories. Propaganda in wartime media, in contrast, disseminated stories about the personal bond between nurses and the injured, sometimes even of dying soldiers to communicate the wounded warrior's heroism.[74] Yet nurses' war accounts tend to abstract from the individual and keep a distance between themselves and the masses of 'badly wounded' or 'slightly wounded', 'head-shots', 'amputated', and those who were 'shot in the lungs'. This terminology dominates even in war accounts which continuously use the leitmotif of the motherly white angel, as Mary Gasch from Bielitz did, who had passed only a three-day course with the Red Cross and some evening classes at the beginning of the war. In her short war account she writes: 'We mainly got slightly wounded and sick soldiers, later also many cases of typhus and dysentery. [...] Already in the first winter we got many with third-degree frostbite. I had to look after two rooms with eight frostbite sufferers.'[75] Industrial warfare even led to the tragedy that there were no corpses left to identify, as Eveline Hrouda describes in haunting words for the months of August and September 1917 at the Isonzo Front:

At dawn I distinguished two wagons which unloaded something in front of the hospital. When I got closer I realized that the terrible smell came from there. 'What's that?' I shouted across. '37 corpses, which we're unloading here', was the answer. But they weren't corpses; arms and legs were scattered about, heads without eyes, torsos without heads and without limbs, half rotted, totally black relics of men as well as pieces of bodies full of worms [...]. The sight was horrible. But we live in the age of humanity.'[76]

This striking example shows, firstly, that nurses of the Austro-Hungarian Army tended to use an elliptic, impressionistic, and staccato-like language in their war accounts to represent war images and experiences, as Higonnet and Das have examined for those of other belligerent countries.[77] It also demonstrates how these narratives were suddenly interrupted by short passages of accusation and harsh critique, which intensify the dramatic rhetoric that seems to correspond with the character of modern warfare. Fessler, in her self-published booklet, strings single episodes together, as this example from early on in her time at the Eastern theatre of war shows:

> Falling in! Provision! Bread, sausage, and – booze. It was on the eve of an assault. Everybody got a water bottle filled with booze (schnapps) – and what kind of booze! It was enough to drive a stone insane. How this horrified me. Poison, pure poison the fatherland gives to his sons! Stupefaction, so that they blindly storm into the hail of bullets! The following night was so horrendous that hell can offer nothing more terrible. How many poor people with shell-shock we had at the first-aid station the next morning![78]

These passages may explain why we can frequently find both explicit and implicit pacifistic statements in nurses' accounts, statements against the war in general or – albeit only vaguely formulated – severe indictments against those who were accused of being responsible for its outbreak and long duration. This includes Pöll-Naepflin's comment that she, though only a 'certainly ignorant' woman, 'condemned' every war and could not see that the warring nations of the First World War really honoured the fallen soldier heroes. If they had, 'no new weapons would have been allowed to be forged' and 'a permanent peace between all nations, as an honouring legacy, would have been established'.[79] Hrouda, on the other hand, uses sarcasm when she mentions the 'age of humanity', and Jarka points out that she lost her faith forever during the war as an obvious consequence of her experiences in those years.[80] Fessler maintained her Christian faith and frequently refers to it in her war accounts, which in many ways can be seen as an attempt to inscribe her experiences on the hegemonic interpretation and legitimization of the war. In contrast to this tendency and her man-like 'standing' during her entire war deployment, which allegedly led to a 'steeled heart',[81] she raises accusations as in the description of an episode of brutal behaviour against POWs she witnessed: '[...] when I remember the poor prisoners of war who have been stripped of everything, everything. And then I am so disgusted at the human race which has incited the war.'[82] And at the very end of her booklet, in its last passage on her 'return home', she extraordinarily accuses the effects of modern nationalism and capitalism, including their 'right hand' – alcohol – of being responsible for what had happened in Europe:

> The four years of service for the fatherland passed by over many a night. Was it possible? In the twentieth century? To force so many millions to take up weapons and to set them at each other like mindless animals? To force them to kill? And what was the driving force of the horrible world war? It was the stock exchange; the bloodthirsty greed for money: the currency trade with its fabulous, effortless profits, benefiting from the confusion of different European languages with which peoples can easily be divided, but most of all it was the alcohol, capitalism's right hand, which is not only most profitable, but can turn people into mere puppets ready to commit cruelty and outrage.[83]

Outlook

In conclusion we can outline some striking, and strong, ambivalences: The women whose texts I have examined in this chapter participated in totalized modern warfare by applying (and transgressing) their ascribed gender role. As shown in their writings and the hegemonic war narratives they used, they were involved in the complex process of 'societalization of violence'.[84] Yet their war accounts also indicate several different tensions. The first, caused by the asymmetry of the hegemonic gender order, was the growing ambivalence between the normative image of nurses' femininity and female or motherly duties (including the opposite; that is, the alleged immorality and mere love of adventure of those women who went to war) and their actual war commitment. A second tension emerged between the nurses' patriotism and their belief that Austria-Hungary was involved in necessary and defensive warfare against reckless enemies, and their growing ethical resentment against the war based on 'transnationalism' and border-crossing humanity. This explains why some nurses even (and secretly) helped soldiers with self-inflicted injuries or wrote about their empathy with the enemy. The last point in particular, which could not be examined here in depth, again seems to be an important and promising topic for future research. The preliminary findings that these tendencies seem to be stronger in unpublished or self-published war accounts should be investigated more closely by comparing various forms, dates of origin, and commemorative contexts of these texts.

What I intended to show is that nursing in the First World War could indeed turn into a nightmare. War violence, with its many dimensions, shaped and influenced nurses' bodies, emotions, and their mental condition as their war accounts prove. Some nurses expressed these experiences more frankly than others, sometimes their accounts have to be read across the grain. These women witnessed the horrible consequences of industrialized warfare with its continuous shelling, the million-fold killing and mutilating, gas attacks, and other war crimes. Nurses themselves became ill, had to bear deprivation, cold, lice, lack of sleep, extreme fatigue, and – in many cases – the all-pervading feeling of helplessness. All this must surely have been traumatizing and affected their lives after the war, especially for those who could not or did not want to continue professional nursing later on. This applies not only to Jarka, with whom this chapter started, but – as far as we know – also to Fessler, who failed to get back into her former, well-acknowledged social work in her home town and went to the United States several times before she finally emigrated to Brazil,[85] and to Pöll-Naepflin, who remained a morphine addict and led a troubled life for many years.[86] In summary it can be said that the nurses' war accounts tell us more about the traumatization they developed during the war than about the permanent work of 'containing trauma' which 'literally "held people together"' and 'permit[ted] their patients to heal', as Hallett has put it.[87] They are indeed similar to the experiences of soldiers, not least in respect to their 'returning home' and related aspects of dis/integration or silencing of what they had had to witness and suffer during war – a topic that further research is called to look for in detail.

This was probably all the more true for former Austria, which together with Germany was defeated and held responsible for the outbreak of the war, since the accounts of nurses not only from Austria but also from Switzerland and the German Empire were more or less completely repressed after 1918. Although their commitment was officially acknowledged during the war,[88] there was no public interest whatsoever in their experiences in the post-war period. Consequently, war nurses never turned into war heroines. Commemorative culture took notice of at most single (and more or less convenient) voices representing the nurses only after many years had passed, as we have seen. One might ask whether the nurses' statements on war violence and their criticism of the war, as well as the war-related gender disorder which they carefully observed, had anything to do with this development. The latter, in particular, clearly did not fit into those interpretations of the war which, after a short period of pacifism, soon became hegemonic in the re-militarized political climate of interwar Austria. To answer this would open a further chapter of the history of the First World War so often forgotten in the European context.

Notes

1. M. Jarka (undated) *Erinnerungen 1889–1934*, typescript of the Dokumentation le-bensgeschichtlicher Aufzeichnungen (Department of Economic and Social History, University of Vienna, 111 pp.), pp. 82 and 106. All quotes from German texts analysed in this chapter are translated by the author.
2. See, for example, R. Schulte (1996) 'The Sick Warrior's Sister: Nursing during the First World War', in L. Abrams and E. Harvey (eds) *Gender Relations in German*

History: Power, Agency and Experience from the Sixteenth to the Twentieth Century (London: UCL Press), pp. 121–41; M. H. Darrow (1996) 'French Volunteer Nursing and the Myth of War Experience in World War I', *American Historical Review*, 101:1, pp. 80–106; M. H. Darrow (2000) *French Women and the First World War: War Stories of the Home Front* (Oxford: Berg), pp. 133–68.

3. See the striking example of a high-ranking Austrian officer who in 1936 published a short text on war nurses written during the First World War. In this text, he not only defined these women as 'honest brave sisters, our sisters, our comrades', but also as 'female soldiers' – by stating that the 'proud' term 'soldier' was the highest 'honorary title' to be assigned. H. Kerchnawe (1936) 'Die Schwester', in B. Breitner (ed.) *Ärzte und ihre Helfer im Weltkrieg 1914–1918* (Vienna: Verlag Amon Franz Göth), p. 246.

4. For France, see Darrow, *French Women*, pp. 1–20.

5. See also A. Fell 'Remembering French and British First World War Heroines', Chapter 7 in this volume.

6. O. Überegger (2011) *Erinnerungskriege: Der Erste Weltkrieg, Österreich und die Tiroler Kriegserinnerung in der Zwischenkriegszeit* (Innsbruck: Universitätsverlag Wagner).

7. A. Fessler (1919) *Aus der Mappe einer ehemaligen Armeeschwester* (self-published pamphlet, Stadtarchiv Bregenz, papers of Agathe Fessler); R. M. Konrad (probably 1922) *Schwestern als Menschen: Aus den Aufzeichnungen einer Armeeschwester*, vol. 1 (Innsbruck: self-published), vol. 2 (Vienna: self-published); M. Gasch (1978) *Im Dienste des Nächsten: Oberschwester Mary Gasch berichtet über ihre Tätigkeit an allen Fronten des 1. Weltkrieges* (Vienna: self-published).

8. M. Pöll-Naepflin (1st edn probably 1933, 3rd edn 1935) *Fortgerungen, Durchgedrungen: Ein erschütterndes Lebensbild einer Krankenschwester aus der Zeit des großen Krieges, der Revolution und der Arbeitslosigkeit* (Constance: self-published). On the inside front page, this book is presented as the 'single oeuvre from a Swiss nurse of the First World War'.

9. H. von Sonnenthal (1918) (ed.) *Ein Frauenschicksal im Kriege: Briefe und Tagebuch-Aufzeichnungen von Schwester Maria Sonnenthal-Scherer. Eingeleitet und nach den Handschriften herausgegeben von Hermine von Sonnenthal* (Berlin: Ullstein); E. Hrouda (1935) *Barmherzigkeit: Als freiwillige Malteserschwester im Weltkrieg* (Graz: Leykam).

10. See, for Germany, Schulte, 'The Sick Warrior's Sister', p. 123.

11. Schulte, 'The Sick Warrior's Sister', p. 123.

12. See the introduction given by C. Hämmerle, O. Überegger and B. Bader Zaar in Chapter 1 in this volume.

13. M. R. Higonnet (ed.) (2001) *Nurses at the Front: Writing the Wounds of the Great War* (Boston: Northeastern University Press), p. x; Darrow, *French Women*, p. 139.

14. This also meant its 'secularization' as nursing for centuries had been the domain of religious congregations. The development towards professionalization was closely connected to activities for a prospective modern war; units of nurses were especially trained for a future war commitment. In France, the first 'école d'infirmières' was opened in Paris in 1907, see Darrow, *French Women*, p. 48; Y. Knibiehler (2004) 'Les anges blancs: naissance difficile d'une profession feminine' in E. Morin-Rotureau (ed.) *1914–1918: Combats de femmes. Les femmes, pilier de l'effort de guerre* (Paris: Éditions Autrement), pp. 47–63, here 48; for the very important case of Britain, see A. Summers (1988) *Angels and Citizens: British Women as Military Nurses 1854–1914* (London: Routledge & Kegan); for other countries such as Australia, New Zealand, and Canada, C. E. Hallett (2009)

Containing Trauma: Nursing Work in the First World War (Manchester: Manchester University Press), p. 7; for Germany Schulte, 'The Sick Warrior's Sister', pp. 123–6.

15. Schulte, 'The Sick Warrior's Sister', p. 123; B. Panke-Kochinke and M. Schaidhammer-Placke (2002) *Frontschwestern und Friedensengel: Kriegskrankenpflege im Ersten und Zweiten Weltkrieg. Ein Quellen- und Fotoband* (Frankfurt am Main: Mabuse), p. 14, mentions 25,000 professional nurses as an official figure of the Red Cross.
16. Darrow, *French Women*, pp. 140–1 and 163, refers to an estimate of even 500,000 French women in all who volunteered for hospital work during the war.
17. S. R. Grayzel (2002) *Women and the First World War* (London: Pearson Education), p. 39.
18. S. Das (2005) *Touch and Intimacy in First World War Literature* (Cambridge: Cambridge University Press), p. 185.
19. Grayzel, *Women*, p. 39.
20. Higonnet, *Nurses at the Front*, p. viii.
21. Grayzel, *Women*, p. 40.
22. Hallett, *Containing Trauma*, p. 1.
23. Though class antagonism did occur among different groups of nurses, for example between paid and unpaid nurses, payment could make nursing jobs attractive also for lower-middle-class and lower-class women, as was the case for example in France until 1916; see Darrow, *French Women*, p. 140–1; Das, *Touch and Intimacy*, p. 186.
24. For the French case this again is convincingly pointed out by Darrow, *French Women*, especially pp. 151–8. In respect to the (albeit not consistent) reproduction of dominant gender and imperialist discourses of nurses involved in colonial enterprises, see A. S. Fell (2011) 'Nursing the Other: The Representation of Colonial Troops in French and British First World War Nursing Memoirs', in S. Das (ed.) *Race, Empire and First World War Writing* (Cambridge: Cambridge University Press), pp. 158–74.
25. See, for example, the trendsetting, psychoanalytically orientated work of K. Theweleit (1978) *Männerphantasien*, 2 vols (Frankfurt am Main: Rowohlt).
26. Mary Borden, a wealthy woman and novelist, worked as a Red Cross nurse at the Western Front and established her own front-line surgical unit under French military authority. For her publication *The Forbidden Zone* from 1929, in which she used this much-cited term in her sketch 'Blind', see Das, *Touch and Intimacy*, pp. 187 and 204, and Higonnet, *Nurses at the Front*, pp. vii–xxxviii and 79–161(reprint), quote on p. 79.
27. M. R. Higonnet (2002) 'Authenticity and Art in Trauma Narratives of World War I', *Modernism/Modernity*, 9:1, pp. 91–107, quotes on pp. 92–3.
28. Das, *Touch and Intimacy*, pp. 177–228; S. Das (2005) 'The Impotence of Sympathy: Touch and Trauma in the Memoirs of First World War Nurses', *Textual Practice*, 19:2, pp. 239–62.
29. Hallett, *Containing Trauma*, p. 13.
30. O. Überegger (2004) 'Vom militärischen Paradigma zur "Kulturgeschichte des Krieges"? Entwicklungslinien der österreichischen Weltkriegsgeschichtsschreibung im Spannungsfeld militärisch-politischer Instrumentalisierung und universitärer Verwissenschaftlichung', in O. Überegger (ed.) *Zwischen Nation und Region: Weltkriegsforschung im interregionalen Vergleich. Ergebnisse und Perspektiven* (Innsbruck: Studienverlag), pp. 179–96; in respect to women's and gender history C. Hämmerle (2013) 'Gendered Narratives of the First World War: The Example of Former Austria', in M. Mondini and M. Rospocher (eds) *Narrating War: XVIth–XXth Century Perspectives* (Berlin: Duncker & Humblot; Bologna: Il Mulino), pp. 173–87.

31. D. C. Angetter (1995) *Dem Tod geweiht und doch gerettet: Die Sanitätsversorgung am Isonzo und in den Dolomiten 1915–18* (Frankfurt am Main: Peter Lang), pp. 231–8; B. Biwald (2000) *Von Helden und Krüppeln: Das österreichisch-ungarische Militärsanitätswesen im Ersten Weltkrieg* (Vienna: ÖBV & hpt), pp. 89–94.
32. See, for example, E. Malleier (1998) 'Jüdische Krankenpflegerinnen im Rudolfinerhaus 1882–1906: Eine In(tro)spektion', in E. Seidl and I. Walter (eds) *Rückblicke für die Zukunft: Beiträge zur historischen Pflegeforschung* (Vienna: Wilhelm Maudrich), pp. 180–207; I. Walter (2004) *Pflege als Beruf oder aus Nächstenliebe? Die Wärterinnen und Wärter in den Krankenhäusern im 'langen 19. Jahrhundert'* (Frankfurt am Main: Mabuse).
33. Research literature only provides figures for minor or special groups of nurses. According to estimates, the Women's Auxiliary Labour Force, which was organized throughout the Habsburg Monarchy from spring 1917 onwards, employed between 33,000 and 50,000 women, ranging from female clerical workers in military units to (auxiliary) nurses; another 107,000 women were engaged in the 'hinterland'; see M. Healey (2004) *Vienna and the Fall of the Habsburg Empire: Total War and Everyday Life in World War I* (Cambridge: Cambridge University Press), p. 204.
34. Angetter, *Dem Tod geweiht*, pp. 190–213.
35. A first nursing school (*Krankenpflegeschule*) was founded in 1882 as part of the 'Rudolfinerhaus', a private hospital with religious affiliation. It was not until 1913 that the main public hospital in Vienna (AKH) and the Red Cross also opened nursing schools – not least due to the dramatic shortage of nursing staff during the Balkan Wars; see B. Bolognese-Leuchtenmüller (1997) 'Imagination "Schwester": Zur Entwicklung des Berufsbildes der Krankenschwester in Österreich seit dem 19. Jahrhundert', *L'Homme: Zeitschrift für Feministische Geschichtswissenschaft*, 8:1, pp. 155–77.
36. See G. Dorffner and V. Kozon (2004) 'Die "Verordnung des Ministeriums des Innern vom 25. Juni 1914, betreffend die berufsmäßige Krankenpflege"', in I. Walter, E. Seidl and V. Kozon (eds) *Wider die Geschichtslosigkeit der Pflege* (Wien: ÖGVP Verlag), pp. 45–65.
37. Angetter, *Dem Tod geweiht*, pp. 190–213; Biwald, *Von Helden*, pp. 153–6.
38. Biwald, *Von Helden*, p. 91.
39. Biwald, *Von Helden*, p. 91; Angetter, *Dem Tod geweiht*, p. 136.
40. Dorffner and Kozon, '"Verordnung"', p. 53.
41. In addition there were also approximately 350,000 wounded POWs. Angetter, *Dem Tod geweiht*, p. 186; Biwald, *Von Helden*, p. 626; G. Hirschfeld, G. Krumeich and I. Renz (eds) (2003) *Enzyklopädie Erster Weltkrieg* (Paderborn: Schöningh), p. 664.
42. Angetter, *Dem Tod geweiht*, p. 186; see also S. Audoin-Rouzeau and A. Becker (2002) *14–18: Understanding the Great War* (New York: Hill & Wang), p. 24.
43. Higonnet, 'Authenticity', p. 98.
44. Audoin-Rouzeau and Becker, *Understanding the Great War*, p. 16.
45. Konrad, *Schwestern*, pp. 4–5.
46. For a broader view on the 'explosion' of auto/biographical writing in both World Wars, see C. Hämmerle (2013) 'Between Instrumentalization and Self-Governing: (Female) Ego-Documents in The European Age of Total War', in F.-J. Ruggiu (ed.) *The Uses of First Person Writings: Africa, America, Asia, Europe* (Oxford: Peter Lang), pp. 163–284.
47. Pöll-Naepflin, *Fortgerungen*, p. 139.

48. See for such an approach originating from theories of the sociology of knowledge, esp. K. Latzel (1999) 'Kriegsbriefe und Kriegserfahrung: Wie können Feldpostbriefe zu einer erfahrungsgeschichtlichen Quelle werden?', *Werkstatt Geschichte*, 22, pp. 7–23.

49. Fessler, *Armeemappe*, p. 4.

50. See, for example, O. Überegger (2002) *Der andere Krieg: Die Tiroler Militärgerichtsbarkeit im Ersten Weltkrieg* (Innsbruck: Universitätsverlag Wagner), especially pp. 256–311; B. Ziemann (2007) *War Experiences in Rural Germany 1914–1923* (Oxford: Berg), especially pp. 82–110.

51. Hrouda, *Barmherzigkeit*, p. 6. Such lamentations on the part of girls and women were apparently quite common.

52. Hrouda, born in 1892 near Lovosice/Lobositz in Bohemia, was the daughter of the director of the Herberstein estate in Pohořelice/Pohrlitz.

53. Hrouda, *Barmherzigkeit*, p. 7.

54. Hrouda, *Barmherzigkeit*, pp. 11–12, where Hrouda quotes a letter from her father.

55. Hrouda, *Barmherzigkeit*, p. 12.

56. Hrouda, *Barmherzigkeit*, p. 20.

57. Hrouda, *Barmherzigkeit*, p. 23.

58. See, for example, L. Musner (2011) 'The Myriad Faces of Battlefield Dynamics', *Recherche - Zeitung für Wissenschaft*, http://www.recherche-online.net/lutz-musner-english.html.

59. Konrad, *Schwestern*, p. 10.

60. Konrad, *Schwestern*, p. 15.

61. Konrad, *Schwestern*, p. 20.

62. See also Pöll-Naepflin, *Fortgerungen*, pp. 34–46 (chapter on her 'fire test': 'Feuerprobe').

63. Pöll-Naepflin, *Fortgerungen*, pp. 12–13.

64. Pöll-Naepflin, *Fortgerungen*, p. 39.

65. Pöll-Naepflin, *Fortgerungen*, p. 41.

66. Pöll-Naepflin, *Fortgerungen*, p. 79.

67. Pöll-Naepflin, *Fortgerungen*, frequently mentions the common use of morphine amongst doctors and nurses; see, for example, pp. 85 and 129; see also Konrad, *Schwestern*, p. 61. Such practice was also widespread at the Western Front.

68. Pöll-Naepflin, *Fortgerungen*, p. 80.

69. Both sides suffered heavy losses in this battle (24 October–2 December 1917). Austrian and German troops were able to break into Italian front lines causing lootings on a massive scale.

70. Jarka, *Erinnerungen*, pp. 71–2.

71. E. Scarry (1985) *The Body in Pain: The Making and Unmaking of the World* (Oxford: Oxford University Press), especially pp. 3–8; see also Das, *Touch and Intimacy*, p. 189.

72. Fessler, *Armeemappe*, p. 20.

73. Hrouda, *Barmherzigkeit*, p. 143.

74. See, for example, Kriegshilfsbüro des k. k. Ministeriums des Innern (no date) (ed.) *Wahre Soldatengeschichten: Erzählt von Roten-Kreuz-Schwestern u. freiwilligen Pflegerinnen 1914–1916* (Vienna: Hermes Buch- und Kunstdruckerei).

75. Gasch, *Im Dienste*, p. 3.

76. Hrouda, *Barmherzigkeit*, pp. 147–8.

77. See notes 27 and 28.

78. Fessler, *Armeemappe*, p. 13.

79. Pöll-Naepflin, *Fortgerungen*, p. 5.
80. Jarka, *Erinnerungen*, p. 77: 'After all the horrible suffering I saw in those years, nobody can tell me that an all-knowing, all-bountiful, all-mighty, and just God exists.'
81. Fessler, *Armeemappe*, p. 61.
82. Fessler, *Armeemappe*, p. 11.
83. Fessler, *Armeemappe*, p. 64.
84. B. Ziemann (2002) '"Vergesellschaftung von Gewalt" als Thema der Kriegsgesellschaft seit 1914: Perspektiven und Desiderate eines Konzepts', in B. Thoß and H.-E. Volkmann (eds) *Erster Weltkrieg – Zweiter Weltkrieg: Ein Vergleich. Krieg, Kriegserlebnis, Kriegserfahrung in Deutschland* (Paderborn: Ferdinand Schöningh), pp. 735–58. The concept of 'socialization of violence' was originally developed by M. Geyer (1986) 'Krieg als Gesellschaftspolitik: Anmerkungen zu neueren Arbeiten über das Dritte Reich im Zweiten Weltkrieg', *Archiv für Sozialgeschichte*, 26, pp. 557–601.
85. M. Pichler (2007) 'Selbstverwirklichung im Dienst an Anderen: Leben und Werk der Bregenzer Sozialarbeiterin Agathe Fessler (1870–1941)', in M. Pichler *Quergänge, Vorarlberger Geschichte in Lebensläufen* (Hohenems: Bucher), pp. 160–87.
86. Pöll-Naepflin, *Fortgerungen*, pp. 161–89.
87. Hallett, *Containing Trauma*, p. 228.
88. See the list in R. Rutkowski (1983) 'Ein leuchtendes Beispiel von Pflichttreue: Frauen im Kriegseinsatz 1914–1918', *Scrinium*, 28, pp. 343–53, here 349–52.

7
Remembering French and British First World War Heroines

Alison S. Fell

Although few are remembered today, the First World War produced scores of heroines who became household names in their respective nations.[1] From summer 1914 onwards, both British and French journalists, artists, and writers sought out women who could be constructed as heroic and lauded them in the press, in posters, and in popular fiction. First World War heroines tended to have a double function: firstly, although cast as exceptional, they were equally set up as gendered embodiments of the finest qualities of a 'race' or a national identity, as role models to bolster morale and mobilize the nation for the war effort. Secondly, their gender was used to underscore the 'barbarous' and 'uncivilized' nature of the enemy. It was usually activities on the front line that marked women out for heroine status. This proximity to the front, along with the patriotic and heroic qualities of courage, devotion, selflessness, tenacity, and sang-froid with which they were endowed, meant that heroines were often discussed in terms normally reserved for male combatants.

However, it is equally notable that in propagandistic and cultural representations of war heroines produced both during and after the conflict, there were clear attempts to redraw the dividing lines between front and rear, and between male and female versions of heroism in wartime. If they had died, their deaths were presented as 'murders' or 'assassinations' rather than as executions or as being 'killed in action', for example. Thus, at the same time as heroines' (temporary) transgressions of gender stereotypes were celebrated, efforts were made in the popular press and in other cultural sources to define their activities within a more traditional understanding of men's and women's roles.

For instance, in 1914 and 1915 in France and Belgium a group of women were singled out as 'invasion heroines': plucky peasants, nuns, and postal workers who defied invading soldiers in order to preserve life or foil attempts to take their territory. Yet in order for these women to function as embodiments of the finer qualities of their nations, journalists consistently emphasized their 'feminine' qualities such as self-sacrifice, frailty, piety, grace, and maternal solicitude. As Margaret Darrow notes:

> [T]he ideal heroine was small, young, pretty and, if possible, orphaned [...].
> If the heroine could not be young and little, she could be simple and above
> all, feminine. [...] The central moment in most of the stories was the con-
> frontation of the frail French woman and the brutal German officer. In tale
> after tale, French civilization, embodied in French femininity, cowed and
> conquered German brutality by its nobility, courage and moral rectitude.[2]

It was for this reason that nursing work of some form featured in many female heroism stories. Nursing allowed women to be close to the front while remaining firmly situated within traditional understandings of the feminized domestic sphere.

In popular representations of female heroism, nurses at the front were not becoming honorary soldiers, they were extending their 'feminine' influence, bringing the home/domestic front to the soldiers, hence the reason why in many popular accounts the nurse functioned as a synecdoche for the lost or absent home. This desire to '(re-)feminize' women who were active at or near to the front explains why the French Resistance heroines I discuss in this chapter, Louise de Bettignies and Emilienne Moreau, were frequently referred to as nurses in wartime and post-war journalistic accounts of their activities, even though neither of them worked in either a voluntary or professional capacity as nurses. Recasting them as nurses also protected Moreau from accusations of being a *franc-tireur* and de Bettignies from an association with long-standing negative stereotypes of female spies as untrustworthy and sexually promiscuous *femmes fatales*, a myth that the First World War successfully revivified. Indeed, as several historians have noted, in the wartime spin on the virgin/whore dichotomy that helped to structure popular understandings of women's relationship to war in both nations, Edith Cavell was the representative par excellence of the virtu-ous virgin-victim, while prostitute-spy Mata Hari was the most notorious embodiment of woman as unscrupulous seductress.[3]

First World War heroines who died in enemy hands became largely symbolic figures, transformed by the artists, writers, and journalists who represented them into idealized martyrs, embodiments of a nation or abstract concepts such as 'Humanity' in the face of barbarism. This was particularly the case with Edith Cavell, executed in 1915, and can also be seen in the example of Frenchwoman Louise de Bettignies, who died while a prisoner of war in Germany. I begin this chapter by outlining the ways in which Cavell and de Bettignies were represented after their deaths, in order to outline some common features of female heroism during and after the First World War. In the autobiographical writings of surviving heroines, however, the relationship to their wartime heroism was represented and reconfigured in more complex terms. After the war, the public perception of the latter depended largely upon the extent to which their wartime activities were understood as transgressive in gender terms.[4] While in some cases wartime heroism enabled women to access public political or cultural life in a way they may not have been able to do otherwise, in other cases their heroic activities were less acclaimed, or even denigrated, in post-war society. In the latter parts of this chapter I concentrate on two case studies: Emilienne Moreau, the French 'Heroine of Loos', and the two British 'Heroines of Pervyse', Elsie Knocker and Mairi Chisholm. I consider, firstly, the ways in which they illustrate the features of popular gendered representations of female heroism and, secondly, the extent to which the women themselves refer to their wartime notoriety in their post-war constructions of self. While the activities of heroines during the First World War have been the focus of a number of popular and scholarly studies,[5] there has been considerably less work on the ways in which those who survived the war extended, adapted, or exploited their wartime roles in subsequent decades. The case studies I have chosen include women who came into the war from very different socio-cultural backgrounds. While during the war their actions allowed them, at least to some extent, to transcend these differences, in the interwar period it proved more difficult to cross class and cultural boundaries. What unites the women I discuss, however, is their frequent use of the war, and of their heroine status, as a key reference point around which their post-war identities were constructed.

Martyr-heroines: Edith Cavell and Louise de Bettignies

In cultural representations of Edith Cavell produced in France and Britain during and after the war, she was made to embody two central (and frequently interlinked) concepts: the brutality of the enemy and the humanity and self-sacrifice of womanhood. These were concepts that many different sections of the national and international community could buy into. The former – that of an innocent nurse mercilessly gunned down by brutal Germans – dominated commemoration during the war, and was instrumentalized by anti-German and, in Britain and the United States, recruitment propagandists who re-imagined her as a young, virginal, and feeble war victim of a brutal oppressor that needed avenging, acting as a proxy for other vulnerable female civilians. Cavell was a 49-year-old experienced professional nurse who ran a training hospital in Brussels, and who pleaded guilty to German charges – she had helped run an escape network for Allied soldiers – before being executed by firing squad in 1915. She appeared at her trial in civilian clothing, yet wartime popular images often depict a much younger Cavell wearing a Red Cross uniform, or with a Union Jack pinned to her breast.[6]

A common myth, which has been shown to be false by the testimony of witnesses to the execution, suggested that she had fainted at her execution and, when the firing squad refused to shoot, a Prussian officer shot her with his handgun.[7] This version of her death allowed Allied propaganda to present Cavell as a feminized victim in a manner reminiscent of atrocity imagery and Germany as guilty of war crimes, literally holding a smoking gun.

Frenchwoman Louise de Bettignies was similarly transformed into an innocent martyr after her death, although in her case she was cast more specifically as an embodiment of the French nation, and more particularly of the northern region of France. In 1914, she was a wealthy, independent, and well-travelled 35-year-old single woman with an aptitude for languages that had made her a good candidate for her role gathering intelligence for both the French and British authorities.[8] However, during the war she was nicknamed the 'Joan of Arc of the North' and in hagiographic wartime propaganda it was her exceptionality, youth, and feminine piety that were emphasized, while her spying activities were underplayed or re-imagined as a quasi-religious vocation, mysterious 'voices' having called her to work for the Intelligence Services.[9] The comparison to Joan of Arc was taken up again in the immediate aftermath of her death while a German prisoner of war, with Bishop Charost's eulogy at her funeral declaring that both heroines shared 'the same love of the fatherland [...], the same solicitude for the wounded, whether friend or foe, the same invincible will to repel threats and accept martyrdom, the same supernatural serenity in the face of death'.[10] It is notable here that Charost highlights her 'solicitude for the wounded', associating her with nursing rather than with intelligence work.

After the war, the nationalist right responded most readily to de Bettignies's story, casting her as an icon of French national identity, the combination of Catholic piety, selfless bravery, and 'instinctive', mystical patriotism that were read into her personal history and death being easily mapped onto their version of Joan of Arc. This interpretation of her identity is evident in the statue unveiled in 1927 and sculpted by nationalist Joan of Arc devotee Maxime Réal del Sarte (Figure 7.1). It features a soldier kneeling in front of de Bettignies, kissing her hand in gratitude. She gazes serenely towards the horizon, indicating not only her bravery in the face of the enemy, but her elevated status as a heroine set apart from the crowd, existing on a higher plane.

It might seem at first glance that the hundreds of memorials and ceremonies that were erected in memory of the heroism of Cavell, and the few that were erected to de Bettignies, subvert or at least challenge dominant gender representations, featuring women as the active heroines of war rather than its passive victims. However, they drew on a long tradition of women as exceptional and transcendent innocent martyrs, especially in France where the cult of Joan of Arc provided a ready vocabulary. While the elevation of fallen heroines to a Christ-like image of selfless martyrdom was broadly

Figure 7.1   Monument to Louise de Bettignies, Lille, unveiled by Marshal Foch, 13 November 1927, Sculptor Maxime Réal del Sarte
Source: © Velvet.

uncontested in both France and Britain, other women who were celebrated in the press during the war had a more mixed reception in the post-war years. Certain of these women continued to maintain, and even accrue, considerable social and cultural capital after the Armistice, but others had a more ambiguous reception from the French and British public.

Emilienne Moreau: the 'Heroine of Loos'

In 1914 Emilienne Moreau was the 17-year-old daughter of a coalminer-turned-shopkeeper in Loos-en-Gohelle (near Lens in the Pas de Calais region of France). She helped her father in the shop while working hard to pass her 'brevet' qualification in order to train to be a schoolteacher.[11] When the Germans invaded, she warned advancing French troops of the positioning of German artillery. The French troops were forced to retreat, however, and the civilian population lived under siege conditions. In December 1914 her father died as a result, according to Moreau's later autobiography, of the 'privations and anguish of the occupation', having been imprisoned for breaking the curfew.[12] The majority of the population having fled, Moreau set herself up as a temporary teacher when the school closed. In September 1915 British troops attacked to retake the town. Again Moreau warned the kilt-wearing Highlanders of the 9th Black Watch of the positioning of German defences. During the battle for the village, Moreau helped a Dr Burns to care for wounded soldiers and, when attempting to move one of them to safety, was fired at by German soldiers. In response, she picked up a gun left by one of the British male nurses and shot back, allegedly killing at least two. Moreau's sister was wounded by shrapnel during the fighting, and when the family took her for hospital treatment in nearby Béthune, they learned that Henri Moreau, Emilienne's brother, had been killed in action in May 1915.

Moreau was awarded medals by both the French and British governments,[13] General de Sailly commenting when awarding her the Croix de Guerre in 1917 that: 'You honour the women of France. For them you are a magnificent and reassuring example.'[14] Moreau's story had all the ingredients the press were looking for, and *Le Petit Parisien*, a powerful newspaper, quickly offered her 5000 francs for an exclusive. Moreau was staggered by the amount, commenting in her memoirs that 'we were living in a precarious financial situation, with a military allowance of 3.50 francs per day and 1.50 to help with the children'.[15] The newspaper paid for Moreau and her mother to stay in a luxurious château in La Maye in Versailles, bought her new clothes, had her photograph taken, and serialized her *Memoirs* of 1914 and 1915, alongside a patriotic popular novel by Jules Mary, *L'Amour dans les ruines* (Love in the Ruins).[16] Her photograph was widely distributed to soldiers, and her portrait was added to the 'Staircase of Heroes' in the enormous French commemorative painting the *Panthéon de la guerre* (Pantheon of the War).[17] Her story was also made into a propagandistic Australian film in 1916, *The Joan of Arc of Loos*, directed by George Willoughby.

A veritable publicity machine thus promoted the image of Moreau as heroine, and she was used by the state for fund-raising and as a symbol of Franco-British *entente*. Looking back at this period of her life in her autobiography, she is lucid about the political and economic uses that were made of her both by the newspaper and the French authorities:

> [W]e weren't [in the château] for pleasure. I had to work. Every day, I would fill the pages of a notebook that one of the newspaper's editors would come and pick up. My mother and I were not permitted to leave the château, as I had become an 'exclusive' for *Le Petit Parisien* and it wasn't willing to share me with its competitors. Later, the newspaper printed enormous posters of one of my photos which decorated the walls of the metro, and then the walls of every town in France. [...] As money was needed to help care for the wounded, it had been decided to appeal to the 'well-known faces' of the war: Fonck, Nungesser, Guynemer[18] [...] and me. Our role was to collect money from wherever it could be found, that is to say, from the rich. So they made me a pretty dress (I wanted

a black one because I was still wearing mourning for my father and brother) and, with Guynemer, I was sent to high-society social occasions.[19]

There are several factors that help to explain the success of Moreau's heroization. The years 1914 and 1915 were extremely costly for the Allies on the Western Front in terms of both losses of territory and casualty rates. The Battle of Loos, for example, saw the 9th Battalion of the Black Watch suffer 700 casualties. It was not easy for journalists to find inspiring and morale-boosting tales of heroism amid such losses. For the French, Emilienne Moreau, poignantly young in her mourning clothes, simultaneously represented stoicism in relation to heavy losses of life and territory, the bravery, resistance and sacrifices made by patriotic civilians, and Allied cooperation under fire. In addition, any young woman fighting for her country against apparently hopeless odds raised the ever-present spectre of Joan of Arc, the ultimate French heroine. Moreau's gender was thus a vital factor in the communication of the different levels of meaning with which her image was charged. While journalists and popular writers focused on quasi-military qualities of courage and coolness under fire, her underlying 'feminine' vulnerability and maternal instincts were equally emphasized. Writers were swift to justify, moreover, her taking up of arms as a defence of the innocent in the face of a 'barbaric' enemy who preyed on civilians or wounded soldiers. Take the following two examples: the first is from a popular published account of the war by Scottish journalist Donald A. Mackenzie:

> She seemed a born nurse, and her gentle words and sweet smile were like a tonic to the stricken soldiers. [...] Through a shattered window in Emilienne's home she had seen a German soldier bayoneting a wounded Highlander in the street. 'They are killing the wounded', she cried. [...] Emilienne remained fearless and composed. For her own safety she took no thought. Her sole concern was for the wounded men under her care.[20]

The second example comes from the French journal *L'Illustration*:

> There was blood everywhere. At her feet, the wounded were moaning. She could see from their striking outfits that they were the famous Highlanders that the Germans so feared. One by one, she picked them up. She wasn't strong, but her will fortified her muscles. She helped some to have a drink and bandaged others. She put them to bed as best she could, and the English surgeons found her leaning over the brave men, many of whose lives she had saved. At the entrance of the village, a song could be heard, sung out by thousands of lungs. It was 'God Save the King'. Mlle Moreau waited. When the national anthem was finished, she sang the Marseillaise at the top of her voice![21]

These two accounts reveal differences between British and French accounts of Moreau's actions. While in Mackenzie's narrative a traditional version of femininity is foregrounded, featuring her as a self-abnegating nurse in the face of German barbarity, in *L'Illustration* it is her patriotism that takes centre stage, endowing her with superhuman strength and will-power, and thereby suggesting that both mobilized and civilian French citizens were admirable friends-in-arms to Britain in the Allied defence of French territory.

However, the contradictions apparent in the construction of a heroine who combined innocent civilian war victim with brave patriotic 'soldier' were not lost on the German press. The German magazine *Des deutschen Volkes Kriegstagebuch* reproduced the French press photograph of Moreau with the caption 'The so-called "Heroine of Loos" who is being celebrated in the English and French press because she murdered five German soldiers in the Battle of Loos', strategically placed next to an article stressing the German nation's desire for peace.[22] Just as Edith Cavell's guilt was emphasized by the German press, so Moreau is presented here as a *franc-tireur* breaking the rules of warfare rather than a brave defender of humanity in the face of barbarism. Indeed, Moreau referred in her memoirs to German hostility in relation to Allied celebrations of her actions, stating that her Croix de guerre ceremony

> was supposed to take place in the Place des Invalides in Paris, but the Germans, who had put a price on my head, had made it known via the King of Spain, Alphonse XIII, [...] that if I was decorated in the Invalides, any civilian captured by their troops would be considered to be a *franc-tireur* and shot. They couldn't stand the fact that military honours were being given, not only to a civilian, but to a woman who had shot German soldiers.[23]

Writing about her experiences many years later, Moreau distanced herself as adult narrator from her former self, whom she presented as a naive young girl, and emphasized a lack of agency not only in her acts of heroism, but in the construction of her public persona by the French and British authorities and media. But she also noted that she gained new experiences and a new perspective from her unexpected notoriety:

> I lived at that time in a kind of whirlwind. Imagine a young girl from the Pas-de-Calais, having always lived quietly, in a peaceful little village, suddenly exposed to everyone's gaze, received and congratulated by bemedalled generals and officials wearing cocked hats, in public squares and golden *salons*... Think, too, that for hours, for whole days, I had to curtsey, smile, answer questions, thank people, make speeches, and congratulate other combatants who were just as intimidated as I was. So, the young girl improvised, tried to always remain calm and simple, opened

her eyes and ears in order to learn from the behaviour of others in such a new world... Slowly, I got used to my role, for I had a role to play. I didn't think for a minute of fleeing, because I knew that my example served to raise soldiers' morale.[24]

Although she presented her past self as overwhelmed by her sudden celebrity, in her later life it was clear that Moreau made use of her prestigious status for both personal and political reasons. Firstly, as she recounted, her wartime role boosted her economic as well as her cultural capital: 'The money from the *Petit Parisien* allowed us to survive. The newspaper also paid for my lessons in an institution in the boulevard Saint-Germain. I did well in my elementary and then advanced qualifications. My dream had finally been realized: I was going to be a teacher!'[25]

In addition to these financial gains that brought about a degree of social mobility, the resonance of her First World War role came particularly into play when the Second World War broke out. Although she had settled into civilian life after 1918, she seems to have been more than willing to take up her symbolic role once again when circumstances changed. For instance, a newspaper report reveals that in March 1940 she attended a football match between British soldiers and a local team from Lens as guest of honour, proudly wearing 'the French and British decorations conferred on her during the last war', and thus revivifying her role as symbol of Franco-British entente.[26]

Having married socialist activist Just Evrard in 1932, the whole family became involved in Resistance work during the occupation, and in 1941 Evrard was arrested and imprisoned. Moreau related in her autobiography that when her house was searched by German soldiers in 1942, they demanded to see her war medals, and when she produced them, 'the officer examined them in a serious manner and then shouted an order to his soldiers "Present arms". I would have willingly gone without this kind of display, but, after all, it was a fine gesture.'[27] She therefore used her past quasi-military status in order to elevate herself above other civilians, implying that the German soldiers treated her with respect because they recognized her as a war heroine. She went on to make further use of her First World War role to help her in her quest to make political gains for the Second World War Resistance movement. In particular, she hoped that her heroine status would add weight to her role as the representative of one of the Resistance networks when she escaped to England in 1944 to seek further support from the British government, and in preparation went to a French police station to get a document certifying the validity of her medals. A 1944 *Times* article reporting her arrival in England overtly linked her First and Second World War roles, using the former to bolster her claims to authenticity and authority in her testimony of conditions in occupied France. The article reminded readers that 'During the battle of Loos in

September 1915, Mme Moreau saved the lives of many English soldiers. [...] She is now a delegate of the Resistance movement to the French collective assembly'. It then quoted her as stating, 'The Germans are no different from what they were in 1914' while reporting that they had carried out summary executions of members of the Resistance movement.[28]

More generally, her autobiographical descriptions of the Occupation openly recalled her First World War experiences, and she adopted the same persona of instinctively patriotic, simple, adaptable, and selfless heroine. Thus Moreau maintained and, at least to some extent, exploited her notoriety in her later life. Moreau's entry into political life was aided not only by her marriage to Just Evrard, but equally by her ability to draw on her status as both First and Second World War heroine. She became General Secretary of the Women's Section of the Socialist Party in the Pas de Calais region in 1934, was one of only six women to be made a Compagnon de la Libération in 1945, and was a member of the Steering Committee of the Socialist Party from 1945 to 1963, as well as being president of a powerful regional veterans' association.[29]

Figure 7.2   Poster, 'L'héroïne de Loos'
Source: © Imperial War Museums IWM PST 6806.

In France, women's resistance activities in the First World War were over-shadowed by the higher profile activities of Second World War resisters. In the 1960s and 1970s, the era in which Moreau published her family memoir, it was proof of Resistance heroism in 1940–44 that was an entry-ticket into public acclaim and, potentially, political power. It is therefore unsurprising that the cover of her autobiography describes her as 'Emilienne Moreau, Compagnon de la Libération' and features a photograph of her meeting General de Gaulle. But the cover also features the famous First World War photograph of her as a 17-year-old wearing mourning clothes that *Le Petit Parisien* had distributed (see Figure 7.2), suggesting that her contribution as a Resistant had not completely effaced her previous identity. Ultimately, it is clear that for many French people she remained a living symbol of resistance in relation to both world wars.[30]

Elsie Knocker and Mairi Chisholm: the 'Heroines of Pervyse'

Another woman who attempted, although less successfully, to instrumentalize her heroine/veteran status by publishing her memoirs in the post-war years was Elsie Knocker, who, along with Mairi Chisholm, was celebrated during the war as a 'Heroine of Pervyse'. Their story is relatively well known, having been rediscovered by the press at the time of a well-attended 1977 'Women at War 1914–18' exhibition at the London Imperial War Museum.[31] In addition, more recently they have been the subjects of a well-researched biography, Diane Atkinson's *Elsie & Mairi Go to War*, that was adapted for a performance at the 2010 Edinburgh Fringe festival, and a historical novel by Jean-Pierre Isbouts, *Angels in Flanders*.[32] In 1914, having met previously because of their shared interest in motorcycling, 29-year-old divorcee Knocker and 18-year-old Chisholm went to the front in Belgium as members of Dr Hector Munro's Flying Ambulance Corps. Munro was a suffragist who was keen to recruit women to prove their worth in a situation of war, although he had little official support and, according to Chisholm, was 'looked upon as a total crank' in Belgium.[33] With the permission of the Belgian authorities they set up, funded, and ran a first-aid post (Knocker was a trained nurse) near to the front lines. Like Moreau, they were awarded medals in a high-profile public ceremony, and only left Belgium after being gassed in 1918.

From the very beginning, their exploits were highly publicized in the French and British press – Mairi Chisholm's diary mentions meeting two journalists and a photographer as early as September and October 1914[34] – who constructed them as heroines. Ellis Ashmead-Bartlett, one of the journalists referenced in Chisholm's diary, who was reporting for the *Daily Telegraph*, wrote in October 1914 that: 'Their names […] should certainly enjoy an immortality associated with the greatest heroines of history' and argued that Dr Munro's Flying Ambulance Corps was 'the most remark-able and useful organization I have ever seen in any campaign'.[35] Their quasi-military virtues of bravery and risk-taking were noted, especially in the British press with headlines such as 'Thrilling adventures with the Belgium Army',[36] but reporters were quick to situate them in relation to more traditional understandings of feminine virtue. They were labelled, for example, 'ministering angels' and 'the Madonnas of Pervyse' by British and French newspapers respectively.[37] More than Emilienne Moreau, though, Elsie Knocker and Mairi Chisholm exploited and to some extent controlled the mediatization of their heroism during the war. They constantly needed funds to keep their first-aid post and ambulances going, and interrupted their nursing work to go on fund-raising lecture tours in Britain. In an interview given in 1977, Chisholm comments on the importance of the press coverage in their fundraising efforts:

> We were tremendously publicized over here you know. You know yourself what the press is. If they get hold of something which they think is very unusual they go to town on it and of course, this was wonderful. Then we both appeared at the Alhambra theatre, which was a very big theatre in Leicester Square, and all the most famous actors and actresses of the day gave their services for us and we had a terrific reception there. It was packed from floor to ceiling and we raised two thousand pounds that afternoon.[38]

In these public appearances, Knocker and Chisholm tended to be introduced and praised according to pre-existing cultural models of female heroism. One report of a public lecture given in Nairn Public Hall (near to Chisholm's family home in Scotland) on 2 May 1916 describes them as 'veritable heroines', suggesting that while Florence Nightingale 'would ever be remembered by the name of the "Lady of the Lamp"', the heroines of Pervyse would 'hereafter be known as the "Ladies of the Ambulance" [applause]'.[39] In contrast, in later writings and interviews, both women are swift to emphasize their lack of conformity to traditional models of femininity. While Mairi Chisholm commented that she felt she was 'a disappointment to my Mother because I wasn't in the least interested in clothes or anything like that. Mechanics interested me enormously', Elsie Knocker scorns those who doubted their ability as women to work close to the front line, recalling the following episode in her memoirs:

> The Red Cross driver [...] flatly refused to take me, adding that it would be bad enough without any women around, since all women panicked at a crisis. Three years later I ran into that driver in Boulogne. He came up to me and said 'I want to apologize, Sister. I have been in comparative safety for the last three years, while you have been up in the front-line trenches'.[40]

However, during the war both Chisholm and Knocker were happy to exploit the feminized 'Florence Nightingale' image for fund-raising purposes, posing for example for photographs in this mode. Like Moreau, a romanticized account of their adventures that they collaborated on, entitled *The Cellar House at Pervyse* (1916), was sold to publicize their cause. The introductory note by author Geraldine Mitton states:

> Of all the things told of the Great War surely this is the most uncommon, that two women should have been at the front with the Belgian Army almost from the beginning. That they should have lived as the soldiers lived, caring for them, tending them, taking cocoa and soup into the trenches and even to the outposts. And this is what has been done by the two British ladies whose names are on the title-page.[41]

The royalties from the book bought a new motorbike ambulance and, more than this, set them up as two of the most high-profile heroines of the war, combining the roles of maternal nurses, mothering 'poor little Belgium', and plucky British lady-soldiers in the public imagination. Their diaries attest to the fact, however, that there was stiff competition for the status of war heroine, even amongst their close colleagues and collaborators. There are hurt and angry entries concerning the jealousy amongst some of the other women they were working alongside when they were awarded medals by the King of Belgium. In addition, they were both furious when American journalist Arthur Gleason's popular account of the Flying Ambulance Corps, *Young Hilda at the Wars* (1915), set up his wife Helen, an original member of the Corps, in a leading role rather than Knocker and Chisholm. In Gleason's account 'Hilda' (Helen) took all the risks, and was responsible for setting up the dressing station at Pervyse, whereas 'Mrs Bracher' (Knocker) was presented as being reluctant: '"Pervyse?", cried Mrs Bracher. "Why, my dear girl, Pervyse is nothing but a rubbish heap. They've shot it to pieces. There's no one at Pervyse." "The soldiers are there", replied Hilda.'[42] Chisholm angrily wrote in her diary after reading Gleason's version:

> I can't understand what he can possibly have been thinking when he wrote it. If only he hadn't mentioned Pervyse by name, & put in Helen's portrait the thing would have been alright. [...] It is the most astounding bit of brazen cheek that has been published for many a long day. [...] Helen, knowing how hurt Gipsy [Knocker] was when Dorothie [Lady Dorothie Feilding] was given the Kudos of Pervyse & how hurt she was re our decorations ought to have been just double careful that nothing further should happen which might aggravate the old wound.[43]

Despite Mitton's declaration in the *Cellar House of Pervyse* that 'the Two had always hated publicity', then, both Knocker and Chisholm jealously guarded their public personae, keenly aware of the potential economic, social, and cultural capital afforded by their mediatization as heroines.[44] Knocker, in particular, was keen to differentiate her work from other wealthy civilians who had travelled to the front, describing the latter in her diary as the 'elderly sightseers on our ambulance column [...]. They are a nuisance & I am not surprised Kitchener gets fed up with women at the front'.[45]

After the war, Elsie Knocker, abandoned by her Belgian aristocratic husband after he discovered she was divorced, struggled to carve out a place for herself in the post-war world: 'The "Heroine of Pervyse" the Press called me, but ten years later it was a different story.'[46] Like many male-authored war memoirs, her autobiography is full of nostalgia for 'the sense of sharing, of comradeship and identification, the hatred of the muddle and waste of war, and then, hard on its heels, the sharp gratitude for being there in the middle of it all to make a tiny corner of sanity [...] Pervyse stood, and stands, for all that is best and most satisfying in my life.'[47] She briefly worked for the newly formed Women's Royal Air Force in 1918 'while the dew of my Pervyse fame was still fresh upon me',[48] but this was soon disbanded. She then embarked on a series of failed projects all involved with helping war veterans, thereby not only exploiting her wartime notoriety but also responding to a psychological need to reaffirm her own sense of her identity as a veteran. Her first successful opportunity to reprise her wartime role came during another national crisis, the 1926 General Strike, when she set up another first-aid post, flying the same Red Cross flag that she had flown at Pervyse, in the working-class Poplar district of London.[49] Like Moreau's descriptions of the Second World War, in her account Knocker deliberately recreated her First World War identity, emphasizing her adaptability and skills in a crisis, and effectively recreating Pervyse in London's East End:

> I went to the British Red Cross and told Eden Paget that work was badly needed in the East End [...] I was given a very dirty, old butchers shop, in Poplar High Street, and settled down to scrub and clean. The crowd were not friendly at all, and big Armoured cars and tanks passed the shop. [...] I flatly refused to move, I said that I had come to do a definite job, and I would do it. [I asked] to bring down two men whom I had known in World War I, and would stay the course.[50]

In the late 1920s, Knocker's veteran status did bring her some economic rewards. The Red Cross offered her a small cottage on the Earl Haig estate in Ashtead, Surrey, that had been created for ex-servicemen. She named it 'Pervyse' and remained there until the final years of her life. She worked for the 'Lest We Forget' organization in the interwar years, giving talks about her war years and helping to fundraise. The Second World War offered her a brief opportunity to shine, and she enjoyed her time as an officer of the Women's Auxiliary Air Force (WAAF). But she was sometimes treated with suspicion by the younger women, and admitted to anxieties that she 'might be considered suspect as an old fogey who lived in a First World War past'.[51] In an interview given in 1977, she remained bitter about the gap between her heroine status during the war and her social status afterwards, claiming that Alexander of Teck, whom she had known during the war, 'would have a fit if he knew the circumstances I am living in now poor darling [...] I can't be a lady in this'.[52]

In contrast, Mairi Chisholm, who came from a more stable and wealthy family, chose not to marry and set up a successful business venture as a poultry breeder. She did not publish war memoirs, but in the 1970s she produced a written account in response to what she described as Knocker's 'racy account of our work in the 1914–1918 War' in order to 'stress the actual facts'. In her description of her war experience, she stressed the bravery and comradeship of the Belgian soldiers: 'Three and a half years of packed incidents; of being privileged to work in danger alongside brave men, and to recognize their immense decency to women in exceptional circumstances.' In this sense, she depicted herself as a war veteran. Yet she also differentiated herself from Knocker, stating that '[u]nlike [the Baroness] I have found much happiness and sense of purpose in peace time. I have been blessed with friendships of both men and women, and although my health has not always been good it has never justified self pity.'[53]

Conclusion

To conclude, ultimately, in contrast to Emilienne Moreau and Mairi Chisholm, Knocker never rediscovered either public acclaim or personal satisfaction in the aftermath of the First World War, and her memoirs express a sense of yearning for the war years, despite their hardships. She implied in her autobiography this was partly for reasons of social class: 'It is always such a pleasure and a privilege when one is shoved through or under or over the class barrier. It's so miserable and anti-climactic when one has to creep back to one's own "station" in life.'[54] Yet what had really changed, and what differentiated Britain and France, was that the greater professionalization and centralization of British women's war work in the Second World War, unlike the informal clandestine Resistance networks that developed in France, allowed less space for individual heroics by women like Elsie Knocker. Women had become accepted as a vital part of the war effort, but this very acceptance meant that the exceptionality that defined the heroines of the Great War was no longer possible. While the high status of French Resistance heroines at the end of the Second World War meant that Emilienne Moreau's social capital only increased, Knocker continued to find peacetime existence an economic struggle, and psychologically unsatisfying. She constructed her autobiography around her First World War activities, nostalgic for a time in which women could join 'schemes, some official, but many, in those far-off untotalitarian days, splendidly freelance'.[55]

Knocker's inability to find a role in the post-war years is matched by other women who blurred the lines between combatant and non-combatant on the front lines during the First World War. French female aviator Marie Marvingt, another war heroine, struggled to find a role in the services or in civilian air industry after the war.[56] The most famous 'she-soldier', Russian Maria Bochkareva, left for America after the Russian Revolution and published her memoirs after the war to some acclaim, but was executed by the Bolshevik regime when she returned to Russia in 1920.[57] British woman Flora Sandes, who enjoyed fame and support during the war working as a volunteer for the First Aid Nursing Yeomanry (FANY) and then fighting for the Serbian Army, faced hostility and criticism on her return.[58] In sum, while the prestige of the heroine-martyrs who had died during the war was assured, and could remain untarnished, it was more difficult for the heroines who survived to maintain their public image in the post-war years. The personal writings of women who had been active during the conflict share many of the characteristics of those of ex-servicemen, but very few women, even those who had enjoyed high public profiles during the conflict, were able to use their veteran status as a platform from which to enter public life in the interwar years. If during the war female heroines on the front line played a vital role in the propaganda messages the belligerent nations wished to communicate, after the war, in a pronatalist climate that encouraged women to return to the domestic sphere, their status as war veterans was generally less welcome.

Notes

1. While in this chapter I concentrate on specific case-studies, it is important to note that the First World War saw the emergence of new or reconfigured heroine 'types', which served as a vital backdrop to the way in which individual heroines were constructed by journalists, artists, and writers. On the British female munitions worker as heroine, see A. Woollacott (1994) *On Her Their Lives Depend: Munitions Workers in the Great War* (Berkeley, CA: University of California Press); D. Thom (1998) *Nice Girls and Rude Girls: Women Workers in World War I* (London: I. B. Tauris). On French nurse-heroines and Resistance heroines, see M. Darrow (2000) *French Women and the First World War: War Stories of the Home Front* (Oxford: Berg). On the influence of both Joan of Arc and Franco-Prussian models of female heroism in *fin-de-siècle* France, see M. H. Darrow (2008) 'In the Land of Joan of Arc: The Civic Education of Girls and the Prospect of War in France, 1871–1914', *French Historical Studies*, 31:2, pp. 263–91.
2. Darrow, *French Women and the First World War*, pp. 109–10.
3. On the representation of Mata Hari during and after the war, see T. M. Proctor (2009) *Female Intelligence: Women and Espionage in the First World War* (New York: New York University Press), ch. 6; Darrow, *French Women and the First World War*, ch. 8. See also C. Antier, M. Walle and O. Lahaie (2008) *Les Espionnes dans la grande guerre* (Rennes: Editions Ouest France).
4. I concur with Tammy Proctor in this context that broadly speaking, '[i]n a climate where "back to normalcy" was the fervent hope of many people in Europe,

honorable she-soldiers and daring women spies had no place'. Proctor, *Female Intelligence*, p. 121. However, this chapter argues that some of these women nevertheless succeeded in recasting their wartime heroism in ways that enabled them to access public acclaim in the interwar years.

5. For France, see J.-Y. Le Naour (2002) *Misères et tourments de la chair durant la Grande Guerre: Les mœurs sexuelles des Français 1914-1918* (Paris: Aubier); J.-M. Binot (2008) *Héroïnes de la Grande Guerre* (Paris: Fayard); Darrow, *French Women and the First World War*. For Britain, see C. M. Tylee (1990) *The Great War and Women's Consciousness: Images of Militarism and Womanhood in Women's Writings* (London: Routledge); S. Ouditt (1994) *Fighting Forces, Writing Women: Identity and Ideology in the First World War* (London: Routledge); J. S. K. Watson (2004) *Fighting Different Wars: Experience, Memory, and the First World War in Britain* (Cambridge: Cambridge University Press); J. Lee (2005) *War Girls: The First Aid Nursing Yeomanry in the Great War* (Manchester: Manchester University Press). On Knocker and Chisholm, see D. Atkinson (2009) *Elsie & Mairi Go to War: Two Extraordinary Women on the Western Front* (London: Arrow books). For a comparative study, see S. Grayzel (1999) *Women's Identities at War: Gender, Motherhood, and Politics in Britain and France during the First World War* (Chapel Hill, NC: University of North Carolina Press).

6. See the photograph of Cavell in civilian clothing at her trial, *Imperial War Museum* (IWM), Edith Cavell Collection, EC 4, C4677, reproduced in K. Pickles (2007) *Transnational Outrage: The Death and Commemoration of Edith Cavell* (Basingstoke: Palgrave Macmillan), p. 31.

7. Darrow, *French Women and the First World War*, pp. 278–9; Pickles, *Transnational Outrage*, pp. 44–5.

8. See Binot, *Héroïnes de la Grande Guerre*, pp. 233–47. A recently published biography of de Bettignies which could not be considered here is C. Antier (2003) *Louise de Bettignies: Espionne et Héroïne de la Grande Guerre* (Paris: Editions Tallandier).

9. Darrow, *French Women and the First World War*, p. 284.

10. H. d'Argoeuves (1956) *Louise de Bettignies* (Paris: La Colombe), pp. 270–1.

11. Binot, *Héroïnes de la Grande Guerre*, pp. 107–26. For a selection of press articles, see 'Dossier Emilienne Moreau', Bibliothèque Marguerite Durand, Paris.

12. E. Moreau (1970) *La guerre buissonnière* (Paris: Solar Editeur), p. 33. This and all subsequent translations are my own unless otherwise indicated.

13. In November 1915, Moreau was awarded the French Croix de Guerre and the Croix du Combattant. In 1916, Moreau was presented with the British Military Medal and the Cross of St John of Jerusalem by Lord Bertie, the British Ambassador in Paris. *British Journal of Nursing*, 5 August 1916, p. 111.

14. 'L'héroïne de Loos reçoit la Croix de guerre', *Le Petit Parisien*, 28 November 1915.

15. Moreau, *La guerre buissonnière*, p. 48.

16. Moreau, *La guerre buissonnière*, p. 49.

17. The *Panthéon de la guerre* was produced by several painters under the leadership of Pierre Carrier-Belleuse and Auguste-François Gorguet. The portraits of 5000 French and Allied heroes are placed on an enormous staircase, and are organized according to rank with generals and other civilian leaders occupying the base. While the vast majority are servicemen, there are several women included in their number. The roll call of French heroines includes the usual suspects of nurses, resistant nuns, and brave employees of the French postal service who defied the enemy advance. Names lauded by the press and decorated by the state, such as Emilienne Moreau, Edith Cavell, and Louise de Bettignies, all feature.

18. René Fonck (1894–1953), Charles Nungesser (1892–1927), and Georges Guynemer (1894–1917) were all famous First World War fighter pilots. In a static war of attrition with few opportunities for significant individual enterprise, it is unsurprising that pilots, with their 'score-sheets' of enemy hits, were amongst the most well known of First World War male military heroes.
19. Moreau, *La guerre buissonnière*, p. 49.
20. D. A. Mackenzie (1917) *From All the Fronts* (Glasgow: Blackie).
21. *L'Illustration*, 20 November 1915, p. 532.
22. *Des deutschen Volkes Kriegstagebuch*, 1915, p. 2009, available online at http://www.greatwardifferent.com/Great_War/Kriegstagebuch/Kriegstagebuch_10.htm. I would like to thank Paul Cooke for the translation of this article.
23. Moreau, *La guerre buissonnière*, p. 45.
24. Moreau, *La guerre buissonnière*, p. 46.
25. Moreau, *La guerre buissonnière*, p. 50.
26. *The Times*, 5 March 1940, p. 7.
27. Moreau, *La guerre buissonnière*, pp. 73–4.
28. *The Times*, 15 August 1944, p. 2.
29. See entry on Emilienne Moreau-Evrard in *Ordre de la Libération*, online at http://www.ordredelaliberation.fr/fr_compagnon/327.html.
30. For example, she has had a school named after her in Lens, and a square named after her in Aubervilliers.
31. An illustrated book accompanied the exhibition. A. Marwick (1977) *Women at War 1914–18* (London: Harper Collins).
32. See http://edinburghfestival.list.co.uk/event/10004151-elsie-and-mairi-go-to-war/; J.-P. Isbouts (2010) *Angels in Flanders: A Novel of World War I* (Santa Monica, CA: Pantheon Press).
33. M. Chisholm (1977) Recorded interview, Liddle Collection, Brotherton Library, University of Leeds, WO 015.
34. IWM, Miss M. M. Chisholm, Diary 1914, 11600 01/42/1.
35. *Daily Telegraph*, 26 October 1914.
36. *The War Budget*, 4 January 1917.
37. 'Les deux madones de Pervyse', *Le Matin*, 17 August 1917.
38. Chisholm, Recorded interview.
39. IWM, Baroness de T'Serclaes, Folder of Press Cuttings, 9029-2 P404.
40. Chisholm, Recorded interview; E. de T'Serclaes (1964) *Flanders and Other Fields* (London: Harrap), p. 50.
41. G. Mitton (2011) [1916] *The Cellar House at Pervyse: A Tale of Uncommon Things* (Milton Keynes: Oakpast), p. 9.
42. A. Gleason (1915) *Young Hilda* (New York: Frederick A. Stokes), pp. 7–11.
43. IWM, Miss M. M. Chisholm (1914), Diary, 11600 01/42/1.
44. Mitton, *The Cellar House at Pervyse*, p. 11.
45. IWM, Baroness de T'Serclaes, Diary, 9029-2 P404.
46. T'Serclaes, *Flanders and Other Fields*, p. 17. Baron T'Serclaes was a Nazi collaborator during the Second World War. See Atkinson, *Elsie & Mairi Go to War*.
47. T'Serclaes, *Flanders and Other Fields*, pp. 68 and 81.
48. T'Serclaes, *Flanders and Other Fields*, p. 104.
49. IWM, Baroness de T'Serclaes, 9029-2 P404; T'Serclaes (1964), pp. 115–30.
50. IWM, Baroness de T'Serclaes, Undated account of the 1926 General Strike, 9029-2 P404.
51. T'Serclaes, *Flanders and Other Fields*, p. 145.

52. Baroness de T'Serclaes (1977), Recorded interview, Liddle Collection, Brotherton Library, University of Leeds, WO 123.
53. IWM, Miss M. M. Chisholm (1975), Typescript, 11600 01/42/1.
54. T'Serclaes, *Flanders and Other Fields*, p. 130.
55. T'Serclaes, *Flanders and Other Fields*, p. 36.
56. R. Maggio and M. Cordier (1991) *Marie Marvingt: La Femme d'un siècle* (Sarreguemines: Pierron).
57. M. Bochkareva (1919) *Yashka: My Life As Peasant, Exile, and Soldier* (New York: Frederick A. Stokes).
58. A. Burgess (1963) *The Lovely Sergeant* (London: Heinemann).

8
The Baby in the Gas Mask: Motherhood, Wartime Technology, and the Gendered Division Between the Fronts During and After the First World War

Susan R. Grayzel

Introduction

In 1916, Marie Donnay published *La Parisienne et la Guerre* in order to pay tribute to the contributions of Parisian women to the war effort. Like many such efforts, this small pamphlet aimed to record and promote the accomplishments made by real French women and girls to war work. She called attention to the 'sublime' efforts of mothers who sacrificed their sons and to all women who helped France endure, even though they could not engage directly in military action on behalf of their beloved nation. In the same short text, Donnay also highlighted one of the war's new heroines, 13-year-old Denise Cartier, who asked those caring for her not to tell her mother that her injuries were serious, despite being gravely wounded by an aerial attack upon Paris in September 1914. Thus, in the early years of the war, Donnay witnessed a transformation in women's relationship to war and the toll exacted specifically upon them. Owing to military technology such as air power, women no longer experienced war merely through damage done to other bodies, through sacrificing their sons. As the example of young Denise Cartier illustrated, wartime technology now brought war home to injure the female population – women and children – directly, well beyond the battle lines.[1]

The innovation that Donnay observed is clearly visible when reading her work against the backdrop of pre-war feminist writings highlighting how women's relational experience of war might shape a particular feminine response. In 1911, feminist Olive Schreiner offered one of the most vivid pre-1914 depictions of the cost of war to women *as* women in her chapter on 'Women and War' in *Women and Labour*. Here she rearticulated the critique that she had made earlier against British intervention in the South African War and asserted that:

> women have in all ages produced at enormous cost, the *primal munition of war*, without which no other would exist. There is no battlefield on earth nor ever has been howsoever covered with slain, which it has not cost the women of the race more in actual bloodshed and anguish to supply, than it has cost the men who lie there. We pay the first cost on all human life.[2]

Moreover, for Schreiner such beliefs were not limited to 'actual' mothers. She continued: 'there is, perhaps, no woman, whether she have borne children, or be merely potentially a child-bearer' who can look at a battlefield strewn with dead and not think 'so many mother's sons'.[3] More significant for the analysis here is Schreiner's equation of 'munition' with flesh, and particularly with the bodies of soldiers. If both men and women bear the cost of war, for Schreiner women bear the greater one. Moreover, the battle zone as she imagines it here is still laden with male combatant and not injured female non-combatant bodies such as that of Denise Cartier.

This particular type of bodily-rooted feminist analysis of war – one emerging from the real and imagined maternal body – remained a potent force in feminist writing and activism both for and against the First World War during its conduct. This was perhaps more evident in feminist anti-militarist writing that emphatically associated male bodies re/produced by women as being war's main munition. For instance, Britain's Frances Hallowes asserted in 1915 that only women can truly value life and protest its being squandered because human beings (soldiers) exist solely through embodied maternal suffering. Thus, for Hallowes: 'Militarism – a masculine invention, holds a man's body [only] as so much hostile stuff to be put into use [...]... Thus the full tragedy of war can only be grasped by those who can imagine the silent agony of the millions of mothers weeping in secret for their sons who were, and are not.'[4]

If 'women' in these accounts have a deep and innate appreciation of the horrors of war, it remains relational – filtered through the damage done to beloved bodies, but not their own. Of course, the figure of the bereaved or potentially bereaved mother could also serve to buttress claims to patriotic self-sacrifice by women, and Donnay supported such attitudes when she praised French mothers who sacrificed their sons in war. As I have argued elsewhere, motherhood led to no *natural* politics.[5] Yet the status of women as mothers, all of whose children are now vulnerable to technologically enhanced warfare, underscores much of the post-First World War reactions to this transformation.

This chapter thus seeks to examine how women's framing of arguments about their relationship to the war-making state shifted due to the First World War's innovations in wartime technology, especially air power, which brought home life under fire. Technological advances in weaponry during the First World War expanded the modern battle zone and turned all homes into potential targets.[6] In so doing, they also altered the relationship – theoretical and actual – between women and war. One of the First World War's many legacies to the post-war world was its more widespread use of technology such as aeronautics and chemical weaponry, both of which were widely condemned as 'atrocities' at the time. While it was overshadowed by the overall carnage of the war years, the damage inflicted by using air power against civilian targets, which invariably included women and children, animated a range of wartime and post-war responses. In particular, they prompted a number of important reflections on the changed wartime status of the mother and child, who could now become direct victims of modern war waged seemingly without geographic limits. Aerial warfare against civilians made it impossible to sustain the illusion that the home front and war front existed in entirely separate realms. It literally placed the home and its inhabitants on the front line.

Extrapolating from the experience of air raids and chemical attacks during the First World War, interwar peace campaigners and government war planners alike assumed that the next war could produce a conflict in which the aerial deployment of chemical weapons would lead to mass civilian casualties. Furthermore, this would be a war that would not discriminate: women and children, the elderly and infants would be as vulnerable to attack as any man serving in the military. Preparing the 'home front' for its new front-line status or protesting vigorously against this prospect preoccupied a range of interwar figures from politicians to journalists to activists. As this chapter's title – 'the baby in the gas mask' – suggests, the sense of innocence under attack became a particularly crucial aspect of these debates. The wartime presence, and renewed post-war prospect, of civilian anti-gas protection for children, and for infants in particular, became a shorthand for the extent to which the state was willing to protect the home/land. At the same time, evocations of the baby in the gas mask became a vital emblem of anti-militarist fears of possibly the *very* worst thing that the First World War had bequeathed to the post-war world.

This study thus begins to explore the transformation of conventional gendered notions of warfare during and after the First World War. After engaging with some of the representations of air power and chemical war against feminized civilians during the First World War, this chapter then investigates some of the strategies and devices developed to protect the so-called home front via measures to prepare a civil population to face aero-chemical warfare. It pays especial attention to the vigorous and multifaceted feminist pacifist response to such measures. Looking particularly at the victorious and democratic states of Britain and France, it assesses the role that new forms of state-sanctioned violence in the First World War played in reshaping gendered assumptions about the home front/front-line divide.

Making the home the front line

The First World War was hardly the first conflict to put civilians under fire. In concrete and abstract ways, European-based and colonial wars of the nineteenth century had caused civilian casualties and disrupted home life. The brutality of colonial warfare, for instance the South African War's abuses that had inspired Schreiner, was not invisible to all European eyes, despite the efforts of participant governments to conceal the mistreatment of civilian populations during the conflict. What was new about the First World War's technology of air power and chemical weapons was the expansion of the potential range and terror accompanying modern warfare.[7]

During the First World War, air raids occurred as early as 1914 as seen in the attacks that injured Denise Cartier that autumn.[8] They continued on and off for the duration of the war, with both Britain and France suffering casualties in their capital cities. While such warfare was restricted by the limits of technology, the prospect of innocent lives under attack soon came to public attention. Discussions of attacks upon civilian targets unleashed during the First World War thus underscored their depravity by showing damage done, particularly to innocents and to 'womenandchildren'.[9]

This can be seen throughout wartime media in the countries subjected to such attacks. An article in Britain's *The Daily Chronicle* in September 1915, under the heading 'The Air Assassins', spoke of the 'senseless and criminal Zeppelin raids' of that month that had 'the usual result that a number of innocent non-combatants have been murdered in their sleep by the Kaiser's emissaries'.[10] As aerial attacks continued on both sides of the Channel, condemnation of the enemy could take visual form. A February 1916 front-page engraving by José Simont appearing in France's weekly *L'Illustration* depicted the prostate bodies of women and children in the foreground with the shadowed images of the ruins of a great city behind them. Highlighting the implicit point of the image, the text below is meant to read as purely ironic; this is how 'their heroes of the air' have attacked the 'fortress Paris'. The airmen killing these ethereal, helpless victims can never be heroes, and the 'fortress' of Paris consists of homes and families, not military fortifications.[11]

How were women now under threat from air power meant to respond to their new engagement in war? Two revealing letters appearing in the same week in *The Times* demonstrate both the potency of the public role of mothers during wartime and that maternity could form the basis for opposite opinions of the new warfare. On 16 June 1917, a letter from 'Bereaved' ('the mother of a beloved son who recently gave his life for his country') insisted that in this 'war of nation against nation – no longer only army against army', the government should use every means possible to respond to air power in kind. This grieving mother's reaction to the loss of life from air raids was to suggest: 'Let us retaliate on their people and cities.' A few days later on 18 June, 'A Mother' (who has 'given two sons to the war') protested that if 'I should live to see Englishmen sent to murder in cold blood German women and children and harmless civilians then indeed I should begin to ask: "Have my sons died in vain?"'[12] What underlies the appeal of both of these mothers, akin to Schreiner's pre-war stance, is an association between women and war that remains relational. It is by having sacrificed their sons that these women can claim a voice to speak on what will happen to them and to other women (and children) during war. The more that women and children faced air power, the more this rhetoric might have to shift.

Along with air power, the unleashing of chemical gas attacks prompted visible reactions to the war's new technology. Germany introduced the more widespread lethal use of poison gas in April 1915, although both sides would come to employ chemical agents. Most striking, perhaps, was the appearance of, first, soldiers and then also civilians, for example in northern France, wearing gas masks. That these masks were worthy of public attention can be seen in a variety of French media. In January of 1916, *L'Illustration* published a series of photographs from regions most directly under threat from new forms of warfare. In an array of striking images, young school children were shown in gas masks, both as individuals and then in a group portrait with their schoolteacher.[13] Such visuals underscored a genuinely *new* horror unleashed by this war; they offered audiences a glimpse of the potential new 'reality' of warfare: no one was safe. Neither age nor gender rendered these figures immune to the horrors of chemical warfare. Furthermore, these distorting, dehumanizing masks revealed the inability of the state to keep the nation's children, literally its patrimony, out of danger.

Even more hauntingly, they appear in a photograph from the commercial photographic agency, Agence Rol, which shows a mother and child in masks in the 'pays bombardé' [bombed country].[14] The jarring juxtaposition in this photograph between the domestic and rustic interior – an iron pot hangs in the fireplace, the child is perched on the mother's lap – and the masks that obscure *all* human features are startling. The viewer can tell nothing about this mother and child, but the image is viscerally disturbing. All such representations depict damage to a literal as well as deeply gendered home front. In this image, the humanity of these potential civilian victims itself disappears; a more frightening *pietà* is hard to imagine.

Some in the United Kingdom, despite the absence of chemical attacks on British soil, played on fears of potentially even more destructive aerial warfare. By early June 1916, the Hospitals and General Contracts Company was advertising a new respirator offering protection against 'asphyxiating gases', under the heading 'Be Prepared for Zeppelin Bombs'.[15] More significantly, this same company mailed a circular to women (the covering letter is addressed, 'dear Madam') that begins with the question:

Having long since disregarded the common Laws of Humanity, will the Germans hesitate to use asphyxiating gases in their premeditated raids on

London? [...] If they abuse the teachings of science, why, let us show them that we are prepared to meet their dastardly attacks in an **Organized and Scientific** way by using a simple but efficient appliance, in effect, a mask that will protect the respiratory organs and eyes against chlorine.[16]

The explicit intention of the advertisement was to sell its product to the woman of the home, as the covering letter reminds her 'an effective mask will save a life, and prevent intense agony', but the entire enterprise does so by underscoring the wartime risk that she and her family might now face directly.

It is unclear how many people received such appeals or took them seriously. However, in a 1916 cartoon depicting a mother and daughter choosing gas masks between one that is 'serviceable' and the other that is 'more becoming', the pre-eminent British humour magazine *Punch* both made light of the marketing of gas masks to civilians, and expressed some of the outrage about the use of chemical weapons. While both masks depicted in the cartoon were potentially ridiculous in appearance, and the idea of asking a mother to choose a device to protect oneself against chemical warfare based on its attractiveness was nonsensical, the cowering daughter reminded the viewer of the less comical aspects of what is under consideration. The choice was seemingly about the type of protection, but the prospect of women and children needing to safeguard themselves from a weapon of such horror was no joke.[17] Moreover, despite the lack of chemical attacks directed at civilian populations, fears that chemical weapons would be launched from the air and used against non-combatants during the Great War did not diminish. In 1917, New Scotland Yard was called to investigate the death of ten-week-old Lillian Alice Trower, whose demise was deemed by the jury at her inquest to have been 'caused by irritant gases caused by bombs dropped from enemy aircraft at Shoreditch during the night of 1 October 1917'.[18] After further inquiry, the Yard concluded that she probably suffocated from breathing air contaminated by leaks from the gas mains during the raid – thus an indirect victim of air power but not chemical warfare as such.[19] Still, given that infants such as this *were* being killed in London by air raids during the war and the repeated use of images of such 'innocent' victims, the legacy of such cases remained in the post-war imperative: how could states protect civilian life in wars to come?[20]

By the end of the First World War, the governments of Britain and France had recognized that the technology by which to wage war against civilians was not going anywhere. They felt that they had no choice but to base planning for a potential future war on the assumption that the war to come would be a war of air power being used to disperse chemical weapons on villages, towns, and cities. As a result, a range of post-war responses, particularly by feminists, translated the abstract danger of war into the *precise* dangers that aerial and chemical warfare posed directly to women and children.

The baby in the gas mask

The terror induced by aerial and chemical warfare had a profound effect on the interwar era. Not only did air power powerfully erode the alleged borders between home and war front, combatant and non-combatant, but in addition, genuinely new threats to homes, to civilians, to women and children far beyond conventional battlefields altered how some interwar proponents of peace and disarmament delivered their message. Despite the international efforts of many advocates in the interwar era to prohibit the use of certain types of weaponry from being used in a future war, the interwar period was filled with writings cautioning that the next war would be one of unprecedented destructiveness. Discussions of the combination of air power and chemical warfare appeared in both public and private texts that cut across lines of gender, class, and political affiliation as well as geography. The particular ways in which the legacy of aerial (and chemical) warfare unfolded in the interwar decades transformed an anti-war message predicated on appealing to women by emphasizing the sacrifice of their sons, into one about the burning and asphyxiation of babes in their mothers' arms, finding especial resonance in startling and evocative images of the mother and child in gas masks.

The post-war era saw the mother and child at home become the quintessential civilian victims of a future war. For instance, the specific legacy of the last war and the imagined horrors of the next war motivated the women who joined activist enterprises of the Women's International League (later for Peace and Freedom), the organization founded out of a gathering of women in The Hague in 1915 to urge an end to the war. At that meeting, women gathered as 'outsiders', barred from participating in the decision-making processes that had led to war. As Jane Addams, the American activist who would become the first head of this new organization, put it in 1915, while different views towards war could be found among women:

> [Q]uite as an artist in an artillery corps commanded to fire upon a beautiful building [...] would be deterred by a compunction unknown to the man who had never given himself to creating beauty and did not know the intimate cost of it, so women, who have brought men into the world and nurtured them until they reach the age for fighting, must experience a peculiar revulsion when they see them destroyed, irrespective of the country in which these men may have been born.[21]

At the moment of the founding of an international body to lobby against war on behalf of all women, the leading figure described the bond tying women together as based on the 'peculiar revulsion' of mothers who, having brought 'men into the world', know something unique about their loss. Such maternity-based anti-war politics did not necessarily diminish, although they did change, in the interwar era.

By May of 1929, when the Women's International League for Peace and Freedom (WILPF) sponsored a conference in Frankfurt on 'modern methods of warfare and the protection of civil populations', it was clear their purview had expanded.[22] The findings of the conference appeared in print soon after, circulating ideas expressed in papers on chemical weapons, poison gas, and the transformation of modern war. While the main goal of these proceedings was to promote disarmament, individual participants consistently called attention to the stakes of future wars. They emphasized that the next war would expose masses of civilians, including women and their children, to the peculiar dangers of the last war: '[T]he worst of the past gives little idea of what would be the horrible reality of a future war', during which 'the civil population [...] will be massacred by gas bombs from thousands of aeroplanes, and peace will only be concluded over the dead bodies of the enemy nation. In comparison even Dante's hell pales into insignificance.'[23]

As we have seen, the possible defence against such attacks – the gas mask – had already been displayed on emblems of innocence during the war, such as the school children in Northern France featured in *L'Illustration*.[24] However, the expert on 'collective and individual protection' from chemical weapons, Dr Nestler, explained that since his time on the German side of the Western Front: 'Gas warfare has been completely transformed in both theory and practice.'[25] Moreover, he noted that there was an especial danger if protection were thought of as an 'individual' problem to be solved with a gas mask. Nestler not only suggested that the costs involved in developing suitable gas masks were exorbitant – a point echoed in the scientific and medical communities – but also emphasized that additional psychological barriers to their effectiveness were also nearly insurmountable. As he elaborated:

> To wear a gas-mask requires extraordinary discipline; people put them on with teeth clenched. If discipline is difficult for trained soldiers, how much more so with civilians. A mother could not endure to hear her child crying under its mask. Women and children will certainly not be able to make full use of protective apparatus; every gas attack would cause a panic.[26]

This dire warning expressed a number of ongoing assumptions about the essential nature of motherhood, as it highlighted one of the obvious limits of any 'rational' form of protection. If despite the known dangers of the type of war to come, women and children could not utilize personalized protection for psychological reasons, there seemed no way for them to survive.

Such grim pronouncements based on assumed gender roles also served to inspire the intensity with which anti-militarists responded to concrete preparations for this new kind of war. By stating categorically 'that all protective measures against modern scientific methods of war were useless', conference speakers urged instead a new commitment to peace and disarmament. For the next war, as Gabrielle Duchêne of the French branch of WILPF asserted, '[was] no longer a question of the clash of mercenary armies or the struggle of young men under arms. [...] At the outbreak of war the civil populations, without distinction of age or sex, would be sucked into the whirlpool.'[27] As conference organizers, the leaders (as well as, one assumes, the members) of WILPF hoped that once they became aware of these grave dangers and, especially, of the uselessness of any government-sanctioned devices to alleviate them, the civilian populations would call upon their nations to halt the progress towards war.

Such a message of course ignored the abundant evidence that the First World War had already exposed 'civil populations' without 'distinction of age or sex' to these new methods of war, and it is precisely the exposure of women and children to this threat that campaigners utilized in garnering support for anti-militarist measures. Nor were they alone in blending two vivid horrors of the First World War – the deployment of chemical weapons and the aerial attacks on civilians. Government planners working on what would become 'civil defence' in Britain and 'défense passive' in France assumed that no one and no place would remain immune. Planners in both states spent the interwar period working on civil defence measures including developing gas masks for civilians of all ages, instructions on turning ordinary dwellings into shelters, complete in the United Kingdom with 'gas proof refuge rooms' and in France with 'abri ballons' or 'balloon shelters'.[28] Those concerned with developing these measures also worried explicitly about civilian morale, about psychology, about panic – especially by women and children. Yet anti-war activists jolted by the idea of a threatened aerochemical war needed to play upon fear, to channel panic into action for disarmament and peace.

Interwar pacifists (using the term very broadly), in their texts as well as images, had to negotiate a different balancing act than their governments. As the 1929 WILPF sponsored conference suggests, they argued that whatever measures states undertook to protect their civil populations, they would ultimately fall short. Those opposed to the idea of any future war because it would constitute a war of annihilation sought ways to convey this message vividly and unforgettably. One means of so doing was to represent this threat via one potent emblem of this danger: the baby in the gas mask.

As already discussed, representations of the mother and child and the gas mask had appeared during the war, but they emerged anew as interwar extra-governmental activists worked against the war to come. Many such activists saw the International Geneva Disarmament Conference (launched under the auspices of the League of Nations) that began in 1932 as providing a singular opportunity to demand the eradication of both aerial and chemical warfare. Strikingly, the French branch of the WILPF – the Ligue Internationale des Femmes pour la Paix et la Liberté (LIFPL) – attached the image of a mother and child in gas masks to their one-page leaflet. The sketch of a mother and baby in masks who appear to be fleeing an attack was meant to provoke the viewer into signing the following statement: 'I refuse to give my government the right to prepare itself and to prepare me for a war of poison, that is to say of universal assassination.'[29] The brief appeal asked citizens to refuse to participate in any drills that might prepare them for a gas war, since this could have only one result, namely the 'reciprocal extermination of peoples'. This exact same image of a terrified mother and child in masks was also reproduced in subsequent printed documents such as a one-page leaflet from the Comité d'action pour le Désarmement total et universel (Committee of Action for Total and Universal Disarmament) asking 'if we will accept this?'. Presumably, the idea of seeing women and children in gas masks was what the audience could not bear.[30]

Many in the interwar scientific community supported such appeals. Scientists on both sides of the Channel condemned not only the idea of aerial chemical war but also any efforts that governments undertook that claimed that they could protect civilians, including the provision of gas masks. Publications from the early 1930s delivered this message with the imprimatur of expert voices. A pamphlet from the French Section of the International Association of Doctors against War, *Une Protection Efficace contre la Guerre Aéro-chimique est impossible* (An Effective Protection against Aero-Chemical War is Impossible), delineated its message succinctly in its title. The British-based Cambridge Scientists Anti-War Group's *The Protection of the Public from Aerial Attack* insisted that gas masks could not work and that there was no real protection, except the abolition of war.[31]

In non-fictional works directly addressing the threat posed by the next war such as the 1932 *La guerre aux civils* (The War against Civilians) and the longer and more detailed *La guerre que revient: Fraîche et Gazeuse* (The War that Returns: Fresh and Gaseous), French anti-militarist Victor Méric expounded upon the imminent dangers of the next war. This would be a war that would transform the lives of citizens through changes in the nature of warfare that made it impossible to distinguish between combatants and non-combatants any longer.[32] Again, Méric evoked the unnatural spectacle of an infant and mother under the heinous conditions of chemical warfare to illustrate the dangers of *not* working against the next war.

As Méric explained in *La guerre qui revient*, mobilization would be 'automatic' for everyone 'without distinction of age or sex'. Indeed, war would become a kind of 'general suicide of civilized peoples', killing the nation. No longer could those waging war separate 'combatants and non-combatants' and 'front' and 'home front' – a refrain he repeated, air raids removed such distinctions and attacked the 'heart' of the nation.[33] His vivid depiction of just what such a future war would entail focused on the devastation wrought upon the mother and child. At the cry of gas: 'women take their little ones and squeeze them to their chests, Where are the shelters and the masks? In a street stained with blood and gutted by fire, vague forms that run, crawling, slipping, collapsing. [...] At a window, a woman leaping over a balcony, jumping into the emptiness.'[34] Until finally: 'A woman, mad with terror, takes her baby and breaks his skull into pieces against a wall. The next day, cadavers in all the streets, the massacre of innocents.'[35] Tellingly, this scene of horror evolved in part because forms of protection seem to be absent; the first cry is 'where are the masks?'. Whether the subsequent tragedy of the scene occurred because the masks and shelters were missing or because they could do nothing was left unclear. What emerged vividly in this spectacle was the image of mothers killing their babies in the face of modern war. This was a potentiality that haunted the interwar popular imaginary.

Nor was such a possibility of the ultimate betrayal of motherhood – the mother driven mad by war who resorts to killing her child – restricted to the imagination of activists like Méric. Such a horror was not without precedent. During the First World War, at least one case of infanticide brought before the Central Criminal Court in England involved a mother who decapitated her child after being under bombardment. The case was dismissed because the mother was found to be suffering from 'air raid shock'.[36]

After the war, when pacifists used images of women and children suffering under attack at home as a kind of shorthand for the terrors of the next war, they were not alone in doing so. Given the failure of international efforts at disarmament, the launching into public life of civil defence measures under what the British called 'Air Raids Precautions' provoked a new urgency in works that sought to imagine and/or prevent the next war. Thus, British organizations ranging from the Union of Democratic Control in its pamphlet on *Poison Gas* to the popular front organization, the British Women's section of Women's World Committee against War and Fascism (WWCAWF), made use of images of domesticity and innocence under threat, personified by women and children, to mobilize action. The WWCAWF did this particularly forcefully on the cover of its 1935 pamphlet exposé *Behind the Gas Mask*, with a disturbing image of a line of babies being handed gas masks by the bloated figure of a capitalist wearing a top hat and brandishing a cigar (Figure 8.1).[37]

It is not surprising that a range of responses to the prospect of the next war appeared in Britain in 1935, as this was the moment when the British government issued its first publicity about Air Raids Precautions. Almost immediately it seemed, Simpson Stokes (pseudonym of Frank Fawcett) decided to engage directly with these issues in his *Air-Gods' Parade* (1935). The novel's frontispiece featured the image of a gas-masked mother and unmasked child beneath a mother and baby monkey. Only the human baby in this engraving does not look simian, and the caption for the entire image reads: 'Twentieth-Century Culture'. The drawing itself reveals the implicit critique of the 'twentieth century', in which culture had been so degraded that it required mothers to wear gas masks. Stokes clearly associated this loss with new forms

Figure 8.1   Cover of the British Section of Women's World Committee Against War and Fascism's (1935?) *Behind the Gas Mask: An Exposure of the Proposed Air Defence Measures* (London) (detail)

of warfare: '[T]hose who wish to read further into this product of twentieth-century culture and illuminating sidelight on what religion, ethics, forbearance, and philosophy have failed to accomplish' need only consult 'The Air Raids Precautions Handbook'.[38]

The new world produced by 'twentieth-century culture' is one where a mother might helplessly try to save her dying infant as it asphyxiates:

> The baby in the pram started to scream [...] and there was a certain note of pain in the screams that every mother knows and instinctively recognizes.

> The mother's heart suddenly contracted, as though an ice-cold hand had gripped it and was squeezing it tight.

By the time the mother is able to respond, 'the baby's body had broken out into sores and there were violent spasms of retching and coughing, followed by the vomiting of fearsome pieces of tissue, looking like blood-stained scraps of dirty rags'. But it was already too late, as 'half comprehending, half crazy', the mother herself unable to cure the 'tortured body' of her infant, succumbs to burning lips 'sticky with some running matter that dribbled from the corners of her mouth' and herself dies a tortuous death.[39]

Ambivalence about the use of the gas mask can be found in a range of interwar texts. The baby in the gas mask, as in this literary work from the late 1930s, becomes the essence of a critique of what society/culture had become. Once again, this is something we see revealed in interwar responses to the growing prospect of war to come. In September 1937, the poem 'Armed for War' appeared in the *London Mercury*. It began by asking: 'Is life on earth a viler thing/ Than ever was known before?'. And continues by pondering who is equipped to answer this question, turning to 'the Baby, three weeks old/ That wears a gas-proof mask/ [...] the Infant armed to meet/ A poisoned earth and sky – A thing too weak to lift its hand/ To rub a sleepy eye'.[40] In this text, the infant in a gas mask comes to epitomize the vileness of modern life in the late 1930s.

It may or may not strike us as ironic that while this poet was evoking the baby in the gas mask as an object of fear, behind the scenes, the poet's government was scrambling to provide anti-gas protection for infants. In 1937, there was no 'gas-proof' mask for babies approved for mass production in the United Kingdom. That same year, in *If Air War Comes: A Guide to Air Raid Precautions and Anti-Gas Treatment*, Dr Leslie Haden-Guest stated matter of factly that '[c]hildren must be protected; and although older children whose growth approaches that of the adult can wear anti-gas respirators, the babies and infants cannot. Little children as well as invalids and the aged must be protected in the home in gas-proof rooms.'[41] Not until early 1938 were British government officials concluding that any device that could protect a mother and child together, such as a gas-proof tent to enclose both, was impractical.[42] Thus the government began to proceed as rapidly as possible with experimental plans to develop individualized anti-gas protection for infants.

Across the Channel, French scientists and medical doctors had been experimenting with their versions of anti-gas protection for babies and young children. Doctoral theses presented to the Faculty of Medicine of the University of Paris in 1936, 1938, and 1939 all tested various refinements of devices to safeguard infants from aero-chemical attack. One of the doctoral candidates praised the 'gas proof cradles' ('sacs berceaux') that provided 'a portable shelter' for young infants. Certainly, the depiction (and idea) of placing a child in a device that resembled a domestic object like a cradle was far less frightening than the baby gas masks of pacifist texts.[43]

Not until the summer of 1938 were British government scientists confident of having models that could be tested – and they ran a number of trials at maternity and child welfare clinics of baby anti-gas protection, notably two devices: baby bags and baby helmets. In his final report, John Macmillan, the Medical Officer of Health overseeing testing in Woolwich in July, commented extensively on each baby, noting for instance that the sole four-month-old baby 'cried continuously', while another boy of ten months 'struggled a good deal' as 'the bag was much too small to allow him full freedom of movement'. Atypically, Macmillan also provided comments from the mothers of these infants. The mother of the youngest baby in the sample noted that she was glad 'to see what was being done [...] as it inspires confidence when one has practical demonstrations of the precautions being taken'. However, while acknowledging this advantage, another mother concluded with the comment: '[M]ay we never have to use them!' These mothers thus demonstrated that one of the goals of those planning for the next war was being realized: despite the popular use of images of babies in masks designed to terrify women into demanding peace, these women were relieved that their government was making plans to protect their children in a war to come.[44] The final result – the baby anti-gas helmet – was perhaps not as comforting as a gas-proof cradle, but it was perhaps far less ominous than the masks of the First World War or the speculative masks of the interwar imagination.

Depictions of the 'baby in the gas mask' or, worse, the baby subject to poison gas without such protection, in the decades after the First World war were employed as 'shock troops' by those, especially feminists, arguing against war: in effect to ask, *how* can we allow this kind of war to occur? Yet, despite vociferous external criticism, government scientists committed themselves to providing protection against the unthinkable. One thing about such preparations was indisputable: a state preparing to protect infants from chemical warfare was a state that had conceded that the home was now a war zone. The relationship of a mother to a child at war was no longer restricted to those who had given birth to a son of military age. All were now at risk.

Conclusion

The First World War succeeded in blurring the firm borders between the 'home front' and the 'front line'. One of the most vivid ways that this occurred was through the aerial bombardment of civilian spaces filled, as contemporary representations would have it, with women and children. Playing upon fears of aerial chemical war in the interwar years, opponents of the further development and deployment of such weaponry used an emotive language – both visual and written – to translate these dangers into ones attacking the essence of home life. The home was still gendered feminine, but its status as full participant in the no longer exclusively masculine domain of war was made viscerally apparent. The implications of the cultural mixing up of civilian/combatant spaces and bodies as a legacy of the Great War merit further concerted attention from scholars seeking to understand the gendered history of this war. For innovative aspects of state-sanctioned violence could help to reshape gendered ideas about the home front/front-line divide.

Perhaps it is too obvious for commentary that the threats to children, to homes, to domesticity, to the almost sacral figure of the mother and baby in arms were the ones that resonated beyond the war years themselves in a range of interwar media to display the fears of, and efforts to prevent, 'the next war'. But there are other ways to display innocence, and other means to rally support against war. Thus it behoves us to pay attention to the texts and images that initially appear during the First War World and that then recur in powerful ways in interwar democracies depicting mothers and children in gas masks to highlight their endangerment by new weaponry. The development of this particular 'next war' discourse both drew upon and subtly altered the gendered rhetoric that accompanied the arrival of air raids in Britain and France during the war. It transformed the stance of women towards war from a relational position as mothers 'producing the primal munition'[45] of war to that of mothers under fire, being trained to operate a baby anti-gas helmet, literally on the front lines of a war that technology had now brought home.

Notes

1. M. Donnay (1916) *La Parisienne et la Guerre* (Paris: Georges Crès), pp. 32–3 and 52. See the discussion of Denise Cartier in S. R. Grayzel (2006) '"The Souls of Soldiers": Civilians Under Fire in First World War France', *Journal of Modern History*, 78:3, pp. 588–622.
2. O. Schreiner (1978) 'Woman and War', in *Woman and Labour* (reprint of 1911, London: Virago), p. 169; my emphasis.
3. Schreiner, *Woman and Labour*, p. 170.
4. F. Hallowes (1915) *An Address to the Mothers of Men and Militarism* (London: Headley Bros), p. 47. See the summation of wartime feminist pacifism in S. R. Grayzel (2002) *Women and the First World War* (Harlow: Longman), ch. 6.
5. For an analysis of the uses of motherhood during the war, see S. R. Grayzel (1999) *Women's Identities at War: Gender, Motherhood, and Politics in Britain and France during the First World War* (Chapel Hill, NC: University of North Carolina Press).
6. Air raids in the First World War were truly novel, and they affected areas closer to active battlefields in northern France, for example, as well as coastal regions in Britain and both Paris and London. Germany first used Zeppelins and later planes to bomb civilian populations, and while the overall death toll was relatively small in comparison to combatant casualties, there was a considerable public discussion and condemnation of these attacks. Detailed information about the First World War's air raids on Britain can be found in S. R. Grayzel (2012) *At Home and Under Fire: Air Raids and Culture in Britain from the Great War to the Blitz* (Cambridge: Cambridge University Press), and on France in Grayzel, '"The Souls of Soldiers"'.
7. See two discussions of contemporary feminist responses to abuses in the South African War in A. Burton (2000) '"States of Injury": Josephine Butler on Slavery, Citizenship and the Boer War' and L. E. Nym Mayhall (2000) 'The South African War and the Origins of Suffrage Militancy in Britain, 1899–1902', both in I. C. Fletcher, L. E. Nym Mayhall and P. Levine (eds) *Women's Suffrage in the British Empire: Citizenship, Nation, and Race* (London: Routledge).
8. See Grayzel, '"The Souls of Soldiers"', for a full discussion of the raids on France.
9. I am following feminist theorist Cynthia Enloe here and using this as a compound noun to suggest how fully integrated these categories had become. See C. Enloe (1992) 'The Gendered Gulf', in C. Peters (ed.) *Collateral Damage: The 'New World Order' at Home and Abroad* (Boston, MA: South End Press), pp. 93–110.
10. 'The Air Assassins', *The Daily Chronicle*, 9 September 1915.
11. *L'Illustration*, 5 February 1916.
12. 'Bereaved', Letter to the Editor, *The Times*, 16 June 1917, and 'A Mother', Letter to the Editor, *The Times*, 18 June 1917.

13. *L'Illustration*, 29 January 1916.
14. 'En Pays Bombardé', Agence Rol Photo 50893, *Bibliothèque Nationale de France*, Paris, online under http://gallica.bnf.fr/ark:/12148/btv1b53004018k.
15. Advertisement for Hospitals and General Contracts Co. Ltd., *Pall Mall Gazette*, 9 June 1915.
16. See letter (16 June 1915) enclosed in diary of Lady Matthews, *Imperial War Museum* (IWM) Department of Documents, Papers of Lady Matthews (09/36/1); emphasis in original.
17. *Punch*, 18 August 1915.
18. 'Air Raid Casualty Inquest', 4 October 1917, *The National Archives* (TNA), HO 45/10883; Shoreditch is a neighborhood in East London.
19. New Scotland Yard Report, 3 November 1917, TNA, HO 45/10883.
20. One of the most infamous First World War raids on London included a direct hit on an infants school in the East End district of Poplar in the summer of 1917. See Grayzel, *At Home and Under Fire*, ch. 2–3 for further discussion of this and other attacks.
21. J. Addams (1999) 'Women and Internationalism' (1915), reprinted in M. R. Higonnet (ed.) *Lines of Fire: Women Writers of World War I* (New York: Plume), pp. 39–40.
22. This was the title of the conference and of the French publication of 1930: *Les méthodes modernes de guerre et la protection des populations civiles* (Paris: M. Rivière); the British publication of the conference findings, also of 1930, was entitled *Chemical Warfare: An Abridged Report of Papers Read at an International Conference at Frankfurt am Main* (London: Williams & Norgate).
23. G. Woker (1930) 'The Effects of Chemical Warfare', in *Chemical Warfare*, p. 45.
24. *L'Illustration*, 29 January 1916.
25. Dr W. Nestler (1930) 'Collective and Individual Protection', in *Chemical Warfare*, p. 75.
26. Nestler, 'Collective and Individual Protection', p. 77.
27. G. Duchêne (1930) 'Conclusion', in *Chemical Warfare*, p. 80.
28. For more on these measures in Britain, see T. H. O'Brien (1955) *Civil Defence* (London: HMSO), and Grayzel, *At Home and Under Fire*. For France, see Ministre de l'Intérieur (1932) 'Instruction Pratique sur La Défense Passive contre les Attaques Aériennes' (Paris: Charles-Lavauzelle), and issues of 1939 of the *Bulletin d'Information de la Défense Passive* (Paris: Min. de la Défense Nationale).
29. Dossier Désarmement, Fonds Bouglé, *Bibliothèque Historique de la Ville de Paris*.
30. See 'Accepterons-nous cela?', in the dossier collected by the French Ministry of the Interior on pacifist activities around disarmament, *Archives Nationales*, F 7 13421.
31. Association Internationale des Médecins contre la Guerre – Section Française (1932) *Une Protection Efficace Contre la Guerre Aéro-Chimique est Impossible* (Paris: Editions du Comité mondial contre la guerre) and Cambridge Scientists Anti-War Group (1937) *The Protection of the Public from Aerial Attack* (London: Victor Gollancz).
32. V. Méric (1932) 'La Guerre aux civils' (Paris: Editions de 'la Patrie humaine'); V. Méric (1932) *La Guerre qui revient: Fraîche et gazeuse* (Paris: Editions Sirius).
33. Méric, *La Guerre qui revient*, pp. 27, 32, 116.
34. Méric, *La Guerre qui revient*, p. 132.
35. Méric, *La Guerre qui revient*, p. 134.
36. See discussion of this case in Grayzel, *Women's Identities At War*, pp. 46–8.

37. Union of Democratic Control (1935) *Poison Gas* (London: UDC); British Section of the Women's World Committee Against War and Fascism (1935?) *Behind the Gas Mask: An Exposure of the Proposed Air Defence Measures* (London: British Section WAWF).
38. Simpson Stokes (1935) *Air-Gods' Parade* (London: Arthur Barron), p. 168.
39. Stokes, *Air-Gods' Parade*, pp. 137–8.
40. W. H. Davies, 'Armed for War', *London Mercury*, September 1937.
41. L. Haden-Guest (1937) *If Air War Comes: A Guide to Air Raid Precautions and Anti-Gas Treatment* (London: Eyre & Spottiswoode), p. 11.
42. Report: concerning the protection of young babies and children, 5 January 1938, TNA, HO 45/17620.
43. See the following doctoral theses submitted to the Faculty of Medicine in Paris: G. Puech (1936) 'La Protection des Enfants et Guerre aero-chimique'; G. Dorey (1938) 'La Protection des Enfants en bas âge contre les Gaz de Combat'; C. Mathieu (1939) 'La preservation des jeunes enfants contre les gaz de combat'.
44. See Report and Appendix to John MacMillan, Report, 20 July 1938, TNA, HO 45/17620. For a further discussion of this, see Grayzel, *At Home and Under Fire*, ch. 9.
45. Schreiner, *Woman and Labour*, p. 169.

9

The Female Mourner: Gender and the Moral Economy of Grief During the First World War

Claudia Siebrecht

On 1 October 1914, the Jena student Fritz Philipps composed a letter of goodbye to his family that was to be opened in the event of his death at the front.[1] It is a short yet emphatic farewell that was clearly written by someone who was expecting death and had come to terms with his impending fate and, as a result, spoke with conviction about what should happen to his body and how his relatives should respond to his passing: 'Please do not repatriate my dead body, leave me buried where I fought and fell. Do not wear mourning dress and do not pressure anyone to do so, but be gracious that you, too, were able to sacrifice on the altar of the fatherland.' Philipps asserted that he did not wish for an end to the war unless it was a victorious one for Germany and insisted that he was happy to give his life as he viewed his participation in the world war as a contribution to world peace. He was killed in Galicia in May 1915 and left a bereaved family to act according to his wishes. His request that his parents should not visibly demonstrate their grief suggests that a stable environment and shared ideal of sacrifice within the family were important to him. The letter also clearly communicates the expectation that his wishes should be respected.

The letter was published in a collection that was edited by the German academic Philipp Witkop, a publication that in its successive editions shifted in purpose from displaying the war enthusiasm of the German youth in its first 1915 edition, to becoming a memorial to their sacrifice by the third and extended edition published in 1928.[2] While the publications and selection of letters naturally reflect the objectives of the editor and while they served to steer the public perception of ideals of heroism and wartime sacrifice, the letters also offer important insights on the war experience of German soldiers in various theatres of war. Urban male youths were among the most fervently patriotic supporters of the national war effort, and their mobilization and self-mobilization for war was largely driven by an identification with the nation and an idealized concept of soldierly masculinity.[3] Some even viewed the outbreak of war as an opportunity for change and the renewal of German society.[4] While these notions are mirrored in the

144

Witkop collection, the content of the letters goes far beyond the criteria the editor had set out for selection. Besides patriotic sentiment and even outright enthusiasm, many of the letters reveal complex emotional processes and testify to a variety of coping mechanisms that soldiers resorted to while at the front. One example is the manner in which some soldiers attempted to address their own fear of mortality and concern for their relations in the event of their death in war. They suggested particular forms of conduct for their families that, after their passing, would demonstrate a reassertion of, and support for, their own wartime sacrifice. In so doing, they might have felt as if they retained some sense of control in a front-line environment in which the agency of individual soldiers was greatly reduced.[5]

The instructions outlined by the soldier-student Fritz Phillips indicate that the conduct of the bereaved carried a certain meaning for those who risked their lives at the front and that the manner in which people performed their grief had a particular relevance in wartime.[6] The visible display of emotions, rites, and rituals acquired a different symbolic power, as death in war was an unfamiliar phenomenon both for those who were facing death and those who were anticipating bereavement. Their needs, moreover, were not necessarily the same. As the letter indicates, the young soldier expressed the wish to remain buried among his comrades, where he could continue to be part of the soldierly community even in death. While this may have offered a certain amount of comfort to the soldier, the geographical distance to the graves of the fallen often compounded the grief of bereaved relatives.[7] In the German Army, moreover, repatriations were rare as the logistics were difficult, the costs high, and the practice considered a medical risk. In addition, military funeral rituals had an established place in military ceremonial and unit cohesion within the army.[8]

The treatment of the war dead and their burial was a point of controversy between the military authorities and the families of the fallen in most of the belligerent states that outlasted the duration of the conflict.[9] In addition to institutional and familial concerns and traditions, the explicitly stated wishes of soldiers could also impact on wartime rites of bereavement. The request for grieving relatives not to wear mourning dress, as in the above example, indicates that traditional customs could acquire a different meaning in the wartime context. As will be seen in this chapter, reflections on the clothing and conduct of the bereaved were quite commonly expressed in soldiers' letters and other personal narrative material. The diary of 15-year-old Agnes Zenker, a schoolgirl from the Ore Mountains in Saxony, for example, offers an interesting perspective on the wartime symbolism of the black dress. Commenting on the demeanour of an acquainted family who had lost a loved-one at the front, she wrote in June 1916: 'Immelmann's parents are true German heroes and set an example for everyone else. They do not wear any outward sign of their bereavement. Surely they are proud of their hero-son.'[10] In war, the entry suggests, the choice not to wear mourning dress was read as a patriotic act and equated with proud bereavement. Yet wearing mourning dress traditionally had the important social function of signalling the grief of the bereaved to the community on the one hand, and affording the bereaved a special status within their communities on the other.[11] Here, the wartime circumstances had reversed the conventional understanding of the custom.

Peacetime burial rites and rituals of bereavement have traditionally served to aid the living in parting from the dead by ritualizing the transition.[12] Funerals, gravesites, and mourning customs are part of long-standing anthropological patterns of people living together and parting from one another.[13] In time of war, in addition to the logistical obstacles faced by those who suffered the loss of a loved one, the cultural and social conventions of bereavement differ from those that pertain in peace. Since burial rituals and rites of bereavement follow quite clearly defined gender patterns in the Western world,[14] the changing meaning of certain customs and symbols in wartime had a different impact on men and women. The moral economy of grief during the First World War, this chapter argues, was highly gendered and placed an expectation on women to bear the weight of their sacrifices with strength and to proudly endure emotional pain. The intention here is not to make a point about a different quality in the emotional experience of wartime loss for women and men, but to suggest that gender, along with age, generation, location, and class determined the context for both the manner in which the bereaved understood their private experience of loss and the public perception of individual grief. Many soldiers, along with the military, political, and religious authorities, civil society, and female intellectuals consistently presented women with a behavioural pattern that left little room for the expression of emotional pain. A historical-cultural tradition of stoic endurance of sacrifice in war also impacted on the manner in which women's roles were cast in wartime. In addition, women themselves felt bound by their loyalty to the soldier and the cause for which he died. Yet emotional conflict and pain, nonetheless, characterized the experience of wartime loss and women's art represented one forum in which these more ambivalent feelings were expressed in Germany.

The dying, the dead and the bereaved

Explicit views on the conduct of the bereaved regularly featured in the correspondence from the front to the home. In a letter written to his parents in May 1916, student Heinz Pohlmann asked his parents not to lament his death, but 'to mourn in a calm and composed fashion that would show that they are Germans who can bear grief'.[15] He explained his national-religious sacrificial logic to his parents and spoke of his belief in a better future as well as his faith in life after death. Pohlmann's willingness to sacrifice himself engendered a sense of moral authority and demanded that his wishes be respected. In this case, the endurance of emotional pain was framed as a national quality. Private emotions and painful experience were interlinked with a political cause and the expectation that patriotic pride should be demonstrated.

Ernst Günter Schallert, another student from Berlin, wrote to his parents about the death of his brother in January 1915 and addressed the differences between what death on the battlefield meant for men in the field and the parents at home.[16] He asserted that for the men in the front lines, death had lost some of its tragedy. While acknowledging that they suffered more, he asked his parents not to mourn for the son they have lost and consider the words from the gospel of St John: 'That no one has greater love than he who gives his life for his friends.' By placing an emphasis on redemption and by stressing that he and his brother identified with the Christian ideal of sacrifice, he offered a potential comfort to his bereaved parents. Yet, alongside the plea 'not to mourn', there was little room for the display of the sort of profound emotions that are perhaps more traditionally associated with the death of a child.

After having learned of a comrade's death, student Herbert Weisser wrote to his mother in May 1915 that it was not death on the battlefield that was difficult to face, as 'the fate of dying alone out in the field was something expected by everyone who had left for the front'.[17] Weisser asserted that what made dying difficult was knowing that the relations were torturing themselves with their own fantasies, picturing the most terrible scenarios while what to them appeared to be the worst fate imaginable, could in fact 'be the most beautiful even if the last hour of our lives'. He continued to counsel his own mother by making a number of general statements about attitudes to death and wrote that 'when one thinks of the death of a son, one should do so calmly and without tormenting images, just as the son would do himself. If one did not comply, one would add bitter drops to the last hour of his life.' Weisser thus concluded his letter with a similarly strong assertion of moral authority and request for loyalty, as in the above examples, by suggesting that a fearful attitude would spoil death on the battlefield. Although his letter is quite general and addresses someone in the third person, it is clear that these sentences are meant for his mother. Weisser died in 1916 and again, the bereaved were to reconcile their emotions with the last wishes of a loved one.

The soldiers writing home were, of course, themselves not spared the experiences of loss and bereavement as many mourned for close relations, friends, and comrades. Men serving at the front occasionally reflected about the degree to which their attitude to death had changed and differed from that of civilians and the letters cited above represent some relevant examples. For a number of soldiers, death in war was often seen as an ordinary incident that was faced by the entire frontline community, and a sense of individual tragedy and despair appeared less prevalent, again an attitude that can be detected in the letters above, but also throughout much wartime correspondence.[18] The written exchange between painter Franz Marc and his wife Maria represents a tragic example, as the matter of death in war represents a constant direct and indirect subtext in their letters. Artists and intellectuals were among those who had eagerly anticipated the outbreak of the war and viewed it as having a potentially cathartic effect on the cultural life of the nation, as a worthwhile national endeavour and also as an extension of personal life experience.[19] While artists were also prone to respond with particular sensitivity to the realities of the war,[20] their initially positive attitude to the conflict and acceptance of its cost is reflected in their personal correspondence, as can be seen in this example. Franz Marc attempted to reason with his wife and described his views on wartime death in lengthy letters, detailing how, to him, death in war was a redemption and a liberation of the spirit and was not something to be feared.[21] Marc was firm in his views and stressed how much he wished that she would understand his position. The subject is clearly a difficult one in the couples' correspondence, while Marc appeared more comfortable with his mother's calm words on death in war and wrote to her of the peace that lies in death.[22] The private communication between Marc and his closest female relatives, his wife and his mother, was infused with evaluations and expectations that built on an ideal of female bravery and negated their fears and worries.

The construct of a heroic sacrificial death was integral to notions of soldierly masculinity and thus part of a model to which many men on active service aspired. Alongside class, age, and generation were also factors that shaped attitudes to dying and mourning, as many of the young soldiers, for example, did not yet have their own families and would not leave dependant children behind. The instructions regarding the conduct of the bereaved indicate, moreover, that soldiers did not want to be responsible for the emotional suffering of those at home. In particular, the request not to visibly express their grief appeared to signify to a number of soldiers that their families could cope without them. The wishes of a relation who had died a sacrificial death put immense pressure on the bereaved to fulfil these as a sign of respect and loyalty. Some of these parting messages were addressed to both parents, but like Weisser's example above, quite often such letters were addressed to the mother and detailed gender-specific norms of conduct. This reflects broader social patterns in funerary customs, which are generally divided into more composed and rational forms of conduct for men and emotionally charged patterns of behaviour for women.[23] Women may therefore have been arguably more acutely affected by wartime codes of conduct for the bereaved that censored the visible and audible expression of emotional pain over loss.

In an open letter from the front to the 'Women of Germany', published in the *Vossische Zeitung* on Christmas Eve in 1914, a Prussian officer formulated a broad appeal to women on the home front: 'Do not cry, do not lament, even if your heart is about to break as you are surrounded by the heroic dead.'[24] He went on to assert that there was no reason for women to mourn, as the spirit of their sons or husbands would live on amongst those who were now standing watch on their behalf. The captain proposed that women's love, care, and prayer should be passed on to fallen soldiers' comrades so as not to waste the well of love. This was presented as beneficial for women as they would experience new joy and, at the same time, the captain emphasized the patriotic nature of his proposed 'adoption scheme':

Away with the tears because you have no one to care for. There is no time to look for graves as Germany's victory also depends on Germany's women and Germany's greatness has its origin in you. You will bring about Germany's peace most quickly with never-failing, never-ending, boundless, honest German motherly and spousal love.[25]

The letter is signed by an officer who had tested 'his boys' in 26 enemy encounters and claimed that he did not think that his 'paternal love' was sufficient to sustain the men through war. His counsel to channel bereavement into constructive and patriotic activism was perhaps sound practical advice, yet it was based on the clear expectation that the duty of bereaved mothers and wives was continued moral support for the troops instead of giving in to despairing emotions. However, highlighting the noble nature of maternal sacrifice was, of course, somewhat contradictory, as bonding with other soldiers and supporting them through their sacrifice also meant the endurance of further emotional pain. In addition, the assertion that there was no time to look for a grave to grieve over shows little consideration for the needs of the bereaved, many of whom suffered as a result of their distance from, or lack of, wartime graves.[26] Nonetheless, the idea that maternal love need not have a biological foundation was quite prominent in feminist thought in Germany, which envisaged a more collective moral and ethical responsibility for women in society.[27] This included the protection of traditions and preservations of family values that were seen to be key to society's progress. After the outbreak of war in 1914, numerous publications produced by women drew strong links between both spiritual and biological maternalism and sacrificial duty to the nation.[28]

Many war letters written by students, artists, and intellectuals express strong emotions and expectations that were projected onto a future version of the nation in which they were prepared to invest.[29] There is a clear class dimension to this contextualization and intellectualization of the war effort, on the part of educated middle-class soldiers in particular. Yet correspondence from other milieus indicates that ideas and patterns developed according to which the war was accepted or rejected, which in turn fed into certain modes of conduct projected onto those at home.[30] One example of particular interest is the correspondence of Anna and Robert Pöhland, a working-class couple from Bremen with five children, who wrote to one another on an almost daily basis between July 1915 and Robert's death at the Somme in October 1916. Their correspondence shows that the motivations for steering the conduct of the bereaved could vary significantly. Concerned that his wife would break at the news of his death, soldier Robert Pöhland reminded her to always consider her duty towards their children, who still depended on her 'motherly help and love'.[31] As a father, Pöhland himself found consolation in the fact that their eldest son would soon be able to contribute to the family income and that his wife and children would then be able to eke out a living in case of his death. Writing to his son Robert in October 1916, he stated that:

> One thought that makes my terrible path easier is knowing that you can soon fill in for me. Dear Robert, should I not return, you could not honour me more than to care, like I did, for your mother and your still so dependent siblings. You are the oldest. This beautiful task befalls on you, fulfil it with pride and strength.[32]

Pöhland was deeply concerned for the future of his family and evoked a sense of duty in his eldest son to take on the care of the family should he not return. At the same time, it was important to Pöhland that his death would be commemorated in a manner that reflected his socialist political beliefs and disdain for the language of wartime sacrifice. He instructed his family to respond to his death in a way that showed clear distance from any symbols that could frame his death as a 'hero's death' in war. In the case of his passing, he asked his wife that neither she herself, nor their children changed into mourning clothes, professing that to him this would be not a tribute, but a mockery of his beliefs: 'Do not comply with other backward people who believe they could honour their loved one no better than by walking around like scarecrows. Do not change your clothes nor those of the children, as this would not be an honour to me, but a betrayal of my principles.'[33] The active radical social democrat wrote that his family could honour him most adequately by continuing to live in the way they used to live together. He asked his wife to be strong and to continue fighting for their cause.

Interestingly, in this unusual case, strength and controlled bereavement were understood as a protest against what were believed to be the root causes of the war: capitalism and the political authorities. Pöhland resented his 'sacrifice for capitalism' and wanted to believe that his offspring would redeem this sacrifice one day. To him, the only way to ensure this was by instilling his beliefs into his children. Although inspired by different political ideals from the soldiers cited at the beginning of this section, the sense that a moral obligation required those on the home front to respect and act according to the wishes of the soldier was also strong in Pöhland's case, albeit for different reasons. The negative affirmation of his sacrifice, by having died for a cause that he did not really believe in, created a deep obligation for those left behind to redeem his fate. Indeed, the legacy of his death was quite profound and is vividly recalled in his daughter's memoirs:

Mrs Lauts immediately brought mourning clothes when this happened with father. But mother said: No. Dad wrote that we should not walk in black if he does not return and we all wore colourful dress – just as for the Kaiser's birthday. We will not show our grief, mother insisted, in front of those up there. But she screamed the whole street down when she got the message; she screamed and screamed – this has never left my ears. But then it was all workers who lived there.[34]

The description reveals both an interesting division and junction of public and private spheres of grief. The wearing of mourning dress was avoided, as the deceased had requested, but within their own familiar class community, different emotional codes pertained and the bereaved woman found an emotional outlet in 'wild screaming'. The idea of not showing grief to those who were held responsible, and not wanting to show that they had been hurt, was possibly born of a desire to avoid exposing the family's vulnerability. The perception of the war as a class conflict and not a national struggle supported by a unified nation is evident; the patriotic narrative of war was resented and the family refrained from adhering to what were seen as class-bound conventions of mourning rituals. The decision not to wear mourning dress was also very clear to the neighbourhood, a working-class community in Bremen, who would have also overheard the mother's screams and to whom the rejection of conventions that were associated with support of wartime sacrifice was thus declared. Yet bereaved women more generally had difficulties in embracing the ideals and conforming to the practices of proud bereavement that were so prevalent in wartime societies.

The daughter further describes how her widowed mother found strength in what she thought would be the 'lifelong task' of the political education of her children and was very active in socialist circles until her death in 1919.[35] This suggests that her bereavement was channelled into political activism, and that class and political ideology could shape the public and private faces of grief. The case of the Pöhland family is particularly interesting, as here the soldier had made very clear that his political loyalty lay elsewhere. In his letters, he confessed small acts of resistance in his daily routine in the army to vent his opposition. Pöhland regularly published articles on socialist politics and insisted that his wife engage with political issues in their correspondence. For the widow, joining the Bremen left-wing radicals and becoming involved in the Internationale Kommunisten Deutschlands further strengthened her support of the socialist cause. This can be seen as an important act of loyalty, following the expressed wishes of her deceased husband. For her, there was no danger of feeling that she had abandoned the cause for which her husband gave his life, as it was made unequivocally clear that he did not understand the conflict as his cause.

Wartime correspondence thus establishes an evident correlation between grief and an enduring loyalty between the living and the dead. The conduct and actions of families, and specifically women, were imagined and controlled so as to enhance the meaning of death in war. As the above letters show, behavioural models were projected onto women and parents that demonstrate how soldiers reflected on the impact their death would have on their families. The fact that soldiers employed the language of redemptive sacrifice, whether for a victorious war or a radical political alternative, suggests that the imagined grief and pain of their close relations were difficult to bear, and perhaps reveals an element of denial and fear that could be contained by counselling their families. To be sure, soldiers' reactions and expectations were by no means uniform. Patterns in responses to their mortality, nonetheless, clearly emerge in their correspondence.

Gendered grief and sacrifice

The codes of conduct communicated both from the frontlines and the civilian authorities did have a considerable impact on men and women on the home front, as they informed gender roles and caused tension and critical reflection. The German military authorities initiated a number of measures designed to influence women's attitudes and to manipulate women's communication with front-line soldiers. It was believed that their views would have significant repercussions both on troop morale and on the cohesion of wartime society. In 1915, the German military and religious authorities published correspondence guidelines for mothers and other female relatives who were writing to soldiers at the front; blueprints which promised the receiver 'strength and brave endurance' in the case of their worst fears being realized.[36] Censorship reports delivered to the Bavarian military authorities in June 1917 expressed concern over the morale of women on the home front and prompted the circulation of propaganda pamphlets and brochures that specifically targeted the female population.[37] The military headquarters in Stuttgart organized special events for women and issued a number of publications that reasserted the unity of the nation and praised women's sacrificial spirit, activities that increased in 1917 and 1918.[38]

In a diary entry written in October 1914, publicist and author Theodor Wolff observed that 'everyone feels the need to boast just to show that he is as brave as our truly remarkably brave soldiers out there.'[39] Wolff describes this tendency as a 'weakness in character' and noticeably resents its opportunism. Yet although Wolff exposes unsubstantiated claims of bravery, his remark also reinforces the ideal of the brave soldier and suggests that they were viewed with admiration and respect. Although a non-mobilized

German male on the home front, Wolff adapted a hierarchical model of masculinity in which the soldier ranked highest.[40] There is possibly also an element of envy, as anger is voiced at the boasting of his fellow civilians, it appears to be an attribute and status reserved for the front-line soldier and his sacrifice.

The impact of behavioural models is also evident in women's wartime writing, and the gendered nature of such responses, though varied, is particularly relevant. As Benjamin Ziemann has shown, concern for the survival of their men meant that women in rural Bavaria were quite pessimistic about the outbreak of the war.[41] Such reactions can be detected on an emotional level, but were also informed by social and material concerns, such as the harvest and personal standing and status in the village. Here, the question of class and region are relevant factors to consider, as other women outspokenly embraced the idea of proud sacrifice. In a letter to the poet Rainer Maria Rilke, the psychoanalyst Lou Andreas Salomé referred to 'a terrible revelation' and claimed that she now understood that 'mankind was in this together and shared a general guilt and pain over death in war'.[42] If she had been a man or had borne sons, Salomé continued, she now realized with astonishment that she would have also fought or given her sons to fight. The letter makes a deliberate statement, emphasizing that Salomé would embrace what she understood as the national duty for women in war.

Many of the letters cited above refer to imagined scenarios, but similar gender patterns appear to have pertained in the condolence messages that were sent to bereaved women. They maintained that women who had suffered wartime loss were expected to bear their fate with an appropriate attitude. The Hamburg-based women's activist and artist Ida Dehmel, for example, received a couple of letters after the death of her son Heinz-Lux Auerbach in January 1917 that were written with genuine concern and offered condolences, while at the same time assuming her proud bereavement. Her friend Gustav Pauli, director of the Hamburg Kunsthalle, wrote: 'May the end have been without pain for your son and may you find some consolation in knowing that you delivered the highest sacrifice a woman can give to the fatherland.'[43] Pauli stated that he felt strongly about contacting her, apologized for disregarding her husband's request for silent respect, yet his words reflect the wartime culture of praise for a mother's heroic sacrifice.

In a similar manner, Dehmel's nephew Ludwig expressed not only concern for Ida and regret for Heinz-Lux's death, but related the personal tragedy to the question of duty in wartime: 'For us, dying is a duty, just as it is a duty for you to bear the losses. The more difficult duty may be yours.'[44] Ludwig wrote that he had four days' leave during which he planned to find the grave where Heinz-Lux was buried and continued: 'I will tell the earth that covers him that you and all of us that he left behind are carrying the pain in a calm and composed fashion.' The wartime situation informed the idea of appropriate social norms and conduct as well as the expectation that the ideal would be met.

There is some evidence suggesting that the ideal of proud and strong sacrifice fed into everyday life's routines and represented a model that others sought to emulate. It unfolded a gendered cross-generational appeal. Fifteen-year old Agnes Zenker, for example, repeatedly wrote in her diary that she wished to do something that would be a 'true sacrifice' for her. Having donated her savings some time before, Agnes decided in September 1915 to give up her two 'dear rabbits Fritz and Liese' and donate them to the Red Cross. This would, she proudly wrote, 'make the lining for a pair of soldier's boots'. She also promised to give two further pets and asserted 'this would be a real sacrifice for me and would also make a difference'.[45] In the end, the Red Cross did not accept the rabbits as they would not have given enough fur, but the fact that a teenager decided to create and suffer her own blood sacrifice indicates that enduring pain was also associated with social convention and prestige. Her understanding was evidently that a sacrifice had to be painful to make a meaningful contribution to the war. The attempt of the teenager to emulate painful bereavement is some evidence for the powerful narrative around sacrifice that had been developed. A study on German women's literature by Hans-Otto Binder demonstrates that the relevance of sacrifice in wartime society and the endurance of grief were ideals re-invented by women themselves.[46] Besides wartime fiction, the morality of the conduct of bereaved women was also at the centre of a discourse among female intellectual elites and the subject of numerous wartime publications and pamphlets. This indicates that these notions were not simply a case of women who conformed to gender stereotypes developed by male political and military authorities.[47]

Between 1914 and 1918, women's bereavement had become increasingly politicized and wartime societies sought to defuse women's distress by honouring their heroic sacrifice. Oliver Janz has argued that a decidedly male-dominated cult of the fallen developed in Italy, where women's emotional anguish was given no public space.[48] In wartime Britain, as Susan R. Grayzel's research has shown, the task of mourning assigned to women was understood as serving to enhance the value of a soldier's death. In September 1914, for example, *The Times* published a number of articles which insisted that bereaved women should dress and act in public in a manner that visibly demonstrated their unfailing patriotism.[49] A similar connection between the display of grief and morale was drawn in Germany. Roger Chickering, for example, describes an incident in wartime Freiburg in which a priest reprimanded a bereaved woman who had broken down in tears before the congregation at a church service.[50] As these examples illustrate, there was no sanction for women's visible and audible display of emotional pain in public and the performance of grief in war was gendered and politicized in various wartime societies. The public discourse on death and sacrifice during the war gave rise to a moral economy that outlined strict guidelines for female bereavement in which a strong emphasis was placed on restraint and dignified composure.

A number of studies have suggested that women embraced the notion of heroic sacrifice and proud bereavement. According to Suzanne Evans, women in Canada and Britain publicly presented themselves as heroic mothers of martyrs and unequivocally supported their sons' sacrifices.[51] Nicoletta Gullace has similarly argued that women found consolation in the language of patriotic motherhood that was so omnipresent in wartime Britain.[52] Yet neither of those studies examines the potential clash between the public and private face of grief that Joan Damousi addresses in her pioneering work on mourning in Australia. Damousi's research outlines the way in which women's shared experience of loss became the foundation for a wartime identity that eventually asserted claims for recognition and compensation.[53] The idea that wartime sacrifices should be borne with pride and that loss had to be endured with silent grace was thus deeply imbedded in German, but also in British, French, Italian, Australian, and US war culture. In Germany, this moral code was constantly reinforced by the army, the churches, the media, and also by leading members of the women's movement.[54]

Emotional conflict

Female civil society in Germany was very much involved in defining the wartime role model of a stoic and proudly bereaved female mourner, emphasizing that it was not a binary gender model that generated this ideal. It was a powerful construct and, to some women offered a certain appeal, while it compounded emotional conflict for others. German women's wartime art offered a medium in which a number of artists expressed women's actions, reactions, emotions, and customs that did not conform to the wartime ideal of stoic bereavement. Instead, these images depict the emotional distress of women in mourning and address the conflict resulting from public expectations and the private needs of the bereaved.

The following illustration (Figure 9.1), by the artist Ansche Fuhrmann, is an interesting example which suggests that women's visual culture allowed more room for ambivalence than much of the rhetoric contained in wartime fiction or other publications. What makes the image particularly relevant is that it was commissioned by the biggest women's wartime trust, the Frauendank (Women's Gratitude), which was founded in 1915 by leading representatives of the major German women's organizations. The trust, in name, founding rhetoric, and advertising, reasserted the idea of proud sacrifice and was a deliberate public effort to express the gratitude of the female population to the German Army.[55]

The appeal for the first round of donations stated:

> We here all suffer from the awareness that we live protected and invulnerably, while every day brings us news of new heroism and new sacrificial death. We all have the burning desire to express our holy pride of so much heroism and painful gratitude for sacrificial death of thousands and thousands in a manner that will outlast these difficult times.[56]

When taking the practical aims of the trust into account, the rhetoric of passive endurance and gratitude for wartime sacrifice stand alongside a scheme to alleviate some of the implications of wartime loss. An article published in the *Frauenfrage* prior to the meeting, details that the idea for a publicly funded trust was also inspired by the wish to offer sisterly support to those women who then needed assistance in bringing up their families and to ensure that their children received an education and had opportunities which the death of their father or his inability to earn a living would have otherwise precluded.[57] Most of the organizations within the German women's movement supported the Frauendank[58] and the trust was a lasting and successful initiative that, by January 1917, had collected 4.5 million marks.[59] Thus, in practice the Frauendank sought to alleviate the social hardship of both widows and their children and disabled veterans. In so doing, it directly addressed the suffering as a consequence of wartime sacrifice.

The image on the postcard shown in Figure 9.1 picks up this element of ambivalence. It was designed on behalf of the Nuremberg women's groups that supported the Frauendank. While the drawing ostensibly shows the very apt motif of a widow and her two small children by a soldier's grave, its atmosphere, the dark colours, and actual contents bear little relation to the language of sacrifice and women's gratitude that described the trust's foundation. Instead, the artist presents a more ambivalent perspective on wartime loss by evoking the widow's loneliness and abandonment. Her long, black mourning gown is an important signifier of grief which, as some of the personal narrative material above indicated, had become problematic in wartime society as it did not communicate emotional strength and patriotic pride. The artist thus appears to have made the deliberate choice of cladding the woman in a mourning gown to emphasize her status as a widow. Yet, the widow is facing the grave in front of her and the viewer only sees her back. Her face as the most evident indicator for her emotional state remains hidden. Again, this is meaningful as it could indicate contempt for displaying emotional pain over loss in a society that expected dignity and composure.

The woman is pausing in front of the grave as if having nowhere to go. The artist thus alludes to the uncertain future of the now fatherless family. This scene is, of course, an imagined scenario and the sole grave and landscape unscarred by war bear little resemblance to the soldiers' graves in and behind the front lines. The family's visit to the grave near the front in what

Figure 9.1   Ansche Fuhrmann (1915) *Kriegsspende: Deutscher Frauendank*[60]

would have been occupied or enemy territory seems very unlikely, but adds to the postcard's emotional appeal. The image establishes a direct connection between the dead soldier, his grave marked by his helmet, and his family, which may have been important as some bereaved women had to face the disdain and resentment of their communities. The artist thus appeals to a sense of solidarity and advertises the Frauendank as a way to channel emotional pain and help to ease material hardship. While the rhetoric of the trust is primarily about women's gratitude, the initiative actually helped those who had fallen through the social net. The postcard evidently does not promote a grateful or proudly bereaved mother, an indicator that the language of sacrifice that was so dominant in women's civil society had its limits. Women's visual culture represents an interesting interface between the public and the private in which feelings of ambivalence over wartime loss were more frequently expressed.

Such feelings can also be detected in women's art more generally and the case of German artist Käthe Kollwitz presents an intriguing example. Both her correspondence and art convey a clear sense of conflict emerging from the strong feelings of obligation and loyalty to her son Peter who died in Flanders in October 1914. Kollwitz's initial artistic reaction was a plan to create a memorial to express gratitude to her son Peter and his generation for their sacrifice. Kollwitz explained to her elder son Hans how she wanted to express her thanks, and how much she respected the sacrifice. Writing in December 1914, her letter is also interesting as it seeks to create a balance regarding the fate of both of her sons in war. She responded to Hans and his perception of having contributed less to the war because he did not die a sacrificial death. Instead, he suffered from the pressure to avoid death on the battlefield. Kollwitz absolved her elder son by describing how, 'in case this had to be', she would place both of her sons on 'the sarcophagus' of her work, but asserted just how difficult that would be.[61] She assured Hans that she would also accept and endure his sacrifice, just as she was enduring that of Peter, thus communicating strength to her son and thereby meeting an ideal of female bravery in war. Hans survived the war, but their conversations about Peter's sacrifice continued and his absence remained a source of emotional agony for both. Her diary and correspondence reveal the fluctuating nature of her emotions on his death. For Kollwitz, these ranged from moments during which she felt at peace and shared her sons' ideas, to pain and guilt.[62] Although she never realized her initial artistic idea, she created a series of art works that address the question of sacrifice and bereavement. Both her writing and her art show that even in the private sphere, conflict arose over personal ideas regarding the nation and one's sense of identity and loyalty.

Conclusion

This emotional conflict expressed by Fuhrmann and by Kollwitz in their art and in their writing was an important subject in women's wartime art more generally. Numerous other German female artists depicted variations of the painfully bereaved female mourner.[63] Their art showed customs, rites, and rituals that asserted painful rather than proud bereavement and expressed conflict and tensions emerging from public and private forms of bereavement, gender roles, associated funerary rites, and the historic tradition of proud mourning, all of which informed the moral economy of grief during the First World War. Correspondence between soldiers and their families was part of that moral economy and the familial bond perhaps added a particular force and moral obligation to comply with the sort of conduct the men expected from women at home. More importantly, however, the model of stoic, composed, and proud bereavement was not only asserted by soldiers, political and military authorities, church figures, and the male-dominated press; sections of the female population also identified with the image of the proud woman who willingly endorsed and endured wartime sacrifice.

To be sure, a gender model that contrasts understandings of masculinity and femininity to one another, such as the double-helix, clearly retains some relevance when attempting to analyse gender relations in war.[64] Yet the 'gendered' nature of wartime role models was more intricate than a male–female divide. Some of the above examples show that women were as involved in determining the parameters for women's wartime identities, just as there were men who critically reflected on hierarchical gender ideals. In addition, the framework for social action for women in war was not necessarily always defined by a quest for advancement, political emancipation, or equality with men. Arguably, something as ostensibly basic as showing and expressing emotions over wartime loss had political implications, as it undermined a dominant role model for women in wartime society. Women's art thus asserts the presence of painfully bereaved women in society, offering a different perspective on wartime loss. By depicting dress, actions, postures, and gestures of mourning women that do not conform to a model outlined by both men and women in wartime society, female artists used the gendered model of the tragically bereaved women to counter the ideal gender role model of the proud female mourner. It was the interconnected nature of gender and the social and cultural meaning of emotions that determined the boundaries of the moral economy of grief during the First World War. Notions of gender thus had a key impact on the way the war was read, processed, communicated, and challenged by those living through the conflict. In turn, the war also changed gender perceptions and identities, and women's art produced over the course of the conflict was one way in which women negotiated their place in wartime society.

Notes

1. Letter F. Philipps, 1 October 1914, in P. Witkop (1928) (ed.) *Kriegsbriefe gefallener Studenten* (Munich: Georg Müller), p. 60.
2. M. Hettling and M. Jeismann (1993) 'Der Weltkrieg als Epos: Philipp Witkops Kriegsbriefe gefallener Studenten', in G. Hirschfeld, G.Krumeich and I. Renz (eds) *Keiner fühlt sich hier als Mensch...: Erlebnis und Wirkung des Ersten Weltkriegs* (Essen: Klartext), pp. 175–98.
3. J. Horne (1997) (ed.) *State, Society and Mobilisation in Europe during the First World War* (Cambridge: Cambridge University Press), pp. 1–17; R. Chickering (2007) '"War Enthusiasm?" Public Opinion and the Outbreak of War in 1914', in H. Afflerbach and D. Stevenson (eds) *An Improbable War: The Outbreak of World War I and European Political Culture before 1914* (New York: Berghahn), pp. 200–12.
4. G. Fiedler (1989) 'Kriegsbegeisterung – Friedenssehnsucht: Reaktionen der deutschen Jugendbewegung auf den Ersten Weltkrieg', in P. Knoch (ed.) *Kriegsalltag: Die Rekonstruktion des Kriegsalltags als Aufgabe der historischen Forschung und der Friedenserziehung* (Stuttgart: Metzler), pp. 186–203.
5. B. Ziemann (1998) 'Die Eskalation des Tötens in zwei Weltkriegen', in R. van Dülmen (ed.) *Erfindung des Menschen: Schöpfungsträume und Körperbilder 1500–2000* (Vienna: Böhlau), pp. 414–18; A. Watson (2008) *Enduring the Great War: Combat, Morale and Collapse in the German and British Armies, 1914–1918* (Cambridge: Cambridge University Press), pp. 85–106.

6. J. Winter (1995) 'Communities in Mourning', in F. Coetzee and M. Shevin-Coetzee (eds) *Authority, Identity and the Social History of the Great War* (Providence, RI: Berghahn), pp. 325–56.
7. G. Holst-Warhaft (2000) *The Cue for Passion: Grief and its Political Uses* (Cambridge, MA: Harvard University Press), p. 15.
8. *Kriegergräber im Felde und daheim. Herausgegeben im Einvernehmen mit der Heeresverwaltung* (1917) (Munich: Bruckmann).
9. L. Capdevila and D. Voldman (2006) *War Dead: Western Societies and the Casualties of War* (Edinburgh: Edinburgh University Press), pp. 37–75.
10. Diary A. Kiendl née Zenker (1900–1991), 25 June 1916 (ed. G. Kiendl, *Nessis Kriegstagebuch aus dem Ersten Weltkrieg*, online at: http://zenker.se/History/nessi_tagebuch.shtml).
11. G. Howarth (2001) 'Fashion and Costume', in G. Howarth and O. Leaman (eds) *Encyclopedia of Death and Dying* (London: Routledge), pp. 190–1; N. Hoefer (2010) *Schwermut und Schönheit - Als die Menschen Trauer trugen* (Düsseldorf: Fachverlag des Deutschen Bestattungsgewerbes).
12. D. J. Davies (1997) *Death, Ritual and Belief: The Rhetoric of Funerary Rites* (London: Cassell).
13. A. C. G. M. Robben (2004) 'Death and Anthropology: An Introduction', in A. C. G. M. Robben (ed.) *Death, Mourning, and Burial: A Cross-Cultural Reader* (Malden, MA: Blackwell), pp. 1–16.
14. J. Hockey (1997) 'Women in Grief: Cultural Representation and Social Practice', in D. Field, J. Hockey and N. Small (eds) *Death, Gender and Ethnicity* (London: Routledge), pp. 89–107; G. Howarth (2001) 'Gender', in *Encyclopedia of Death and Dying*, pp. 205–7.
15. Letter, H. Pohlmann, 25 May 1916, in Witkop, *Kriegsbriefe gefallener Studenten*, pp. 153–4.
16. E. G. Schallert, 10 January 1915, in Witkop, *Kriegsbriefe gefallener Studenten*, p. 74.
17. H. Weisser, May 1915, in Witkop, *Kriegsbriefe gefallener Studenten*, p. 83.
18. P. Walther (2008) (ed.) *Endzeit Europa: Ein kollektives Tagebuch deutschsprachiger Schriftsteller, Künstler und Gelehrter im Ersten Weltkrieg* (Göttingen: Wallstein); Witkop, *Kriegsbriefe gefallener Studenten*.
19. W. J. Mommsen (1997) 'German Artists, Writers and Intellectuals and the Meaning of War, 1914–1918', in Horne, *State, Society and Mobilisation in Europe during the First World War*, pp. 21–38.
20. A. Becker (2000) 'The Avant-Garde, Madness and the Great War', *Journal of Contemporary History*, 35:1, pp. 71–84.
21. F. Marc to M. Marc, 23 June 1915, in F. Marc (1966) *Briefe aus dem Felde* (Munich: List), pp. 74–6.
22. F. Marc to S. Marc, 17 February 1916, in Marc, *Briefe aus dem Felde*, pp. 133–4.
23. V. Clark (2001) 'Family', in *Encyclopedia of Death and Dying*, pp. 187–90; Holst-Warhaft, *The Cue for Passion*, pp. 4–8.
24. 'An Deutschlands Frauen, Offener Brief aus dem Felde', *Vossische Zeitung*, 24 December 1914.
25. 'An Deutschlands Frauen'.
26. Holst-Warhaft, *The Cue for Passion*, p. 15
27. A. T. Allen (2000) *Feminismus und Mütterlichkeit in Deutschland 1800–1914* (Weinheim: Deutscher Studienverlag), English original 1991: *Feminism and Motherhood in Germany, 1800–1914* (New Brunswick, NJ: Rutgers University Press).

28. E. Metzdorf-Teschner (1914) *Die allgemeine Wehrpflicht der Frau während des Krieges* (Leipzig: Neueste Frauen-Korrespondenz); H. Lange (1915) *Die Dienstpflicht der Frau: Vortrag gehalten auf der Kriegstagung des Allgemeinen Deutschen Lehrerinnenvereins Pfingsten 1915* (Leipzig: Teubner); C. Usborne (1988) 'Pregnancy is a Woman's Active Service', in R. Wall and J. Winter (eds) *The Upheaval of War: Family, Work and Welfare in Europe, 1914–1918* (Cambridge: Cambridge University Press), pp. 389-416; E. Domansky (1996) 'Militarisation and Reproduction in World War I Germany', in G. Eley (ed.) *Society, Culture and the State in Germany* (Ann Arbor, MI: University of Michigan Press), pp. 427–63.
29. Hettling and Jeismann, 'Der Weltkrieg als Epos', pp. 175–6.
30. N. Buschmann (1997) 'Der verschwiegene Krieg: Kommunikation zwischen Front und Heimatfront', in G. Hirschfeld, G. Krumeich, D. Langewiesche and H.-P. Ullmann (eds) *Kriegserfahrungen: Studien zur Sozial- und Mentalitätsgeschichte des Ersten Weltkrieges* (Essen: Klartext), pp. 208–24; B. Ziemann (2007) *War Experiences in Rural Germany 1914–1923* (Oxford: Berg).
31. R. Pöhland to A. Pöhland, 1 August 1916, in D. Kachulle (2006) (ed.) *Die Pöhlands im Krieg: Briefe einer sozialdemokratischen Arbeiterfamilie aus dem Ersten Weltkrieg* (Cologne: Papyrossa), p. 179.
32. R. Pöhland to R. Pöhland, 17 October 1916, in Kachulle, *Die Pöhlands im Krieg*, pp. 225–6.
33. R. Pöhland to A. Pöhland, 1 August 1916, in Kachulle, *Die Pöhlands im Krieg*, p. 179.
34. K. Krebs, 'Erinnerung an meine Eltern', in Kachulle, *Die Pöhlands im Krieg*, p. 42.
35. K. Krebs, 'Erinnerung an meine Eltern', in Kachulle, *Die Pöhlands im Krieg*, pp. 42–5.
36. 'Mutter- und Freundesbrief ins Feld', in B. Ulrich (1997) *Die Augenzeugen: Deutsche Feldpostbriefe in Kriegs- und Nachkriegszeit, 1914–1933* (Essen: Klartext), pp. 165–6.
37. Stv. Generalkommando, Kommandierender General v. d. Tann an die Pressepolizeibehörden, 11 June 1917, *Bayerisches Hauptstaatsarchiv, Kriegsarchiv*, München, Stv. Gen K. I. Armee Korps 1709.
38. *Landesarchiv Baden-Württemberg, Hauptstaatsarchiv Stuttgart*, Stellv. Gen-Kommando M 77/1 482.
39. Diary T. Wolff, 8 October 1914, in Walther, *Endzeit Europa*, p. 87.
40. J. Tosh (2004) 'Hegemonic Masculinity and the History of Gender', in S. Dudink, K. Hagemann and J. Tosh (eds) *Masculinities in Politics and War: Gendering Modern History* (Manchester: Manchester University Press), pp. 41–60.
41. Ziemann, *Front und Heimat*, pp. 45–6.
42. L. Andreas-Salomé to R. M. Rilke, Göttingen, 12 September 1914, in Walther, *Endzeit Europa*, p. 68.
43. G. Pauli to I. Dehmel, 16 January 1917, *Staats- und Universitätsbibliothek Hamburg*, DA: Br: P 567.
44. Ludwig to I. Dehmel, 12 January 1917, *Staats- und Universitätsbibliothek Hamburg*, DA: Br.
45. Diary A. Kiendl née Zenker, 26 September 1915.
46. H.-O. Binder (1997) 'Zum Opfern bereit: Kriegsliteratur von Frauen', in Hirschfeld, Krumeich, Langewiesche and Ullmann, *Kriegserfahrungen*, pp. 107–28.
47. R. Anderson (1914) *Wie können sich Frauen in der Kriegszeit nützlich machen?* (Trier: J. Lintz), p. 4.
48. O. Janz (2002) 'Zwischen privater Trauer und öffentlichem Gedenken: Der bürgerliche Gefallenenkult in Italien während des Ersten Weltkriegs', *Geschichte und Gesellschaft*, 28:4, p. 570.

49. S. R. Grayzel (1999) *Women's Identities at War: Gender, Motherhood, and Politics in Britain and France during the First World War* (Chapel Hill, NC: University of North Carolina Press), pp. 227–9.

50. R. Chickering (2007) *The Great War and Urban Life in Germany: Freiburg 1914–1918* (Cambridge: Cambridge University Press), p. 323.

51. S. Evans (2007) *Mothers of Heroes, Mothers of Martyrs: World War I and the Politics of Grief* (Montreal: McGill-Queen's University Press).

52. N. F. Gullace (2002) *'The Blood of Our Sons': Men, Women and the Renegotiation of British Citizenship during the Great War* (Basingstoke: Palgrave Macmillan), p. 69.

53. J. Damousi (1999) *The Labour of Loss: Mourning, Memory and Wartime Bereavement in Australia* (Cambridge: Cambridge University Press), pp. 65–78.

54. For example A. M. Wagner (1915) *Der Krieg und die Aufgabe der deutschen Mutter* (Gotha: F. A. Perthes); M. Feesche (1915) *Vom segnenden Leid in harter Zeit: Gedichte* (Hannover: Feesche); E. Le Seur (1916) *Die Aufgabe der deutschen Frau im Krieg: Vortrag von Pastor Le Seur* (Stuttgart: Steinkopf).

55. Protokoll der Gründungssitzung der 'Kriegsspende deutscher Frauendank 1915', *Landesarchiv Berlin*, HLA 2749.

56. Protokoll der Gründungssitzung der 'Kriegsspende deutscher Frauendank 1915'.

57. *Die Frauenfrage*, 16 June 1915, *Landesarchiv Berlin*, HLA 2750.

58. *Die Frauenfrage* 1 January 1917, *Landesarchiv Berlin*, HLA 2750.

59. M.-E. Lüders (1936) *Das unbekannte Heer: Frauen kämpfen für Deutschland, 1914–1918* (Berlin: Mittler & Sohn), p. 66.

60. The postcard was published by the Berlin-based publishing house Albert Frisch in 1915. The postcard is from the author's collection.

61. K. Kollwitz to H. Kollwitz, 18 December 1914, in J. Bohnke-Kollwitz (1992) (ed.) *Käthe Kollwitz: Briefe an den Sohn, 1904–1945* (Berlin: Siedler), p. 92.

62. On Kollwitz's sacrifice see also: R. Schulte (1998) *Die verkehrte Welt des Krieges: Studien zu Geschlecht, Religion und Tod* (Frankfurt am Main: Campus), pp. 117–51.

63. Artists Sella Hasse, Katharina Heise, Martha Schrag, and Käte Lassen, for example, all produced images of bereaved women, see C. Siebrecht (2013) *The Aesthetics of Loss: German Women's Art of the First World War* (Oxford: Oxford University Press).

64. M. R. Higonnet and L.-R. P. Higonnet (1987) 'The Double Helix', in M. R. Higonnet, J. Jenson, S. Michel and M. Collins Weitz (eds) *Behind the Lines: Gender and the Two World Wars* (New Haven, CT: Yale University Press), pp. 31–47.

10
French Boys and Girls in the Great War: Gender and the History of Children's Experiences, 1914–1918

Manon Pignot

Working on childhood requires the historian to interrogate the use of gender as a tool for analysing the characteristics of children's wartime experiences.[1] It makes more sense to use the plural 'children' than the generic term 'childhood', since the first corresponds more closely to the diversity of the issue. However, this chapter will not merely juxtapose individual stories. The nature of the sources presented here, including diaries, letters, and drawings as well as secondary sources such as oral testimonies, involves a very intimate level and a micro-historical perspective – 'au ras du sol' as Jacques Revel has called it.[2] This allows us to constitute a corpus of personal sources in which various dimensions become apparent, in particular in terms of expressions of gender. Even in sources that at first appearance seem to be rather disparate, we can recognize specific patterns such as similar representations and a consistent imagery. This 'cultural flow' stresses that all these children belong to the same *generation*. Transposing the mentioned personal sources can shed light on the 'singular normal' (the 'normal unusual') of wartime childhood.[3]

This chapter will consider children's *experiences* of the Great War and examine the variations between boys and girls, using the example of France.[4] Yet most of the findings are also true for other countries at war; the variation between them is due to the degree of mobilization in the respective countries.[5] Women's and gender history has shown how the war reinforced gender barriers; consequently, the same can be said about young people. Studying children's lives during the war reveals deep divisions between boys and girls at specific moments or in specific places of war. It also demonstrates that the way the war was witnessed was widely determined by gender. From the perspective of an intimate history of children, gender appears as a relevant concept in order to comprehend wartime experience. Along with geographic, social, or cultural criteria, gender is essential to understanding how children perceived the Great War, as it plays a crucial role in the representations and practices of war.

Children's experiences of the Great War must be examined in terms of the 'places of war' (*lieux de guerre*): 'real places' such as home front or occupied territories, school and family home as well as 'metaphorical places' in the press and literature, and so on. For some of these places, gender is not necessarily a primary operating concept. At the home front, for instance, everyday life and food supplies were more affected by the economic and social situation of the family than by gender. In contrast, there were 'places of war' where social or economic aspects played a less important role and where 'gender' is an absolutely crucial criterion to understand the nature of children's experience. To illustrate this, the chapter will focus on three such 'places'. The first *lieu de guerre* is a discursive one: it refers to the discourses on war and on mobilizing youth. The second aspect draws on the material mobilization in which girls got deeply involved. Finally, the *lieu de guerre* can be seen geographically; here, I will examine the occupied territories of Northern and Eastern France.

Boys and girls and the discourse on war

As Stéphane Audoin-Rouzeau has shown,[6] the discourse on war addressing children did not appear *ex nihilo* in August 1914: it belonged to a cultural context from pre-war times when gender distinctions were strong. Children's fiction and non-fiction in press and literature in France since the beginning of the twentieth century offer a good example. A wide range of periodicals reached Paris and parts of the provinces (by subscription). All social strata would find something to their liking – among them the Catholic *Etoile noëliste* published by the Assumptionists, the bourgeois *Semaine de Suzette* (Gautier-Languereau), and publications such as *L'Epatant* (Société Parisienne d'Edition, published by the Offenstadt family). Jean-Paul Sartre, a great reader of French 'illustrés', commented on the rapid 'mobilization' of the magazines he used to read: 'Colonial novels of the pre-war years gave way to war novels, inhabited by *mousses* [ship's apprentices], young Alsatians, orphans, and mascots.'[7] Only a few months after the war had started, stories, games, and other items such as toys, were contaminated by the discourse on war, sometimes in a very violent fashion. There are two explanations for the success of 'illustrés' regarding the mobilization of children. The first is linked to the cultural history of the *Belle Époque*: At the outbreak of the Great War, children's magazines had, over almost ten years, been substantially developed and had become extremely popular.[8] The low price of the publications – five centimes per week – contributed to their success and diffusion into all strata of society and created a new readership.[9] Secondly, in the new context of conflict, 'illustrés' played a key role in mobilizing children, because they made warrior values more accessible and transposed them into everyday life: the authors 'had put heroism within easy reach of everyone, courage and self-sacrifice became daily virtues', wrote Sartre.[10]

More than literature, school – compulsory from the age of six to thirteen years – was a privileged means of access to children; it was therefore the best way to mobilize a whole generation. Since 7 August 1914, a series of circulars from the Minister of Public Instruction Albert Sarraut had been sent to school inspectors which entailed the supervision of children and the establishment of a 'school of war', that is to say, an adaptation of programmes and exercises in terms of the new context of war.[11] Yet rather than examining the *content* of this discourse on war which was based on patriotic exaltation and hatred of the enemy,[12] I will concentrate on its *effects* on children.

The war discourse that addressed children had two functions: it valorized children as sons and daughters of heroes ('valorization'), and at the same time made them feel guilty about the soldiers who gave their lives for them ('culpabilization'). Its main theme was sacrifice. How could children compensate for the blood shed by the soldiers? The assignment of guilt to the children implied two consequences: it imposed the obligation on them to work hard at school and to abstain; that is, to make a sacrifice. A drawing from the rich collection of the Musée du Vieux Montmartre (Paris),[13] most likely made by a ten-year-old boy during the war, expresses the issue of sacrifice as well as the 'valorization' of the 'home front's little heroes': 'Everyone at work: with munitions / at the front / at school' (see Figure 10.1).

Figure 10.1 Everyone at Work.
H. Bourgois, 'Tout le monde au travail', 1 December 1916
Source: Fonds Sainte Isaure, Musée du Vieux Montmartre, Paris.

The drawing in Figure 10.1 illustrates the allocation of workstations to each part of French society: the 'poilu' in the centre, framed by the woman at the ordnance factory on one side and the child at school on the other. The school desk appears as the equivalent of the workbench, but it is also a civilian parallel to the trench, as suggested by the presence of the map behind the students. Children were told that they played an important role in the war effort by being disciplined and useful.

For girls, the feelings of guilt necessarily worked differently and went deeper. Admittedly, all children were in an unequal situation in relation to the soldiers. They could offer hard work and small sacrifices (no candies, no toys), but they still were in the soldiers' debt who were giving their blood, their lives. Yet, within this unequal situation, girls seemed to be even 'more unequal', so to speak. To support the feelings of guilt about this 'blood credit', and eventually to defy it, boys had their own military future: one day, they, too, would be soldiers. At school, gym lessons encouraged boys to think of themselves as prospective soldiers and to see exercise as preparation for military life, as the drawing in Figure 10.2 illustrates:

Thus, boys saw school and the battlefield as similar worlds. They used the same vocabulary to describe battles and exams: 'While my father is killing

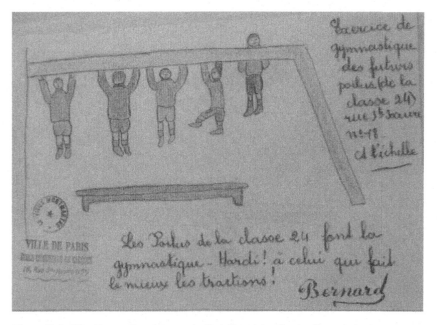

Figure 10.2 The Future Combatants (*poilus*) Exercising in the Gym
Bernard, 'Exercise de gymnastique des futurs poilus', s.d.
Source: Fonds Sainte Isaure, Musée du Vieux Montmartre, Paris.

Figure 10.3   While My Father is Killing a *Boche,* I Have My Own Victory
Jolivet, 'Pendant que mon père tué un Boche, je remporte la victoire (la mienne)',
July 1916
Source: Fonds Sainte Isaure, Musée du Vieux Montmartre, Paris.

a Boche, I have my own victory', the pupil Jolivet wrote according to this
logic (Figure 10.3).

At the same time, girls were not in the position to consider themselves as
potential soldiers: Although one day they would not be too young to fight,
they would still be women. Girls lacked the possibility of relying on their
future in order to alleviate their feelings of guilt, which were, in contrast
to those of boys, eternal. Society allowed them only forms of consolation.
Girls were expected to behave at school, to sacrifice small things – just like
boys. Yet, they were also supposed to be good, helpful, and useful. Their
role model was the nurse: 'The girls, who have been less affected by disorder, have rather been moved by charity. As for our women, their task was
much clearer than the boys' duties', observed the Société libre pour l'étude
psychologique de l'enfant, an association of French pedagogues, in 1917.[14]
A little 'disorder' might be acceptable for a future combatant at the front
line, but not so for a prospective nurse or mother. Charity always served
a second purpose, which was to console women and girls.

Writing from the front, fathers asked their daughters to behave well and
comfort their mothers and in doing so they repeated the demands of the

school: 'What makes me most happy is that you are very affectionate to your little mother and that you know how to console her when she is sad', wrote the schoolmaster Emile Auneau to his young daughter Paulette, placing the task of consoling her mother over academic success.[15] In each letter sent to Paulette, Emile Auneau asked her to take care of her mother.

According to the discourse on war, boys and girls had different roles to fulfil – which is not surprising. Yet private sources also show how children internalized these topics of war culture, with more or less spontaneity. This could, however, cause some contradictions for girls, as we can see, for instance, in the exercise book of Marcelle Lefebvre. This young girl from Boulogne-sur-mer imagined a dialogue between two soldiers, of whom one was mutilated: 'I feel pity for this poor crippled man who forgets all his suffering by thinking of his vanished comrades. He is proud to have lost his leg, for the fatherland.' She expressed her feelings towards this soldier with the word 'pity', but the teacher crossed out the word in red ink and changed it to 'admiration'.[16] In the same class, another student described soldiers who were getting out of a train: 'Some poor soldiers, exhausted, can barely get out [of the train], they are laden with bags and luggage.' Once again, the teacher criticized the child's sympathetic perspective, and in so doing contradicted a core principle of the war discourse aimed at girls. She commented: 'They had a rest in the train!'.[17]

Girls must be useful: material mobilization

Besides working hard at school, children were expected to make themselves useful in terms of the economic war effort. This requirement concerned all children. In the cities, both boys and girls were sent out to queue at the shops; at school, they were told to collect money in the streets on 'patriotic days' or to work in the 'school gardens'. In rural areas, they were supposed to help with the harvest. However, contrary to other countries like Germany or the Austrian Empire, boys were not much involved in patriotic collections of materials such as glass or scrap metal for the war.[18] Adults mainly expected boys to behave themselves, at school and in the streets. Girls with an urban background, on the other hand, had additional tasks to fulfil and were deeply involved in the economic war effort. Our sources inform us that they were expected to make themselves 'useful' from the age of four, when they were at nursery school (*école maternelle*). At the nursery school in Chaptal Street in Paris, girls made 'lint for the pillows of the hospital trains'.[19] Very young girls were not exempt from this requirement. On the contrary, 'big girls aged six and a half helped us with [knitting] and the little ones aged four took the skeins and made balls of wool'.[20] By making girls knit, sew, or collect money for the soldiers, the school offered them the opportunity to prove their patriotism; yet it was also a substantial way to obtain money and products necessary for the war.

The next example is representative of our sources. Between October 1914 and April 1915, the Cours Spinoza in Paris sent the following items to the front: '70 sweaters, 33 flannel waistcoats, 306 underpants, 40 flannel belts, 190 shirts, 143 pairs of socks, 103 balaclavas, 88 scarves, 90 shirt fronts, 89 pairs of gloves, 229 handkerchiefs, 104 towels, 24 pairs of slippers, 41 soaps, 100 iodine phials'.[21] Three observations are noteworthy in this context: firstly, the fact that the mobilization of schoolchildren began immediately with the start of the new school year in October 1914. Secondly, the contributions of these school workshops were not negligible, even if they were not professional. Thirdly, the use of child labour, which technically had been prohibited in the Third Republic for all children under the age of 13 years since 1880, was practically suspended.

Knitting, sewing, and collecting money in the streets were tasks imposed by teachers. However, according to girls' diaries and letters, it seems that they internalized the demands. The welcome change to the monotony of school lessons caused by crafting and needlework, the competition between schools, the pleasure of making real clothes and not just single patterns as was common practice before the war, the feeling of duty – all these aspects were crucial to develop the mass of production by children at the beginning of the war. Françoise Dolto, a famous French child psychiatrist born in 1908, described the process of internalization of guilt in her childhood memories:

> I was very skilful with my hands at a very young age [...] I loved doing embroidery, crocheting, knitting, drawing, in short, I was very indus- trious with my hands; and when the war came we made [scarves] for the soldiers [...]. I liked that but, at the same time, it bothered me to be forced to do it. [...] So, I knitted scarves because the soldiers needed them, and they had to be one metre or one metre twenty long, and it was a lot of work to do. So, at night, I tried to hook it to the chairs with pins or hairpins and I pulled it to make it longer, up to one meter and twenty, and I moistened it; but when it dried it became short again, or the chairs fell down. [...] Naturally, I was very annoyed, I spent my time knitting, I couldn't play anymore because that made me feel guilty, the soldiers were waiting, or so they said. There was a poor combatant in the trenches who was waiting for my scarf and who would freeze to death if I did not finish it.[22]

Françoise Dolto was six years old at the beginning of the war. Her letters confirm her later memories: 'I did eight rows of my scarf today, Miss told me I've done half of my scarf so I'm happy.'[23] In 1915, aged seven, she wrote to her father:

> I promised two scarves to the hospital and both of them are done, and now I'm making a scarf for Uncle Pierre [her uncle and godfather]. When

we return to Paris, I will try to work hard so that you will be happy and not too sad, because you have to work more to make shells to kill the dirty *boches*[24] who hurt the poor French who suffer from the evil *boches* who are cruel and who kill children who are one and two years old, who suffer and cry.[25]

What Françoise Dolto describes here, reveals a real *obsession* with crafting and needlework along with self-imposed demands regarding her school-work and a feeling of duty towards her father and, by extension, towards all combatants.

The occupied territories

As we have seen, differences linked to gender become clearly apparent in regard to discursive places at the home front. In everyday life – in terms of hunger or bombing – the differences between boys' and girls' experiences were mainly determined by social and geographic aspects: for instance, depending on whether the family was wealthy enough to acquire food apart from the official rations or on how far away the family lived from the front. The situation was completely different in the occupied territories of northern and eastern France. Though the whole population in this area was isolated, children seemed to have been even more detached than others: no school, no social life, and no possibility of walking in the streets on their own due to the presence of German soldiers.

Girls in particular appeared to be affected by the forced seclusion. Their diaries describe a life under occupation lived vicariously, in which the boys' accounts played an important role. The Congar family is a good example: Marie-Louise Congar was born in 1902 and her brother Yves in 1904. According to their war diaries, they seem to have been very close to each other. Yet, mostly, Yves describes what he has seen, whereas Marie-Louise tells about what her brother has reported.[26] Comparison between the diaries of boys and girls from the occupied territories gives us some further hints as to which perspectives each gender focused on. For instance, girls noticed the sexual dimension of the occupation process more carefully than boys. In their diaries, girls often mentioned what we might call 'symbolic rapes' during the occupation. They noted how the Germans used nudity as a weapon against women and girls: 'They came and took the water, some of them having a shower under the pump being naked, without even bothering about us.'[27] Girls also paid attention to physical aggression specifically aimed at females. They were shocked by the body searches in the middle of the street: 'I have kept many painful and distressing memories of the Great War that I hope I will forget [...] In 1915, I went to St Vaast, and on the road I met two Germans who were hunting, they arrested me, searched me, took my name and the name of my parents, my street, the number of the house and sent me back. I was so affected that I became ill, confined to bed for six months', a schoolgirl remembered in 1920.[28] Gynaecological examinations were sometimes imposed on very young teenagers, as in Lille in 1916.[29] Finally, one of the most recurrent cases of aggression was to harness girls to the plough as Marie-Louise Congar, already mentioned above, noted: 'The Germans are now trafficking in girls. They make them work in the fields and everywhere.'[30] Her brother wrote a few months later: 'In Remilly, they harnessed 15 girls to a road roller. In Fleigneux, women up to 45 years were working at the plough.'[31] The aim of this aggressive behaviour against girls, whether it was symbolic or real, was to soil their bodies: girls' bodies represented virginity as an equivalent to the unraped country; femininity, which stood for reproduction; and youth, as a symbol for the future of the nation. By demeaning a girl's body, it was the soldiers' aim to soil the whole occupied nation.[32]

Finally, girls noticed attacks on houses and homes in their diaries, whereas boys did not mention any such incidents. Marie-Louise and Yves Congar belonged to the same generation, to the same family, but they did not share the same views on the war and on occupation. For instance, Marie-Louise Congar observed very carefully whenever a German soldier or officer left his faeces in the bedroom: 'Arrival of another captain Nemnich. This pig has left his pee and poo in the chamber pot.'[33] Her brother Yves never did so. This is understandable given the fact that the house, as a domestic space, was the *domaine réservé* of girls and women. Soiling the house was a metaphoric way to hurt the nation.

Unlike the home front, where male values were glorified, the occupied territories seem to have been a feminized battlefield, focused on the domestic sphere. Invasion and occupation led to a reversal of the traditional gender roles, a process which was noticed by children at the time. The girls often described men as cowards in their diaries, whereas women were shown as being brave in their attempts to resist the invaders. For example, the young Henriette Thiesset, born in 1902, reported how her mother tried to prevent a German soldier from requisitioning a piece of furniture:

> Mum called him a thief, a barbarian, a coward, a Prussian, while holding tight to the sofa. Without any compassion for a woman, he twisted her hand to make her release it. She repeated that it was a family heirloom [...], but in vain. It was the only furniture that we had saved. Grandfather was very concerned that we would have to pay a fine of thousand marks for this offence, but that never happened.[34]

Oral sources also tell of the courage, not to say boldness, of mothers who faced dangerous situations: 'We knew that French planes were coming. Then, Mum told us: "Get out into the street, wave your handkerchief to let them know we are civilians." [Question: were you afraid?] No, with Mum, we could not be afraid.'[35] Mothers and their gestures of resistance, some-times against their husband's will, seemed to have been role models for the girls: 'It was Mum who had hung up maps [author's note: to follow the troops]. She had maps on the wall [...] When the officer who lived with us had gone out, Mum used to take the German newspapers to the doctor; after that, she put them back carefully.'[36]

We can observe that girls of 12 to 14 very often used the word 'us' when referring to women. They had developed a feeling of admiration towards women, particularly mothers, rather than towards men: 'I'm 14 today. Another birthday with the *Boches*. [...] Ah! I wish women could be soldiers, Sedan would have been recaptured long ago and we would be in Germany. Unfortunately, this is not *our* role.'[37] Since women played a major role in the occupied territories until 1918, we can observe a posi-tive affiliation of girls with their world. Again, the comparison between the two diaries of the Congar children is very helpful: Marie-Louise described a demonstration of women in the streets of Sedan who demanded more food. Her report emphasized their heroism, when the 250 women enforced the dismissal of the mayor: 'Women of Sedan, about 50 to 250, I don't know exactly, angry because we did not have enough to eat, showed up at the City Hall and threatened Grand Pierre. Thereupon Benedict [the mayor] resigned. The women had slippers in their baskets and were pre-pared to throw them in case the mayor would not comply.'[38] In contrast, her younger brother Yves gave a different version of the same scene in his diary: 'It seems that a hundred women, armed with slippers and brooms, presented themselves at the City Hall to force the mayor to give up the food supplies that he had saved because of the American events! [Yves probably refers to the US entering the war.] What kind of people will there be after the war, what a firm hand will the police need in order to handle the crowd!'[39]

The difference between the diaries of the two children reveals how girls identified themselves with women in the occupied territories, who for them appeared to be, in a way, combatants on the domestic front. This is a distinctive feature of the experiences of girls in the occupied territories, which differs extremely from that of girls in the rear area. While boys often expressed their desire to take part in combat, girls at the home front rarely mentioned anything of the kind. The difference between the occupied territories and the home front was to a certain extent caused by a growing gender imbalance in the occupied territory, which affected the nature of the experience as much as its interpretations by the children themselves. Thus, invaded and occupied space can be seen as a place where gender is a major variable in the child's wartime experience. It is true that boys and girls shared the same feelings of hunger and boredom. However, their gendered way of everyday life and their interpretations of the occupation caused a significant divergence between their lives.

Conclusion

Our French sources offer a vast variety of experiences. It made a difference whether an individual came from the southeast, from Paris or from the north. The war was not the same in these parts of France. A French girl and a German girl of the same age who lived in the occupied territories had certainly more in common than two French girls from different regions of France. Thus, examining the role of children in the First World War implies a comparative perspective. Beyond the particularities of each belligerent country (the particularly difficult economic situation in Germany or the Austrian Empire for instance), children's experiences across borders had a lot in common. The *place* where the war was experienced – not the *country* or the nationality – was essential. In this respect, our French sources appear to be quite representative. A careful reading of intimate sources has shown the significance of gender as a decisive variable in children's experiences of the conflict. For instance, we can observe that in certain places and at certain moments, boys and girls shared experiences of the war, but represented them differently in their diaries. However, gender should not be taken as an absolute determinant.

Notes

1. Special thanks to Susan Grayzel and Christine Brocks for helping me with the translation.
2. J. Revel (1989) 'L'histoire au ras du sol', preface to G. Levi *Le pouvoir au village: Histoire d'un exorciste dans le Piémont du XVIIe siècle* (Paris: Gallimard), pp. i–xxxiii.
3. J. Revel (ed.) (1996) *Jeux d'échelles: La micro-analyse à l'expérience* (Paris: Gallimard-Le Seuil).
4. See M. Pignot (2012) *Allons enfants de la patrie: Génération Grande Guerre* (Paris: Le Seuil).
5. See, for example, C. Hämmerle (ed.) (1993) *Kindheit im Ersten Weltkrieg* (Vienna: Böhlau); A. Gibelli (2005) *Il popolo bambino: Infanzia e nazione dalla Grande Guerra a Salò* (Torino: Einaudi); A. Donson (2010) *Youth in the Fatherless Land: War Pedagogy, Nationalism and Authority in Germany 1914–1918* (Cambridge, MA: Harvard University Press); S. R. Fisher (2011) *Boys and Girls in No Man's Land: English-Canadian Children and the First World War* (Toronto: University of Toronto Press). For a synthesis, see M. Pignot (forthcoming 2013) 'Children', in J. Winter (ed.) *The Cambridge History of the First World War* (Cambridge: Cambridge University Press).
6. S. Audoin-Rouzeau (1996) *La guerre des enfants* (Paris: Armand Colin).
7. J.-P. Sartre (1964) *Les mots* (Paris: Gallimard), p. 177.
8. A. Fourment (1987) *Histoire de la presse des jeunes et des journaux pour enfants, 1788–1988* (Paris: Eole).
9. M. Lyons (1997) 'Les nouveaux lecteurs au XIXe siècle: femmes, enfants, ouvriers', in G. Cavallo and R. Chartier (eds) *Histoire de la lecture dans le monde occidental* (Paris: Le Seuil), pp. 365–401.
10. Sartre, *Les mots*, p. 179.

11. A. Sarraut (1917) *L'Instruction publique et la Guerre* (Paris: H. Didier).
12. Audoin-Rouzeau, *La guerre des enfants*, ch. 'Une école de guerre', pp. 24–37.
13. M. Pignot (2004) *La guerre des crayons: Quand les petits Parisiens dessinaient la Grande Guerre* (Paris: Editions Parigramme). This unique collection of 1146 drawings was created between 1914 and 1918 by the students of two schools – école Sainte Isaure and école de la rue Lepic – in the eighteenth arrondissement of Paris. The children were from two classes. The largest number of drawings came from the 'upper *cours*' of the school Sainte Isaure (where the students were about ten years old). Done in class, often to illustrate essays, these drawings were ordered by the headmaster; most are titled, dated, and signed. A second set of pictures was drawn by year two of the school in Lepic; that is, schoolchildren aged about six years. They are particularly important because they were probably the only means of expression for these young children. Drawings, which were also used by paediatricians long before the war, are valid historical sources. Like objects, they offer an alternative approach in examining the role of children during the war.
14. C. Chabot (1917) *Nos enfants et la guerre: Enquête de la Société libre pour l'étude psychologique de l'enfant* (Paris: Félix Alcan), p. 73.
15. Emile Auneau, letter to Paulette, 30 December 1916, *Historial de la Grande Guerre*, Péronne, Centre de Documentation, carton n°1/22969–22990.
16. Exercise book of Marcelle Lefebvre, school Pierre Bertrand, Boulogne-sur-mer, February 1916, *Bibliothèque de Documentation Internationale Contemporaine*, Nanterre (BDIC), F°Δ 1126 / 8 Cx 001.
17. Exercise book from the school Pierre Bertrand, Boulogne-sur-mer, February 1916, BDIC F°Δ 1126 / 8 Cx 001.
18. Hämmerle, *Kindheit im Ersten Weltkrieg*, pp. 265–98.
19. J. Combarieu (1916) *Les jeunes filles françaises et la guerre* (Paris: Armand Colin), p. 53.
20. Combarieu, *Les jeunes filles françaises*, p. 54.
21. Combarieu, *Les jeunes filles françaises*, p. 26.
22. F. Dolto (1986) *Enfances* (Paris: Le Seuil), p. 28.
23. F. Dolto (1991) *Correspondances* (Paris: Hatier), letter to Suzanne Marette, 27 August 1915, p. 42.
24. *Boches* was a pejorative term for Germans widely used in France during the Great War.
25. Dolto, *Correspondences*, letter to Henry Marette, 21 September 1915, p. 51.
26. The diary of Marie-Louise Congar is in the author's personal collection. Yves Congar's diary has been published: Y. Congar (1997) *Journal de la guerre 1914–1918* (Paris: Editions du Cerf).
27. H. Thiesset, *Journal de guerre 1914–1920*, BDIC cote FΔ 1126 / 7 C 695.
28. Exercise book of Sophie Manet, school Saint-Python, BDIC F°Δ 1126 / 2 B 312.
29. A. Becker (1998) *Oubliés de la Grande Guerre: Humanitaire et culture de guerre, populations occupées, déportés civils, prisonniers de guerre* (Paris: Noêsis), p. 70.
30. M.-L. Congar, *Journal de guerre*, 14 May 1917.
31. Y. Congar, *Journal de la guerre*, p. 186 (27 December 1917).
32. According to S. Brownmiller (1975), rape is a violent act of degradation and physical humiliation: *Against Our Will: Men, Women and Rape* (New York: Simon & Schuster). On the invasion as a 'gender process', see: J. Horne and A. Kramer (2001) *German Atrocities 1914: A History of Denial* (New Haven, CT: Yale University Press), pp. 198–9. See also J.-Y. Le Naour (2002) *Misères et tourments de la chair durant la Grande Guerre: Les mœurs sexuelles des Français 1914–1918* (Paris: Aubier).

33. M.-L. Congar, *Journal*, p. 21 (4 September 1914).
34. Thiesset, *Journal de guerre*, 1 March 1916.
35. Oral recollection of Marie-Thérèse L., interviewed by the author in March 2004 in Labège.
36. Oral recollection of Marie-Thérèse L., interviewed by the author in March 2004 in Labége.
37. M.-L. Congar, *Journal*, p. 99 (6 September 1916); emphasis added.
38. M.-L. Congar, *Journal*, p. 114 (14 April 1917).
39. Y. Congar, *Journal de la guerre*, p. 168 (14 April 1917).

11

Towards a New Internationalism: Pacifist Journals Edited by Women, 1914–1919

Bruna Bianchi

Within a few weeks after the declaration of war, the organizations which had always considered themselves as last bastions of peace – the Socialist International and the International Peace Bureau – disbanded. Most socialists, who had never condemned war in itself and had never questioned the possibility of distinguishing between defensive and aggressive warfare – in particular those with a democratic and liberal background – considered their respective countries to have been unjustly attacked. As well as several pacifists, they aligned themselves with their governments.[1] Only a minority of absolute pacifists sought to reinforce internationalist aspirations which were threatened by the war, and to give expression to all the 'free voices' that emerged from the war-affected countries.[2] Placed under strict surveillance, they endured arrest and expulsion, their bases were closed, their publications censored, their homes searched, and their passports withdrawn.[3]

Still, those turbulent years, which marked the defeat of liberally and democratically oriented socialism and pacifism, were at the same time a hotbed of ideas, practices, and contacts which paved the way for a new pacifism in the post-war period. In Geneva, Romain Rolland and his work with the Agency for Prisoners became an international point of reference.[4] In London, three committees came into being which aided foreign nationals from enemy countries and assisted civilian victims (the Emergency Committee for the Assistance of Germans, Austrians and Hungarians in Distress; the Fight the Famine Committee; and the Friends War Victims Relief Committee which was part of the Society of Friends).[5] In Berlin, Elisabeth Rotten founded the Auskunfts- und Hilfsstelle für Deutsche im Ausland und Ausländer in Deutschland (Information and Assistance Bureau for Germans Abroad and for Foreigners in Germany) in 1914.[6] New pacifist organizations surfaced in various countries:[7] the Nederlandsche Anti-Oorlog Raad (Dutch Anti-War Council) emerged in Holland in October 1914; Albert Einstein, Elisabeth Rotten, Kurt von Tepper-Laski, and Helene Stöcker founded the Bund Neues Vaterland (New Fatherland League) in November 1914 in Germany; and in Britain, the Union of Democratic Control[8] was established during the first days of the First World War to establish parliamentary control of British foreign policy, and the No-Conscription Fellowship against compulsory conscription was formed in autumn 1914.[9]

In this chapter, I argue that a new pacifism emerged during the war, inspired by conferences, activities of newly formed organizations, and writings published in journals that were edited by women. Pacifist feminists insisted on basing decision-making and international relations on the 'female' disposition of nurturing. It was an absolute pacifism which regarded all war as intrinsically wrong, and had finally abandoned trust in the proposals for arbitration. Antithetical to militarism, it was based on the concept of strong womanhood and motherhood. The latter, considered as the strongest support of the military effort by governments, journalists, and propagandists, was reversed in the discourse of pacifist feminists. Rather than settling for their confinement to a narrow domestic sphere, they turned traditional women's roles such as nurturing and caring into a vital force that would be able to counter some of the more destructive effects of a 'man-made world'. According to this view, only women would be able to eradicate the principle of brute force in international affairs and society. As historian Jo Vellacott writes: 'That some feminist opponents of war claimed that their stand was based on the special experience of women as the givers of life should not blind us to the radical departure they were making from the expected and approved role of women.'[10] This new direction was visible from the beginning of the conflict.

Washington and The Hague 1915: towards a new internationalism

At the Washington conference for all American women's organizations in January 1915 the Women's Peace Party was formed. On that occasion, concrete proposals were presented in order to end hostilities and to build international relations on new foundations. In her presidential address, *What War is Destroying*, Jane Addams declared that war was jeopardizing women's values such as protection, nurture, and conservation. Thus, women had the right and the duty to protest. Addams believed that this protest was grounded in the 'soul of every woman all over the world'.[11] She emphasized society and culture rather than biology as important aspects in women's opposition to war. Consequently, women were depicted not only as bearers of life, but also as 'custodians' who have been assigned by society with the care of others. She thought that women were tired of seeing their contributions to society destroyed and that their anger over this destruction would bring about their opposition to war.

In order to be heard and to come up with specific suggestions to put an end to the military conflict, an international peace conference at The Hague was organized in April 1915. The congress, with 1000 representatives from various countries, was a key event for pacifism on an international level. Chaired by Jane Addams, America's most 'revered' feminist and reformer, it laid the foundations for the first international peace organization: the Women's International League for Peace and Freedom (WILPF).[12] In her opening address, Jane Addams stated that the forces that had led women of various nationalities to gather in the Dutch city represented the spirit of an internationalism that had survived the war and was constantly penetrating everyday life and human relationships, breaking down national barriers: 'We have many evidences at the present moment that inchoate and unorganized as it is, [internationalism] may be found even in the midst of this war constantly breaking through its national bounds. The very soldiers in the opposing trenches have to be moved about from time to time, lest they come to know each other, not as enemy, but as individuals, and a sense of comradeship overwhelm their power to fight.'[13] Like the soldiers from opposing trenches who had met in no man's land during the Christmas festivities in 1914, women should find a way to express the feeling of universal brotherhood, or rather sisterhood, allowing it to take effect around the world: 'We have come to this congress not only to protest', she pronounced, 'but furthermore we would fain suggest ways by which this large internationalism may find itself and dig new channels through which it may flow.'[14] Now that men were reduced to silence in the trenches, it was women's turn to speak out; their voices alone could climb above the hubbub of propaganda, and only women could use a language able to uphold universal principles. The words spoken by the women in The Hague were 'clear and solemn': 'For three days we have met together, so conscious of the bloodshed and desolation surrounding us, that all irrelevant and temporary matters fell away and we spoke solemnly to each other of the great and eternal issues as do those who meet around the bedside of the dying.'[15]

The Congress revealed a constructive and courageous feminist activism in marked contrast to the silence and the passivity of the peace societies led by men, which were dissolved in 1914.[16] Women claimed that they could do much for the healing of the spiritual wounds which the nations were inflicting upon each other. They opposed the idea of women's passivity and their need for protection, and claimed the right to speak for themselves as well as for men.

Women's voices in pacifist journals published in Switzerland

For the entire duration of the war, women's pacifism found many channels to express itself. A fundamental means for spreading ideas and keeping up contacts with pacifist women of different nationalities were journals. In 1917, for instance, two new journals which were edited by women appeared: in France, *La mère éducatrice*, edited by Madeleine Vernet; and in Philadelphia, *Four Lights: An Adventure in Internationalism*, published by the American branch of the WILPF and edited by Crystal Eastman. Other significant journals which had emerged in the early years of the twentieth century survived censorship, such as Helene Stöcker's *Die Neue Generation* (founded in 1903) and *Jus Suffragii*, the journal of the International Woman Suffrage Alliance, established in 1906 and edited by Mary Sheepshanks from 1913 onwards. In addition, women's writings, particularly those which were censored or which provoked waves of protest in their homelands, were welcomed and circulated by pacifist journals published in neutral countries.

In Switzerland, the hub of anti-militarism and artistic avant-garde, new journals came into being in 1916: *Demain*, published in Geneva and edited by Henri Guilbeaux, who worked with Romain Rolland, and *Les Tablettes*, published in Lausanne by the anarchist Jean Salives. Last but not least, the journal *Coenobium*, which had begun publication already in 1906, was edited in Switzerland by Enrico Bignami[17] and printed in Italy during the war. Supported by Romain Rolland's involvement, these periodicals kept the internationalist ideal alive, gave a voice to feminist pacifism, advocated conscientious objection and professed the idea of non-violence. In many cases, copies of the journals managed to cross the Swiss borders and reached the war-affected countries.

In Italy, copies of the journals appeared among the pages of *Coenobium*, thanks to Enrico Bignami's contacts. The Italian socialist acted as an intermediary between the Milanese pacifist Rosa Genoni, German pacifists, and international women's organizations; he released passages drawn from pacifist texts (such as Olive Schreiner's *Women and War* and Marcelle Capy's *Une femme dans la mêlée*) and, above all, papers and appeals for peace which were censored abroad. In October 1914, Clara Zetkin's *An Appeal to the Socialist Women of all Countries* was published which in Germany had led to the confiscation of the *Gleichheit*, the journal Zetkin had edited since 1892. Moreover, a plea by Louise Saumoneau, *To the Women of the Proletariat*, found a place in the journal. In summoning French women to action, Saumoneau stigmatized their passivity and their 'need to hate' that was born out of suffering and ignorance, and claimed that their 'intelligence was left to lay dormant'.[18]

In February 1915, a piece by Ellen Key, entitled *Santa insurrezione* (Holy Insurrection), appeared in *Coenobium*. 'The only ray of light', she wrote, 'will come from women's hatred of war', from 'the holy insurrection of motherhood'. 'For too long mothers have been treated like the earth. The earth is supposed to endure everything and give everything without tiring. Humankind has learned that this is a mistake. Yet, as long as the patience of women lasts, men will continue to exploit it. The war, however, has exhausted this patience and has driven women to their furthest limits.'[19] In Key's view, the war was shedding blood, tearing women apart and trampling over the 'world's great protective and creative powers', which alone might have made humankind truly human. All that men had achieved, she wrote the same year in *War, Peace, and the Future*, had counted for nothing in terms of the self-fulfilment of humankind.[20]

Ellen Key also introduced the concept of the mother as educator capable of instilling the values of nurturing and preserving life, a topic which was central to Madeleine Vernet's journal, *La mère éducatrice*, published from October 1917. Women who had limited their love to the small family circle and had looked lightly upon the warlike games of their own sons, as Key pronounced, should have weeded out their patriotic feelings which were fuelled by hatred and pride. In so doing, 'the mother-educator would be fit to purify her children's souls'.[21] In June 1915, Marguerite Gobat, too, discussed the issue of women's responsibility in an article proclaiming the formation of the Universal Union of Women for International Harmony on 9 February in Geneva, by the American Clara Guthrie Cocke and by 36 other women from various countries. This organization was geared to promote peace through education.[22] Gobat returned to this topic in the summer of 1917, in an article in which she reminded women of their duty to break their silence and encouraged them to join the new international organization:

> With some rare exceptions, women have still not spoken on the issue of 'war or peace'. Not only have they not spoken, they still have not understood the essence of their role in the disaster. They have been told that violent conflict is innate to human nature and that as long as there are men upon earth, they will fight. Overwhelmed by this male prejudice and thus unable to react, they have considered war as an inevitable evil which can be defied just as little as illness and death. Rather than opposing this false view and asserting what is innate to them as creators of humanity, they retreated within the walls of their homes.[23]

Embracing such appeals, *Coenobium* covered international events concerning women's pacifism in detail: the International Women's Conference in Bern in March 1915 and the gathering held in The Hague in April of the same year. In summer 1915, the journal published the complete Hague resolutions and the key aspects of the conference proceedings as well as a letter written by Jeanne Halbwachs and other French pacifists.[24]

The journal *Demain* undertook an extended translation project. Its first issue from January 1916 included Helena Swanwick's essay 'Les femmes et la guerre' (Women and War), published in the previous year in London by the Union of Democratic Control. In this piece, the British pacifist described the consequences of war on the lives of women (mothers, refugees, and workers), the impact of women's involvement in politics on peace and the connection between militarism and female degradation. Swanwick identified the 'physical force mentality' as the deep roots that nourished conflicts, obstructed democracy, and strengthened domination over women: 'I felt that men had abandoned their aims and had left the responsibility of life upon women's shoulders while they played that foolish and bloody game of massacring women's children.'[25]

In October 1916, the tale 'Le brouillard' (The Mist), written by Selma Lagerlöf for the Neutral Conference of Stockholm and promoted by Henry

Ford, was printed in *Demain*. In the same month Ellen Key published a story entitled 'La supplication des mères', which was written especially for *Demain*. At the heart of the tragedy, and inspired by Euripides' suppliant women, a chorus of mothers bemoan the futility of their responsibility to conceive, to care for, and to love sons whose lives will be cut short by war. Millions of mothers suffered in the context of modern warfare just as much as the weeping women of Argos had suffered. Weeping and moaning were not signs of weakness, but the voice of reason and nature which demanded respect for women's fundamental rights. Thus, Euripides expressed the conviction that peace was consistent with a profound sense of existence, as well as with reason and love, and that war emerged from human inactivity. According to Key, the principal task of human kind was to transform 'the chaos from discord and stupidity into a cosmos wherein reason and harmony become the spontaneous expression of human nature'.[26]

In March 1917, *Demain* published Marianne Rauze's manifesto 'Aux féministes socialistes', which, as it says in the introduction, had been censored in France. The example of a woman, twice widowed, with one son born to a French and another to an Austrian father, prompted reflection upon the relationship between women, state, and nationality. Rauze pronounced that no nation would ever have the power to control women's ability to give life, and that no law could limit a mother's fertility. Mothers would always be the bond between all homelands, 'the powerful, invincible, and eternal bond between human societies and the great natural laws'. Rauze concluded that women would never recognize borders. Women, without having political rights, were above the events, they were the 'judges' who denounced militarism, violence, and the disastrous discipline which dominated the socialist parties unchallenged, herds led by shepherds who would not shy away from betrayal.[27]

Finally, *Les Tablettes*: This periodical, which advocated a non-violent pacifism and an anarchical and individualistic vision, published a vast number of literary and poetical texts. In May 1917, it started the French translation of Vernon Lee's work *The Ballet of Nations* (1915) which had caused uproar in her homeland, Britain, and had alienated many of her friends. In this text, Vernon Lee (a pseudonym for Violet Paget) carried out a detailed analysis of the 'war mentality' and of its psychological mechanisms. According to Lee, 'the devil of war' mobilizes the most noble sentiments such as indignation, pity, and sense of justice, and this with the only purpose of beginning the massacre and continually justifying it. With Claire Studer's book *Die Frauen Erwachen* in 1918, the Lausanne journal returned to the topic of women's responsibility for not being able to oppose the war.[28]

The texts of the journals published in Switzerland between 1915 and 1918 focused on topics which reflected on the relationship between women and war. These pacifist publications made women's thought and organizational activities accessible to a broad public in some war-affected countries. At any rate, the periodical which was the most significant one in keeping women's internationalism alive and cultivating it was *Jus Suffragii*.

Jus Suffragii

Jus Suffragii, founded in 1906 and published by the International Woman Suffrage Alliance (IWSA),[29] was edited from 1913 to 1919 by Mary Sheepshanks.[30] The London-based edition was released in the English language, the one based in Geneva in French. Sheepshanks was responsible for the pacifist character and the international quality of the periodical. As early as October 1914 she apologized to suffragists from 'enemy' countries, in case she had failed to present their situation appropriately:

> The editorial office being in a belligerent country, all news from other countries is subject to censorship [...]. It appears almost inevitable that news from England, America and neutral countries should predominate, and though, of course, the policy and sympathy of the paper is and must be entirely international and untainted by national or partisan bias [...]. We appeal earnestly to readers in neutral countries to furnish news and articles, especially news of women's doings in Germany and Austria, and if the paper reaches our German and Austrian subscribers, we appeal to them not to attribute the dearth of news from their countries to anything but its true cause, the impossibility to obtain news.[31]

There were many replies to the appeal from readers of neutral countries committed to keeping in contact with suffragists from the warring nations and to sending news and reports.

Radical pacifism made its appearance in the journal on 1 August 1914, in an article by Rosika Schwimmer entitled 'The Bankruptcy of the Man Made World War'.[32] 'The curtain of the European stage is raised to show the last act of the greatest tragedy ever performed on this stage. The catastrophe of a European war has not taken us by surprise. This terrible event is the logical consequence of all the former acts of the play called "The Making of the State". In this hour of disaster, greater than any imagination is able to grasp, we accuse men and women alike.'[33]

According to Schwimmer, women, too, were to be blamed for having contributed to this process and for having neglected their 'sacred duties as mothers of the human race'.

It was not without opposition that *Jus Suffragii* managed to retain its pacifist and internationalist perspective. Millicent Fawcett, Vice-President of the IWSA, protested against what was viewed as an inappropriate tendency, as the journal's role was supposed to focus exclusively on suffrage-related issues. Yet for the time being, the suffrage campaign was over, and in many countries women had started with relief work for civilians, refugees, and prisoners.[34]

From the first weeks of the war, the journal became the base for a new international organization: the International Women's Relief Committee which was geared to assist and support families of imprisoned foreign nationals from enemy states as well as Belgian refugees in Holland. Thus, the publication introduced Elizabeth Rotten's work in Germany.[35] In the course of the war, the journal regularly published news about social work by women in Austria, Germany, and Hungary, intending to establish a sense of community in everyday life and to lift, in Vernon Lee's words, 'the monstrous iron curtain of war, which has completely separated people from one another'.[36]

In an article entitled 'Bach's Christmas Music in England and Germany' from 1 January 1915, a few days after the fraternization between 'enemy' soldiers from opposing trenches, Vernon Lee imagined that German and British women alike went to church to listen to the same music by Bach, and that mothers, sisters, and girlfriends brought along 'soldier-lads' to celebrate Christmas, 'perhaps their last Christmas on earth'. These women from two warring countries were united in the same hope, the same fear, and the same prayers.[37] The bond between women from 'enemy' nations is perhaps the most recurrent topic, certainly the most intensely heartfelt. At around the same time, an open letter appeared in the journal by Emily Hobhouse,[38] entitled 'To the Women of Germany and Austria' and signed by more than 100 Quaker and Suffragette women:

> Sisters, some of us wish to send you a word at this sad Christmastide though we can but speak through the press [...]. Do not let us forget that our very anguish unites us, that we are passing together through the same experiences of pain and grief [...]. We hope it may lessen your anxiety to learn we are doing our utmost to soften the lot of your civilians and war prisoners within our shores, even as we rely on your goodness of heart to do the same for ours in Germany and Austria. [...] As we saw in South Africa and the Balkan States, the brunt of the war falls upon non-combatants, and the consciousness of the world cannot bear the sight.[39]

Help and support for the 'enemies' was a fundamental feature of women's international political commitment. The suffragists' task, Mary Sheepshanks wrote on 14 November 1914 in 'Patriotism or Internationalism', was to prepare for international reconstruction. Suffrage should not be understood in a narrow-minded sense, purely political and limited to national borders.[40] The president of the IWSA, Carrie Chapman Catt, discussed this subject in an article from 1 September 1914 entitled 'Women and War'.[41] Only women's votes and the establishment of an international parliament could open the door to peace. 'It is apparent', the Irishwoman Louie Bennet wrote in December 1915, 'that women cannot take part together with men in the government of a militarist state [...] and it therefore follows that the Suffrage campaign will have to be united with anti-militarist propaganda'.[42]

During the war a new convergence between pacifism, anti-militarism, and suffrage arose. Women were to reflect on the causes of war, to make every possible effort to keep the internationalist spirit alive, and to examine the meaning of patriotism and militarism. According to this view, the glorification of the principle of power and the contempt for physical weakness, sensitivity, and compassion, inevitably led to a contempt for femininity. As Grace Isabel Colborn wrote in the New York journal *The Woman Voter* in 1914: 'The military point of view is that of contempt for woman, of a denial to her of any other usefulness than that of bearing children. It is this spirit of militarism, the glorification of the brute force, and this alone, that has kept woman in political, legal and economic bondage throughout the ages.'[43]

In 1915, *Jus Suffragii* featured a series of articles, subsequently published as a pamphlet entitled *Militarism versus Feminism*, in which Mary Sargant Florence and Charles Kay Ogden demonstrated the utter incompatibility between female dignity and militarism, the extreme expression of male domination. To support their stance, they turned to history, anthropology, theology, and classical studies:

> Militarism has been the curse of women, as women, from the first dawn of social life. [...] Violence at home, violence abroad; violence between individuals, between classes, between nations, between religions; violence between man and woman: this it is which, more than all other influences, has prevented the voice of woman being heard in public affairs until almost yesterday. War has created Slavery with its degrading results for women [...]. War has engendered and perpetuated that dominance of man as a military animal which has pervaded every social institution from Parliament downwards.[44]

In the February edition of 1915, after the American Women's Peace Conference in Washington, Lida Gustava Heymann made her vibrant appeal to European women: 'Women of Europe, where is your voice, that should be sowing the seeds of peace? [...] Strive at least to put a spoke in the bloody wheel of Time, with the strength, courage, and humanity worthy of your sex.'[45] This was followed, in the March edition, by another appeal by Aletta Jacobs,[46] in which she called for participation in the Hague Conference. Over the following months, the journal published some papers from the conference, the resolutions, Jane Addams's opening speech, letters, and solidarity statements from Austria.[47]

The conference raised hopes of a new internationalism. In 1916, Mary Sheepshanks opened the June edition with an article in which she asked women not to join those who had declared internationalism dead. She warned that by continuously repeating this, in her view false statement, it would eventually manifest itself. In contrast, it was necessary to recognize that women's contribution to internationalism had increased, and would still increase in the future:

> Women of all countries have this task before them. Unenfranchised, unequal before the law, suffering from innumerable disabilities and injustices, they will preserve the bond of their common sisterhood. The ideal which unites them is a greater one than any for which men have fought; it is no less than the spiritual freedom of the half of the race. The immemorial, the world-wide wrongs of women transcend those that have ever inspired warriors or poets; no mere national wrongs can touch them in duration or extent.[48]

Therefore, women were supposed to pursue their commitment to obtaining civil and political rights throughout the world. This was a topic to which the journal *Jus Suffragii* devoted a great deal of space over the following years.

La mère éducatrice

On 1 August 1914, the day after the assassination of Jean Jaurès in Paris, Madeleine Vernet[49] left the Orphelinat ouvrier (Worker's Orphanage), which she had founded in Épône, and went to Paris. She was convinced that a spontaneous reaction by the people and the workers' movement would halt mobilization. Contrary to her expectations, she witnessed hate-filled demonstrations against the Germans, lootings, socialists' resignation, and the tears of those who set off for the front: 'As the men – whether ignorant or knowing, villains or heroes, dominated by events or unable to resist them – went away towards the abyss and towards their deaths, there still remained one sacred, irrevocable task: to save the children from the disaster. In this, at least, I did not want to fail.'[50] Vernet stated that the 'evil force', which was holding the majority of people in its sway, had age-old origins and deep roots; it had been cultivated from childhood, from that moment on when the little child was given 'the first toy-soldier, the first rifle'. Afterwards, in school, the child was told that the world was divided into different homelands. Vernet considered this a powerful force, as it was able to destroy everything: family, happiness, love.[51] Individuals had to rid themselves of hatred and vengeful feelings in order to live together again and to initiate a new internationalism. Thus, getting involved in education for her meant acting politically against the roots of evil.

To deal with this task, Vernet founded the journal *La mère éducatrice: Revue mensuelle d'éducation populaire*. The first issue came out in October 1917, the hardest year of the war. Since spring, war weariness of soldiers and civilians

alike had been on the increase and resulted in unrest and riots in every belligerent country. The journal, comprised of just a few printed pages, was written in plain language and addressed working-class mothers. It offered help
to boost their self-confidence, to accomplish their role as moral educators,
and to take up their rightful place in society.[52] The disavowal of the mother's
role was, in Madeleine Vernet's opinion, the main cause of the spiritual
impoverishment of society. War as the supreme insult to motherhood, 'the
denial of the beauty of women's achievement of love', had to be opposed
by affirming the inviolability and strength of motherhood. According to
Vernet, motherhood was above society as it was the only basis for rights
and justice, it was uncoercible, and it would submit neither to the plans of
nations nor the will of men. The values of motherhood had been distorted
by nationalism and women were forced to support the war effort. Sacrificing
one's own sons, a common propaganda topic, meant to comply with the
symbolic order of death, a male perception, which dominated the minds of
the people, particularly in times of war. In contrast to this, women should
reassert the idea of a strong and free motherhood which was solely inspired
by the impulse to protect and preserve life; a motherhood that was joyously
experienced in times of peace, but was capable of rebelling in times of war.
War, in fact, had also revealed the weakness and the errors of mothers: 'How
have the mothers of the latest generation brought up their sons? To respect
and admire military glory, the sword, and force.'[53] Women were part of the
tragedy which was shaking the world and, as one reader put it in a letter to
the editorial staff, their hands were not clean. If women's hands had produced ammunition, then why should they not hold guns? By addressing the
responsibility of women in the military conflict, which was a recurring topic,
the journal did not intend to blame or dishearten but rather to encourage
awareness. Besides, it would have been quite unreasonable to blame women
who were inferior and deprived of social and political rights, excluded from
education, and marginalized in the working environment. In every aspect of
life, women had always been told of their weakness and inferiority.

Unlike other writers who confined themselves either to disapproval or to
abstract appeals for action, Vernet offered motivation and support for non-
violent education, based on love of life and joy: 'The truth, in fact, lies only
in life, the rest is lies and deceit.'[54] In addition to journals with a focus on the
condition of women and mothers within the social and political spheres, on
topics of war, militarism, and women's organization, *La mère éducatrice* also
provided mothers and teachers with didactic tools such as stories, poems,
and songs.

Yet it was only in the aftermath of the war and in the face of the triumph
of militarism, the celebration of martyrdom and the myth of resurrection,
in contrast to individual experiences of horror and death, that Madeleine
Vernet's pacifism became more radical. Three events in particular led to
her decision to propose a women's peace organization: the 'rowdy, stupid,

and vulgar' celebrations of the news about the armistice, the indifference of working-class men and women to the suffering of children in Central Europe due to the continuing naval blockade, and the profanation of death at the memorial ceremony for the unknown soldier. In November 1918, the announcement of the end of the conflict had not only prompted feelings of joy and liberation, it had also provided opportunity to give vent to feelings of aggression and the desire for revenge: 'What frightens me, you know, is the growing wave of hate. This crowd that wishes to enjoy itself is in need – in order to stifle the secret voices that rise against the conscience – of someone responsible for all the evil that has occurred over these four years [...]. That victim will be the vanquished people.'[55] Throughout the pages of the issue, Madeleine Vernet made an appeal to send 'a peaceful fraternal greeting' to the German people, the women and children on Christmas Day.[56] She considered all borders places of violence, which separated nations, classes, men, and women.

Hatred and ill-feeling towards an entire population did not spare the children. In June 1920, questions arose on the living conditions of hundreds of thousands of children in Central Europe. After five years of war, children were still affected by its repercussions and atoned for the crimes committed by men. While Herbert Hoover, head of the US Food Administration during the war and later president of the United States, estimated the number of children in Europe facing starvation to be between four and five million,[57] politicians and the media ignored this tragic fact.

What little information that filtered through about the repercussions of the naval blockade during the war could be read in a publication edited by a woman: 'Notes on the Foreign Press', a supplementary feature edited by Dorothy Jebb Buxton for *The Cambridge Magazine*. In May 1919, Dorothy's sister, Eglantyne Jebb, founder of Save the Children, had been arrested in Trafalgar Square for handing out leaflets which showed images of young victims of the blockade. Edith Pye had made the same pictures public in France.[58] Vernet writes:

> I saw the photographs and read the reports from Austria, Germany, Russia, Hungary, and our departments in the North, and I was chilled by fear when I saw those living skeletons that looked as if they had just risen from their graves, had there not been their eyes, those large eyes, those large feverish, encircled eyes, big and wide-open, testifying to the fact that life had still not left the body. But what life could inhabit such a shell? One of incessant torture, the lingering death of a plant deprived of its lifeblood.[59]

Vernet added that she had not taken up her pen to collect money, but to ask individuals to face up to the events and to remind them of their duties. She blamed men and women alike; among them mothers who had taught their sons that children beyond the border belonged to a race different to their own. This, Vernet thought, was the only explanation for the wide-spread insensitivity of working men and women and of the French trade unions, who refused to purchase the French one-franc postage stamp issued by the General Confederation of Labour for the benefit of European children. Very few people were willing to help the little 'boches'. Once again, Madeleine Vernet asked mothers to teach their children a sense of solidarity with Central European children, to recognize the suffering that the war had brought upon the most vulnerable.

The greatest offence to mothers, as Vernet saw it, was inflicted by the French government in November 1920, when the remains of a soldier were exhumed from the battlefields of the Western Front and buried at the foot of the Arc de Triumph in Paris. To placate the wrath of the working classes, Vernet wrote, the government leaders 'turned into hyenas': They invented a 'macabre comedy' and 'entertained the populace with a skeleton'. In a long essay entitled 'À la "Mère inconnue" du "soldat inconnu"' ('To the Unknown Mother of the Unknown Soldier'), which appeared in the November edition, Vernet recalled the torment of that unknown mother: her pain at the moment of separation, the waiting, the silence, the resignation, and then the gruesome digging up of the remains and, eventually, the rowdy and unseemly celebrations:

> Oh, unknown mother of the unknown soldier, due to the necessities of life I was travelling across Paris on the very day when the abominable play was enacted [...] I heard the fanfares, the singing and the shouting of the celebrating crowd. I saw the river of people flooding out onto the streets, eager to go and watch the grim procession, proudly escorting the sad remains of the poor unnamed boy who had been snatched from the holy peace of the grave.[60]

An anti-war association was needed, which Vernet would finally set up on 10 May 1921 as the Ligue des femmes contre la guerre:

> Now, we mothers demand the abolition of regular armies. We demand the general disarmament which was promised to our martyrs. We demand the end of the current regime which crushes us, this republican imperialism which is not satisfied with making the people sweat to provide luxuries for an idle handful, but also exterminates our sons, making fun of their remains and insulting our holiest feelings.[61]

From then on, the journal opened up to topics concerning international pacifism. During 1922, many articles outlined the situation and developments of pacifism in Great Britain, the United States, Germany, Belgium, and Austria. It provided information on the activities and conferences of the WILPF and, at the same time, the collaborative work of pacifists from other countries, particularly Germany (Helene Stöcker, Lida Gustava Heymann, Lilli Jannasch) was repeatedly featured in the journal.

On 13 November 1921, *La mère éducatrice* declared the internationalism of the *Ligue*'s official policy. Many close ties were established with other associations in Great Britain and in Germany, 'with a view to a federation of all pacifist and anti-militarist associations which focused their activities on the rejection of any kind of participation, direct or indirect, in war'.[62] Women, too, were directed to refuse work in ammunition factories and any other employment that supported war. Everyone had blood on their hands, Vernet wrote in the association newsletter on 22 January 1922: 'The only heroic gesture is complete refusal.'[63] In summer 1922, the secretary of the WILPF's French division, Andrée Jouve, announced the *Ligue*'s participation in the international women's organization for peace and freedom.

Conclusion

Due to the internationalist spirit, which a minority of feminist pacifists endeavoured to keep alive during the war, new important international organizations developed significantly in the post-war years. The idea of motherhood, in feminist theoretical reflection, was at the heart of this new internationalism. This concept was understood as an experience with a culturally and socially transformative impact, which would eradicate the principle of brute force in society, politics, and international relations. Therefore, feminist pacifists opposed the idea of women's passivity and their need for protection, and claimed the right to speak for themselves as well as for men. They pointed out that the true nature of modern warfare was violence against civilians. Indignation over the naval blockade, a weapon that deliberately hit the civilian population and inflicted enormous suffering on mothers and children, gave feminist pacifism a power of persuasion stronger than it had ever been before.

During the post-war years, another international organization came into being, the Save the Children Fund. The topics of motherhood and desecrated childhood, which had already been widely discussed by pacifist women during the First World War, became the cornerstone of a new internationalism and a new understanding of politics from 1919 on. This was stressed by Eglantyne Jebb in her appeal to British women in 1919. Only women's international solidarity, only their independent and direct action could repair and clear up war damage. Politics as understood, conceived, and enacted by men could never have done so. Jebb appealed 'to my fellow country women to help me to lift the whole question of the saving of the child life of Europe out of the political region altogether. Let the women of this country take the lead in a work which the men, in their political groupings, seem powerless to carry forward'.[64] According to Jebb, this was not a question of charity, but of giving women's social and voluntary actions international responsibility. In so doing, there was hope that new international relations could be built on basic human needs and on a politics of compassion. On 19 May 1919, when the foundation of the Save the Children Fund was announced at the Royal Albert Hall, Dorothy Buxton, while shaking a can of condensed milk, declared that 'there is more morality in this can than in all the creeds'.[65] Children became the symbol of a new internationalism and their suffering an indictment against the politics of men. Along these lines, Dorothy Buxton and Eglantyne Jebb, in a privately produced and circulated pamphlet, wrote on the developments in Paris, where the destiny of the world was being decided:

> Paris is very self-important. It believes it is making a new Europe, that it is writing history with a large and firm hand, but history is being made elsewhere. It is being made in 1000 hospitals, in innumerable humble homes all over Europe. The cry of the child for bread is hushed in a nameless grave, but surely his voice will waken again. It will resound down our century. All shall hear it. It will become a voice of thunder which shall send statesmen and politicians, Parliament and Churches to their doom.[66]

Notes

1. On this issue, see G. Procacci (1989) *Premi Nobel per la pace e guerre mondiali* (Milano: Feltrinelli), pp. 82–111; S. E. Cooper (1991) *Patriotic Pacifism: Waging War on War in Europe, 1815–1914* (Oxford: Oxford University Press); V. Grossi (1994) *Le pacifisme européen 1889–1914* (Bruxelles: Bruylant), pp. 385–401. On pacifism in France, S. E. Cooper (1991) 'Pacifism in France, 1889–1914: International Peace as a Human Right', *French Historical Studies*, 17:2, pp. 359–86. On Italian pacifists, B. Bianchi (2012) 'I pacifisti italiani dalla guerra di Libia al primo conflitto mondiale (1911–1919)', in F. Degli Esposti, L. Bertucelli and A. Botti (eds) *I conflitti e la storia: Studi in onore di Giovanna Procacci* (Roma: Viella), pp. 187–207.
2. Those who condemned war itself denied the existence of a non-aggressive patriotism, advocated the abolition of all forms of military organization and proposed conscientious objection. They were mostly Christian anarchists who were heavily influenced by the thoughts of Tolstoy. Among those who posed the question of war and peace at the international congress in Amsterdam in 1907 were Rudolf Grossmann and Domela Nieuwenhuis, since 1904 the head of the International Anti-militarist League. On Grossmann, see R. R. Laurence (1999) 'Rudolf Grossmann and Anarchist Antimilitarism in Austria before World War I', *Peace & Change*, 14:2, pp. 155–75. On Tolstoy's influence in Europe and Russia, see B. Bianchi (2004) 'Tolstoj e l'obiezione di coscienza', in B. Bianchi, E. Magnanini and A. Salomoni (eds) *Culture della disobbedienza: Tolstoj e i Duchobory 1895–1910* (Roma: Bulzoni), pp. 9–122.
3. On the hostility towards pacifists in Germany, see Procacci, *Premi Nobel per la pace e guerre mondiali*; in Great Britain, J. Bell, *We Did Not Fight: 1914–1918 Experiences of War Resisters* (London: Cobden-Sanderson); in the United States, B. Wiesen Cook (1973) 'Democracy in Wartime: Antimilitarism in England and the United States', in C. Chatfield (ed.) *Peace Movements in America* (New York: Shocken); see also J. Addams (1922) *Peace and Bread in Time of War* (New York: Macmillan), p. 142.

4. On the activities and contacts of French pacifists, see R. Rolland (1960) *Diario degli anni di guerra 1914–1919: Note e documenti per lo studio della storia morale dell'Europa odierna*, 2 vols (Milano: Parenti).
5. On the Friends War Victims Relief Committee, which was funded by the Society of Friends, A. R. Fry (1926) *A Quaker Adventure: The Story of Nine Years' Relief and Reconstruction* (London: Nisbet); D. Detzer (1948) *Appointment on the Hill* (New York: Henry Holt); B. Bianchi (2008), '"Una grande, pericolosa, avventura": Anna Ruth Fry, il *relief work* e la riconciliazione internazionale', *DEP. Deportate, esuli, profughe: Rivista telematica di studi sulla memoria femminile*, 9, pp. 23–54, online at http://www.unive.it/dep. On the Emergency Committee for the Assistance of Germans, Austrians and Hungarians in Distress, founded by Stephen Hobhouse in September 1914, see A. Braithwaite Thomas (1920) *St. Stephen's House: Friends' Emergency Work in England, 1914 to 1920* (London: Emergency Committee for the Assistance of Germans, Austrians and Hungarians in Distress).
6. On Elisabeth Rotten's activities during the war, see M. Stibbe (2007) 'Elisabeth Rotten and the "Auskunfts- und Hilfsstelle für Deutsche im Ausland und Ausländer in Deutschland", 1914–1919', in A. S. Fell and I. Sharp (eds) *The Women's Movement in Wartime: International Perspectives, 1914–1919* (Basingstoke: Palgrave Macmillan), pp. 194–209.
7. M. Ceadel (1980) *Pacifism in Britain 1914–1945: The Defining of a Faith* (Oxford: Clarendon) On the UDC, see H. Swanwick (1924) *Builders of Peace, Being Ten Years' History of the Union of Democratic Control* (London: Swarthmore); S. Harris (1996) *Out of Control: British Foreign Policy and the Union of Democratic Control, 1914/1918* (Hull: Hull University Press). On the Bund Neues Vaterland, see P. Grappin (1952) *Le Bund Neues Vaterland (1914–1916): ses rapports avec Romain Rolland* (Lyon: IAC). On the Netherlands, see R. Jans (1952) *Tolstoj in Nederland* (Bussum: P. Brand), pp. 130–40. On the Bond van Christen Socialisten, see Foundation for Information on Active Nonviolence (1990) *Bart De Ligt (1883–1938): Peace Activist and Peace Researcher, His Life and Ideas* (Den Haag: Foundation for Information on Active Nonviolence).
8. Until 1924, the UDC was presided over by Edward Dene Morel (1873–1924). When Morel was arrested in 1917 for sending a pacifist leaflet to Romain Rolland, the UDC's membership numbered 650,000. H. Hanak (1963) 'The Union of Democratic Control During the First World War', *Historical Research*, 36:94, pp. 168–80.
9. In the post-war period, the conscientious objector Fenner Brockway, who initiated setting up the organization, was among the founders of War Resisters International (WRI), the most important and radical pacifist organization between the two wars, which was focused on conscientious objection and on the refusal to support the war effort. In the late 1930s, WRI was represented in 24 countries. C. Chatfield (ed.) (1975) *International War Resistance through World War II* (New York and London: WRI).
10. J. Vellacott (1993) 'A Place for Pacifism and Transnationalism in Feminist Theory: The Early Work of the Women's International League for Peace and Freedom', *Women's History Review*, 2:1, p. 27.
11. J. Addams (1976) 'What War is Destroying', in A. F. Davis (ed.) *Jane Addams on Peace, War, and International Understanding, 1899–1932* (New York: Garland), p. 63.
12. Much has been written about the Hague Conference and about the WILPF's pacifist internationalism. Apart from A. Wiltsher (1985) *Most Dangerous Women: Feminist Peace Campaigners of the Great War* (London: Pandora), see also

L. B. Costin (1982) 'Feminism, Pacifism, Internationalism and the 1915 International Congress of Women', *Women's Studies International Forum*, 5:3/4, pp. 301–15; Vellacott, 'A Place for Pacifism and Transnationalism in Feminist Theory'; L. J. Rupp (1994) 'Constructing Internationalism: The Case of Transnational Women's Organizations, 1885–1945', *The American Historical Review*, 99:5, pp. 1571–600; A. Wilmers (2008) *Pazifismus in der internationalen Frauenbewegung (1914–1920): Handlungsspielräume, politische Konzeptionen und gesellschaftliche Auseinandersetzungen* (Essen: Klartext).

13. J. Addams (1976) 'Presidential Address, International Congress, The Hague', in Davis, *Jane Addams on Peace, War, and International Understanding*, p. 69.

14. Addams, 'Presidential Address', p. 71.

15. Addams, 'Presidential Address', p. 71.

16. The Bureau International de la Paix (BIP) and the Inter-Parliamentary Union for Peace (IPU) postponed their commitment to peace until the years after the war and devoted themselves to humanitarian work. The international organizational network disintegrated. The only tenuous link between the various members of official pacifism during the war was represented by the Organisation Central pour une paix durable, established in The Hague in 1915, which excluded by statute the elaboration of proposals to hasten the end of the conflict. Grossi, *Le pacifisme européen 1889–1914*, pp. 385–401; B. Bianchi (2009) 'La dissoluzione del pacifismo e la nascita di un nuovo internazionalismo', in B. Bianchi, Laura De Giorgi and Guido Samarani (eds) *Le guerre mondiali in Asia Orientale e in Europa: Violenza, collaborazionismi, propaganda* (Milano: Unicopli), pp. 53–72.

17. Enrico Bignami was the founder of the socialist periodical *La Plebe* (1868–1883) and the first to spread the word of Marx and Engels in Italy; subsequently, he moved towards Benoît Malon's 'integral socialism'. In 1868, he joined the Union de la paix, promoted by Felice Santallier and one of the first and most radical peace organizations. After the Italian uprising of 1898 (*moti per il pane*) and the resulting harsh repression by the government, he settled in Lugano.

18. L. Saumoneau (1915) 'Al proletariato femminile di Francia', *Coenobium*, 9:12, pp. 92–3.

19. E. Key (1915) 'Santa insurrezione', *Coenobium*, 9:2, p. 18.

20. E. Key (1916) *War, Peace, and the Future. A Consideration of Nationalism and Internationalism, and of the Relation of Women to War* (New York: Putnam), p. 162.

21. E. Key, 'Santa insurrezione', *Coenobium*, 10:2, p. 16.

22. M. Gobat (1915) 'L'Union mondiale de la femme pour la concorde internationale', *Coenobium*, 9:6/7, pp. 26–7.

23. M. Gobat (1917) 'Les femmes et la paix', *Coenobium*, 11:6/7, p. 53.

24. 'Congresso internazionale femminile', *Coenobium*, 11:6/7, pp. 64–8.

25. H. M. Swanwick (1935) *I Have Been Young* (London: Gollancz), p. 241.

26. E. Key (1916), 'La supplication des mères', *Demain*, 1:10, p. 280.

27. M. Rauze (1917) 'Aux féministes socialistes', *Demain*, 2:1, pp. 8–10. In 1913, Marianne Rauze (1875–1964) founded Equité which welcomed middle-class and socialist feminists. In 1923, she adopted absolute pacifism and became the leader of the French section of War Resisters International.

28. On Studer's stories, see I. Sharp (2007) 'Blaming the Women: Women's "Responsibility" for the First World War', in Fell and Sharp, *The Women's Movement in Wartime*, pp. 67–87.

29. S. Oldfield (2003) 'Mary Sheepshanks Edits an Internationalist Suffrage Monthly in Wartime: *Jus Suffragii* 1914–1919', *Women's History Review*, 12:1, pp. 119–31.

30. Mary Sheepshanks (1872–1960), born in Liverpool, was engaged in social work, first in Liverpool and afterwards in London. She joined the National Union of Women's Suffrage Societies (from 1908 to 1913) and then the IWSA. Straight after the outbreak of the war, she went to the Netherlands to help Belgian refugees and later assisted German families in England. After the war, she became secretary of the Fight the Famine Council and, in 1927, secretary of the WILPF; in Geneva she edited the journal *Pax International*. In 1929, Mary Sheepshanks organized the first international scientist's conference on the consequences of aerial bombardments on civilians and, in 1930, Europe's first conference on statelessness. At the beginning of the 1930s she went secretly to East Galicia to record the atrocities committed by Poles in Ukraine. S. Oldfield (1984) *Spinsters of this Parish: The Life and Times of F. M. Mayor and Mary Sheepshanks* (London: Virago).
31. M. Sheepshanks (1914) '*Jus Suffragii* and the Crisis', *Jus Suffragii*, 1 October, p. 171.
32. Rosika Schwimmer (1877–1948), a Hungarian suffragist, was committed to peace and internationalism during the Great War. She held conferences in the United States and in Europe and participated in the organization of the Hague Conference. In the aftermath of the war she went into exile to Vienna and then to the United States, where she was denied citizenship because of her pacifism. H. Josephson (ed.) (1985) *Biographical Dictionary of Modern Peace Leaders* (Westport, CT: Greenwood), pp. 862–5.
33. Rosika Schwimmer (1914) 'The Bankruptcy of the Man Made World War', *Jus Suffragii*, 1 August, p. 148.
34. On women's international commitment to relief work, see Bianchi, '"Una grande, pericolosa, avventura"', pp. 23–54.
35. See note 6.
36. V. Lee (1915) 'Bach's Christmas Music in England and Germany', *Jus Suffragii*, 1 January, p. 218.
37. Lee, 'Bach's Christmas Music in England and Germany', p. 218.
38. There are a vast number of research studies on Emily Hobhouse (1860–1926), the British pacifist who first raised the question of concentration camps in the South African war and who, in 1916, secretly went to occupied Belgium and to Berlin 'in the interests of truth, peace and humanity'. For a brief biography, see S. Oldfield (2001) *Women Humanitarians: A Biographical Dictionary of British Women Active Between 1900 and 1950: 'Doers of the Word'* (London: Continuum), pp. 102–6.
39. The reply by German women was published in March 1915, with dozens of signatures included, *Jus Suffragii*, p. 249.
40. *Jus Suffragii*, 14 November 1914, p. 184.
41. *Jus Suffragii*, 1 September 1914, p. 164.
42. L. Bennet (1915) 'To the editor', *Jus Suffragii*, 1 December, p. 44.
43. G. I. Colborn (1914) 'Women and the Military Spirit', *The Woman Voter*, 5, p. 9, cited by L. B. Costin (1982) 'Feminism, Pacifism and the 1915 International Congress of Women', *Women's Studies International Forum*, 5:3/4, p. 305.
44. C. K. Ogden and M. S. Florence (1915) 'Militarism versus Feminism', Supplement to *Jus Suffragii*, 1 March, pp. 79–86. In 1915, articles by Romain Rolland, Norman Angell, Lida Gustava Heymann, Olive Schreiner, Emily Greene Balch, Paul Henri d'Estournelles de Constant, Helena Swanwick, and others were published in the journal.
45. L. G. Heymann (1915) 'Women of Europe, when will your cry ring out?', *Jus Suffragii*, 1 February, p. 232.

46. Aletta Jacobs (1854–1929) was the first woman to be admitted to a Dutch university, where she was awarded a degree in medicine. A reformer and pacifist, she decided to independently organize a peace conference in the Hague in spring 1915, after IWSA's refusal to call an international conference.
47. On the activities and pacifist thought of Jane Addams, see B. Bianchi (2006) 'Discours de paix: Les interventions publiques et les écrits de Jane Addams contre la guerre (1915–1919)', in S. Caucanas, R. Cazals and N. Offenstadt (eds) *Paroles de paix en temps de guerre* (Paris: Privat), pp. 181–94.
48. M. Sheepshanks (1916) 'Is Internationalism Dead?', *Jus Suffragii*, 1 June, p. 319.
49. Madeleine Vernet (1878–1949) founded l'Avenir Social, a school for children of the poor, in 1906. In 1909, the school moved to Épône and was renamed Orphelinat ouvrier. Vernet wrote several poems against the war; many of them circulated clandestinely, others appeared on postcards and were widely distributed in the trenches. By 1917, she had founded *La mère éducatrice*, a journal she published until 1939. In 1928, Vernet wrote *De l'objection de conscience au désarmement*.
50. Quoted from G. Fraisse (2010) *Les femmes et leur histoire* (Paris: Gallimard), p. 490.
51. M. Vernet (1922) 'Au seuil de l'Epouvante', *La mère éducatrice*, 5:10 Supplement, p. 82.
52. M. Vernet (1917) 'Au femmes, aux mères!', *La mère éducatrice*, 1:1, p. 3.
53. M. Vernet (1920) 'La grande misère des enfants d'Europe', *La mère éducatrice*, 3:6, p. 67.
54. Vernet, 'La grande misère des enfants d'Europe', p. 67.
55. M. Vernet (1918) 'Noël', *La mère éducatrice*, 2:12, p. 18.
56. Vernet, 'Noël', p. 18.
57. D. Buxton and E. Fuller (1931) *The White Flame: The Story of the Save the Children Fund* (London: Longmans), p. 5.
58. Edith Pye (1876–1955) was a trained nurse and midwife and from 1908 a member of the Society of Friends in London. From 1914 to 1919, she lived in France and from 1921 to 1922, in Vienna. In response to her appeal, a committee was set up in France including, among others, Gabrielle Duchêne, Jeanne Alexandre, and Madeleine Rolland.
59. Vernet, 'La grande misère des enfants d'Europe', p. 66.
60. M. Vernet (1920) 'À la "Mère inconnue" du "soldat inconnu"', *La mère éducatrice*, 4:2, p. 12.
61. M. Vernet (1920) 'Une proposition', *La mère éducatrice*, 4:2, p. 14.
62. 'Ligue des femmes contre la guerre', *La mère éducatrice*, 5:2 (1921), p. 13.
63. 'Les femmes contre la guerre', *Bulletin de la Ligue des femmes contre la guerre*, 1 Janvier 1922, p. 2, Bibliothèque Marguerite Durand (Paris), Dossier Madeleine Vernet.
64. C. Mulley (2009) *The Woman Who Saved the Children: A Biography of Eglantyne Jebb, Founder of Save the Children* (Oxford: Oneworld), p. 243.
65. Mulley, *The Woman Who Saved the Children*, p. 245.
66. Mulley, *The Woman Who Saved the Children*, p. 231.

12
'A foolish dream of sisterhood': Anti-Pacifist Debates in the German Women's Movement, 1914–1919

Ingrid Sharp

In 1914, before the outbreak of the First World War, the dominant discourse within women's organizations was of the natural pacifism and the international solidarity of all women, especially among those who were working to improve their social, professional, and political situation.[1] The women's movement since the turn of the century had become increasingly international and even the German women, at first reluctant to cooperate beyond their own borders, had been drawn in.[2] International congresses were held in Berlin in 1896, 1904 – at which the International Women's Suffrage Alliance (IWSA) was founded, and 1912, with a further meeting planned there for 1915.[3]

Yet in all combatant nations, the majority of organized women supported the war policies of their government and suspended their international contacts for the duration of the war: only a very small minority of women in each nation opposed the war and retained or strengthened their international contacts. This was certainly the case in Germany, where the women's coordinated war effort, the Nationaler Frauendienst (National Women's Service, NFD) was controlled by the nationally minded umbrella group of bourgeois women's organizations, the Bund Deutscher Frauenvereine (Federation of German Women's Associations, BDF) led by Gertrud Bäumer. In Germany, as elsewhere, the women most likely to maintain international links and to work for peace during the war were also the most enthusiastic suffrage campaigners such as Lida Gustava Heymann and Anita Augspurg of the Deutscher Frauenstimmrechtsbund (German Women's Suffrage Federation), who played an active role in the IWSA, and Helene Stöcker and Lili Jannasch of the pacifist organization Bund Neues Vaterland (New Fatherland League), formed in November 1914.[4]

Pacifist campaigners saw working for peace and the prevention of future wars and female suffrage as inextricably linked: without the influence of women in government, the strongest moral impulse for peace would be lacking. On the other hand, political rights meant little if war was to be allowed to destroy any progress towards a fairer, more just and representative society. When it became clear that the meeting of the IWSA planned for Berlin in 1915 could not take place, an alternative congress was planned jointly by women from England, Holland, Belgium, Hungary, and Germany. In April 1915, nine months after the start of the First World War, over 1000 women from combatant and non-combatant nations met at The Hague to discuss ways of mediating between the warring nations, stopping the war and finding ways of resolving future conflict without recourse to violence. At the Congress, the transnational organization the International Committee of Women for Permanent Peace (ICWPP), later renamed the Women's International League for Peace and Freedom (WILPF) was formed. The Congress brought the underlying divisions within the women's movement into sharp focus in many nations, dividing opinion in England and France as well as in Austria and Germany and creating a rift that continued well after the end of hostilities. Nowhere was this more acute than in Germany, where the debate between the BDF and the congress organizers was played out in the public arena.

The Hague Congress has been widely discussed in feminist scholarship,[5] and most women's historians have agreed with Leila Rupp's 1997 claim that 'the Congress of women, bravely convened in The Hague during the first year of the Great War, is probably the most celebrated (and was at the time also the most reviled) expression of women's internationalism.'[6] Most have also concurred with Jennifer Davy's 2002 assessment that the peace campaigners of the First World War provide a historic point of identification and a political legacy that is far more palatable than the patriotic war work undertaken by the majority of organized women.[7] With the exception of Annika Wilmers, who offers a more even-handed account, most commentators writing about Germany have presented the controversy as the attempt by the powerful leadership of the BDF to crush dissent within its ranks[8] and to 'denigrate the difficult attempt of courageous women to find a way of bringing the great slaughter to an end, by presenting them as a group without a mandate and lacking any expert knowledge'.[9] For Sabine Hering, the BDF's cooperation with government policies during the war placed them on the side of might as opposed to right: '[t]he battle lines are clear. Socialist and pacifist women are on the other side. The BDF, however, is on the side of power and tries to couch even its criticism according to the rules of the powerful.'[10] Yet hostility to Bäumer and condemnation of her stance often fail to take account of the fact that her position was shared by the majority of organized women in combatant and non-combatant nations – for example, women within the Conseil national des femmes françaises (National Council of French Women, CNFF) were even more publicly outspoken in their criticism and even more ruthless in their expulsion of pacifist elements from their ranks.[11]

As well as ignoring the international context, much of the criticism also fails to take account of the national context in which the women were operating; for example, the particular pressure on the BDF caused by the fact that there were four German women among the Congress's organizing committee, making the need for distancing strategies especially acute.[12] Scholarship tends, too, to place the blame for a lack of sisterly solidarity entirely with the BDF, overlooking the highly limited sympathies and lasting resentment displayed by women from the pacifist camp to those who did not share their convictions. Davy states that '[t]he BDF publicly opposed the participation of German women in the Hague Congress and condemned their pacifist activities',[13] but it is equally true that the pacifist women condemned the BDF for their response to the war: in 1920, Heymann described them as 'chauvinistic women, steeped in the spirit of militarism, whose sense of true womanliness had been clouded by war psychosis'.[14]

By examining the strategies and arguments employed by both groups of women to distance themselves from one another and claim the exclusive right to represent German women, this chapter seeks to challenge the one-sided way the controversy has been received. Drawing on a wide range of contemporary German press responses to the Hague Congress and to the aims of the women's organizations before, during, and immediately after the war, I will seek to show that the context in which the German women were operating was one of long-standing negative attitudes to feminist goals.[15] I will argue that this climate of suspicion and disapproval reflected in and fostered by the mainstream press was a major factor in forcing the BDF into publicly adopting an anti-pacifist position over the Hague Congress, thus creating a dichotomy that had far-reaching and highly damaging consequences for the women's movement in the Weimar Republic.

Different responses to the war

The fundamental paradox facing the organized women's movements in wartime was how they could justify activities that would release more men to fight and be injured or killed. The BDF justified their war service by stressing the inevitability of war and its nature as a great test from which the nation would emerge stronger, as well as the redemptive nature of the deaths and the sense of service to a higher ideal that overrode individual concerns. From the outset, the women of the BDF laid claim to a parallel war experience in which women played a pivotal role. First, this was through their role as mothers and wives of the fighting men: 'We mustn't ever forget that it is not just military training that is being put to the test out there in the trenches and at sea, at the gun emplacements and in the air, but also German mothers' upbringing and German wives' care.'[16] Secondly, this was through a coordinated war effort captured in the expression 'seelische Mobilmachung' ('mobilization of the soul').[17] Through the NFD, women schooled in the women's movement were able to apply their motherly care to the needs of the nation in the familiar fields of social welfare, employment, and education.[18]

The BDF believed they were laying down foundations for peacetime acceptance of women's competence, and it is clear that they set great store by the closeness to government and decision-making at state level that they achieved. As Alice Salomon put it: 'if these had not been times of war, the limitless power given to women would have fulfilled our wildest ambitions.'[19] Despite this, the findings of my press survey show that there was little public sympathy for the women's movement during the war, and, despite the women's integration into government policy, there is no evidence that this was seen as anything but a temporary arrangement with no expectation that it would be carried over into the post-war social order.[20] For example, the Kaiser's Easter Message of April 1917, in which he promised to repay the loyalty and courage of working-class men with political concessions that would express the new bond of trust between the social classes, made no mention at all of the contribution made by women.[21]

The pacifists, however, did not accept the necessity or inevitability of this or any war, seeing it instead as a man-made disaster, a further instance of the failure of male government and demonstration of the necessity of women's involvement in the state. For Heymann and Augspurg: 'The world war has proved that the male state, founded and built up on force, has failed all along the line; we have never seen clearer proof of its unfitness. The male principle is divisive and, if allowed to continue unchecked, will bring about the total destruction of humanity.'[22] In this context, deaths could not be meaningful or redemptive, they were merely pointless and all the more pitiable because they were unnecessary and avoidable. Pacifists dwelt on the horror of war deaths in order to undermine the elevated language of redemptive sacrifice used by the women of the BDF and other supporters of the war.

In contrast to Bäumer's almost mystical connection with the German nation,[23] the pacifists felt strongly that internationalism in this context overrode the national interest: as war – a global phenomenon with national and local consequences – destroyed all that women's work had built in the local community, women must work together across national borders to oppose it. This remained the central pillar of their conviction, and the motivation for the Hague Congress and the activities of the ICWPP and WILPF.

Despite the BDF's increasingly direct involvement in the war, Bäumer was convinced that theirs remained a specifically womanly contribution motivated by love, and saw no contradiction between women's nurturing role and the organization's success in fuelling the war machinery with workers and soldiers. For Bäumer, as for so many others, August 1914 was a shared emotional experience of great power and intensity which, she remained sure, revealed the underlying connectedness of German society. In 1915, she claimed that '[t]here is not one of us who doesn't feel that this time, whatever it may bring, whatever it demands of us, is for our generation the pinnacle of our existence'.[24]

According to their own account, Heymann and Augspurg felt nothing of this elevated mood, feeling themselves clear-eyed yet isolated amidst all the fellow-feeling: '[t]he great crime, war, achieved in 24 hours a unity that had eluded the efforts of rational people for decades. This behaviour appeared repulsive to us, not glorious.'[25] A tiny minority within the women's movement, these women saw themselves as the voice of reason amidst a howling storm of insanity. While they very clearly saw their duty as trying to stop the war, they were realistic enough to realize that few would be willing to hear a dissenting voice in the early moments of 'war psychosis': 'The German people felt like a mighty Colossus, united in its purpose of defying the whole world. [...] Anyone who had dared to openly oppose this unity would have been trampled, crushed, lynched.'[26]

Both groups used a discourse of motherhood to support their position; for Bäumer, it was precisely as a mother that a woman could 'understand from the innermost depths of her heart that a generation has been granted the task of winning with their blood a richer and more worthwhile life for those who are to come',[27] while for Heymann and Augspurg, women's role as bearers of life made their implication in any aspect of war work that led to men's deaths deeply unnatural and abhorrent: 'Women are, just because they are women, against all forms of brutal force that seek to pointlessly destroy what has grown, what has become. They want to build up, to protect, to create anew.'[28] Even the fact that a majority of women worked for and supported the war did not shake this conviction: writing in 1919, Heymann refers to the BDF's pro-war stance as 'the aberration of a few women' set against 'millions and millions who turn away from these women in disgust and were, are, and remain opponents of this war out of the deepest conviction'.[29] While the women's responses to the war and emotional connection with the nation were radically opposed, it is clear that there were sufficient similarities in the roots of their arguments to make the association highly problematic: both groups used maternalist discourse, and both claimed that their actions were motivated by a woman's natural predisposition to love.

Context: press coverage of women's role in wartime

Although press reporting is by no means a fully reliable indicator of public opinion, it both reflects and forms it, and a consideration of the discourse in the media will give an indication of public attitudes.[30] This study therefore will use an analysis of German press coverage of the three key, interlinked ideas associated with the Hague Congress; suffrage, internationalism, and pacifism in relation to the activities of the women's organizations between 1914 and 1919 to offer an insight into the public discourse surrounding feminist goals.[31] I will argue that in this context, in order to remain true to her vision of national service and to protect the long-standing goals towards which she was working, Gertrud Bäumer was compelled to distance herself and the organization she led from the wartime activities of German pacifist women.

There were considerable restrictions placed on publication during this period: in effect, the German press and publishing policy was in the hands of the military, who determined whether a particular publication was harmful to the German war effort.[32] These measures especially affected the pacifist women's writings, which could hardly be published or disseminated at all within Germany between 1914 and 1918, while the few pamphlets and publications expressing pacifist views that were produced in neutral countries, such as Switzerland, had a very limited circulation. In order to gain a better overview of their response, I will therefore consider publications from outside Germany, such as the IWSA's journal, *Jus Suffragii,* and post-war publications, in which pacifist women were keen to give a delayed account of their anti-war activities.

Pre-war coverage of suffrage had been complicated by widespread reporting of suffragettes' violent actions in the United Kingdom, such as the slashing of Velasquez's Rokeby Venus by Mary Richardson on 10 March 1914. The destruction of the beautiful Venus by the 'ugly' feminist was presented as highlighting the contrast between 'deviant' suffragettes and 'normal' women. The suffragettes' tactics were reported as a seven-year war against men, a 'Reign of Terror'[33] that led to questions about the masculinity of English men and the vitality of the English race: 'in powerlessly knuckling under they are showing a *slackness* that points to degeneration, a lowering of national willpower.'[34]

This coverage also reflected and influenced attitudes to feminist aims and activities in Germany, as can be seen, for example, in the *Berliner Volkszeitung* on 11 March 1914, in which a report on English extremism was used to criticize what were seen as similar tendencies in German society: 'our entire public life is suffering from a sinister and generally damaging feminism.'[35] Writing in *Die Hilfe* on 10 June, Gertrud Bäumer complained that 'even liberal newspapers' were conflating the suffrage movement with the activities of one extreme group and using this negative association to condemn the entire campaign for women's rights.[36] However, there are also examples where the negative coverage of English feminists had a positive effect on German women's feminist campaigns, as they were presented as moderate and unpolitical compared to the crazed English deviants.[37] Fears of suffragette extremism spreading to Germany could also be used to advance the German women's cause; for example, Bertha von Kröcher-Winzelberg, President of the Association of Conservative Women, argued that Conservative parties should allow women more influence within their ranks in order to counter the appeal of the left, who were wooing women with 'false promises of political equality and the vote'.[38]

Even before the outbreak of war, democracy itself was presented as a weak, unmanly form of government and many objected to female suffrage on the grounds that it would so compromise the nation's strength that it would not be able to defend itself against aggressors. Throughout the war, women's suffrage continued to be associated with the imposition of an alien, un-German form of government upon a nation proud of its military prowess. The English suffragettes were sometimes invoked to reflect badly on the enemy's military resolve: from September 1914 there were widespread reports of a suffragette battalion arming itself to defend England, supposedly because Lord Kitchener was unable to find English men to fight: '[i]n the English war ministry they are firmly convinced that German soldiers will be just as incapable of dealing with mad women as the gentlemen of the island realm.'[39]

With the front soldier elevated in press coverage to the level of mythic hero, any assertion of women's rights or suggestion that women were seeking recognition for their wartime service was seen as distasteful and inappropriate. In the light of men's bravery and suffering, women could not credibly press their own demands: in 1917, the *Deutsche Tagesblatt* reminded readers that 'when the hour of danger for the nation strikes, everyone, men and women, do their bit and anyone crying out for a reward is not thinking like a German.'[40] In fact, the BDF believed that through organizational efficiency, national-mindedness, and a rhetoric of service, women would demonstrate their value to society and fitness for civic and political rights, but these aims could not be openly articulated without negative response. Even as late as 1917, when constitutional reform was being openly discussed and the BDF had sent a position paper in favour of female suffrage to the Reichstag, female suffrage was presented in the press as a selfish, deeply unpatriotic demand, inappropriate during wartime.[41]

The need for caution was exacerbated by the sensitivity surrounding women's moral behaviour, which took on national significance during the early war years. Press reports show that women and girls' education and behaviour, competence as mothers and housewives, and their consumption habits (notably of unpatriotic luxuries like cake and international fashion items) were under close scrutiny throughout the war.[42] As early as August 1914, the hysterical response to thinly evidenced reports that some German women and girls had been approaching French prisoners of war and offering them food and comforts is a case in point: scores of articles appeared with variations on the title 'würdelose Weiber' ('shameless hussies') and the responses outdid themselves to condemn these girls and suggest increasingly harsh punishments for their transgression: For the *Berliner Tageblatt*, their behaviour was 'nothing short of treason';[43] while the *Berliner Volksblatt* suggested a spell in the stocks for these 'Ungeziefer' ('pests') on the symbolic national oak.[44] Freifrau von Klöcker wrote that 'only harlots could do such a thing and harlots are international [...] we would like to publicly denounce ["brandmarken", literally "brand"] those who through behaviour devoid of breeding and morality dare to cast doubt on our honour as German women!'[45] It is likely that there was a strong class element to this aristocratic lady's condemnation of these women, but the opprobrium was in no way restricted to the lower classes. Although by 2 September 1914 the initial reports were seen to be greatly exaggerated, responses continued: on 10 September, the *Deutsche Tageszeitung* printed letters from serving soldiers under the heading 'Pfui Deibel!' ('For Shame!') including one that urged: 'pass the horsewhip and then harder, harder.'[46]

Unsurprisingly, 'German' came to signify entirely positive attributes, while 'international' was purely negative. War was seen as a teacher, and its lesson for women was that they must learn 'to feel and think in a German way again [...] drive everything foreign from your hearts [...] let the spirit of purity and nobility in once more, hold onto German simplicity, breeding, and morality'.[47] The *Berliner Lokalzeitung* spells out the task for women: 'be national, think German, feel German, act German in everything, be aware of your Germanness in the smallest as in the biggest things'.[48] This recurs throughout the war – in 1917 there is a veiled threat in the *Hamburger Korrespondenz* about what might happen 'when the men come back from bloody battles and deprivations and ask the first question in judgement: what were you doing while we bled, froze, huddled in dugouts, fought and – were victorious?'[49]

Coverage of the Hague Congress, with its emphasis on international cooperation, was overwhelmingly negative: one response was mockery of the delegates, firstly, as childless spinsters using the discourse of motherhood to claim their mission for peace; secondly, as women trespassing on the domain of men; and thirdly, as a sex deemed incapable of rational discussion attempting formal debate. The inability of 181 English women to secure papers or passage to attend the congress was also widely reported as hilarious.[50]

Another response was outrage at the women's lack of national feeling and, especially, at their analysis of the war as 'mass psychosis'. This was seen as a particular betrayal of the soldiers, especially as it came from the very women they were defending with their lives. In response to an anti-war pamphlet by Frida Perlen, the *Hamburger Nachrichten* claims that while soldiers are in the field fighting for German women, 'at home behind their backs a suffrage lady under the flag of peace is inciting the most abominable war of all, the war of the sexes'.[51] The *Vossische Zeitung*, although not as hostile as many papers, nonetheless expressed the suspicion that the women were more interested in securing political advantages for themselves than in world peace.[52]

It is notable that neither the BDF nor the majority of the press felt obliged to engage with the content of the women's resolutions. Merely the fact of German women discussing the war with the women of enemy nations was enough to fuel the outrage.

The Hague Congress as catalyst

From the outset the plans for the Congress resulted in greater public activity by the pacifists and greater public notice of their ideas by the press.[53] The BDF was keen to downplay the significance of the Congress for the women's movement and did not wish to enter into a debate that attracted further attention to it, but this was difficult to sustain as German women were playing a well-publicized role in its organization. The call for Congress participation in February 1915, which was widely distributed and reproduced in the German press, set out the pacifist women's principles clearly, condemning the war as a product of male politics and openly demanding women's suffrage as the only way of preventing future wars:[54] 'We women declare the war, the last word in men's statesmanship, to be madness. War is only possible in the life of nations in the grip of a mass psychosis, for it seeks to destroy everything that the creative forces of humanity have built up over centuries.'[55]

The Hague women's commitment to peace was not passive at all, nor was it domestic: instead, it was confrontational, attacking the war, attacking men and their fitness to govern, and even attacking the nation state. Moreover, these women claimed the authority to speak for *all* women, undermining the BDF's careful public position of disinterested patriotic service to the *Volksgemeinschaft* and associating it with the highly negative concepts of suffrage, internationalism, and pacifism discussed above. The BDF therefore felt compelled to distance itself from the pacifist women and vigorously assert their counter-claim that they were the sole authoritative voice of the organized women's movement in Germany. In fairness to the BDF, there was some justice to this claim. For one thing, the BDF was numerically far the biggest women's organization in Germany,[56] but more importantly, its leadership of the NFD meant that at that time it could truly claim to be representative of the German women's movement. Working closely with the Red Cross, the NFD coordinated all women's activities, whether voluntary work, charity work, or paid employment, and included socialist women's organizations in its ranks: the early months of the war saw a wave of 40,000 middle-class volunteers but also of 1400 working-class women.[57] In contrast, the pacifist women failed to find support even from within the ranks of the German suffrage organizations, and international as well as national women's organizations overwhelmingly rejected the idea of the Congress.

The BDF's own press release appeared in the national press in April 1915, and stressed that the Congress was neither organized nor endorsed by the women's movement and that it was 'absolutely out of the question for any serious women's organization to participate in this Congress'.[58] Bäumer was at pains to make clear that individual women attending did so without any representative function and that the German women's movement had 'no wishes other than those of our whole nation',[59] and therefore would not be associated with the 'special requests' (that is suffrage) demanded at the Congress. The BDF expressed its strongest objection to the analysis of the war as madness and mass psychosis, seeing in this a denigration of the soldiers' fighting spirit:

> Should German women deny the moral strength that is calling their husbands and sons to their deaths by declaring the courage and

self-sacrifice of our menfolk to be 'madness' and 'psychosis'? Should we, whom they are defending, spiritually stab our men in the back by despising and denigrating the inner values that they are fighting to uphold?'[60]

In her *Heimatchronik* of 28 April 1915, Bäumer makes clear that for her, this moral duty applied to women in all the warring nations and that international discussions about the war were only morally possible for women of neutral countries.[61] In her letter of refusal to Congress organizer Aletta Jacobs of 4 April, Bäumer repeatedly asserted her claim to speak for German women by using the formulation 'die deutschen Frauen': 'German women' could not attend a congress at the present time, 'German women', even those who supported the peace movement, were not in agreement with the Congress' resolutions: 'it is obvious to us that during a national struggle for existence we women belong to our nation and *only* to our nation.'[62]

Behind the scenes, too, the struggle to assert the rival claims was being fought, each side accusing the other of being the first to go public.[63] In a letter to the BDF leadership of 29 March 1915, the organizing committee of the Congress decisively rejected 'the example of the BDF leadership: to offer up the public spectacle of women squabbling at this time'. The committee also objected strongly to the BDF leadership's claim to speak for all women in the combatant nations, and their attempt to impose their 'narrow-minded' and 'one-sided' vision on other women: 'they should, however, not judge others by their own lack of knowledge and understanding of broader affairs.'[64] During this time, an internal BDF memo was circulated, stating that attendance at, or support for, the congress was 'incompatible with the patriotic sentiments and national duties of the German Women's Movement' and 'with any position or area of responsibility within the BDF',[65] effectively forcing members such as Alice Salomon to choose between their international connections and BDF office. To Bäumer's irritation, this directive was leaked to the press and widely interpreted as a boycott of the peace conference and a slur on the patriotism of the organizers. Bäumer was in the difficult position of appearing to be against peace and found herself under fire from her fellow liberals, notably the pacifist Ludwig Quidde.[66] In a letter sent on 16 May 1915, he accused Bäumer of high-handedly restricting BDF members' freedom of conscience. Referring to their shared pre-war condemnation of *ad personam* political tactics, he went on: 'and now out of our own ranks and even worse, out of the women's movement, comes an attack against comrades and countrywomen that adopts these methods, just because these women have different views from the majority about their patriotic duty and what their patriotism demands of them.'[67] For Quidde, 'the worst male organization could not have acted worse!'[68]

Throughout the war, Bäumer continued to stress that the women's movement had not been represented at the congress. In a letter to the Silesian branch of the BDF, whose leader, Marie Wegner, was critical of the leader-ship's response, she referred to 'a congress of haphazardly thrown together individuals' with no authority or competence to debate questions of inter-national politics.[69] Bäumer's article in *Die Frauenfrage* of September 1915 offered the most thorough and critical account, in which Bäumer attempted to clarify that it was not the pacifists' desire to fight for peace that was 'incompatible with national feeling' but the form this took and the aims and timing of the Congress. In this article, she adopted a position similar to that of the IWSA, that the war had interrupted 'but not destroyed' international connections within the women's movement, and that 'German women have no intention of seeking to disavow this common ground', but that the Congress itself was ill-advised.[70] In support of her stance, Bäumer cited the views of a Dutch woman, Fräulein Dr von Dorp, who had attended the congress and concluded that 'these women have not the slightest concept of their own superficiality.'[71]

In the BDF's view, the pacifist women were lost in the realm of abstrac-tion, their analysis naive and their responses sentimental and superficial. Even honest hatred of the enemy was preferable to the (to them) inauthen-tic expressions of sisterly love that characterized the pacifist discourse: 'Love and hatred belong together. [...] The more we are capable of becoming one with our nation, the more we feel its enmities as our own. [...] It would be senseless, even cruel and inhuman, if we German women could [...] stand before Germany's enemies with the lacklustre objectivity of the neutrals.'[72] Bäumer used words such as 'blass' ('pallid'), 'blutarm' ('anaemic'), or even 'blutleer' ('bloodless')[73] to stress the abstraction and intellectualism of the pacifists' response in contrast to full-blooded emotions felt directly and passionately. Writing in *Die Frauenfrage*, Bäumer states: 'We cannot make ourselves "international"! We cannot – we women least of all – cast off the deepest, strongest, warmest experiences that burn within us from 9 to 1 and from 4 to 8 and, theoretical ghosts of ourselves, ascend into an international fourth dimension.'[74] For the BDF, then, the ability to maintain international contacts suggested a lack of rootedness and an ability to intellectualize that denied real; that is, patriotic, feeling. In October 1915, Bäumer accused the pacifists of seeking to avoid sharing Germany's destiny, of wanting to breathe 'rather than the bitter air of our German fate [...] the soft air of a shallow fraternization'.[75]

The claim to true depth of feeling was an important element in the discourse of the BDF even before the Hague congress emerged. Writing in 1914, Helene Lange differentiated between women's general peaceableness and 'peace at any price': 'if the question is war or the stalemate of German development, death or the suffocation of German life, then the answer of German women is without question: war and death.'[76] Even before the war, Lange had expressed her discomfort with the 'superficiality' and the 'empty phrases' of international meetings, stating robustly in 1900 that '[t]rees need their own soil to take root in: only parasites can eke out their short-lived existence on alien organisms'.[77] For veteran campaigner Lily Braun, for whom the war meant the restoration of national strength and a strict gender hierarchy, too, the pacifists were unpatriotic sentimentalists, ready to accept a cringing peace at any price because of 'their sentimental pacifism, their foolish dream of the sisterhood of all people of the female sex'.[78]

For the pacifist women, however, the discourse of love between the international members was far from sentimental folly, but played a significant psychological role during the war years. Women pacifists were doubly isolated in their own community – by attitudes to nation that saw pacifism and internationalism as unpatriotic, and by rejection by other women's groups – so the sense of belonging and shared values available through their international ties were especially important. For Heymann, the Hague Congress was 'a rest after months of anguish, a rest among those who felt the same',[79] and the Zurich Congress of 1919 'a delightful oasis amidst a vast desert', a respite among like-minded women from the hostility and isolation of everyday life.[80] Throughout the war, French, German, and English women exchanged emotionally charged greetings;[81] for example, in December 1915 French women wrote to German women: 'We know that the majority among you think as we do and that is why we want to say to you that we are sisters and that we love you.' German women replied: 'We think as you do! We feel as you do! We suffer like you with our hands tied and must, like you, remain silent!'[82] As well as providing the women with vital emotional support, the deliberate stressing of ties of love maintained a sense of the shared humanity of the enemy, and women were thus able to maintain channels of communication not open to men both during and in the aftermath of the conflict. The warm messages and gestures of mutual support and understanding that reached these isolated women or were displayed during rare meetings served to create a network of personal friendships and trust amounting to a 'fictive kinship',[83] a dream of sisterhood that their opponents dismissed as 'foolish' but which sustained them in their vision of building a lasting peace in times of war.

The pacifists felt deeply hurt by the lack of recognition for their efforts at bringing peace, expressing particular bitterness that the BDF had organized a reception in Berlin in May 1915 for Congress President Jane Addams and Congress organizer Aletta Jacobs, while 'the German participants [...] were boycotted and declared beyond the pale by the very same women'.[84] While many of the pacifists had themselves been members of the BDF up until 1915, the controversy over the Hague Congress caused them to break their last ties with the organization.[85] The consequences of the rift continued into the post-war period, with Heymann and Augspurg taking every opportunity to scoff at and undermine the BDF's attempts to bring women's influence to bear in the troubled waters of the Weimar Republic. Even in 1927, Heymann described the BDF as 'pathetic remnants of the women's movement' who were 'dragging out their fossilized existence'.[86] The rift never healed, and the pacifists' continued attacks on the BDF demonstrated little or none of the love, inclusion, and mutual understanding that supposedly formed the basis of the universal female principle. In fact, the German women's movement emerged from the war more divided than it had ever been, and throughout the Weimar Republic, the BDF was squeezed between nationalist women on the one hand, who despised them for what they saw as their weak, conciliatory interaction with former enemies, and left-wing radicals on the other, who condemned them for what they saw as their unquestioning, jingoistic response to the war.[87] In this climate, and with continued negative press coverage of female suffrage, it is not surprising that the women's movement failed to make full use of the enfranchisement of all German women over the age of 20 that came into effect in 1918.[88]

Post-war congress, Zurich 1919

In May 1919, at the same time as women were excluded from the actual peace negotiations in Paris, the pacifist women met again in Zurich to formulate their own vision for a sustainable peace and to offer a model for the peaceful and productive cooperation of nations.[89] However, even though the delegates were drawn only from among those women who had shown support for pacifist ideas during the war, the harmonious face they presented to the world hid tensions that threatened the unity of the congress.[90] For example, most of the Belgian women refused to attend the congress at all, stating that it was pro-German, and the belief that it was a 'Verliererforum' ('a forum for losers') was widespread.[91] There were also tensions over the extent to which German women could be held responsible for German war crimes or blamed for their apparent failure to speak out against the occupation of Belgium and France.[92] Hidden, too, was the French women's organizations' refusal to intervene on behalf of the women and children affected by the starvation blockade that continued until the signing of the peace treaty, the physical effects of which were all too visible in the dramatic weight loss and fatigue of the German and Austrian delegates.[93] We have seen that much of the criticism levelled at Gertrud Bäumer was due to her intolerance of dissenting views within the ranks of the BDF and her 'ruthless exclusion of dissidents',[94] but it is evident that even the sustaining community of WILPF had to be artificially constructed by the exclusion of or refusal to acknowledge dissenting voices.

Conclusion

During the war years, it was in the interests of both the leadership of the BDF and the pacifist organizers and supporters of the Hague Congress to distance themselves from the ideas and attitudes of the other, and both showed themselves to be equally intolerant of dissent and equally harsh in their judgement of those with different views. For the pacifist women, the existence

of a majority of women who supported the war undermined their view of
the innate pacifism of women, on which their own claims to full female
citizenship rested. For the women of the BDF, association with suffrage, internationalism, and of course pacifism itself, threatened to undermine their
own unstated war aims, tacitly geared towards demonstrating a fitness for
involvement in the life of the state and full acceptance in the national community. The BDF leadership's high-handed stifling of open debate over the
1915 Congress was a bid to present a harmonious public front that precluded
any expression of support within the organization for these unpopular ideas.
However, their public display of animosity surrounding the Hague Congress
and their apparent rejection of previously professed ideals did much to
discredit the women of the BDF at home and abroad, compromised their
ability to re-enter the community of the international women's movement
after the war, and undermined their attempts to maintain focus and unity
within the German women's movement during the difficult post-war period.
Post-war society in Germany was economically, politically, and culturally
unstable, violent, and traumatized by the defeat and the terms of the peace,
and the BDF saw its primary post-war mission as overcoming these deeply
damaging inner divisions.[95] In January 1919, Bäumer wrote that 'there is
nothing more valuable than the creation of an inner unity of our people
[...] no national demand is more important than this.'[96] In May 1919, she
stressed community as the highest priority of public life, setting spiritual,
inner values against the violence and materialism of the times and claiming
a central role for women in this endeavour.[97] It is clear that the women of
the BDF felt that the post-war inability to transcend personal interests and
ambition, prejudices and political infighting represented the greatest threat
to Germany's recovery, so it is ironic that they were hampered in one of their
key aims by divisions within their own movement.[98]

We have seen that the public discourse as reflected in and fostered by the
German press was hostile to and highly suspicious of feminist, specifically
pacifist, activities and aims, and that this was a major factor in compelling
the BDF to distance itself so irrevocably and so publicly from the aims of the
Hague women. We have seen that there were very real differences between
the two groups' responses to war and their relationship to the nation
state, but there is no doubt that the public controversy over the Hague
Congress not only exposed but also deepened these divisions, forcing an
irreconcilable rift with far-reaching consequences for the German women's
movement.

Notes

1. For more on pre-war pacifism and internationalism in the women's organizations,
   see S. Cooper (1987) 'Women's Participation in European Peace Movements:
   The Struggle to Prevent WWI', in R. Pierson (ed.) *Women and Peace: Theoretical,*

Historical and Practical Perspectives (London: Croom Helm), pp. 51–75; J. Vellacott (1987) 'Feminist Consciousness and the First World War' in Pierson, *Women and Peace*, pp. 114–36; A. Gelblum (1998) 'Ideological Crossroads: Feminism, Pacifism, and Socialism', in B. Melman (ed.) *Borderlines: Genders and Identities in War and Peace 1870–1930* (New York: Routledge), pp. 307–27.

2. When asked to join the International Council of Women (ICW) in 1888, the leading German women's organization at the time, the Allgemeiner Deutscher Frauenverein (ADF), had refused, stating that '[i]n Germany we have to work with great tact and conservative methods', but by 1897 the BDF, of which the ADF remained a leading member, was a member of the ICW and involved in international exchanges. Cited in U. Gerhard (1993) '"National oder International?" Frauengeschichte im Spiegel der internationalen Beziehungen der deutschen Frauenbewegung', *Ariadne*, 24, p. 51.

3. Gerhard, '"National oder International?"', p. 52.

4. Other key German pacifists were Frida Perlen, Emma von Schlumberger, Margarete Selenka, Auguste Kirchhof, and Getrud Baer.

5. See A. Wiltsher (1985) *Most Dangerous Women: Feminist Peace Campaigners of the Great War* (London: Pandora Press); S. Hering (1990) *Die Kriegsgewinnlerinnen: Praxis und Ideologie der deutschen Frauenbewegung im Ersten Weltkrieg* (Pfaffenweiler: Centaurus); L. J. Rupp (1997) *Worlds of Women: The Making of an International Women's Movement* (Princeton, NJ: Princeton University Press); J. Vellacott (2001) 'Feminism as If All People Mattered: Working to Remove the Causes of War, 1919–1929', *Contemporary European History*, 10:3, pp. 375–94; A. Wilmers (2008) *Pazifismus in der internationalen Frauenbewegung (1914–1920): Handlungsspielräume, politische Konzeptionen und gesellschaftliche Auseinandersetzungen* (Essen: Klartext); K. E. Gwinn (2011) *Emily Greene Balch: The Long Road to Internationalism* (Urbana, IL: University of Illinois Press). There are some critical voices; A. Wilmers (2005) argued that we have to look beyond the Hague women's own assessment of the significance of the Congress: 'Zwischen den Fronten: Friedensdiskurse in der internationalen Frauenfriedensbwegung 1914–1919', in J. Davy, K. Hagemann and U. Kätzel (eds) *Frieden – Gewalt – Geschlecht: Friedens- und Konfliktforschung als Geschlechterforschung* (Essen: Klartext), pp. 123–43, and S. Cooper pointed out in 'Women's Participation in European Peace Movements' that the women's ideas were not in themselves new, but rather built on a long tradition of peace activism and analysis.

6. Rupp, *Worlds of Women*, p. 3.

7. J. A. Davy (2002) 'German Women's Peace Activism and the Politics of Motherhood: A Gendered Perspective of Historical Peace Research', in B. Ziemann (ed.) *Perspektiven der Historischen Friedensforschung* (Essen: Klartext), p. 114.

8. M. Bereswill and L. Wagner (1998) 'Nationalism and the Women's Question – The Women's Movement and Nation: Orientations of the Bourgeois Women's Movement in Germany during the First World War', *European Journal of Women's Studies*, 5:2, p. 242.

9. M. Walle (1993) 'Die Heimatchronik Gertrud Bäumers als weibliches Nationalepos', *Ariadne*, 24, p. 20.

10. Hering, *Kriegsgewinnlerinnen*, p. 104.

11. Wilmers, *Pazifismus*, pp.169–70, discusses the treatment of pacifist women in the pages of *La Française*, journal of the CNFF.

12. These were Heymann, Augspurg, Perlen, and von Schlumberger.

13. Davy, 'German Women's Peace Activism', p. 115.

14. In Internationale Frauenliga für Frieden und Freiheit/Deutscher Zweig (ed.) (1920) *Völkerversöhnende Frauenarbeit während des Weltkrieges, Juli 1914 – November 1918* (Munich: Heller), p. 6.

15. My survey draws on the collection of newspaper cuttings held in the Federal archives (*Bundesarchiv*) at Lichterfelde, Berlin (R8034/II). These cuttings were collected between 1893 and 1945 by the Reichs-Landbund, a powerful, highly conservative agrarian lobby, with the aim of keeping a close eye on any potentially disruptive social movements. Ordered thematically, this comprehensive collection has the advantage over research in individual newspapers of breadth of coverage – the relevant articles have already been selected from a wide range of daily newspapers – but the disadvantage of possible selector bias and incompleteness, not to mention the missing page numbers and handwriting problems that make attribution problematic at times. For this chapter, I particularly consulted volumes 11–19 (7965–7973) that deal with the topic 'Stellung der Frau/ Frauenbewegung' between 1914 and 1921.

16. G. Bäumer (1914) 'Der Krieg und die Frau', in E. Jäckh (ed.) *Der deutsche Krieg: Politische Flugschriften* (Stuttgart: Deutsche Verlagsanstalt), p. 11.

17. G. Bäumer (1914) 'Zur seelischen Mobilmachung der Frau', *Die Frauenfrage*, 16 (October), pp. 105–6.

18. G. Bäumer (1915) 'Die Frauen und der Krieg', in E. Altmann-Gottheiner (ed.) *Kriegsjahrbuch des Bundes Deutscher Frauenvereine 1915* (Leipzig: B. G. Teubner), p. 2.

19. Cited in B. Clemens (1988) *'Menschenrechte haben kein Geschlecht!' Zum Politikverständnis der bürgerlichen Frauenbewegung* (Pfaffenweiler: Centaurus), p. 107.

20. For a discussion of the extent of women's integration into government policy during wartime, see M.-E. Lüders (1937) *Das unbekannte Heer: Frauen kämpfen für Deutschland 1914–1918* (Berlin: E. S. Mittler & Sohn), and U. Daniel (1997) *The War from Within: German Working-Class Women in the First World War* (Oxford: Berg), pp. 73–80.

21. H. Lange (1917) 'Der Oster-Erlaß des Kaisers und die Frauen', *Die Frau*, 24 (May), pp. 449–54.

22. L. G. Heyman (1980) [1917/22] 'Weiblicher Pazifismus', in G. Brinker-Gabler (ed.) *Frauen gegen den Krieg* (Frankfurt am Main: Fischer), p. 65.

23. See A. Schaser (1996) '"Corpus mysticum": Die Nation bei Gertrud Bäumer', in Frauen und Geschichte Baden Würtemberg (ed.) *Frauen und Nation* (Tübingen: Silberburg), pp. 118–32.

24. Bäumer, 'Die Frauen und der Krieg', pp. 6–7.

25. L. G. Heymann and A. Augspurg (1992) [1972] *Erlebtes Erschautes: Deutsche Frauen kämpfen für Freiheit, Recht und Frieden 1850–1940* (Frankfurt am Main: Ulrike Helmer), p. 137.

26. Heymann and Augspurg, *Erlebtes Erschautes*, p. 138.

27. Bäumer, 'Der Krieg und die Frau', p. 10.

28. L. G. Heymann and A. Augspurg (1919) 'Was will "Die Frau im Staat"?', *Die Frau im Staat*, 1 (February), p. 1.

29. L. G. Heymann (1919) *Völkerverständigung und Frauenstimmrecht* (Leipzig: Verlag Naturwissenschaften), p. 12.

30. J. Verhey (2000) states in his influential study of press response to August 1914 that 'the press could with some justice be considered the voice of public opinion', in *The Spirit of 1914: Militarism, Myth and Mobilization in Germany* (Cambridge: Cambridge University Press), p. 15.

31. See note 15 for details of the sources used.

32. See K. Kosyk (1968) *Deutsche Pressepolitik im Ersten Weltkrieg* (Düsseldorf: Droste Verlag), pp. 20–30, and J. Horne (2012) 'Public Opinion and Politics', in J. Horne (ed.) *A Companion to World War One* (Chichester: Wiley-Blackwell) pp. 279–94.
33. *Berliner Volkszeitung*, 13 March 1914, and *Berliner Tageblatt*, 10 June 1914.
34. *Leipziger neueste Nachrichten*, reported in *Deutsche Tageszeitung*, 9 June 1914. See S. Adickes (2002) 'Sisters, Not Demons: The influence of British suffragists on the American suffrage movement', *Women's History Review*, 11:4, pp. 675–90, for an account of how the suffragettes were reported in the American press and the negative effect of this on the domestic campaign for female suffrage.
35. *Berliner Volkszeitung*, 11 March 1914.
36. *Die Hilfe*, 10 June 1914.
37. *Kreuzberger Zeitung*, 10 June 1914.
38. *Hallesche Zeitung*, 13 March 1914.
39. *Berliner Lokalanzeiger*, 5 September 1914.
40. *Das Deutsche Tageblatt*, 14 January 1917.
41. This paper *Die Stellung der Frau in der politisch-sozialen Neugestaltung Deutschlands* was sent to the Reichstag and regional parliaments in October 1917. For a discussion of press coverage of female suffrage during and after the war, see I. Sharp (2014 forthcoming) 'Post-suffrage strategies in the organized German women's movement', *Women's History Review*.
42. B. Davies (2000) discusses the negative views of the *Kriegerfrauen* (warriors' wives) who, supposedly made rich by the money paid to their husbands, wasted national resources by eating cake, while their poor cooking skills also made them dependent on bread for family meals: *Home Fires Burning: Food Politics and Everyday Life in World War I Berlin* (Chapel Hill, NC: The University of North Carolina Press), pp. 22–45. This is also discussed by B. Kundrus (1995) *Kriegerfrauen: Familienpolitik und Geschlechterverhältnisse im Ersten und Zweiten Weltkrieg* (Hamburg: Christians), while U. Daniel provides evidence of working class women's actual economic situation in *The War from Within*, pp. 24–32.
43. *Berliner Tageblatt*, 18 August 1914. Daniel also discusses the negative press reaction to German women's alleged soft treatment of French prisoners in *The War from Within*, pp. 23–4.
44. *Berliner Volksblatt*, 19 August 1914.
45. *Deutsche Tageszeitung*, 21 August 1914.
46. *Deutsche Tageszeitung*, 10 September 1914.
47. *Thüringer Landeszeitung*, 15 August 1914.
48. *Berliner Lokalzeitung*, 3 May 1915.
49. *Hamburger Korrespondenz*, 14 April 1917.
50. See, for example, 'Der Friedenskongress ohne "Ladies"', *Rheinisch Westfälische Volkszeitung*, 2 May 1915. See also Wilmers, *Pazifismus*, p. 230, for a discussion of press responses.
51. *Hamburger Nachrichten*, 23 March 1915.
52. *Vossische Zeitung*, 30 April 1915 and 1 May 1915.
53. Gelblum, 'Ideological Crossroads', p. 312.
54. As well as writing reports for *Jus Suffragii* in February and May 1915, Heymann published a direct appeal to German women as mothers to resist the man-made war, in 'Frauen Europas, wann erschallt Euer Ruf?', *Die Frauenbewegung*, February 1915, p. 14. In consequence, Heymann's activities were severely restricted.

55. Anita Augspurg et al. (February/March 1915) 'Call for Attendance at the Women's International Congress', *Landesarchiv Berlin*, Helene Lange Archiv, microfiche 2754.

56. Hering gives figures of 46 member organizations and 500,000 members, *Kriegsgewinnlerinnen*, p. 100.

57. See M.-E. Lüders, *Das Unbekannte Heer*, pp. 21–2; Hering, *Kriegsgewinnlerinnen*, pp. 48–9, and Daniel, *The War from Within*, pp. 73–80.

58. *Die Frauenfrage*, 17, 16 March 1915. It was followed up in April 1915, printed in the press on 29 April, and appeared in translation in *Jus Suffragii* in June 1915, alongside other reports on the Congress.

59. G. Bäumer (April 1915) 'Zum internationalen Frauenkongreß im Haag', BDF Press release, *Landesarchiv Berlin*, Helene Lange Archiv, microfiche 2753.

60. Bäumer, 'Zum internationalen Frauenkongreß im Haag'.

61. G. Bäumer (1915) 'Heimatchronik, 28 April 1915', *Die Frau*, 23 (June), pp. 559–60.

62. Letter to Aletta Jacobs, 4 April 1915.

63. For a full account of the debate, see Wilmers, *Pazifismus*, pp. 110–12.

64. Letter from the organizing committee to G. Bäumer, 29 March 1915, *Landesarchiv Berlin*, Helene Lange Archiv, microfiche 2753.

65. Reprinted in G. Bäumer (1915) 'Zu dem Plan eines internationalen Frauenkongresses', *Die Frauenfrage*, 17 (16 March), p. 82.

66. L. Quidde (1979) *Der deutsche Pazifismus während des Weltkrieges 1914–1918* (Boppard am Rhein: Harold Boldt), pp. 297–302.

67. Quidde, *Der deutsche Pazifismus*, p. 299.

68. Quidde, *Der deutsche Pazifismus*, p. 299.

69. Letter to the Silesian Women's Associations, 19 January 1916. See also Wilmers *Pazifismus*, pp. 116–17.

70. G. Bäumer (1915) 'Der Bund deutscher Frauenvereine und der Haager Frauenkongreß', *Die Frauenfrage*, 17 (1 September), p. 83.

71. Bäumer, 'Der Bund deutscher Frauenvereine und der Haager Frauenkongreß', p. 84.

72. G. Bäumer (1915) 'Vaterlandsliebe und Völkerhass', *Die Frauenfrage*, 17 (1 January), p. 1.

73. Bäumer, 'Der Bund deutscher Frauenvereine und der Haager Frauenkongreß', p. 83.

74. Bäumer, 'Der Bund deutscher Frauenvereine und der Haager Frauenkongreß', p. 83.

75. G. Bäumer (1915) 'Zwischen zwei Gesetzen', *Die Frau*, 23 (October), p. 39.

76. H. Lange (1914) 'Frauen und Friede', *Die Frau*, 22 (November), p. 66.

77. H. Lange (1928) [1900] 'National oder International', in H. Lange *Kampfzeiten*, vol. 1 (Berlin: Herbig), p. 271, cited in Gerhard, '"National oder International?"', p. 52.

78. L. Braun (1915) *Die Frauen und der Krieg* (Leipzig: E. Hirzel), p. 11.

79. L. G. Heyman (1915) 'A German View of the Congress', *Jus Suffragii*, 9 (June), p. 304.

80. Heyman and Augspurg, *Erlebtes Erschautes*, pp. 197 and 241.

81. Wilmers, *Pazifismus*, p. 43.

82. See Heymann, *Völkerversöhnende Frauenarbeit*, pp. 23–4.

83. J. Winter (2006) discusses his concept of a 'fictive kinship', whereby familial bonds are echoed within a community of individuals who share the same sorrows in *Remembering War: The Great War Between Memory and History in the Twentieth Century* (New Haven, CT: Yale University Press), p. 136.

84. *Mitteilungen des deutschen Frauenstimmrechtsbundes* (May–June 1915), nos 5 and 6, pp. 5–6; see also Wilmers, *Pazifismus*, pp. 161–6.

85. See Hering, *Kriegsgewinnlerinnen*, p. 110.
86. L.G. Heymann (1927) 'Freie Menschen', *Die Frau im Staat*, 9 (January), p. 1.
87. For a discussion of right-wing women's opposition to the ideals of the BDF, see C. Streubel (2007) 'Raps across the knuckles: The extension of War Culture by Radical Nationalist Women Journalists in Post-1918 Germany', in A. S. Fell and I. Sharp (eds) *The Women's Movement in Wartime: International Perspectives, 1914–19* (Basingstoke: Palgrave Macmillan), pp. 69–88. Women within the Socialist parties were also reluctant to make common cause with the liberal Bäumer.
88. For a detailed discussion of post-war press response to the women's movement and to suffrage in particular, see Sharp, 'Post suffrage strategies in the organized German women's movement'.
89. See E. Kuhlman (2008) *Reconstructing Patriarchy after the Great War: Women, Gender, and Postwar Reconciliation between Nations* (New York: Palgrave Macmillan), and E. Kuhlman (2007) 'The Women's International League for Peace and Freedom and Reconciliation after the Great War', in Fell and Sharp, *The Women's Movement in Wartime*, pp. 227–43.
90. See Wilmers, *Pazifismus*, pp. 181–7.
91. Wilmers, *Pazifismus*, p. 187.
92. Wilmers, 'Zwischen den Fronten', pp. 129–30.
93. The French women's refusal was published in *La Française* on 30 November 1918 and makes clear that German women were being punished for their stance during the war. See Wilmers, *Pazifismus*, pp. 188–9.
94. Bereswill and Wagner, 'Nationalism and the Women's Question', p. 233.
95. See I. Sharp (2011) 'The Disappearing Surplus: The Spinster in the Post-War Debate in Weimar Germany 1918–1920', in I. Sharp and M. Stibbe (eds) *Aftermaths of War: Women's Movements and Female Activists, 1918–1923* (Leiden: Brill), pp. 152–3.
96. G. Bäumer (1919) 'Die Frauen in der deutschen Demokratie', *Die Frau*, 26 (January), p. 105.
97. G. Bäumer (1919), 'Hoffnungen und Aufgaben', *Die Frau*, 26 (May), pp. 230–3.
98. Helene Lange (1920), 'Politische Zerstörungsmethoden', *Die Frau*, 27 (April), p. 194.

13

War Activities and Citizenship Rights in and outside the Occupied Zone: Lithuanian Women During the First World War

Virginija Jurėnienė

Throughout The First World War, Lithuanian women were active both in charity and for women's rights. In so doing, they continued a long history of organized commitment both to alleviating the situation of women and accelerating the process of emancipation which had begun in the nineteenth century and was strongly intertwined with Lithuanian national aspirations against subjection to Russian rule. Their activities were, however, hampered to a certain degree during the war. Having been under Tsarist rule since the end of the eighteenth century, Lithuania was automatically involved in the conflict, when, in August 1914, Germany and the Habsburg Monarchy declared war on Russia. Large parts of Lithuania were occupied by German troops from March to September 1915. Consequently, political and most social activities were prohibited in the occupied zone. Initially, women's organizations could campaign only in the unoccupied parts of Russia. As a result, the process of emancipation and the implementation of citizenship rights took a different course in both areas. This situation finally ended in February 1918 when Lithuania gained independence in the course of the peace negotiations between Germany and Bolshevik Russia.

This chapter, firstly, analyses the activities of organized and non-organized Lithuanian women during the First World War, focusing on those emphasized in the press and other contemporary sources.[1] So far, this topic has largely been ignored both in studies on Lithuania under German occupation (for example, by Vejas Gabriel Liulevicius and Pranas Čepėnas)[2] and in historical research on Lithuanian émigré activities in Russia. Secondly, the demands for women's inclusion into citizenship, which again emerged in 1917, are examined as well as the question of how they were connected with the movement for independence. The chapter starts off with some background information on the pre-war situation of Lithuanian women's movements in order to contextualize women's demands.

The beginning of the Lithuanian women's movements

A Lithuanian state existed from the thirteenth until the eighteenth century. Yet, due to partitions of the Polish-Lithuanian Commonwealth, Lithuania lost sovereignty and fell under Russian rule in 1795. During the nineteenth century, Lithuanian noblewomen started to play an important role in society.[3] They became involved in numerous newly created charity organizations, which mostly had a confessional background and were either Catholic, Jewish, or orthodox Russian and focused on different ethnic groups.

In the second half of the nineteenth century, the commitment of noblewomen intensified along with the rise of the national movement, which was directed against the Russification politics of Tsarist Russia after the Second Revolt in 1863–64. All social strata of Lithuanian society, and both men and women, were involved in this revolt. In reaction, the Tsarist government banned Latin script in the area, restricted the activities of the Catholic Church, and started to actively colonize the region in an attempt to turn Lithuania into a Russian state. This, in turn, provoked Lithuanian resistance, in which women worked side by side with men. Female teachers, for instance, taught the national Lithuanian language in secret schools. Thus the Lithuanian women's movement emerged as part of the nationalist movement.

In this context, women's demands for political rights were a result of self-education and followed demands for a better education of girls and women. As in the rest of Europe, education was the primary goal, and literacy among Lithuanian women was quite high by the end of the nineteenth century.[4] Women actively fought for equal rights, for women's suffrage, for equal education, and for equal access to the professions at the beginning of the twentieth century. The political parties which were founded at the turn of the century also declared their support for women's equal rights.

On 22/23 September 1905, the Association of Lithuanian Women (Lietuvos moterų sąjunga) came into being in Vilnius. The association's agenda was geared towards obtaining autonomy for Lithuania within its ethnic boundaries; this included the demand for a Lithuanian parliament (Seimas) elected by universal, equal, secret, and direct suffrage. In addition, it demanded equal rights for women and men, and acknowledged equal membership of both sexes. Though the government of Tsarist Russia did not approve the statutes of the association, this very first organization of Lithuanian women was active until the First World War.

On 6 and 7 October 1907, the First Women's Congress was organized by Catholic priests in Kaunas, one of the biggest cities in Lithuania at the beginning of the twentieth century and developing into an alternative cultural centre next to Vilnius. The priests' objective was to use women's public activities to their own purpose and to the benefit of the Church. The

Association of Lithuanian Women of Vilnius, however, also maintained its own interests and decided to change the Women's Congress of Kaunas into a Women's Congress of entire Lithuania. It adopted the following decisions: to create a union that would fight for the rights of women and join similar unions in other countries; to create associations geared towards improving housework conditions; to work together with men as well as separately; and to elect an executive committee of the union. The latter finally consisted of both Catholic and Liberal representatives. The First Lithuanian Women's Congress was a hugely important event in the public life of the region. It was widely reported on in the Lithuanian and the foreign press, and it influenced the establishment of both the first union of women's associations and the creation of a Catholic women's movement. It did not, however, manage to unite women in their common objective – women's rights.

The Lithuanian Catholic Women's Association (Lietuvos katalikių moterų sąjunga) was founded on 26 April 1908. Its aim was to unite all women of Lithuania in terms of cultural and economic work, to promote self-respect towards Lithuanian society as a whole, to reform education, to seek improvement of the situation of girls and women, and to fight for the political and civil rights of women. With the support of the Church, which in contrast to the Social Democratic and Liberal Parties quickly understood the significance of women's organizations for the political development of the country, the association expanded its activities in Kaunas and in the provinces. This included the establishment of agricultural schools for rural girls and charity work. The Catholic Women's Association was the most influential of all women's organizations in Lithuania, both in the pre-war period and during the war. It was also the only legal women's association until the war since other organizations, such as the Association of Lithuanian Women, were not officially acknowledged by the Tsarist regime. And, crucially, it supported the Lithuanian Christian Democrats. The leaders of the women's association were, for instance, appointed as members of the party's central committee.

Apart from the Catholics, Liberal and Social Democratic women also championed women's rights. In 1908, their Association of Lithuanian Women was renamed as the Lithuanian Women's Union (Lietuvos moterų sąjunga). The education of young women and the promotion of the ideas of the women's movement were its major goals. In 1910, the Union even discussed the question of establishing a women's party. But, with the German occupation of Lithuania during the First World War, the activities of all women's organizations in the occupied zone were suspended.

Women's activities in occupied Lithuania until 1917

After the outbreak of the war, many Lithuanians moved further into Russia, and Lithuanian parties, women's organizations and schools were established there. The Lithuanian women's organizations of Moscow and Saint Petersburg were especially active, as will be described later in this chapter. Those who stayed in the occupied zone had to bear a difficult situation. When the Germans began to occupy Lithuania, an undertaking which took until September 1915 to complete, they banned all organizations and the military administration of 'Ober Ost' introduced several measures geared towards the economic exploitation and colonization of the area. All parts of the civilian population were affected, even children, who were obliged to work from the age of ten years. From the beginning of the occupation, the inhabitants of Lithuania had to face numerous restrictions and prohibitions enforced by the military government. It was, for instance, forbidden to bake cakes, brew beer, leave one's own neighbourhood or go to another county without a passport, or to go out at night-time. The number of market days were reduced and priests were urged to celebrate Mass early in the morning only so that village people could work on Sundays as well.[5] In the course of the war, the Germans introduced requisitions; for instance, of cattle, horses, household implements, and even hens. According to statistics gathered after the war, 90,000 horses, 140,000 cattle, and 767,000 pigs were requisitioned during the occupation of Lithuania up to February 1918. Lithuanian researchers estimate that the military administration removed resources worth 338,606,000 marks during this period, while importing goods and materials at a cost of 77,308,000 marks.[6]

As announced shortly after the beginning of the occupation in 1915, women had to carry out all the duties imposed upon them by the Germans, just as well as men.[7] They were punished for any failure to comply with these orders. Prisons were overflowing. There was a special women's jail in Panevėžys with about 300 women prisoners.[8] According to an order by the German administration from mid-1916, all adult men and women in the territory could be forced to work. In addition, women faced special requisitions. Observers and travellers reported that skirts woven by women, in particular skirts from the area around Prienai, which was famous for its weavers' clothes and belts, were taken away, allegedly for military purposes, but more likely as presents for the wives and mothers of German soldiers.[9] Women had to collect nettles and down for the production of clothes, and were even forced to give their hair. If they refused to do so, they had to pay fines.[10] Nevertheless, although the situation in Lithuania during the German occupation was very difficult for the people – most of them wished for the Russians to return – observers stated that the Germans treated Lithuanian women better than men.[11]

Lithuanian women tried to improve the situation during the occupation period. Their activities during the First World War can be differentiated and classified in terms of: (a) the place (Lithuania or Russia); (b) the degree of organization (individual or organized activities); and (c) the type of activities. In this context, four particularly important periods can be distinguished, according to military and political events as well as to the nature of the activities and tasks: Firstly, in August 1914, with the beginning of the war, Lithuanian women's organizations reoriented their activities towards military affairs. New women's organizations were founded. Secondly, the period between March 1915 and the end of 1917 – the years of German occupation when all organizational activities in Lithuania were forbidden and women could only work individually to alleviate the suffering caused by the war. Women's organizations moved to Russia. Thirdly, the year 1917 as a turning point in the Lithuanian women's movement when leaders of women's organizations raised the question of equal political and civil rights. Fourthly, 1918, the last year of the war, when women's organizations moved their activities back to Lithuania, which re-established its sovereignty. Women, then, demanded full political and civil rights, including equal representation in government, legislation, and administration.

Hard times 1914

There is no contemporary source of any kind which accurately describes the activities of women in Lithuania at the beginning of the war. We can only observe that the population adapted to the conditions of war and that many Lithuanians moved to Russia. Those who stayed helped one another, and women acted both individually and within organizations. In 1914, Viktorija Rukuižytė-Landsbergienė received permission from the commander of the region of Vilnius to establish a committee For the Support of War Sufferers (Nukentėjusiems nuo karo šelpti). As Landsbergienė remembers, she 'did not chair the committee for a long time, we just started and I passed the leadership on to A. Smetona [...] Our story ends where men start to work and lead. The work of women, even though it is public, remains unnoticed.'[12] A further Association for the Support of Prussian Lithuanian War Sufferers (Nukentėjusiu nuo karo mūsų tautiečių iš Prūsų Lietuvos šelpti organizacija) was founded in Vilnius at the beginning of 1915, with Felicija Bortkevičienė as chairwoman. Since 1903, Bortkevičienė had been leader of the organization The Light (Žiburelis) which was involved in teaching and supporting gifted children. On 9 June 1915, however, she left the occupied part of Lithuania and moved to Saint Petersburg, later to Siberia. After five months of work, Bortkevičienė submitted an announcement to the consul of the United States in Moscow in which she indicated that it was necessary to support Lithuanians and to let them return home.[13] Apart from this organization, the committee for the Support of War Sufferers also worked in Saint Petersburg from September 1915 onwards. The ties of the Lithuanian women's movement to Russia were close. Many of the women active in the movement had graduated from Russian educational institutions. In addition, the Lithuanian women's movement had cooperated with its Russian counterpart since its beginnings.

After all organizations in occupied Lithuania had been banned in the autumn of 1915, women worked on their own initiative and helped their fellow countrymen to survive the difficulties of the war. They fed prisoners, organized the nursing of wounded soldiers, sewed clothes and raised funds for those who had suffered from the war – the injured, the paralysed, and the homeless. Here are a few examples of women's individual work: Juzefa Višinskienė was engaged in providing donations for refugees in Lithuania. In 1916, she moved to Minsk, Russia, and later to the Crimea. In 1915, Felicija Grincevičiūtė established a canteen for Lithuanians in Vilnius and continued to support Lithuanians during the entire German occupation.[14] E. Vasiliauskienė, a schoolteacher, organized evening events for Lithuanians in Šiauliai from 1915 onwards. At these meetings, which were regarded as patriotic, the audience was urged not to give in to the Germans. Furthermore, in 1916 Vasiliauskienė and Petras Bugailiškis established a children's shelter and a school which accommodated 13 boys and 17 girls; 80 children attended school at the shelter in 1917.[15] A further example of women's initiatives is St Zita's Society, which worked underground in Vilnius. Its members nursed wounded Lithuanian soldiers and took care of prisoners.[16] The German women of Kaunas – there had been a strong German community since the fifteenth century – also organized themselves, together with Russian women, in the Evangelical Women's Society (Moterų evangelikių draugija) in 1916. It was the strongest and largest organization of women during the war. It established a Protestant Girls' Society and arranged concerts and dancing parties in order to promote manners and morality.[17]

In August 1917, the German military administration allowed the Catholic women's movement, now re-established as the Lithuanian Catholic Women's Society, to resume its activities. The liberal women's movement also revived its work. The founder of The Light, Gabrielė Petkevičaitė, offered weekend classes for young adults in the rural Panevėžys region, which also took place in other Lithuanian areas. Petkevičaitė passed on pedagogical knowledge for teachers and explained special features of this work.[18] Others acted individually, such as Sofija Smetonienė who helped Lithuanians who had returned to Vilnius to get permission from the military government to visit their relatives. In addition, she donated food, money, and shelter for many people.[19] In order to raise people's spirits during wartime, women organized so-called 'evening parties' which were supposed to increase national and unifying, as well as anti-German, sentiments. Unsurprisingly, Germans were not allowed to take part.[20] The fact that the German occupiers first gave the Catholic women's organization permission to renew its activities can be seen as the wish to support Catholic activities as an antidote against Russian and Polish influence in the region, according to the assumption that piety encouraged obedience and submission.

The fight for women's rights by Lithuanians in Russia

As mentioned above, many Lithuanian women transferred their organizations, schools, and activities to Russia when the war started, especially to

Voronezh, Moscow, and Saint Petersburg. In Russia, they felt secure and were able to intensify their activities. For instance, St Zita's Society, located in Saint Petersburg, was engaged in charity, self-education, and self-support, and helped the Saint Petersburg division of the committee for the Support of War Sufferers. In Voronezh, a group of Lithuanian women, whose primary goal was to unite and educate the Lithuanian people, was granted permission by the local government to establish two Lithuanian high schools.[21] The group leader, Sofija Čiurlionienė, taught Lithuanian language at high school and gave talks to the Lithuanian community, to young people in particular.

1917 was a significant year for Lithuanian women in Russia. On 6 March 1917, the Lithuanian Women's Freedom Union (Lietuvių moterų laisvės sąjunga) was established in Moscow. It united both non-party and party women (such as the Lithuanian Social Democrats, the Unity Party Santara, and the Christian Democrats). Ona Mašiotienė was the leader of the Union. Its primary objective was to fight for women's equal rights and to raise their consciousness by giving talks in the Lithuanian communities in Russia.[22] Mašiotienė organized such lectures and meetings, and urged the political parties to guarantee women's equal rights in the future free state of Lithuania.

The women's movement did not forget its key demand for women's civil and political equality during the war. The leaders emphasized this particular point in the Lithuanian Parliament (Seimas), which consisted of emigrant representatives and held sessions in Saint Petersburg. On 13 March 1917, the Lithuanian National Council was formed in Saint Petersburg. It appointed a Provisional Committee for Lithuania's administration to prepare a constituent assembly. In its first session, the Council issued a declaration which included the equality of political and civil rights for women and men in its sixth and seventh articles. The sixth article declared equal civil rights: 'The broad guarantee of freedom must be the foundation of the administration of Lithuania: equality of all citizens before the law, freedom of nations, religion, conscience, and political opinions [...].' The seventh article addressed political rights: 'The Provisional Committee for Lithuania's administration has to take care of the preparation of the constituent assembly of Lithuania without gender distinctions, on the basis of equal rights and secret suffrage [...].'[23] On 19 April 1917, the Lithuanian National Council decided to convene the Seimas of Russian Lithuanians in Saint Petersburg for the end of May. Felicija Bortkevičienė was the only woman on the organizing committee and a member of the subdivision for education. The organizing committee issued a proclamation to all Lithuanians living in Russia which stated that 'representatives are to be elected by all Lithuanians, men and women, who are 18 years of age and older'.[24] The proclamation also promised equal and secret suffrage. Yet, although women were enfranchised, only nine of the 330 delegates overall who were elected to the Saint Petersburg Seimas from the different Lithuanian colonies in Russia were female. The weakness of the women's Social Democratic and Liberal movements was certainly one reason. Even more important was the fact that most women were not organized.

At the meeting of the Saint Petersburg Seimas from 27 May 1917 until the beginning of June greetings were read from the Lithuanian group in Voronezh, signed by Sofija Čiurlionienė and others.[25] The group announced that women were willing to work with men in order to achieve improvements. The delegate Ona Mašiotienė, chairwoman of the Lithuanian Women's Freedom Union, greeted the Seimas and declared that the decisions of the Great Seimas of Vilnius (1905) and the Lithuanian National Council were to be carried out by acknowledging full civil and political rights for women. Mašiotienė also stated: 'I hereby congratulate the women representatives on the beginning of their solid, thorough work in the social and political field.'[26] She explained how women's activities could be supported until the Lithuanian state re-established its sovereignty. Various women's unions were to be founded to bring women together and to give them an understanding of free, responsible citizenship. As women were active members of parties, the representatives of the parties supported these demands. During the debates in the Seimas, it became obvious that women did not act as a united group but as members or supporters of different political parties. Nevertheless, despite political differences women communicated in a respectful manner. The resolution accepted by the Seimas declared that 'in the independent democratic Republic of Lithuania equal civil rights must be acknowledged regardless of nationality or gender [...] The administration of Lithuania and the state system must be established by the Constituent Seimas of Lithuania based on universal, equal, and secret suffrage.'[27] Even left-wing members of the Seimas, such as Santara, Social Democrats, and Populist Social Democrats who had separated themselves from the other parties, accepted this last point of the resolution.

We can summarize that the Saint Petersburg Seimas declared equal political and civil rights for men *and* women. As in some other European countries, political change triggered by the First World War accelerated the political emancipation process of Lithuanian women. They did not raise the question of political rights during the early period of the war. Rather, they substituted for the men, who went to war, in all spheres. However, in the Saint Petersburg Seimas, which aimed at re-establishing Lithuanian sovereignty, women reminded their fellow male countrymen of their demands for political and civil rights. And here, the Lithuanian women's movement was acknowledged.

The Vilnius conference of 1917 and its disregard of political and civil rights for women

At the same time, the situation in occupied Lithuania was completely different. As mentioned above, the Lithuanian Catholic Women's Society obtained permission to resume its activities, and also the Liberal women's movement revived its work. German occupation policy had slightly changed during 1917. Instead of strict administrative pressure in the occupied zones in Eastern Europe, more autonomy was granted. In the course of this development, the Vilnius conference took place from 18 to 22 September 1917. Because of the war, conference participants were not elected but appointed upon invitation by the organizing committee of the conference; 200 men took part, but not one woman was invited, even though women could also have contributed to the task of re-establishing Lithuania's sovereignty. The fact that women did not participate was criticized in the press: 'Is it possible that in Lithuania there are not even a couple of women who could be selected, even for political issues? No one can say that.'[28] At the start of the conference, even the Lithuanian Catholic Women's Society submitted a note of protest to the organizing committee, requiring an explanation why women had not been invited to the conference. The petition was signed by 128 supporters. A similar petition was also submitted by women from Šiauliai. Women based their demands primarily on the fact that they formed the majority and always worked together with men in all kinds of activities.

The women's protests provoked discussions at the conference. The organizing committee did not provide a full explanation why women had not been invited. Jurgis Šaulys, one of the founders of the Lithuanian Democratic Party, stated that the organizing office could not be blamed for the misunderstanding.[29] The press expressed the hope that the Lithuanian nation, becoming more and more democratic in the future, would allow all its members political and civil rights, regardless of gender, social class, and property.[30] In the press, women also discussed how they did not have the opportunity to participate in the Lithuanian Council, even though the conference had provided that the Council could be complemented by co-optation and that there was a number of women who had graduated not only from high school, but also from university and who, therefore, would have been perfectly qualified to work in the Council.[31] The Council of Lithuania was elected at the Conference of Vilnius. Its 20 members were to conduct negotiations with the German occupation administration to take over educational affairs, re-establish the university of Vilnius, and help emigrants who had moved to Russia and to other states during the war to return to their homeland.

How can we explain the reluctance of the Vilnius conference to include women? As illustrated above, circumstances of women's activities and subsequently the intensity of their work in 1917 clearly differed in occupied Lithuania on the one hand and Russia on the other. The party leaders, who had emigrated to Russia at the beginning of the war, were more tolerant and far-sighted than those who stayed in Lithuania. Lithuanian society was very patriarchal. The most active women's organization in the occupied zone was the Lithuanian Catholic Women's Society. It was strongly influenced by the

Catholic Church and championed principles of maintaining morality and supported women's education and women's crafts and needlework. Most of the representatives of the liberal women's movement, such as Bortkevičienė, Mašiotienė, or Ona Puidienė, were not in Lithuania during this period. Bortkevičienė in particular, who lived in Stockholm at the time, did not witness the disregard of women's rights at the Vilnius conference.[32]

The debate on women's rights rekindled at the Conference of Vilnius within a new historical context. Towards the end of 1917, events in Lithuania were influenced not only by the changed military situation of the war, but also by the Russian Bolshevik revolution. After coming into power, Lenin announced decrees on peace, the self-determination of nations, nationalization, and so on, and passed laws introducing gender equality and those concerning women's labour. Many Lithuanian women observed these changes very carefully. Their self-confidence had grown during the war when they took over men's positions in the public sphere – though we should not forget that a critique of stereotypical patriarchal gender roles and the process of women's emancipation had already begun at the turn of the century. Moreover, for Lithuanian women, the developments within the Russian women's movement served as a model. They had always been strongly influenced by the women's movements of the surrounding nations and minorities (Russians, Poles, Latvians, Estonians, Germans, Jews), especially by the Russian movement. There was, however, no actual cooperation with Polish women, due to resentments originating from the experience of the common state between the sixteenth and eighteenth centuries and the wish to create an independent state that would in no way be connected with Poland. Besides, leaders of Polish women's organizations had tried to include Vilnius and its vicinity into the Polish women's movement at the beginning of the twentieth century by founding Polish organizations or at least single branches in the Lithuanian capital. Russian women, in contrast, were not perceived as a threat to Lithuanian national aspirations which were fully supported by Lithuanian women.[33]

Women's activities until the end of the war

The fourth period of women's wartime activities – from the beginning of the year 1918 until the end of the war on 11 November – was characterized by the re-establishment of women's organizations or their return from Russia to Lithuania. At the beginning of 1918, the press stated that it was necessary to restore women's organizations as women lacked organizational skills. Associations should initiate and support activities and set up branches in the entire country, so that 'even in the most remote areas of Lithuania, the issue of women's education and mutual understanding will be discussed'.[34]

The Lithuanian Catholic Women's Society opened schools for girls and re-established societies that had already existed before the war. On 17 February

1918, it convened a meeting in Kaunas, which prepared a petition demanding the co-optation of women representatives to the Lithuanian Council, who would participate in all Council meetings in order to restore 'the dear Motherland Lithuania'.[35] Again the women argued that statistics indicated that there were more women in Lithuania than men. Besides, they had always worked together with men for the restoration of Lithuania and its culture. The Catholic Women's Society managed to collect 20,000 signatures for the petition in the parishes, and the Council's chairman, Antanas Smetona from the Lithuanian Democratic Party, promised to solve the issue of the lack of women's participation in the Council.[36] This, however, turned out to be only a tactical move by Smetona in order to sooth the women and give them hope. As his lectures of 1917 show, he did not really intend to give in to women's demands: 'Today, society is aware that a woman must be treated as an equal person in all spheres just like a man. In any case, in regard to public and political professions this goal can only be achieved gradually [...], not immediately.'[37]

In the summer of 1918, the Catholic women's movement split.[38] A further association had been founded in Vilnius in June, and both the Kaunas and the Vilnius organization argued on whether to establish the centre of the association in the capital Vilnius or to retain it in Kaunas, negotiations which lasted until the beginning of 1919. In the meantime, the two organizations worked separately.

Lithuanian independence and women's citizenship

On 16 February 1918, after the peace negotiations of Brest-Litovsk between Germany and Russia, the independence of Lithuania was declared. Several provisional constitutions, issued between November 1918 and 1920, formally granted women full citizenship.[39] Nevertheless, by the end of 1918, an ambiguous situation regarding the implementation of women's political rights had developed in Lithuania. Though women were granted civil and political rights by constitutional law, they did not participate in governing the state. The question arises why women's rights were not fully realized until 1920. We can assume that Smetona, Chairman of the State Council of Lithuania, did not include women in government because he doubted their skills. Smetona was convinced that women's roles were confined to activities in humanitarian organizations and the commitment to the family.[40] This became obvious in the beginning of November 1918, when the first Lithuanian cabinet was announced. F. Bortkevičienė, an experienced politician and member of the central committee of the Democratic Party, was not confirmed as Minister for Food. Most of the male members of the Lithuanian State Council voted against her appointment.[41] Generally, Lithuanian society was highly patriarchal and agrarian – approximately 80 per cent of the population lived in small villages in the countryside – and therefore showed little inclination to accept women in government.

From November 1918 until 15 May 1920, the Council of Lithuania served as a legislature. After that, the Constituent Seimas started its work. During its entire existence, women had not been included in the Council. To be sure, Article 22 of the first Provisional Constitution,[42] issued by the Council on 2 November 1918, declared that all citizens, irrespective of their gender, were equal before the law. The Constituent Seimas, which had to decide on the political system and to adopt the constitution, was to be elected by universal, equal, and direct suffrage and by secret ballot, as specified in Article 27. The Provisional Constitution of 1918 thus declared democratic principles for elections, and, while establishing gender equality, enshrined women's suffrage. Identical provisions were included in the second Provisional Constitution of 1919.[43] On 20 November 1919, the Council of Lithuania adopted the Law on the Elections to the Constituent Seimas,[44] thus implementing the provisions of the provisional constitutions. Article 1 of the law accordingly specified the principles of suffrage and Article 2 stipulated that all men and women who were Lithuanian citizens and 21 years of age should be enfranchised, regardless of religious and ethnic affiliations. Article 5 conferred the right to be elected to all Lithuanian citizens who were at least 24 years old. Suffrage was not specifically mentioned in the third Provisional Constitution of 1920 which was adopted by the Constituent Seimas, but the general principle of equality was defined in Article 15 of the Constitution in the same way as in the previous provisional constitutions.

Around thirty political parties and groups campaigned for the elections of the Constituent Seimas in 1920 and presented lists of candidates. Most of them included women. In only one district, however, was the first candidate on the list female – Gabrielė Petkevičaitė. Most women candidates were active and well-known leaders of the women's movement, and most of them were young. Six women were elected among the Lithuanian Christian Democrats,[45] one – Gabrielė Petkevičaitė – from the Lithuanian Socialist Populist Democrats and the Lithuanian Peasant Union,[46] but no female Social Democrats entered the Constitutent Seimas. Seven out of 112 members of the first Parliament of independent Lithuania were women, an equivalent of 6.25 per cent. They were teachers or headmistresses of primary and secondary schools or governesses. Since Gabrielė Petkevičaitė was the oldest member of the Constituent Seimas (she was 60), she chaired its first session, a great sensation in Europe at this time.[47] The session secretary, Ona Muraškaitė-Račiukaitienė, was also a woman – at 24 years of age, one of the youngest members of the Constituent Seimas. The group of six female Christian Democrats was called the women's fraction in the Constituent Seimas though it did not separate itself from the block of Christian Democrats. It was led by Magdalena Galdikienė. The Christian Democratic women were members of several Parliamentary committees and prepared amendments to the laws. They were concerned that women's rights would be narrowed in the new Constitution of Lithuania of 1922 and in the laws adopted from Russia. Striving for gender equality, the women developed a manifesto which was supposed to be realized in the independent state.[48] Thus, the female members of the Constituent Seimas, elected in 1920, played a substantial role in the preparation of the legal basis of the restored independent state.

Conclusion

Like women in other European countries involved in the war, Lithuanian women were engaged in relief work. Due to the German occupation, however, they faced specific conditions. Many women, who remained in the occupied zone, had to work individually or underground as their organizations had been banned by the German military administration. They established schools, took care of children, nursed patients, opened canteens, delivered food to hungry citizens, and carried out other charity work. Unlike women in non-occupied European countries, Lithuanians also helped their fellow citizens to endure German occupation. Due to the lack of historical sources, it is impossible to get a complete overview of women's activities, but we can summarize that Lithuanian women showed a strong commitment to the survival of the nation during the war and to the restoration of an independent Lithuanian state.

On the other hand, there were some organizations which were allowed to continue or renew their work during German occupation. The German Protestant women's organization, for instance, was supported by the Ober Ost government, which intended to spread its influence in occupied Lithuania. Moreover, the German administration cooperated with the Lithuanian Catholic Church. The Lithuanian Catholic Women's Society had been the most important – and only legal – women's organization in the pre-war period and was permitted to take up its activities again in 1917. In this context it also supported women's citizenship rights and protested against the exclusion of women from the Vilnius conference in September 1917 and from the Lithuanian National Council. In Saint Petersburg, in contrast, where Liberal and Social Democratic women's organizations had been able to survive, a convention of Lithuanian émigrés had emphasized the demand for women's civil and political rights in May 1917. Still, the Catholic Women's Society remained powerful, as was to be revealed by the Christian Democrats whose political power strongly depended on women after independence. Catholic women were the most active voters in the elections of the Constituent Seimas in 1920, in which the Christian Democrats gained the majority.

As in other central European countries, the demands of the Lithuanian women's suffrage movement for civil and political rights were only accomplished along with national independence after the First World War. A certain characteristic of the Lithuanian women's suffrage movement has to be emphasized: It was inextricably linked to the national movement and directed against Tsarist Russia, later against the German occupier. Most women who participated in this movement were intellectuals (teachers, writers, advocates, publishers), who worked together with men for national independence and believed that the survival of their nation was as significant as their position in society.

Women's war efforts had some impact on achieving civil and political rights as they had shown that women were capable of engaging in humanitarian activities and managing factories as well as public, political, financial, economic, social, and other affairs in difficult times. During the war women's self-confidence increased immensely and by the end of the war, they demanded the right to politically participate in decisions regarding the re-establishment of the state. The resolutions of the Saint Petersburg Seimas declaring gender equality in political and civil affairs were particularly important steps. In general, women's suffrage in Lithuania has to be analysed in the context of regional and worldwide events. Most Lithuanians who had moved to Russia during the war were influenced by the revolutionary events of 1917 and 1918. In addition, contemporary developments and ideas of other Central European and Baltic countries affected the members of the Lithuanian State Council, who prepared a provisional constitution on 4 November 1918. The policies of gender equality conducted by Czechoslovakia, Poland, and Latvia in particular directly influenced Lithuanian politicians who included women's suffrage in the first Lithuanian Provisional Constitution of 1918. Historical sources from Lithuania do not indicate that this can be attributed to internal efforts entirely, as similar measures were undertaken in England and the United States. Thus external factors were decisive for the implementation of women's enfranchisement. In general, however, formal rights for women did not change Lithuanian society itself, which remained traditional at least until the 1930s.

Notes

1. In this chapter I primarily refer to the memoirs of J. Nainienė-Petrauskaitė about Sofija Čiurlionienė during The First World War in Russia, Voronezh (F. 4–912), at the Lietuvių literatūros ir tautosakos institutas, Rankraščių skyrius (Institute of Lithuanian Literature and Folklore, Department of Manuscripts [LLTI RS]). Abundant material on the Lithuanian women's movement can be found at the Lietuvos mokslų akademija, Rankraščių skyrius (Lithuanian Academy of Sciences, Department of Manuscripts [LMA RS]). The Department of Manuscripts also holds the archive of F. Bortkevičienė and G. Petkevičaitė (F. 30–26, F. 30–1143).

2. P. Čepėnas (1986) Naujųjų laikų Lietuvos istorija [A History of Modern Lithuania], 2 vols (Chicago, IL: Dr Kazys Griniaus Fondas); V. G. Liulevicius (2000) War Land on the Eastern Front: Culture, National Identity, and German Occupation in World War I (Cambridge: Cambridge University Press).

3. For this section see the following accounts on the Lithuanian women's movement: V. Jurėnienė (2006) *Lietuvos moterų judėjima XIX amžiaus pabaigoje – XX amžiaus pirmojoje pusėje* [The Lithuanian Women's Movement from the End of the Ninteenth to the Middle of the Twentieth Centuries] (Vilnius: Vilniaus universiteto leidykla), and V. Jurėnienė (2006) 'The Lithuanian Women's Movement at the Beginning of the 20th Century', in E. Saurer, M. Lanzinger and E. Frysak (eds) *Women's Movements: Networks and Debates in Post-Communist Countries in the 19th and 20th Centuries* (Vienna: Böhlau), pp. 457–74.

4. E. Aleksandravičius and A. Kulakauskas (1996) *Carų valžioje Lietuva XIX amžiuje* [Lithuania under the Reign of the Czars in the Nineteenth Century] (Vilnius: Baltos Lankos), p. 359.

5. Čepėnas, *Naujųjų laikų Lietuvos istorija*, vol. 2, p. 86.

6. Liulevicius, *War Land on the Eastern Front*, p. 73.

7. P. Žadeikis (1925) *Didžiojo karo užrašai* [Records of the Great War], vol. 1: *1914–1915–1916* (Klaipėda: Rytas), p. 104.

8. Čepėnas, *Naujųjų laikų Lietuvos istorija*, vol. 2, p. 113.

9. J. Šilietis (1922) *Vokiečių okupacija Lietuvoje 1915–1919 m., paveikslėliuose ir trumpoise jų aprašymuose* [German Occupation in Lithuania, 1915-1919, in Pictures and Short Descriptions] (Kaunas), p. 190; M. Gudaitis (1925) *Lietuva 1917 metais: Kelionės po Lietuvą vokiečių okupacijos metu* [Lithuania in 1917: Travelling through Lithuania during German Occupation] (Klaipėda: Rytas), p. 33.

10. Šilietis, *Vokiečiu okupacija Lietuvoje*, p. 9; Žadeikis, *Didžiojo karo užrašai*, vol. 2: *1917–1918–1919*, p. 114.

11. Šilietis, *Vokiečiu okupacija Lietuvoje*, p. 149.

12. Quoted in: O. Beleckienė (1938) 'Lietuvės Vilniaus Golgotoje', *Naujoji vaidilutė*, 7:153, p. 413. When exactly A. Smetona took over the leadership of the organization is unknown, but it is likely that it was in autumn 1914.

13. LMA RS, F. Bortkevičienė, A. O. Liudkevičiūtė-Povickienė, 1922, f. 192–22, l. 3.

14. LMA RS, F. Bortkevičienė, Filomena Grincevičiūtė, 5 Oktober 1941, f. 192–159, l. 2.

15. *Šiaulių miesto istorija/ iki 1940 m.* (1991) [History of Šiauliai City until 1940] (Šiauliai), p. 124.

16. LMA RS, A. Ambraziejūtė-Steponaitienė, Už lietuvybę [For Lithuanianship], f. 12–3078, l. 174.

17. 'Moterų evangelikių draugija' [Protestant Women's Society'] (1917), *Kownoer Zeitung*, 196, p. 1.

18. O. Voverienė (2000) *Žymiosios XX amžiaus Lietuvos moterys* [Famous Lithuanian Women in the 20th Century] (Kaunas: Naujasis Amžius), p. 94.

19. O. Mašiotienė (1938) *Moterų politinis ir valstybiniai-tautiškas darbas 1907–1937 m.* [Women's Political and National Work 1907–1937] (Kaunas: Mašiotienė), p. 18.

20. LMA RS, A. Ambraziejūtė-Steponaitienė, Už lietuvybę, f. 12–3078, l. 154.

21. LLTI RS, J. Nainienė-Petrauskaitė, 'Iš mano atsiminimų apie rašytojos S. Čiurlionienės-Kymantaitės asmenybę' [From my Memoirs about the Personality of the Writer S. Čiurlionienės-Kymantaitė], f. 4–912, l. 30.

22. 'Lietuvių moterų laisvės sąjunga' [Lithuanian Women's Freedom Union] in *Lietuviškoji tarybinė enciklopedija* [Lithuanian Soviet Encyclopedia], vol. 3 (Vilnius: Vaga), p. 535.

23. 'Pirmas Steigiamasai Lietuvių Tautos Tarybos, 1917, posėdis kovo 13', *Santara*, 19 March 1917, p. 6.

24. 'Visiems Rusijos lietuviams', *Santara*, 24 August 1917, p. 1.

25. 'Lietuvos moterys ir Seimas', *Santara*, 17 June 1917, p. 2.

26. 'Lietuvos moterys ir Seimas', p. 2.
27. V. Vaitiekūnas (1957) 'Rusijos lietuvių seimo 40 m. sukaktį minint', Į laisvę, 13, p. 49.
28. 'Lietuvių konferencija', Darbo balsas, 15 November 1917, p. 5.
29. Lietuvos Valstybės Tarybos protokolai, 1917–1918 [Minutes of the Lithuanian State Council 1917–1918] (1991) (Vilnius: Mokslas), p. 124.
30. 'Lietuvių konferencija', Darbo balsas, 15 November 1917, p. 5.
31. O. Byliunaitė (1918) 'Ar turime moterų tinkamų į Tarybą?' [Do We Have Suitable Women For The Council?], Moterų balsas [Women's Voice], 10 October, p. 55.
32. LMA RS, F. Bortkevičienė (1917) 'Iš mano ypatingų užrašų' [From My Special Records], f. 190–19, l. 1.
33. Jurėnienė, Lietuvos moterų judėjimas, p. 58.
34. M. Šveikauskytė (1918) 'Į Lietuvos moteris' [To the Women of Lithuania], Lietuvos aidas [Lithuania Echo], 7 February, p. 2.
35. O. Gratkauskienė (1936) 'Darbo skruzdės' [Working Ants], Naujoji Romuva [New Romuva], 27 September, p. 3.
36. O. Beleckienė (1938) 'Moterų teisės Lietuvoje' [Rights of Women in Lithuania], Naujoji vaidilutė, 11:373, p. 271.
37. Lietuvos Centrinis Valstybės Archyvas (LCVA) [Lithuanian Central State Archive], A. Smetona, 'Paskaitos' [Lecture], f. 1686, ap. 1, b. 64, l. 10.
38. Jurėnienė, Lietuvos moterų judėjimas, p. 66.
39. For more detail on the political realization of women's rights, see Jurėnienė, 'The Lithuanian Women's Movement at the Beginning of the 20th Century', pp. 469–73.
40. Jurėnienė, Lietuvos moterų judėjimas, p. 77.
41. LCVA, 25/12-1918, Ministrų kabineto posėdis [The Cabinet meeting] f. 923, b. 9, l. 35.
42. V. Andriulis, R. Mockevičius and V. Valeckaitė (eds) (1996) Legal Acts of the State of Lithuania (1918.II.16–1940.VI.15) (Vilnius: Centre of Legal Information), pp. 2–3.
43. V. Jurėnienė and T. Birmontienė (2009) 'Development of Women's Rights in Lithuania: Recognition of Women's Political Rights', Jurisprudencija: mokslo darbai, 116:2, p. 32; Andriulis, Mockevičius, Valeckaitė, Legal Acts of the State of Lithuania, pp. 6–7.
44. Andriulis, Mockevičius, Valeckaitė, Legal Acts of the State of Lithuania, pp. 41–6.
45. These were Magdalena Galdikienė, Emilija Gvildienė, Morta Lukošytė, Vida Mackevičaitė, Ona Muraškaitė, and Salomėja Stakauskaitė.
46. On 22 January 1921, when Gabrielė Petkevičaitė refused the mandate in Parliament, she was replaced by Felicija Bortkevičienė.
47. In her opening speech on 15 May 1920, Petkevičaitė greeted the Constituent Seimas: 'I am happy to do this as an old fighter for my nation's freedom, as a woman who has gained the desired equal rights, as a member of society who did not cease to fight against any enslavement of nations, social status, capital. While the representatives are doing remarkable work, let us do it without forgetting even for a moment that we here are only the ministers of our people's will.' Quoted in Čepėnas, Naujųjų laikų Lietuvos istorija, p. 367.
48. The manifesto stated that (1) the family was to be based on the equality of both genders, allowing the family to develop on a new foundation of humanism instead of on enslaving each other; (2) the principle of equality was also to be realized with regard to the economy, in particular in terms of equal pay for equal work, irrespective of gender; (3) women's housework and education of the children have to be

appreciated to the same extent as men's earnings. See *Steigiamojo Seimo darbai* [Works of the Constituent Seimas], 2 March 1922, session 177, p. 13. Thus, the manifesto ironically demonstrates how similar it is to current demands and problems. The women also tried to pressure the Seimas to implement the manifesto and proposed bills for the abolition of regulations on prostitution, the restriction and prohibition of the distribution of alcohol, the revision of articles in civil law stating the inequality of men and women, and amendments to the law on a patients' bill.

14

Love for the Nation in Times of War: Strategies and Discourses of the National and Political Mobilization of Slovene Women in Carinthia from 1917 to 1920

Tina Bahovec

In the years before the First World War, national tensions in the Habsburg Monarchy were on the rise. This was also true for Carinthia, a province with a mixed ethnic German- and Slovene-speaking population. According to the census of 1910, the Slovenian-speaking community of the whole province accounted for 21 per cent of the population, but they were under-represented in the upper social strata. Due to an electoral system based on property qualifications, they were, in consequence, politically less influential. With the outbreak of the war, this antagonism increased. Persecutions of Slovenes as allegedly 'pro-Serbian' strengthened their demands for a fundamental reorganization of the Habsburg Empire.

On 30 May 1917, the South Slavic deputies in the chamber of representatives of the Austrian parliament (*Reichsrat*) proclaimed the May Declaration demanding the unification of the Habsburg South Slavs in an independent state under Habsburg rule. A movement, in the form of mass meetings and endorsements by municipalities, associations, and individuals, began in autumn 1917 to support the declaration. It reached Carinthia in January 1918, after the representatives of the Catholic Political and Economic Society for Slovenes in Carinthia (Katoliško politično in gospodarsko društvo za Slovence na Koroškem) had declared their support of the declaration. The German-speaking population as well as the Austrian government, however, disapproved of the declaration's demands.

In summer 1918, the South Slavs' struggle for separation from the Habsburg Empire gained momentum. On 29 October 1918, an independent State of the Slovenes, Croats and Serbs was constituted on the territory of the former Habsburg Empire. As this state did not gain international recognition, it sought unification with Serbia. On 1 December 1918, the Kingdom of Serbs, Croats and Slovenes was established under the sceptre of the Serbian Karadjordjević which was renamed as Yugoslavia in 1929.

Both the Kingdom of Serbs, Croats and Slovenes and the Republic of German-Austria, founded on 12 November 1918, laid claim to the southern parts of Carinthia, where Slovene speakers made up 69 per cent of the population. After military conflict over the disputed territories between autumn 1918 and summer 1919, which prolonged wartime conditions in the area, the border question was to be resolved by a two-stage plebiscite as laid down by the Paris Peace Conference and the Treaty of St Germain. Southern Carinthia was divided into two plebiscite zones 'A' and 'B'. Zone A in the south was to vote first; zone B, including the capital Klagenfurt/Celovec, was supposed to go to the ballot box only in case the result of the plebiscite in zone A was in favour of Yugoslavia. On 10 October 1920, Austria won 59 per cent of the vote and Yugoslavia 41 per cent, thus zone A and Carinthia as a whole became part of Austria.

This politically exciting period saw the first massive organization and politicization of Slovene women in Carinthia, who in the years from 1917 to 1920 played an important role in the May Declaration movement for the unification of the Habsburg's South Slavs as well as in the campaign for the Carinthian plebiscite. Studies on women's national and political mobilization and organization in the war and its aftermath are scarce.[1] However, they are an important contribution to the understanding of the gendered concepts and processes of state- and nation-building[2] in general, and in the (Carinthian) Slovene case in particular. This chapter analyses discourses and strategies used in the organization and mobilization of Slovene women of Carinthia. It is based on sources such as public speeches by women, newspaper articles in Slovene and Carinthian Slovene (women's) papers, pro-Yugoslav and pro-Austrian propaganda material, and so on. After an overview of the role of women in the declaration movement and the plebiscite the chapter focuses on the following. Firstly, tracing the gendered meanings of duties to the nation and rights as citizens in peace and war, it asks how certain concepts emerged in the propaganda in general; that is to say, the concept of both national/political and female/ male duties and rights as well as the notion of war and peace. Secondly, it explores the emphasis which was put on (women's) voting rights and (men's) military duty in particular, as suffrage and military service are important means of political inclusion and participation with regard to both state and nation. And thirdly, the chapter examines the imagery related to gendered concepts of heroism and the military. In particular, it considers the questions of how the image of the 'heroic mother' and the image of a 'women's army', which was repeatedly attributed to the Carinthian Slovene women's organization, were linked to notions of gender, war, and nationalism. The concluding section summarizes the ambiguous results of women's national and political activities, offers a comparative glance at pre- and post-war gender relations in Southern Carinthia and poses some questions for future research.

A gendered view of the May Declaration of 1917 and the Carinthian plebiscite of 1920

A gendered view of the declaration movement[3] reveals the differing roles of men and women in the Slovene national political arena: The political representatives formulating the national programme were solely men, due to the exclusion of women both from national (and partly local and provincial) suffrage and from membership in political associations in the Habsburg Monarchy.[4] At the mass meetings for the declaration, attended by both women and men, men and a few women gave speeches, and men, but also women, were involved in the sometimes violent eruptions. It was mostly women who collected signatures and signed the people's support declarations, as most men, having been called up, were away from home.

As early as December 1917, two well-known female public figures issued an appeal asking women to support the declaration. The first was Franja Tavčar, leading representative of the Slovene liberal women's movement and wife of the prominent Liberal mayor of Ljubljana, Ivan Tavčar; the second was Cilka Krek, a representative of the Catholic women's movement and sister of the well-known Conservative politician Janez E. Krek. Their joint appeal illustrates two characteristics of Slovene women's national activism: For one thing, the women involved were often wives, sisters, or daughters of male activists. For another, women's movements, although often cooperating, were split along the main political and ideological divides.[5] Following the appeal, women collected over 200,000 female signatures with the support of the clergy, public media, and women's associations, and handed them over to the male political representatives at a festive ceremony on 24 March 1918.

In Carinthia, German opposition against the Slovene declaration movement was particularly strong. As media coverage[6] and parliamentary debates show, it was directed against the women involved. On 28 February 1918, a Parliamentary interpellation by South Slavic representatives regarding the involvement of public administration and courts in the agitation against the declaration cited the case of two Slovene women as an example. They had collected 200 signatures in Jezersko/Seeland. Afterwards, they were visited by a community official and two police constables with fixed bayonets. One of them told the women that they had committed an indictable offence, because they 'were working towards separation from Austria. This was high treason! He threatened the teacher with losing her job if she had participated in the collection [of signatures]. He took the details of the two "delinquents" and demanded the collected sheets.'[7]

Similar to the declaration movement, women's participation in state and national affairs was crucial for the Carinthian plebiscite on 10 October 1920,[8] when men and, for the first time, women[9] had the right to vote and to decide if they wanted to be citizens of either the Kingdom of Serbs, Croats and Slovenes or the Republic of German-Austria. Prior to the plebiscite, two 'battles' were fought: The first was an armed border conflict, accompanied by sexual violence against women and the reinforcement of a soldierly masculinity which defined manliness in relation to militaristic values of honour and courage.[10] As a result, parts of Southern Carinthia were temporarily under Yugoslav control. The second battle was a propaganda war of words and images to win over the plebiscite voters. Both sides actively involved and addressed women. Since summer 1919, National Councils (*Narodni sveti*), the Slovene political and propaganda mouthpieces, had started to include female representatives. The novelty of this involvement of women is illustrated by the wording of the 'Declarations of Commitment' which were signed by all members of the National Councils: The printed form used only the male gender and the signatory had to commit 'himself with his man's word' to work for the victory of the plebiscite.[11]

The National Councils also initiated the foundation of the Association of Women's Societies in Carinthia (Zveza ženskih društev na Koroškem), the first political Slovene women's organization in the province. Founded in autumn 1919, it grew to include up to 7000 members, mostly rural women, in 56 local societies. Men were not excluded from membership as at least one local society had a male founding member and hoped for further men to join them.[12]

A major aim of these societies was to win women's plebiscite votes for the Yugoslav state, followed by aspects of social welfare, women's education, and the struggle for equality. To reach these goals, the societies organized national demonstrations, charity festivities, cooking courses, and so on. From April to October 1920, the Association published *Koroška Zora* (Carinthian Dawn), the first women's magazine for Slovenes in Carinthia. It emphasized Slovene and South Slavic patriotism and was geared towards the political and nationalist mobilization of women. At the same time, it supported the traditional female roles of housewife and mother. The first editors were female teachers, who in general played an important role in organizing women's societies.[13] The Carinthian Association was also supported by women's societies in Slovenia and other parts of Yugoslavia, thus creating new bonds of Slovene and South Slavic sisterhood.

Discourses on duties versus rights and on war versus peace

The already mentioned public appeal to Slovene women of December 1917, which asked for support of the May Declaration for a united Yugoslavia within the Habsburg Monarchy, contained recurring references to gender(ed) roles. It read:

> In the terrible war our hearts bleed from thousands of wounds, our beloved husbands, sons, fathers, brothers and bridegrooms are dying

on the battlefields, at home the misery and anguish of our families lays unbearable burdens upon us. Our tears, our grief [...] may not be in vain. We put our misery on the altar of our nation. [...] Being aware of our duty as guardians of the hearth in the Slovene home, we demand the unification, liberty and independence of all our people [...].[14]

As we can see, women were addressed as the actual and symbolic keepers of the hearth – the fire and cooking place, as the caring and nursing heart and soul of the family and the nation. This view was in accordance with concepts of social motherhood and care as they were discussed in the whole of Europe and in Slovenia, too, at the beginning of the twentieth century.[15] By transferring the idea of personal maternity to the concept of motherhood of the entire nation women were held responsible for the future of their own children and of the children of the entire nation. Furthermore, following the dichotomy of women as passive, suffering beings and men as the active, fighting sex, a distinction was made between men, who put their blood and life on the altar of the homeland, and women, who offered their misery and tears – a common construction of gendered identities in wartime.[16]

One of the first appeals to the Slovene women of Carinthia to support the declaration was the letter 'To Slovene Women and Girls' published in the newspaper *Mir* in March 1918. The anonymous female author put a similar emphasis both on women as keepers of the home during the war and on the present and future national political system, revealing an outspoken nationalist point of view:

In Carinthia, the Germans rule. [...] We [Slovenes] are underprivileged everywhere, without rights [...], scorned [...]. Shall it stay like that [...] after the war? Never! [...] Every nation shall decide if it wants to be its own master [...], if it wants to elect its own government, its own domestic officials, in one word if it wants its own state or rather wishes to stay subordinate to other nations, foreigners. [...] Each to their own! To the Germans what is theirs and to the Slovenes what is ours, then there will be peace. [...] We will stay loyal to Austria, loyal to our [...] Emperor, but we will have an independent state [...].

While politics was seen as the domain of men, who govern and represent the state, women were the ones to follow and give support, as the second part of the letter stresses:

To all Slovene women [...] let us declare ourselves for the Yugoslav state under our emperor and let us sign that. In doing so, we also show that we agree with our Slovene representatives who demand that peace is made immediately. Slovene women [...] let us help to gain a better life, a better future for our soldiers when they return from the battlefields![17]

In July 1919, when the mobilization of Slovene women in Carinthia for the plebiscite began, Alojzija Modic, later secretary of the Association of Women's Societies and second editor of the association's paper, urged for women's support for Yugoslavia. Her article in *Korošec*, one of the major Carinthian Slovene newspapers which supported the plebiscite, discussed the rights and duties of women in the private and public sphere during the war and in times to come by using the same arguments as contemporary women's movements did in Slovenia and elsewhere.[18] On the one hand, she emphasized traditional female responsibility for the domestic sphere in general and in troublesome times of war in particular. On the other hand, she referred to women's national activities during the war, which legitimized women's involvement in the public sphere, and consequently demanded women's future political participation both as a duty and a right derived from women's war effort and sacrifices:

> Carinthian women! [...] You have stayed at home alone, without your husbands and sons, and due to [...] your perseverance [...] the farms did not suffer. Yet you have also proven something else – that your work is not restricted only to the home, that women, too, have rights and duties in public life. Even before the collapse of Austria you collected signatures for the Yugoslav declaration [...]. You had clearly realized that this is our only salvation, our future. And towards you, who did all this, I direct my call! It is the first duty of the wife to make her husband happy; the biggest concern of the mother to make the children happy. Now you hold the happiness of your husbands and children in your hands. Think of that and do not abandon the work you started. Step into the public! We can hope that our Parliament in Belgrade will give women the right to vote! Prove now that you are mature enough for political activity. You suffered enough during the war, now it is time to demand your rights.[19]

Before discussing women's suffrage in detail, let's have a look at a speech given by 'our sister, Miss Pantar' at various women's meetings and published in the paper of the Association of Women's Societies in June 1920. In reference to the changes during the war, Pantar compared private and public concerns and the activities of women and men with an ironic tone by pinpointing fashion as a female preoccupation and the affairs of the world as a male one:

> We live in strange, completely unexpected times. Until now, women used to cook and perform various tasks at home and in the fields. [...] Apart from that, we cared for [...] fashion. We were curious [...] how the modern hat has to be rolled up [...]. We weren't interested in what was happening outside of our home, in the municipality, in the country, in the world. That was the concern of [...] men, who thought that they were

the only ones who had the brain and the skills; they even took this right for granted.

Pointing out the failure of men who had led the world into war, Pantar demanded the right of women to participate and decide in public and political matters and thereby prevent future wars:

> By God, if we women were the ones wearing the trousers, we would be downright ashamed for the fiasco the world has been experiencing because it was led by smart men. They slaughtered and killed each other, while we women at home suffered [...] and waited for these insane men to come to their senses. [...] Yet during these long years we women swore that in future we, too, want to have our say in the public, want to have a word about the administration of the municipality, the country and the state. We will pay a bit less attention to modern [...] hats and cardigans, we will instead pay attention to how we will live [...], so that we all [...] will be content and happy, and that men will not again get us into this complete mess called war [...].

In the second part of her speech, Pantar explained how to achieve these goals: All women should unite and join the women's association. They should show the right attitudes regarding their beliefs, hopes, and love, and especially should have faith in their strength as well as their just cause, their love for God and their homeland. Thus, in order to save 'our good mother, the beautiful Slovene Carinthia, with the ballot paper in our hands we will show that this our land always was and forever will be ours, Slovene. So help us God!'[20]

Voting rights and military duties

The May Declaration movement addressed issues such as national and political rights, the form of government, home rule, and so on. Women's suffrage was not a demand directly mentioned, although the declaration explicitly called for a state on a democratic basis. The nation was the main cause women rallied for. For the first time, they got involved in the fight for a political idea on a large scale. Some historians, therefore, have interpreted their activism as the first politicization of Slovene women and as an epoch-making step in their emancipation.[21] Press coverage in 1917/18 and later also marked the importance of women's commitment. In March 1918, the leading conservative Slovene newspaper, *Slovenec*, called the collection of numerous female signatures 'a political document and proof of the maturity of our nation and a political and tactical weapon'.[22] At the tenth anniversary of the declaration in 1927, a female author in *Slovenec* referred to Slovene womanhood as 'the bearer of the idea of national liberation' during the period of the declaration movement. Reminding readers that until then, women 'had lacked political rights and consequently had not been politically active', she wondered how women had had 'such political awareness, such political faith in a completely new era'. She concluded that Slovene womanhood 'showed admirable political maturity in the fateful years 1917 and 1918'.[23] Nevertheless, as historian Marta Verginella has phrased it, 'women's commitment to the May Declaration and their massive participation in the declaration movement remained without any political acknowledgment', as women in interwar Yugoslavia did not get the right to vote.[24]

Focusing on Carinthia, it is interesting to further compare journalistic and historiographic discourses on women's political involvement in the declaration movement. In May 1918, the newspaper *Mir* interpreted women's signatures for the declaration as a form of exercising the right to vote. *Mir* took up the old debate about women's intelligence and sound mind as a precondition for political rights and, on the other hand, emphasized women's courage putting it on the same level as men's courage on the battlefield:

> *Long hair – small brain*, this saying implies that women have long hair and a small brain. [...] A woman's mind has always been judged in this manner until now. Yet this war has shown that a woman's brain is not so small, despite her long hair. Women replaced men in many occupations [...]. It comes as no surprise that now they [...] demand political equality with men and the right to vote [...]. Even before the state granted them this right our women have already voted and still vote with their signatures for their new homeland Yugoslavia [...]. In doing so, women showed a lot of brains. They [...] immediately comprehended that it was their national duty as conscious and reasonable Slovenes to sign for our free Yugoslav homeland under the Habsburg dynasty. They are not ashamed to admit they are Slovene; what they are they also admit without fear. [...] They showed that they *not only have a reasonable mind, but also courage*! They are worthy comrades of our soldiers who have proven themselves as fearless heroes in bloody battle. [...] *Honour is due to them, they are real heroines!*[25]

The 'value' of women's political commitment was, however, disputed between Slovene and Austrian historians in the 1970s in some polemics on the declaration movement in Carinthia. Referring to the Austrian scholar Martin Wutte and his 'epigones',[26] the Slovene historian Janko Pleterski wrote in 1970:

> One of the arguments which are supposed to devalue the Yugoslav declaration movement is the claim that mainly women, especially those

organized in church associations, actively took part in it. Let us leave aside that such a line of argument distinctively reveals the conservative nature of this approach, as it contradicts the democratic principle of equal political rights for women. What is more, the argument is pointless, because [...] the purpose of the movement was to collect signatures merely among women and only in some regions and by individual initiative was it extended to the male population.

Yet as if Pleterski was not convinced of his own reasoning about the equality of women, he then stated that it is nevertheless 'also interesting to look at the data about the gender structure of the signatures'. Listing the localities where only women signed, he explained the gender imbalance by pointing out that 'due to war conditions many men were away from home and could not participate in the declaration movement'. Pleterski compared the number of female and male signatures for ten Carinthian municipalities and rural communities, where data is available. Based on his findings of 57.2 per cent female signatures in these areas, Pleterski suggested that it was fair to assume the same ratio for the rest of the territory.[27] By stressing the participation of men, he tried to valorize the importance of the movement and to strengthen the Slovene national interpretation. Yet in so doing, he also contradicted his initial statement that it was mainly a women's movement.

For the plebiscite itself as well as for its propaganda, women's right to vote was a key factor and an important topic. Due to the novelty of women's suffrage, members of women's societies were given precise instructions not only for whom to vote, but also how to carry out voting itself:

Every male and every female voter will receive their ballot paper [...] one white and one green. The white one is for Yugoslavia [...]. The green one [for Austria] has to be torn apart, the white one remains whole. Both are then to be put in the envelope [...]. Teach this especially to our older sisters, who are not used to paper and envelopes. Get yourselves a piece of white and a piece of green paper and some envelopes and practise it [...]. Not one of our votes should be lost![28]

The pro-Austrian propaganda in Carinthia constructed the image of the 'uncivilized Balkans' with references to gender relations and repeatedly referred to the subordinate position of women in the Yugoslav state in general and in politics in particular. The journal *Kärntner Landsmannschaft* stated that in Austria, as in all 'civilized states' in Europe, 'a woman is legally equal to a man with regard to political rights' and 'has passive and active suffrage like a man', whereas in Yugoslavia 'she has no suffrage at all' and 'is not considered [...] mature enough to share political rights with men.'[29]

In Yugoslavia, women's suffrage was already a widely discussed topic during the founding period from 1918 until the constitution of 1921. Slovene women's organizations as well as the main political parties supported women's suffrage on similar grounds as in other countries; they stressed the democratic principle itself, women's sufferings and achievements during the war, the necessity of women's maternal care for society, and so on.[30] Yet women's suffrage was not a common goal of the political parties throughout Yugoslavia. In November 1920, women did not have the right to vote for the constituent assembly, as electoral law was based on Serbia's patriarchal pre-war legislation. On the municipal level, women's suffrage was initially granted in May 1920, but then abolished in February 1921.[31] The Yugoslav constitution of 1921 gave the right to vote to every male citizen at the age of 21, whereas women's suffrage was to be settled by law (there was an identical clause in the constitution of 1931). Since such a law was never passed, women remained without the right to vote until the Second World War, when they participated in elections for the committees of the resistance movement, and finally, the introduction of universal and equal suffrage by the Yugoslav electoral law of 22 August 1945.[32] Thus, women's suffrage continued to be a main topic of women's movements in interwar Yugoslavia.

Back to Carinthia and the plebiscite: Slovene propaganda in favour of opting for Yugoslavia was obviously aware of the dispute over women's suffrage and therefore hardly ever mentioned this topic. However, it is striking that the Carinthian Slovene newspaper *Mir*, which was in favour of the option for Yugoslavia, published an enthusiastic article in May 1920 on the achievement of municipal suffrage for women in Slovenia, greeting 'our fellow [female] combatants, who, notably during the war, spread the Yugoslav idea from doorstep to doorstep' as new voters: 'With such enthusiastic members of the municipal council, zealous for all that is good, we will get along well and there is no danger that a war of men against women and of women against men will erupt. Hail to women's suffrage!'[33]

In general, the question of women's suffrage in Yugoslavia was under-represented in Slovene (women's) papers and in the propaganda in Carinthia. Some articles in *Koroška Zora* referred to women's rights and equality, for example by identifying the 'struggle for equality' as a goal of women's associations.[34] Yet only one author focused on the question of female suffrage in a report about the convention of the National Women's Alliance of Serbs, Croats and Slovenes (Narodni ženski savez Srba, Hrvata i Slovenaca) in Zagreb in July 1920, which had been attended by two representatives of the Slovene Association of Carinthia. The main topics at the convention were the nation, education, and charity; but after one of the speakers had demanded a campaign for women's suffrage, the convention approved a resolution that the representatives of 200 Yugoslav women's societies 'indignantly demand that all political and civic rights, enjoyed by the citizens of male sex, be guaranteed to them'. Describing her impressions from the gathering, the author (most likely one of the Carinthian representatives) summarized women's duties and future activities, among them 'the task of fighting for their political rights and not to desist from their demand until they reach their goal'.[35]

Contrary to the scarce mentioning of female suffrage in Yugoslavia, the call for Slovene women's right – and national duty – to contribute their votes in the plebiscite (in favour of Yugoslavia, as a matter of course) was, as we have seen, widely disseminated. In the propaganda clamour, the Slovene side even insinuated that the Austrians wanted to deny women this right, as the paper *Korošec* wrote:

> Rumour has it that Carinthian Germans and German-friendly persons have demanded from the voting commission that you, Slovene women and girls, should not be allowed to vote. And do you know why? The show offs [...] say that you are not yet mature enough to vote. [...] The Germans deny you maturity, because they know that you will all vote for your Slovene homeland! So, when the voting day comes, show them that you are more mature than all the stupid German-friendly people [...].[36]

The pro-Austrian newspaper *Kärntner Landsmannschaft* denied this allegation emphatically by calling it 'the culmination of the filthiest and meanest lying demagogy' and asked: 'How desperate must the expectations for the plebiscite be in the "Narodni Sveti" [National Councils] that such bold lies are supposed to support the "sentiment" for Yugoslavia!'[37] We can only speculate if the question of their future suffrage was a decisive rationale for some women and their plebiscite vote.

After having examined women's voting rights, we turn to the role of men's military duty and to militarism and war as propaganda arguments. Numerous textual as well as visual propaganda materials on these topics were addressed both to men and to women. An entire chapter of the pro-Austrian brochure 'Wie werden die Frauen und Mädchen der Zone A am 10. Oktober wählen?' (How will the women and girls of Zone A vote on 10 October?) is devoted to this matter and states:

> You [women] have got to know the horrors of *war* more than enough. Do you want to experience them again? You know how tense the relations between Yugoslavia and Italy are. Sooner or later there will be [...] a war between the two states. If [...] Carinthia will not be part of neutral Austria [...] *your homeland* [...] *will become an area of military deployment and a war zone.* [...] You know *that in Yugoslavia conscription still exists.* [...] Do you once again want to let your husband or father, brother, son or bridegroom take up arms, go to war and maybe bleed to death on the battlefield? Do you want to experience once again the fear and despair [...] that depressed you so terribly during the war? If you decide in favour of Yugoslavia at the polls, then you have to brace yourselves for all of this.[38]

After the experiences of the World War, this warning must have appealed to many women. Similarly to the question of female suffrage, conscription and possible war in Yugoslavia were topics the Yugoslav side could not easily invalidate. Two examples illustrate how it dealt with this propaganda problem. In the pamphlet 'A letter of Carinthian girls to the [nationally] conscious young men!', the writers regretted that some boys 'let themselves be frightened' by the Germans who 'made up the scarecrow' of military service. The pamphlet stated that girls, who 'have always made bouquets of flowers for the handsome soldiers', also 'have the right to say something about military service'. They especially would not understand that before and during the war, 'the Germans had worshipped and hailed military service the most. They had praised [...] the bloodthirsty generals to the skies, but now, after they have been beaten [...], suddenly they no longer like military service.' In the second part of the pamphlet, previous military events are mentioned to point out the lessons learned. The (Yugoslav) military is described as a defensive and protecting force:

> Once *the Turks attacked our region*, six years ago the Germans attacked the Serbs, last year *the Volkswehr*[39] *marauded* [...]! *Are we women supposed to put on trousers and to drive off such bandits? Soldiers are necessary to uphold peace and order*, to chase the enemy out of the country. Certainly soldiers should not attack others. Yugoslavia *does not intend to attack anyone*, as it has *won and achieved what it wanted*. Only the Germans are not satisfied, only they still think of war!

Consequently the pamphlet demanded that Carinthian boys should not be 'wimps' and predicted: '*If Yugoslavia has good soldiers, everyone will leave it in peace*. And we Carinthian girls will sing to you "*darn soldiers, how handsome you are*", we will prepare rosemary and carnations "when the regiment marches along the road" [refers to a popular folk song]!'[40] As we can see, the pamphlet stressed men's soldierly masculinity as defined by soldierly courage, and women's acquiescence to patriotic militarism by singing songs and giving flowers. Furthermore, the pamphlet's rhetorical question of whether women were supposed to put on trousers and to join the army, ridiculed gender roles and underlined the 'unnaturalness' of a women's army.

The newspaper *Slovenec* emphasized a further aspect of women's commitment to patriotic militarism a few days before the plebiscite, when it appealed to the patriotism and honour of Slovene mothers referring to their sons:

> The [...] enemy is trying to fool you by saying: Mother, vote for the republic of Austria, so you will not have to give up your son to the Yugoslav army. Fool! The Carinthian Slovene mother, if the need arises, will be proud to give her brave sons to Yugoslavia [...]. These sons will

carry her honour [...] into the whole world! The brothers, friends and enemies will admire the courageous sons of the Carinthian Slovene mother. And now the Carinthian woman, out of fear for her sons serving the Yugoslav homeland, should betray her homeland and her sons and vote for Austria [...]? How blind must the enemy be to expect something like this![41]

Such propaganda could itself be viewed as 'blind', since it ignored genuine concerns about the perils of warfare and military service and offered abstract patriotic phrases instead. As such, it probably had little effect. Along these lines, we can interpret the report of a Slovene agitator. He had tried to persuade a Slovene family with a considerably high national consciousness not to vote for Austria. Yet the mother allegedly told him: 'I have two sons, former Austrian soldiers. In Austria they do not have to join the army. Yugoslavia will fight against Italy. [...] What if in this war both sons die? It would burden my conscience, if I had voted for Yugoslavia.'[42]

The 'heroic mother' and the 'women's army'

The examples given above have already indicated how women were asked to prove their patriotism in times of war by their readiness to sacrifice their family, namely their sons, as 'heroic mothers'. The significant role model of the heroic Serbian mother was presented to the Slovene women of Carinthia in June 1920. We should bear in mind, though, that Serbia had been pictured in the Habsburg Monarchy as the heinous enemy during the war; just a few months later, Carinthian Slovenes were asked to feel brotherly or rather sisterly love for Serbia. *Koroška Zora* repeatedly highlighted Serbian topics, among others the battle against the Ottomans on the Kosovo field on 28 June (St Vitus day) 1389. After a vivid description of the battle, the male author depicted the tradition of folk songs that 'preserved the memory of the heroic Serbian women of those times', namely the memory of the Kosovo maiden and the mother of the Jugovići, who are 'a role model of love for the homeland'. The article then summarizes the ancient tale which was an essential part of Serbian historical memory, but rather unfamiliar to Slovene readers in Carinthia: Bogdan Jugoviči and his wife had nine sons, all married. When Bogdan and his sons went into battle, the mother and the daughters-in-law stayed at home waiting for news from the battlefield. When they learned of the death of Bogdan and the nine sons, the daughters-in-law started crying, but the 'heroic mother' consoled them: 'Why do you cry, my daughters-in-law [...]? I did not raise my sons to lie on soft cushions, but to defend their homeland against enemies. And if the enemy has killed our sons [...] we will raise the children [...]. Our tribe will not vanish.' Nevertheless, the mother's 'loving heart' was still hoping for the return of at least her youngest son. But when she realized that he, too, was dead, 'her heart shattered with grief, and without a word, without lamentation, she collapsed dead to the ground. This is the image of the heroic mother of the Jugoviči, who loves her children, but loves her homeland even more.' The article finished with a patriotic call:

> Slovene Mothers, girls, sisters! You, too, have proven innumerable times that you love your language, that you love your homeland no less ardently than the mother of the Jugoviči, the Kosovo maiden 500 years ago. You will not have to sacrifice your husbands, nor sons, nor bridegrooms. But for the freedom of our homeland you will gladly sacrifice some effort [...]. Therefore step into the light, you Carinthian mothers of the Jugoviči, you Carinthian Kosovo maidens![43]

Similar calls urging Slovene women to fulfil their patriotic obligation towards the fallen soldiers and to show their national commitment by voting for Yugoslavia in the plebiscite were made both in a speech by the prominent plebiscite activist Angela Piskernik and in a newspaper appeal by Maša Puncer. She was the sister of Srečko Puncer, who had died in border fights between the Kingdom of Serbs, Croats and Slovenes and the Republic of German-Austria in 1919. Maša Puncer described the loss of her brother as 'unfathomable, yet as he died for the homeland we find solace in his sacrifice and do not mourn'. Consequently, she demanded that Carinthian women who:

> have lavished flowers on Srečko's grave [...] and remembered him on his last path [...] with innumerous bouquets [...], now prove yourselves as courageous, conscious, and proud Slovenes who will do everything so that Carinthia will be united with its mother Yugoslavia. When the Yugoslav flag will flutter on the Gosposvetsko field, then you will have accomplished your duty, Carinthian Slovene [woman]![44]

As the historical centre of the early medieval Slavic principality of Carantania, the Gosposvetsko polje/Zollfeld was of great importance to Slovene national ideology. Therefore, the pro-Yugoslav plebiscite propaganda recurrently referred to it and put it on the same level as the Kosovo field in terms of historical significance. At a large gathering of women's societies in Velikovec/Völkermarkt in April 1920, Angela Piskernik demanded support for the plebiscite in order to not 'betray our martyrs'; that is, the Slovene soldiers who gave their lives fighting for freedom (naming Srečko Puncer as one of them): 'The soil in which these heroes [...] rest is holy soil. We shall not let it fall into the hands of our sworn enemy.'[45]

In contrast to the sometimes passive enduring patriotism of the 'heroic mother', the image of a 'women's army', attributed to the Slovene women's societies of Carinthia, was closely connected with women's active involvement in the 'political battle' of the plebiscite. Commenting on the women's gathering in Velikovec/Völkermarkt mentioned above, a male author wrote in *Mir*:

> The Carinthian elite army is marching, every Carinthian patriot is shouting out with joy [...]. But what kind of army is this – after all, our general Maister [leader of Slovene armed forces in the border conflict] has sent his heroes home 'on holiday'? You all [...] listen: the Carinthian women's army is marching – so tautly [...] that [...] not only the Carinthian mountains, but all of Yugoslavia, the whole world today hears the firm will of the Carinthian peasant women [...] who want to vote unanimously for Yugoslavia.

The author then stated that 'a new epoch – a new political life' of all Carinthian Slovenes – had begun with the women's gathering and that the women's organization had 'crossed the threshold of the peasant home' and 'stepped into the public' with a clear intent and goal.[46]

Evaluating the gathering in Velikovec/Völkermarkt and a second one in Pliberk/Bleiburg, *Koroška Zora* declared that the meetings had strengthened the pride of women, enhanced their courage to act publicly and taught the enemies respect. Given that 'women's votes alone count for more than half of the votes, and all of them are for Yugoslavia', supporters of the Germans feared women 'like the devil fears the cross' and therefore would try to fight 'our proud women's army'.[47] A few weeks before the plebiscite, *Koroška Zora* tried to give women courage for the 'main battle' of the referendum by asking:

> Sisters! Is there anyone [...] who can intimidate [...] us, who have seized the rifle, to throw it back into the fields so even one of us would faint-heartedly flee the main battle or stay at home? No, there is no one like that among us! We are so many and we are so strong, no one can overcome us. Behind each of us stand thousands and thousands of sisters who would horribly avenge every injustice. Our weapon is invincible. Do you know what it is called? It is called love, love for the homeland and the nation. [...] It knows no fear [...], it knows no obstacle, but follows its goal until it reaches it.[48]

Conclusion

The key objective of Slovene women as phrased in the May Declaration movement, a South Slavic state, was achieved, albeit in a somewhat different form. The Slovene goal of the plebiscite – Carinthia as part of Yugoslavia – was not realized, Carinthia became a part of the newly established Austrian Republic. Thus the Slovene population was separated. As citizens of Yugoslavia,

Slovene women had gained national freedom, yet many other rights, including suffrage, were withheld from them. As citizens of Austria, Slovene women in Carinthia gained new political rights, including suffrage, but their national rights where contested.

The propaganda strategies and discourses addressing Slovene women in the years 1917–20 were an ambiguous mixture of old and new gender(ed) virtues, roles, and images. They indicate a period of change in which the gender order became fragile and gender(ed) boundaries permeable. At the same time, the European system of states was in flux, loyalties to old and new nations were conflicting, national allegiances shifted and borders were contested. Thus, the interactions between gender, nation, and state were complex. I have tried to visualize these complexities in the following map that depicts, besides the territories and states in question, women's political rights and organizations as well as various national, dynastic, and other allegiances mentioned in the sources.

As we have seen, Slovene women were urged to enter the public and political sphere, albeit first and foremost for the benefit of the nation, less for their own sake. The novelty of this large-scale mobilization becomes even more evident when we consider gender relations in Slovene Carinthia before the war: Compared to other Slovene regions the organization of

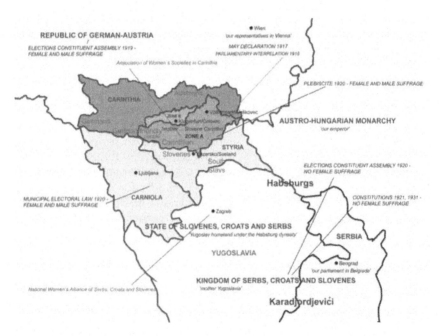

Map 14.1   Gender, Nations, and States: Organization, Representation, Participation
Source: ©Tina Bahovec, design by Ryan Gormley.

women was belated and their inclusion into the national movement weak. The latter was highly conservative and the leading role of the clergy pronounced, which strengthened the influence of patriarchal images of the Catholic Church. In the struggle against (German) liberalism, the patriarchal peasant family as the pillar of Slovenedom was to be preserved, a woman's national duty thus fulfilled in her traditional roles as (house-)wife and mother. The organization of women in the Slovene Christian-Social Union for Carinthia (Slovenska krščansko-socialna zveza za Koroško) began only a few years before the First World War and operated within the traditional framework of national ideology, summarized as the concept of 'mother – homeland – God'.

In view of these circumstances, the mobilization of Slovene women of Carinthia from 1917 until 1920 was quite astonishing. The years after 1920, however, were characterized by a re-traditionalization of the gender order. The leaders of the Slovene minority in Carinthia were focused on preservation and tolerated and supported the mobilization of women only for the national good. The activities of women's societies from the pre-plebiscite period ceased. The Slovene Christian-Social Union, re-established in 1922, included a women's and a girls' union, but their activities, such as Mother's Day festivities and cooking courses, underlined traditional gender roles. As women were enfranchised in Austria, the Slovene party of Carinthia tried to gain their support and actually received more female than male votes, but the political representatives of the minority were male. The traditional divide, 'the public sphere as a male domain – the private sphere as a female domain', was also disseminated by the minority newspaper *Koroški Slovenec*. Here, Carinthian Slovenes could read that it was 'not inborn to the woman to act in public and to take part in discussions of municipal assemblies',[49] whereas the man 'commands and leads in economy and education, in religion and in social life'.[50]

Supporting the finding that Slovene history in general and the period of the First World War, in particular, still lack a gendered approach,[51] my research for this article has raised questions, which need to be examined in more detail. To name but a few: Did the women who campaigned in the declaration movement also get involved in the Yugoslav plebiscite propaganda and in women's societies? Did German women and women's associations take part in the opposition against the declaration movement and if so, in what way? And, taking into account that the key objectives of the Slovene national movement in the Habsburg Monarchy were national equality, freedom from (German) oppression and emancipation from subordination, why were the concepts of equality and emancipation so reluctantly applied to gender relations? But then again, a common demand of the Slovene national movement was to be the master of one's own house – and the master of the house in patriarchal society is traditionally male.

Notes

1. Cf. T. Bahovec (2010) 'Engendering Borders: The Austro-Yugoslav Border Conflict Following the First World War', in A. Schwartz (ed.) *Gender and Modernity in Central Europe: The Austro-Hungarian Monarchy and Its Legacy* (Ottawa: University of Ottawa Press), pp. 219–33.
2. See, for example, N. Yuval-Davis (1997) *Gender & Nation* (London: Sage); B. Melman (1998) 'Introduction', in B. Melman (ed.) *Borderlines: Genders and Identities in War and Peace 1870–1930* (New York: Routledge), pp. 1–25; I. Blom (2000) 'Gender and Nation in International Comparison', in I. Blom, K. Hagemann and C. Hall (eds) *Gendered Nations: Nationalism and Gender Order in the Long Nineteenth Century* (Oxford: Berg), pp. 1–26.
3. V. Stavbar (2003) 'Vloga žensk v deklaracijskem gibanju na Spodnjem Štajerskem' [The Role of Women in the Declaration Movement in Lower Styria], in N. Budna Kodrič and A. Serše (eds) *Splošno žensko društvo 1901–1945: Od dobrih deklet do feministk* [The General Women's Society 1901–1945. From Good Girls to Feminists] (Ljubljana: Arhiv Republike Slovenije), pp. 504–13; I. Selišnik (2006) 'Podoba ženske v letu 1918 skozi prizmo političnih člankov' [The Image of a Woman in the Year 1918 through the Prism of Published Material], *Zgodovinski časopis*, 60, pp. 139–56.
4. B. Bader-Zaar (2012) 'Gaining the Vote in a World of Transition: Female Suffrage in Austria', in B. Rodríguez-Ruiz and R. Rubio-Marín (eds) *The Struggle for Female Suffrage in Europe. Voting to Become Citizens* (Leiden: Brill), pp. 191–206; I. Selišnik (2012) 'Female Suffrage in Slovenia', in Rodríguez-Ruiz and Rubio-Marín, *The Struggle for Female Suffrage in Europe*, pp. 339–55.
5. See, for example, V. Jalušič (1999) 'Women in Interwar Slovenia', in S. P. Ramet (ed.) *Gender Politics in the Western Balkans: Women and Society in Yugoslavia and the Yugoslav Successor States* (University Park, PA: Pennsylvania State University Press), pp. 51–66; N. Budna Kodrič (2003) 'Žensko gibanje na Slovenskem do druge svetovne vojne' [The Women's Movement in Slovene Territory up to World War II], in Budna Kodrič and Serše, *Splošno žensko društvo*, pp. 16–27.
6. For example, *Mir*, 22 February 1918, p. 35.
7. *Stenographische Protokolle über die Sitzungen des Hauses der Abgeordneten des österreichischen Reichsrates* (Anhang), 22nd sess., 66th meeting, 28 February 1918, pp. 6517–18.
8. Bahovec, 'Engendering Borders'.
9. Women in Austria were enfranchised in December 1918, but the first Parliamentary elections in February 1919 were not held in the parts of Southern Carinthia under Yugoslav control. For the 1919 elections in Carinthia see, J. Pleterski (1970) 'O prvinah in o značaju plebiscitne odločitve' [On the Elements and the Nature of the Plebiscite Decision], in J. Pleterski, L. Ude and T. Zorn (eds) *Koroški plebiscit: Razprave in članki* [The Carinthian Plebiscite. Treatises and Papers] (Ljubljana: Slovenska matica), here pp. 221–3.
10. Cf. J. Nagel (1998) 'Masculinity and Nationalism: Gender and Sexuality in the Making of Nations', *Ethnic and Racial Studies*, 21:2, pp. 242–69.
11. Arhiv Republike Slovenije, AS 660, Narodni svet za Koroško, šk. 2.
12. *Koroška Zora*, 8 July 1920, p. 8.
13. A. Vode (1998) 'Aktivnost slovenskih učiteljic [The Activities of Slovene Female Teachers]', in A. Vode *Spol in upor* [Gender and Revolt] (Ljubljana: Krtina), pp. 217–341; T. Bahovec (2003) 'Zur Rolle der slovenischen Frauen in der Ära

der Nationalisierung', in T. Bahovec (ed.) *Eliten und Nationwerdung: Die Rolle der Eliten bei der Nationalisierung der Kärntner Slovenen/Elite in narodovanje: Vloga elit pri narodovanju koroških Slovencev* (Klagenfurt/Celovec: Hermagoras/Mohorjeva), pp. 345–85.
14. C. Krekova and F. dr. Tavčarjeva (1917) 'Slovensko ženstvo za deklaracijo' [Slovene Women for the Declaration], *Slovenski narod*, 15 December, p. 1. See also Selišnik, 'Podoba', pp. 151–2.
15. Cf. I. Selišnik (2003) 'Socialno materinstvo: Koncepti državljanstva in argument skrbi pri uveljavljanju žensk v javni sferi na začetku 20. stoletja' [Social Motherhood: Concepts of Citizenship and the Argument of Care in Connection with the Assertion of Women in the Public Sphere at the Beginning of the 20th Century], *Teorija in praksa*, 50:6, pp. 1155–66.
16. Cf. C. Tacke (2000) 'Geschlecht und Nation', in S. Kemlein (ed.) *Geschlecht und Nationalismus in Mittel- und Osteuropa 1848-1918* (Osnabrück: fibre), pp. 15–32.
17. *Mir*, 1 March 1918, p. 45. The phrase 'Yugoslav state under our emperor' refers to the South Slavic state as demanded in the May Declaration; that is, a state of Slovenes, Croats and Serbs on Habsburg territory under the Habsburg sceptre, which would have been an implementation of the tripartite concept.
18. Cf. Selišnik, 'Podoba'; Bader-Zaar 'Gaining the Vote'.
19. A. Modic (1919) 'Koroškim ženam in dekletom' [To the Carinthian Women and Girls], *Korošec*, 16 July, p. 1.
20. *Koroška Zora*, 10 June 1920, pp. 6–7.
21. Selišnik, 'Podoba', p. 152.
22. *Slovenec*, 22 March 1918, p. 1.
23. I. Klem[enčič?] (1927) 'Slovensko ženstvo in majniška deklaracija' [Slovene Women and the May Declaration], *Slovenec*, 29 May, p. 5.
24. M. Verginella (2006) 'Od narodnih dam do emancipiranih deklet' [From National Ladies to Emancipated Girls], in M. Verginella *Ženska obrobja: Vpis žensk v zgodovino Slovencev* [Women on the Margins: Inscribing Women into the History of Slovenes] (Ljubljana: Delta), p. 123.
25. *Mir*, 10 May 1918, p. 105. Original emphases here and in following quotes.
26. As an example, Pleterski cites M. Wutte (1943) *Kärntens Freiheitskampf*, 2nd edn (Weimar: Böhlau).
27. J. Pleterski (1970) 'Koroški Slovenci med I. svetovno vojno' [Carinthian Slovenes during World War I], in Pleterski, Ude and Zorn, *Koroški plebiscit*, pp. 105–6.
28. *Koroška Zora*, 7 October 1920, p. 4.
29. *Kärntner Landsmannschaft*, 21 September 1920, p. 5; 19 June 1920, pp. 4–5.
30. Selišnik, 'Podoba', pp. 143–50; Selišnik (2008) *Prihod žensk na oder slovenske politike* [Women's Entry into the Arena of Slovene Politics] (Ljubljana: Sophia).
31. V. Melik (1962) 'Izid volitev v konstituanto 1920' [The Results of the Elections to the Constituent Assembly 1920], *Prispevki za zgodovino delavskega gibanja*, 3:1, pp. 3–4; S. P. Ramet (2011) *Die drei Jugoslawien: Eine Geschichte der Staatsbildungen und ihrer Probleme* (München: Oldenbourg), pp. 89–91.
32. M. Verginella, 'Naše žene volijo: O volilni pravici žensk v povojni Jugoslaviji in Sloveniji' [Our Women Vote: On Women's Suffrage in Postwar Yugoslavia and Slovenia], in Verginella, *Ženska obrobja*, pp. 53–71, especially pp. 53–4.
33. *Mir*, 27 May 1920, p. 94.
34. *Koroška Zora*, 13 May 1920, p. 7; 27 May 1920, p. 3.
35. *Koroška Zora*, 22 July 1920, pp. 3–8.
36. *Korošec*, 8 June 1920, p. 1.

37. *Kärntner Landsmannschaft*, 19 June 1920, p. 4.
38. 'Wie werden die Frauen und Mädchen der Zone A am 10. Oktober wählen?', Arhiv Republike Slovenije, AS 1083, Zbirka Koroški plebiscit.
39. The *Volkswehr* were Austrian armed forces deployed in the border conflict. They were volunteers and raised by limited conscription. Cf. E. Steinböck (1963) *Die Volkswehr in Kärnten unter Berücksichtigung des Einsatzes der Freiwilligenverbände* (Vienna: Stiasny).
40. Arhiv Republike Slovenije, AS 1194, Zbirka plakatov, letakov in koledarjev, t.e. O.
41. *Slovenec*, 7 October 1920, pp. 2–3.
42. Pleterski, 'O prvinah in o značaju plebiscitne odločitve', p. 243.
43. Kompoljski (1920) 'Vidov dan' [Vitus Day], *Koroška Zora*, 24 June, pp. 9–10. See also S. Slapšak (2005) 'Women's Memory in the Balkans: The Alternative Kosovo Myth', *Anthropological Yearbook of European Cultures*, 14, pp. 95–111; M. Bokovoy (2006) 'Kosovo Maiden(s): Serbian Women Commemorate the Wars of National Liberation, 1912–1918', in N. M. Wingfield and M. Bucur (eds) *Gender and War in Twentieth-Century Eastern Europe* (Bloomington, IN: Indiana University Press), pp. 157–70.
44. M. Puncerjeva (1919) 'Koroškemu ženstvu' [To the Carinthian Women], *Korošec*, 1 October, p. 1.
45. *Koroška Zora*, 13 May 1920, pp. 6–7; *Korošec*, 24 April 1920, p. 1.
46. Carantanus junior (1920) '18. april 1920', *Mir*, 30 April, p. 69.
47. *Koroška Zora*, 27 May 1920, p. 3.
48. *Koroška Zora*, 2 September 1920, pp. 1–2.
49. *Koroški Slovenec*, 19 July 1939, pp. 3–4.
50. *Koroški Slovenec*, 11 March 1936, p. 3. For a gendered perspective on Carinthian Slovene history, see T. Bahovec (2010) '"Die Frau muss Frau bleiben und darf die von der Natur gegebenen Grenzen nicht überschreiten": Geschlecht und Nation in der Kärntner slowenischen Geschichte', in W. Berger, B. Hipfl, K. Mertlitsch and V. Ratković (eds) *Kulturelle Dimensionen von Konflikten: Gewaltverhältnisse im Spannungsfeld von Geschlecht, Klasse und Ethnizität* (Bielefeld: transcript), pp. 54–71.
51. M. Verginella (2006) 'Na poti k matrilinearni genealogiji?' [On the Way to a Matrilinear Genealogy?], in Verginella, *Ženska obrobja*, pp. 179–91; M. Wakounig (2010) 'Ženske v prvi svetovni vojni' [Women in the First World War], in V. Rajšp (ed.) *Soška fronta 1915–1917: Kultura spominjanja* [The Isonzo Front 1915–1917: The Culture of Memory] (Vienna: Slovenski znanstveni inštitut na Dunaju/Slowenisches Wissenschaftsinstitut in Wien) pp. 43–50.

Select Bibliography

M. C. Adams (1990) *The Great Adventure: Male Desire and the Coming of World War I* (Bloomington, IN: Indiana University Press).

P. Antolini, G. Barth-Scalmani, M. Ermacora, N. Fontana, D. Leoni, P. Malni and A. Pisetti (eds) (2007) *Donne in guerra, 1915–1918: La Grande Guerra attraverso l'analisi e le testimonianze di una terra di confine* (Rovereto: Centro Studi Judicaria, Museo storico italiano della guerra).

A. S. Belzer (2010) *Women and the Great War: Femininity under Fire in Italy* (Basingstoke: Palgrave Macmillan).

B. Bianchi (ed.) (2006) *La violenza contro la popolazione civile nella Grande guerra: Deportati, profughi, internati* (Milano: Unicopli).

J. Bourke (1996) *Dismembering the Male: Men's Bodies, Britain and the Great War* (Chicago, IL: University of Chicago Press).

D. Cohen (2001) *The War Come Home: Disabled Veterans in Britain and Germany, 1914–1939* (Berkeley, CA: University of California Press).

U. Daniel (1997) *The War from Within: German Working-Class Women in the First World War* (Oxford: Berg).

M. H. Darrow (2000) *French Women and the First World War: War Stories of the Home Front* (Oxford: Berg).

B. Davis (2000) *Home Fires Burning: Food, Politics, and Everyday Life in World War I Berlin* (Chapel Hill, NC: University of North Carolina Press).

A. Fell and I. Sharp (eds) (2007) *The Women's Movement in Wartime: International Perspectives, 1914–19* (Basingstoke: Palgrave Macmillan).

S. R. Grayzel (1999) *Women's Identities at War: Gender, Motherhood, and Politics in Britain and France during the First World War* (Chapel Hill, NC: University of North Carolina Press).

N. Gullace (2002) *'The Blood of Our Sons': Men, Women, and the Renegotiation of British Citizenship During the Great War* (Basingstoke: Palgrave Macmillan).

C. Hämmerle (2013) *Heimat/Front: Geschlechtergeschichte(n) des Ersten Weltkrieges in Österreich-Ungarn* (Vienna: Böhlau).

M. Healy (2004) *Vienna and the Fall of the Habsburg Empire: Total War and Everyday Life in World War I* (Cambridge: Cambridge University Press).

M. R. Higonnet, J. Jenson, S. Michel and M. C. Weitz (eds) (1987) *Behind the Lines: Gender and the Two World Wars* (New Haven, CT: Yale University Press).

J. Horne (ed.) (1997) *State, Society and Mobilisation in Europe during the First World War* (Cambridge: Cambridge University Press).

B. Kundrus (1995) *Kriegerfrauen: Familienpolitik und Geschlechterverhältnisse im Ersten und Zweiten Weltkrieg* (Hamburg: Christians).

H. J. W. Kuprian and Oswald Überegger (eds) (2006) *Der Erste Weltkrieg im Alpenraum: Erfahrung, Deutung, Erinnerung / La Grande Guerra nell' arco alpino: Esperienze e memoria* (Innsbruck: Universitätsverlag Wagner).

P. Lerner (2009) *Hysterical Men: War, Psychiatry, and the Politics of Trauma in Germany, 1890–1930* (Ithaca, NY: Cornell University Press).

É. Morin-Rotureau (ed.) (2004) *1914–1918: Combats de femmes. Les femmes, pilier de l'effort de guerre* (Paris: Éditions Autrement).

D. S. Patterson (2008) *The Search for Negotiated Peace: Women's Activism and Citizen Diplomacy in World War I* (New York: Routledge).

I. Sharp and M. Stibbe (eds) (2011) *Aftermaths of War: Women's Movements and Female Activists, 1918–1923* (Leiden: Brill).

F. Thébaud (1994) 'The Great War and the Triumph of Sexual Division', in F. Thébaud (ed.) *A History of Women in the West 5: Toward a Cultural Identity in the Twentieth Century* (Cambridge, MA: Belknap Press), pp. 21–75 (French original of 1992: 'La Grande Guerre: Le triomphe de la division sexuelle', in F. Thébaud (ed.) *Histoire des Femmes en Occident 5: Le XXe siècle* (Paris: Plon), pp. 31–89).

J. Vellacott (2006) *Pacifists, Patriots and the Vote: The Erosion of Democratic Suffragism in Britain During the First World War* (Basingstoke: Palgrave Macmillan).

A. Wilmers (2008) *Pazifismus in der internationalen Frauenbewegung (1914–1920): Handlungsspielräume, politische Konzeptionen und gesellschaftliche Auseinandersetzungen* (Essen: Klartext).

N. M. Wingfield and M. Bucur (eds) (2006) *Gender and War in Twentieth-Century Eastern Europe* (Bloomington, IN: Indiana University Press).

A. Woollacott (1994) *On Her Their Lives Depend: Munitions Workers in the Great War* (Berkeley, CA: University of California Press).

B. Ziemann (2007) *War Experiences in Rural Germany 1914–1923* (Oxford: Berg).

Index

abortion, 28, 98
abstinence, sexual, 55
Addams, Jane, 133, 177–8, 184,
   194n.47, 206
aerial warfare, 127, 129–33, 135–6, 140,
   193n.30, *see also* air raids
aesthetics, 38, 47, 77
Agence Rol, 131
Agency for Prisoners, 176
aggression, 41, 47, 170–1, 187
agricultural production, 17–21, 30
agricultural sector, 18
Air Raids Precautions, 137–8
air raids, 5, 16, 22, 98, 127, 129–30, 132,
   136–9, 141n.6, *see also* aerial warfare
Airoldi, General, 23
alcoholism, 19
alcohol, 101, 230n.48
Alexandre, Jeanne, 194n.58
Allgemeine Rundschau, 55
Allgemeiner Deutscher Frauenverein
   (ADF), 209n.2
Alphonse XIII, 115
Alps, 5, 23, 26, 34n.43
alterity, 76
American Women's Peace Conference,
   184
ammunition, 23, 26, 51n.24, 186, 189
androgyny, 84
Angell, Norman, 193n.44
anti-heroism, 73
anti-militarism, 179, 184
antiquity, 40
Aquileia, 29
armistice, 112, 187
art, 5, 146, 155, 157–9
artillery, 25–6, 72, 112, 133
artists, 39, 108–9, 123n.1, 133, 148–9,
   153, 155–9
Ascoli, 20, 22
Ashmead-Bartlett, Ellis, 118
Ashtead, 121
Association for the Support of Prussian
   Lithuanian War Sufferers, 218

Association of Conservative Women,
   200
Association of Lithuanian Women,
   215–16
Association of Women's Societies, 236
Associazione Agraria Friulana, 18
Atkinson, Diane, 118
Audoin-Rouzeau, Stéphane, 164
Auerbach, Heinz-Lux, 153
Aufhauser, Dr, 55–6
Augspurg, Anita, 195, 198–9, 206,
   209n.12
Augusterlebnis, 40
Auneau, Emile, 168
Auneau, Paulette, 168
Auskunfts- und Hilfsstelle für Deutsche
   im Ausland und Ausländer in
   Deutschland, 176
Australia, 103n.14, 155
Austria-Hungary, 90, 94, 101
Austria, 2, 12n.3, 93, 97, 102, 182–4,
   187–8, 196, 232–6, 239, 241–4,
   246–7, 248n.9, *see also* Habsburg
   Empire; Habsburg Monarchy
Austro-Hungarian Supporting Medical
   Corps Organization, 93
autobiography, 6, 49n.12, 81, 89–90, 92,
   112–13, 116, 118, 121–2

baby helmet, 139–41
Baer, Gertrud, 209n.4
Bahovec, Tina, 11
Balkan Wars, 93, 105n.35
Balkan, 8, 183, 239
baptism of fire, 43, 95, 97
barbarism, 109, 115
Baron de Constant, Paul Henri
   d'Estournelles, 193n.44
Barthes, Roland, 78
Battalion of Death, 3
Bäumer, Gertrud, 195–6, 198–200,
   203–5, 207–8
Bavaria, 58, 152–3
behaviour pattern, 21–2, 26, 146, 148